Community Organizing for
Urban School Reform

Community Organizing for Urban School Reform

Dennis Shirley

University of Texas ◆ Austin

BJ V 5428- 6/2
API - 420

Library of Congress Cataloging-in-Publication Data

Shirley, Dennis, 1955–
Community organizing for urban school reform / Dennis Shirley. —
1st University of Texas Press ed.
p.   cm.
Includes bibliographical references (p.   ) and index.
ISBN 0-292-77718-3 (cl : alk. paper).—ISBN 0-292-77719-1 (pa : alk. paper)
1. Education, Urban—Texas—Case studies.   2. Community and
school—Texas—Case studies.   3. Public schools—Texas—Case
studies.   4. School improvement programs—Texas—Case studies.
I. Title.
LC5132.T4S55 1997
370′.9764′091732—dc21   96-52806

For Shelley

Contents

Acknowledgments

G rateful acknowledgment is made of grants which supported this research from the Mellon Foundation, the Ford Foundation, and the American Academy of Arts and Sciences. I am especially thankful to Allen Matusow of the School of Humanities at Rice University, Theda Skocpol of the Department of Sociology at Harvard University, and Robert Wilson of the Lyndon Baines Johnson School of Public Affairs at the University of Texas for their roles in gaining that support.

I wish to thank the many community organizers, parents, teachers, principals, and clergy who hosted my visits in their homes, schools, churches, and offices. They include Ernesto Cortés, Jr., Joe Higgs, Father John Korcsmar, Oralia Garza de Cortés, Alejandro Mindiz Melton, Claudia Santamaria, and Toña Vasquez in Austin; Lady Coleman Byrd, Odessa Ravin, and Reverend Nehemiah Davis in Fort Worth; Sister Maribeth Larkin, Dolores de Avila, Manuela Cadena, Robert Hemphill, and Elsy Fierro-Suttmiller in El Paso; Robert Rivera, Emily Cole, Stela Balderas, Louisa Meacham, and Javier Parra in Houston; Archbishop Patrick Flores, Sister Consuelo Tovar, Pamela Ahart Walls, Estela Saunders, Richard Alvarado, Sharon Eiter, Cynthia Castillo, Adalia Perez, Linda Holloman, Marcia Welch, David Semrad, Juanita Zamarripa, Norma Vinton, Julia Lerma, Father Will Wauters, and Joe Rubio in San Antonio; Sister Christine Stephens and Melvin Traylor in Dallas; and Sister Mignonne Konecny in Beaumont. Keri Kinsey, a graduate student at Rice University, played an indispensable role in helping me to begin the research during an unusually demanding period of my work at Rice University.

I also wish to thank the following readers for taking the time to read preliminary drafts of the book and offering their criticisms and recommendations: Stela Balderas, Zenaido Camacho, Edward Cox, Chandler

Davidson, Jean Bethke Elshtain, Marshall Ganz, Howard Gardner, Elnora Harcombe, Elizabeth Heckelman, Jeffrey Henig, Bill Hobby, Marvin Hoffman, Ray Marshall, Allen Matusow, Louisa Meacham, Deborah Meier, Robert Putnam, Seymour Sarason, Peter Skerry, Armando Trujillo, Angela Valenzuela, Mark Warren, Gary Wehlage, Barbara Willis, Robert Wilson, and Emilio Zamora. I also thank my colleagues in the Department of Education and my students in Will Rice College at Rice University for their interest in this project.

I especially wish to express my gratitude to my wife, Shelley, and our two children, Skye and Gabriel. They provided me with joy and love in my private life which everyone desires but few are blessed to receive in such plenitude. Their companionship reminded me of that which is truly important in life, and gave me inspiration to return to my writing with renewed passion and commitment.

Fig. 1 The IAF developed community organizations in every major city and region of Texas.

Fig. 2 Principal Odessa Ravin worked with Allied Communities of Tarrant to transform the relationship between Morningside Middle School and its community. *The Fort Worth Star-Telegram,* photo by Beatrice Terrazas.

Fig. 3   COPS delegation at an assembly in San Antonio, 1992. Photo by Alan Pogue.

Fig. 4   Ernie Cortés has received national recognition for his community organizing work in the Southwest. Photo by Alan Pogue.

Fig. 5 Ann Richards spoke at numerous assemblies of the Texas IAP in the early 1990s. Photo by Alan Pogue.

Fig. 6 Marcia Welch played a major leadership role in developing IAF strategies concerning education, housing, and job training in San Antonio. Photo by Alan Pogue.

Introduction

Picture this: you are a first-grade teacher at an inner-city elementary school in San Antonio, Texas. You live in the suburbs and have taught at the school for ten years. You love children and you love teaching. You are proud of your profession and are admired by your peers and your principal for your dedication, enthusiasm, intelligence, and creativity.

Recently, your school has begun working with a community-based organization which has sought to broaden teachers' awareness of the relationship between education within the school and the dynamics of the immediate neighborhood. Your approach to the collaborative is skeptical but open-minded; you've seen lots of coalitions come and go in your school. Still, you know that the organization has planned a large community assembly in the school in the coming weeks, and you're willing to let yourself be educated. So you take some initiative, and one day, in a light-hearted and experimental mood, you ask your children to draw some pictures representing how they see their community.

What you receive from the children changes your experience of teaching ✓ *forever.* You learn that one boy's seventeen-year-old brother was killed on his front lawn in a drive-by shooting the previous week. Two students depict the explosion in a neighborhood bank during a recent robbery. Another student shows himself being offered drugs. Two students depict scenes from their homes after they were burglarized. For each child, you write down his or her verbal description of the event on a blank spot of the picture: "A sad man threw a bottle through my window and broke it." "Some gangs are using some white stuff. They asked me to try it." "A gang came to my yard. My aunt chased them away." "Someone hit my cousin with a gun." The violence and poverty of the children's lives shakes you to the core. *Not a single child in your class represents his or her community in a way that could be interpreted positively—as depicting the wonder, innocence, and excitement of childhood.*

Troubled as you are by your students' artistic representations of their neighborhood, you're even more disturbed about yourself and your lack of awareness of the realities of your children's lives outside the school. Nothing in your teacher education program compelled you to take a hard look at the community surrounding your school. Your training, your institution, and your pride in your profession strike you as collective delusions devastatingly remote from the lives of desperation experienced by the children in your classroom.

The scenario described above is not fictional. Estela Saunders is the teacher; Herff Elementary in San Antonio is the school; October 1992 is the time. Yet Estela Saunders' lost illusions are far more vast than the world of Herff Elementary School. All three of the major educational documents issued by presidential commissions, governors, presidents, and secretaries of education in the last dozen years are premised on the atomistic fallacy that fixing education means fixing schools. For the first five years after the publication of *A Nation at Risk* in 1983, a wave of reforms raised standards and teacher salaries, but did nothing to coordinate education within the school with development within the community. When the research results from that first wave were disappointing, a second wave ensued, which placed an emphasis on "restructuring" rather than "reform," intending to change patterns of teaching, curriculum development, governance, and assessment in public schools. Both waves, however, kept their distance from alarming new social trends: the greatest surge of income inequality in American history, the doubling of juvenile crime rates in the central city, and the increasing destabilization of the family. Although each wave was marked by the politics of the moment, neither had an explicitly political dimension.[1]

Jonathan Kozol began his 1991 *Savage Inequalities* with an indictment of the apolitical, fragmented nature of the efforts to improve public schooling in the 1980s. After touring the nation from coast to coast, Kozol commented,

> In many cities, what is termed "restructuring" struck me as very little more than moving around the same old furniture within the house of poverty. The perceived objective was a more "efficient"

ghetto school or one with greater "input" from the ghetto parents or more "choices" for the ghetto children. The fact of ghetto education as a permanent American reality appeared to be accepted.

In Kozol's account, the signal characteristic of school reform in the 1980s—regardless of which wave of reform one intended—was its staggeringly *introspective* quality. American educators appeared to believe that one could ignore the larger deterioration of young people's lives in civil society and simply focus on changing their schools with felicitous results.[2]

Assume for a moment that Kozol's analysis was correct. From one vantage point, educators were responding as best they could to a difficult situation. Friends of public schools found themselves placed on the defensive in the 1980s and 1990s, suffering stinging attacks from both the Right and the Left. Leading conservative, liberal, and even radical thinkers promoted the idea that our public school system was so dysfunctional that it needed to be scrapped altogether. In its stead every possible pablum was offered to troubled educators and communities. School choice, privatization, teacher career ladders, and "autopsies" of public education were the tonics which captured policymakers' imaginations and the media headlines. Blended together with a heady mixture of "total quality management," information superhighways, and vouchers, the brave new world of education looked very different from the traditional democratic conception of public schooling for children from all social classes and ethnic backgrounds.[3]

The traditions of Americans, like virtually all forms of cultural inheritances, are based on a complex blend of arguments and agreements that we have had with one another. In spite of variances, one strong democratic thread has animated American education for over three centuries. Beginning in the seventeenth century in New England, and spreading west and south throughout the following centuries, Americans have come almost universally to embrace the idea of public schooling for their children. Opposing tendencies always existed: aristocratic obscurantism, or the premise that the poor should be kept ignorant, in seventeenth-century Virginia; codes which prohibited slaves from learning to read and write, in the antebellum South; cultural expectations that women should know less than men, and that even when they did know more, it was improper to show it; segregated schools for African Americans, Native Americans, and Mexican Americans up to the early 1970s. Many problems have existed along the way, which have limited numerous lives; many blessings have also been conferred, which have uplifted and ennobled others. In spite of many obstacles, the broader national and historical trajectory has been toward inclusion. As an aggregate, within ethnic groups, along gender lines, and within social classes, greater percentages of Americans are graduating from high schools than ever before.[4]

Public schools in the United States were born out of the conviction that education is not an individual affair but a public matter, one of deep import for the cultivation of social order, civic liberty, and democratic vitality. In spite of phenomenal obstacles—not the least of which is the lack of any provision for public education in the Constitution, an anomaly among industrialized nations—the United States now has over eighty thousand public schools teaching over fifty million students in more than fifteen thousand local school districts. Those schools reflect the ability of local and state governments to promote education with limited interventions from the federal government. Yet for a variety of reasons, the vitality of those institutions, and the ideas which undergird them, are under assault. Even American parents with children in public schools are critical of them; a majority would prefer to send their children to private schools, if they could afford to do so.[5]

This book argues that the metaphorical "autopsy" of public schools demanded by their critics is premature. Yet it will not do to suggest that the various criticisms of public education, in and of themselves, are simply wrong. Rather, one must demonstrate that public education, even in inner-city neighborhoods, can be a source of academic achievement, community engagement, and civic renewal. We must learn about forms of community self-mobilization and political action that not only confront the despair which haunts our urban schools, but also address Kozol's question about the presence of the ghetto itself. Detailed, empirical description must show that Americans, who surpass virtually every industrialized nation in the world in the richness of their voluntary associations, possess the civic force to reclaim their urban public spaces.[6]

The following account describes the efforts of a number of community-based organizations which have formed coalitions with educators like Estela Saunders in places like Herff Elementary School to revitalize urban public schools. Since the assembly in November 1992, Herff Elementary School and its neighborhood initiated a process of dramatic cultural change. The school's principal, its parents, and its teachers have insisted on the enforcement of code compliance laws to close down vacant neighborhood buildings from which drugs were sold; they have won funding for an after-school program which engages the community on behalf of children suffering from "latchkey" isolation; they have gone from an atmosphere of hatred toward the police to community policing and a new relationship of mentoring and collaboration; they have fought for and succeeded in developing an integrated housing strategy which has enabled low-income tenants to become homeowners; and they have acquired the skills needed to meet with city council members, the mayor, code compliance officers, the police department, and school board members to get the results that they need to enhance the lives of their children.

The promising new initiatives at Herff Elementary School and its surrounding neighborhood are far from perfect or complete. The problems confronting low-income urban communities are complex and tenacious, and long-term change will come about only as a result of an ensemble of many different factors working together. Economic development, quality health care, affordable housing, parent education programs, preschool programs, and after-school programs for children whose parents work an eight-hour day are some of the most salient factors which must be brought together to produce sustained educational development in inner-city schools and neighborhoods. Nonetheless, the transformation at Herff represents a significant break with the past insofar as it signals that the school is developing a new civic culture with higher standards, mutual accountability, and united community advocacy of the needs and rights of children.[7]

Of key importance to understanding Herff's development is the recognition that Herff did not change its internal culture or its community on its own. Herff Elementary School has joined an alliance with the Industrial Areas Foundation (IAF), which is struggling to improve education in urban schools and neighborhoods throughout Texas. The account which follows is a description and analysis of those collaboratives. In a nutshell, I shall argue that the experience and achievements of those collaboratives are sufficiently intriguing and powerful that they present a new and singular challenge to the orthodoxies of the current school reform movement. School restructuring as commonly practiced seeks to evade the political realities of urban schools and cities, but the Texas IAF teaches low-income parents and urban teachers the political tools that they must use to enhance the quality of education for their children and students. Most school restructuring envisions no role for churches or synagogues in the process of school change, but the Texas IAF works closely with religious institutions, developing collaborations that are instrumental in mobilizing urban political and economic elites to improve the conditions of the working class. Internal school restructuring is an important part of Texas IAF educational collaboratives, but it acquires a distinctive flavor and potency because of the complex mixture of political activity and congregational support with which it is engaged. And although the collaboratives are relatively new, encouraging results are there, measured in increased student attendance, improved teacher retention, enhanced academic achievement, and new forms of school innovation and community uplift.[8]

Case studies of individual school development and neighborhood improvement make for compelling reading, and in the accounts which follow I have sought to give optimal attention to the complex manner in which individual schools can evolve from islands of bureaucracy to centers of civic activism. At the same time that individual case studies can enrich our understanding of school change, however, I have deliberately sought to avoid much of the antitheoretical and noncontextual character of much contemporary writing on urban school reform. It is good to recognize heroes and heroines such as Jaime Escalante, Madeline Cartwright, and LouAnne Johnson, who have become household words in the educational community, but we also need to describe the extraordinary efforts of ordinary teachers and parents who can and do improve urban public schools. Having participated in a number of school reform wars of my own, I have observed that most of the failings of contemporary efforts have little to do with lack of goodwill toward the plight of low-income youth or lack of extraordinary effort. Goodwill is available in abundance, and so is hard and vastly undercompensated work. What is needed is a more powerful and explanatory conceptual framework and far more sensitivity to the full range of ways in which the social and historical context influences the process of education. For that reason, this volume begins with both conceptual and contextual issues, which provide essential preconditions for the kinds of multifaceted understanding that can promote democratic agendas of school change and neighborhood revitalization.[9]

A key part of the contextual nature of this presentation has to do with its regional setting in Texas—rarely the site of noteworthy educational innovations in American history. Although the predominantly Anglo-American revolutionaries who won independence from Mexico in 1836 explicitly condemned Mexico for having "failed to establish any public system of education," the first public schools, of which there were four, were not established until 1853. Ironically, the funds for the schools were drawn from lands given to San Antonio by the Mexican congress before Texas' independence.[10]

As was the case in all of the South, public schools in any meaningful sense of the term were created for the first time in Texas during Reconstruction and were fiercely opposed by the majority of White citizens. As soon as federal control was withdrawn, one of the first acts of male Anglo-American Texans—the only group to enjoy the uninhibited exercise of the franchise—was to abolish the schools. Public schools were recreated in Texas in 1876 after a long and protracted battle, but with tremendous restrictions. Localities were prohibited from raising local taxes to pay for the schools; the boundaries of school districts were undefined; every school had to reapply to a county judge each year to be eligible for funding; and local districts could not choose to operate racially integrated schools.[11]

Eventually a form of public education was created in Texas, largely due to the efforts of Governor Oran Roberts in the late 1870s and early 1880s. But the new system was strongly marked by the attitudes of Anglo-Americans toward racial and ethnic differences, and by the beginning of the twentieth century, Texas had developed a full-blown caste system of education, with separate schools for Anglo-Americans, Mexican Americans, and African Americans. Segregation, attended by a vastly uneven distribution of resources to students, made a mockery of the concept of public education and prepared students for an ethnically segmented labor market and segregated neighborhoods—with geographic, economic, and political ramifications that still mark the state strongly today. In the postwar period Texas' state department of education dictated a phenomenal number of detailed admonitions to individual teachers and schools, and its state board of education hearings became notorious nationwide for the ready ear given to extremist right-wing groups demanding changes in social studies, science, and English textbooks.[12]

Texas' aberrant politics of education resulted in nightmarish academic and social consequences. For years Texas had the most unequal school funding plan of all fifty states; in the early 1990s affluent districts allocated over nineteen thousand dollars in per-pupil spending per year to their schools while impoverished districts struggled by with a meager two thousand dollars per pupil. More students drop out of high school between the ninth grade and their expected graduation date in Texas than in any other state. While 47 percent of the adults in the United States struggle with basic literacy skills, the situation is even more extreme in Texas, where more than half of the adult population is functionally illiterate.[13]

In spite of its undistinguished past in regard to education, Texas, like all of the sunbelt states, is changing, and changing fast. Passage of the Voting Rights Act and its enforcement created far more diverse and inclusive political constituencies than in the "primitive years" of Anglo-American hegemony. The Texas myth of the frontier continues to influence the popular imagination—but Texas surpassed New York as the second most populated state in the union in 1994, and over 87 percent of Texans reside in large metropolitan areas. The popular association of Texas with machismo did not prevent the election of women to the governorship of Texas and mayoralty of San Antonio, Houston, Dallas, Fort Worth, El Paso, Austin, Galveston, Nacogdoches, and Corpus Cristi in the late 1980s and early 1990s. In addition, the Texas myth of overwhelming conservatism ignores a dynamic regional history of agrarian populism, Chicano militancy, and African American resilience. Most relevant for this volume, a coalition of working-class and middle-class Texans engendered one of the few community groups—the Texas IAF—in the early 1970s that has not only survived to the current day but has also recruited and organized thousands of citizens through the social matrices of their religious institutions. Given this achievement, one may speculate whether urban Texas may be generating new sites for a regeneration of public schooling that may provide one source for a broader recovery of national nerve as to the purposes and promise of public education.[14]

In the presentation which follows, I first describe the economic dislocations, decline in political participation, and social disorganization which characterize our current national predicament. Next, I provide background on the origins of the IAF in Texas, the nature of the organization's philosophy of education, and its strategies of community organizing around issues of school change and neighborhood development. The narrative then moves to case studies in which local organizations of the Texas IAF have sought to mobilize low-income citizens to forge new kinds of social networks among parents, clergy, parishioners, teachers, administrators, and civic leaders. The case studies are not restricted to individual schools, but encompass both citywide and statewide initiatives which reflect the capacity of community-based organizations to develop political power and to expand their strategies from protest around local issues to governance on issues of regional and national import.

The schools in which the Texas IAF is organizing are engaged in intense and sometimes wrenching struggles to transform their cultures. To idealistic teachers and administrators it sometimes seems that there is an insurmountable array of impediments that can block school improvement. Bureaucratic mandates from state departments of education, teacher resistance to parental engagement, limited job opportunities, and the rise of youth gangs—which drive neighborhood residents out of public spaces and into private seclusion—all can undermine community support of public schools. Not one of the schools described in this account has fully overcome the myriad problems that confront low-income neighborhoods.

In spite of their problems, each school described in the pages which follow has made a bold and sustained effort to attack civic disengagement and to recreate schools as centers of their communities. For this reason, I consider each school to be an emergent "laboratory of democracy"—a civic site in which parents, teachers, students, and community leaders struggle to overcome the many obstacles to civic participation and educational improvement in low-income neighborhoods. Each of the schools described in the following accounts may be construed as a *laboratory* which is intensely involved in experimentation both within the school and in its relationship to its immediate community—and that experimentation will produce successes as well as failures. Each school manifests principles of *democracy* insofar as the nature of its experimentation is rooted not in the directives of bureaucracies but in the deliberations of unusually large numbers of parents, teachers, and community leaders. In spite of the ongoing and unresolved nature of many of their most serious challenges, these "laboratories of democracy" have established enough of a track record to earn a substantial place in contemporary discussions of school reform, community organizing, and civic renewal. Their struggles challenge us to reflect anew about the relationship between education in the school and in the community, and about the benefits rather than the threats entailed in developing civic solidarity across class and ethnic lines.[15]

I
Origins

The Contemporary Context

U rban public schools are often blamed for many problems whose roots lie not in the classrooms and corridors of educational institutions but in the broader fabric of civil society—in workplaces, on city streets, and in homes. If we are to avoid the widespread tendency to confuse the causes and effects of social disorganization as they are played out in city schools and neighborhoods, we must illuminate some of the major social, political, and economic trends of recent decades that have had profound ramifications for public schools and our nation's civic infrastructure. The structure of American society has changed dramatically in the last two decades. Economic growth, while positive in and of itself, has come at a tremendous cost to our most disadvantaged and vulnerable citizens. Political participation has declined. Family structures have changed in a manner which has produced a dramatic rise of either single-parent households or homes in which both parents are working; the consequence for the children is a dramatic decrease in the amount of close adult attention available to them. Although Americans continue to uphold values of equal opportunity, the intensification of social stratification in recent years has been unparalleled in American history and threatens to continue in the future. Although there have been countervailing tendencies, they have been weak at best. Working-class Americans feel the economic pressures, lack of political accountability, and challenges to their job security, wage stability, and overall quality of life on a relentless daily basis.

Americans have responded to economic transformations with dramatic changes in their social lives. A whole generation of women entered the waged labor force in the 1980s, but even the rise of the two-income family was no guarantee of a middle-class life style. In the past twenty-five years the manufacturing sector has declined, service industries without fringe benefits have expanded, and the minimum wage has fallen precipitously when adjusted for inflation. The degree to which middle-class and working-class Americans have suffered in terms of a decline in their standard of living is not always apparent because family income may remain stable, but that stability is often gained by the entry of women into the labor force.

For a variety of reasons—the cost and inflationary consequences of the war in Vietnam, the OPEC oil embargo, the inevitable plateau of the unprecedented expansion of the economy in the post–World War II economy—the early 1970s marked the beginning of a decline in the fortunes of middle-class Americans. Between 1973 and 1990 the median real income of young families, with a parent under the age of thirty, declined by 32 percent. Entry-level hourly wages declined for high school dropouts, high school graduates, and college graduates alike, placing phenomenal pressures on younger families. Traditional young families, with only a male working and no college diploma, experienced entry-level wage declines of over 30 percent from 1973 to 1993. As a result, the poverty rate among young families doubled in the same period, from 20 to 40 percent, and home ownership among young families declined 10 percent in the 1980s.[1]

Analyses of the declining economic fortunes of young families differ. Most economists view the middle and latter years of the 1970s as a period of stagnation and inflation. The 1980s was a period of economic revitalization which benefited the most affluent Americans while enabling the upper middle class to hold its own. *The bottom 70 percent of Americans, however, have experienced declines in their incomes in recent years when these are adjusted for inflation.*[2]

Who or what is responsible for the decline of the standard of living for the vast majority of Americans? Paradoxically, a Democrat such as Robert Reich saw the globalization of the economy—and the attendant devaluation of unskilled labor in the United States—as the major culprit, while a Republican like Kevin Phillips blamed the fiscal policies of Presidents Reagan and Bush for what he described as the "Brasilianization" of American incomes. Some economists emphasized the technological transformation of the workplace in increasing income stratification; others stressed the decline in union membership and clout; others attributed declining blue-collar wages to high rates of immigration from

Asia and Latin America. Whichever interpretation was correct, the numbers were the same—as were their real-life ramifications for the middle class. *By 1995 every other industrialized country in the world had a stronger middle class and less stratified economy than the birthplace of modern democracies, the United States.* The correlation for American youth was simple and direct: a cross-national study completed in 1995 found that *poor children in the United States are worse off than children in low-income families in fifteen other industrialized nations*—even *without including* the heavily subsidized child-care services and medical care available in most European countries.[3]

Increasing class stratification has not been the only worrisome trend of the past two decades. Electoral participation steadily dropped from 1960 to 1988 to a point at which only one of every two enfranchised citizens exercised his or her right to vote. In recent years, a wave of democratic revolutions has swept the world from the Philippines to Eastern Europe to South Africa to Latin America, but citizens in the United States appear to have grown more cynical and disengaged rather than rejuvenated by the dramatic transformations of global politics.[4]

Economic changes and political alienation might strengthen family ties, but in the United States in the last quarter century, the opposite has occurred. The percentage of children born out of wedlock has grown each year, and roughly 40 percent of American children go to bed each evening without their father in the home. Although feminism reshaped social mores by promoting women's *right* to work outside of the home, millions of American women have felt *compelled* for economic reasons to work rather than to attend to their young children. In 1991, about 60 percent of married women with preschoolers worked outside of the home as opposed to the 18 percent of three decades earlier. The net effect of these social changes has been a dramatic reduction of the amount of time parents spend with children on a weekly basis, from thirty hours in 1965 to only seventeen hours two decades later.[5]

The institution of marriage, the social foundation for the vast majority of Americans of all ethnic groups for centuries, has been devastated in our country in recent years. The United States has the highest divorce rate in the world, and about half of all first marriages now end in divorce. The majority of American children now grow up for a period in a family headed by a single parent. Managing the emotional disruption of divorce is tremendously difficult for children, and an emerging body of research suggests that the effects of divorce are far graver than had previously been assumed. In addition, a growing body of evidence links the absence of fathers in the home to greater behavioral problems and lower academic achievement in schools. The children of unwed adolescent mothers appear to be especially prone to a wide range of psychological and educational disorders.[6]

The emotional strains of divorce both reflect and compound the economic disparities in American society. Couples living in poverty are almost twice as likely to separate as those above the poverty line. The average mother's standard of living falls 30 percent in the first year after divorce, while the father's often increases 10 to 15 percent. In 1992 the median income for father-absent homes with young children was $9,000, less than a quarter of the $41,000 earned by married couples with preschoolers.[7]

Sociologists are at odds with one another about the best ways to interpret the changes in family structure in the past quarter century. Economic explanations emphasize the impact on the family of the decline of wages and the high rates of unemployment for men in the central cities, which have combined with the greater fiscal independence of women to weaken the economic necessity of marriage for women with children. Cultural explanations point to the sea change in public attitudes toward sexuality since the 1960s and the increasing public acceptance of children born out of wedlock. Those who favor economic explanations emphasize job creation as a strategy to restabilize families, whereas those who favor cultural explanations note that the take-off period in the rise of single parenthood was during the economically robust 1960s. They contend that self-defeating cultural norms which tolerate licentious behavior and an overall lack of responsibility to others must be confronted and overcome to bolster family ties.[8]

Questions of family structure are closely related to issues of social class. There is no question that affluent parents, who can provide their children with excellent nannies in infancy and private schools later on, have found ways in which both parents can work that enable their children to grow up happily with all of their basic needs well met. For the vast majority of American children, however, changes in the marketplace, culture, and social structure translate into preschool care that is affordable but unprofessional, public schools that are besieged by social problems, and precious little time with either parent. The careful time and attention which children need for nurturance, comfort, and encouragement is frequently passed on to a series of surrogates who cannot provide children with a sense of stability, some control of their environment, and lasting attachments. A vast array of research demonstrates that poverty and unemployment are strongly associated with psychological distress among adults, which is in turn associated with depression and behavioral problems among their children.[9]

In addition to growing economic polarization, declines in voting, and the disorganization of the family, crime rates rose dramatically in the United States from the 1970s onward. No other industrialized nation begins to approach the levels of criminal violence in the United States. The homicide rates in New York City for 1993 alone were greater than during a quarter century of civil war in Northern Ireland from 1969 to 1994. The number of homicides involving handguns committed by youths increased fivefold from 1984 to 1993. As a result of the soaring rise in crime, rates of incarceration more than doubled in the 1970s and 1980s. Americans jail a larger proportion of their population than any other western industrialized nation, and Texas alone jails more people than either France or Germany, in spite of its much smaller population. Americans spend close to $5 billion annually on security, but a recent Justice Department report estimates that the sum total of out-of-pocket costs caused by crime—such as lost time at work, legal expenses, and debilitating psychological consequences—exceeds $450 billion a year.[10]

The ramifications of political alienation, fragile families, and social instability have changed the quality of life throughout the country since the early 1970s. In addition to all of these problems, recent findings in social science identify dramatic declines in PTA participation, union membership, church-related groups, and fraternal and veterans' associations in the United States. According to Robert Putnam, "The average number of associational memberships has fallen by about a fourth over the last quarter century." The net effect is that the United States is a society moving away from strong social ties and energized voluntary associations toward civic disengagement, declining social trust, and individual opportunism.[11]

The Southwest has enjoyed generally favorable trends compared to the rest of the country, but it has hardly been immune to the negative economic and social developments of the last quarter century. Texas did far better than other states in the 1970s because of the high prices of oil and natural gas, but the collapse of oil prices in 1982 changed everything. The free fall of artificially high prices, compounded by speculation in real estate and encouraged by the deregulation of the savings and loan industry, generated a multifaceted crisis in the southwestern economy. Over one hundred thousand jobs disappeared in Houston, Texas' largest city, as a direct result of the crisis of the oil industry between 1981 and 1986, and the rippling effect throughout the city's economy meant a loss of over $4 billion in purchasing power in the same period.

Texas dropped from sixteenth to thirty-fifth among states in per capita income from 1983 to 1991. The percentage of Houstonians living below the poverty level rose from over one-eighth to over one-fifth between 1980 and 1990. The state's struggling economy in the late 1980s meant that many Texans were hard pressed to invest financially in their children's futures, and many of the aspirations expressed in education reform bills passed in the 1980s were diluted to relieve the state's struggling taxpayers. Even when communities voted to raise their property tax rates, the drop in property values often left the schools poorer than they had been before the oil bust. Hard economic times also hit the state's teachers; by 1996 close to one third of them worked second jobs to make ends meet. In the 1990s more than a quarter of all children in Texas were growing up in poverty.[12]

The economic distress Texas suffered in the 1980s was accompanied by an intensification of social disintegration. Juvenile crime increased by 53 percent between 1980 and 1990. In a survey conducted in 1991 by the Association of Texas Professional Educators, three quarters of the teachers surveyed stated that violence had intensified in their schools. In major urban centers such as Houston, arrests of juveniles committing felonies rose from under three thousand in 1985 to over five thousand in 1993. And, while our society's expectations of our teenagers' academic achievement appear to rise higher with each passing day, we have failed to pay attention to their most elementary needs for personal security. Seventy percent of all public school students in Houston report that they do not feel safe in their schools. Nationally, one third of students in high-crime neighborhoods report that they have stayed away from school on at least one occasion because of their fear of crime.[13]

Economic polarization has been matched with racial segregation; in

urban Texas, "intensely segregated" schools with over 90 percent minority enrollment are common, while schools with a balance of White
and minority enrollment are rare. Although trends toward economic
polarization and racial segregation in schools have been noted by many
observers on a national level, the weakening of the middle class in sunbelt states like Texas has been particularly brutal because of the lack of
a social infrastructure typical of northern states. For decades Texas has
ranked close to the bottom or at the absolute bottom of all fifty states in
safety-net features such as the level of unemployment compensation
payments, annual expenditures to students, Aid to Families with Dependent Children, and percentage of the population eligible for state welfare
and actually receiving it.[14]

It would be disingenuous to suggest that all of the developments in
the past two decades have been negative. In the 1980s and 1990s the
United States experienced the largest peacetime expansion of the
economy in its history. The incomes of the top 20 percent of Americans
rose steadily and a revolution in information technology created dynamic new industries with a wealth of career opportunities for the college educated. In spite of the decline of voting nationally, the enfranchisement of African Americans and Latinos and the struggle for and
enforcement of the Voting Rights Act have resulted in a far more diverse
and representative sampling of our population in our legislatures than
existed a quarter of a century ago. Women and minorities have economic opportunities scarcely imaginable a generation ago, as well as
avenues of legal recourse when they are the subjects of illegitimate discrimination. While political alienation may be high, record numbers of
Americans volunteer in charitable activities on a regular basis. The
economy has recovered since 1992, crime rates are slowly declining,
and the nation is at peace. Although declining civic participation is a
serious concern and should be arrested, the United States still possesses
a richer associational life and higher levels of civic engagement than
most other industrialized countries. In an ethnically heterogenous, politically pluralistic, and capitalist nation such as our own, uneven development is inevitable, and can encourage a cultural ferment entirely
appropriate to a free and democratic polity.[15]

In spite of those reassuring observations, however, a host of thought-
ful analysts from across the political spectrum agree that civil society in
the United States in the 1990s is in critical condition. The current pre-

dicament is particularly striking when contrasted with traditional interpretations of American exceptionalism vis-à-vis other western nations, which often have centered on the vitality of civic and political associations in the United States. The classical interpretation of American uniqueness in this regard was formulated by Alexis de Tocqueville, who traveled throughout the United States in the early 1830s and articulated his findings in his magnum opus, *Democracy in America*. Because Tocqueville's analysis is so central to all considerations of civil society in the United States today, a brief excursus into the essence of his presentation is warranted here.

When Tocqueville visited the United States in the early 1830s, he marveled at the vitality of civic and political associations in our country. "Americans of all ages, all stations in life, and types of disposition are forever forming associations," Tocqueville observed. "There are not only commercial and industrial associations in which all take part, but others of a thousand different types—religious, moral, serious, futile, very general and very limited, immensely large and very minute." With uncanny insight, Tocqueville linked the propensities of Americans to enter associations with the restless energy and passionate commitment to freedom which characterized civil society in the United States. By joining associations, Tocqueville observed, Americans learned to identify their self-interests and to advance them in combination with those of others. To the degree that associations promoted social solidarity on a local, face-to-face, and intermediary level of society, they functioned as "great free schools" which taught citizens how to "freely associate for little purposes as well as great." Even if those associations were strictly apolitical, Tocqueville observed, "civil associations pave the way for political ones," because the same organizational skills, habits of mind, and disposition to collaborate cut across both civil and political associations. Associations help citizens to develop out of purely privatized identities into a larger public role, which promotes social solidarity and expands the polity's intellectual horizons: "A political association draws a lot of people at the same time out of their own circle; however much differences in age, intelligence, or wealth may naturally keep them apart, it brings them together and puts them in contact." [16]

Tocqueville understood that the "art of association" was "a dangerous liberty." Individuals could conspire to subvert democracy. They could plot against one another for purposes of self-aggrandizement.

They could combine to support authoritarian kinds of populism that would suppress the rights of minorities. "One must understand that un-limited political freedom of association is of all forms of liberty the last which a people can sustain," he wrote. "If it does not topple them over into anarchy, it brings them continually to the brink thereof." In spite of these dangers, Tocqueville was a resolute champion of voluntary asso-ciations. Contrasting the American situation with that of his native France, Tocqueville claimed that *etatist* traditions in his motherland opened up a void in society in which the isolated individual confronted the state as an impotent vassal. Without the ferment of a powerful and self-regulating civil society mediating the relationship between the indi-vidual and the state, individuals could not help but surrender their pub-lic identities and fall into privatized existences which would leave them vulnerable to every machination of centralized state authority.[17]

Democracy in America was written against the historical backdrop of a French monarchy which had smashed the decentralized and interme-diary power of the nobility in the seventeenth and eighteenth centuries and juxtaposed itself as an absolutist regime against which individuals of the most diverse social backgrounds had meager appeal. More tragic than the collapse of the aristocracy itself in Tocqueville's account were the habits of servitude and civic disengagement which the atrophying of mediating institutions brought in its wake. Tocqueville's interpreta-tion of the collapse of voluntary associations and the political central-ization in France which ensued was described in detail in *The Old Régime and the French Revolution,* a pessimistic late work. According to Tocque-ville, "The segregation of classes, which was the crime of the late monarchy, became at a late stage a justification for it, since when the wealthy and enlightened elements of the population were no longer able to act in concert and to take part in the government, the country be-came, to all intents and purposes, incapable of administering itself, and it was needful that a master should step in." For Tocqueville, it was a supreme irony of history that the French Revolution, which promised to create a new reign of republican virtue, further centralized adminis-trative and political power and perpetuated the incompetency of local voluntary associations. In the United States, in contrast, Tocqueville felt that he discovered a countervailing force in the modern world which could refortify civil society, energize citizens to take charge of their own affairs, and carefully circumscribe the boundaries of the state.[18]

For all of the power of Tocqueville's analysis—which continues to offer one of the most compelling interpretations of American culture ever written—his presentation had several shortcomings. His analysis of American freedoms dealt only in the most marginal way with the massive and glaring reality of slaveholding in the South; the bulk of his time was spent describing New England townships and projecting their high levels of civic participation on to the rest of the nation. Tocqueville was most impressed by small towns and paid scant attention to the growth of manufacturing and commerce along the eastern seaboard. He valorized the role of women in educating their children to become productive citizens, but he neglected to address the exclusion of women themselves from the franchise.[19]

Perhaps the gravest error in Tocqueville's analysis relates to his failure to articulate a positive role for the state in his political theory. The relationship between voluntary associations and the state in Tocqueville's analysis is largely one of mutual animosity. Empirically, however, many if not all of the social policies which have been created by the federal government in the United States in its history have been the result of organized citizen advocacy. Veterans' and women's associations mobilized massive civic campaigns in the late nineteenth and early twentieth centuries to provide pensions and state subsidies to soldiers and widowed mothers; virtually all of the ambitious legislation passed during the New Deal was the result of tenacious organizing by labor unions; all of the Great Society legislation crowned years of advocacy and self-mobilization by voluntary associations made up of African Americans, unions, and professional groups. By neglecting to articulate a positive role for the state in his political theory, Tocqueville repudiated the central role of government in promoting a common civic culture as espoused in classical political theory; he also failed to develop a synthetic theory of civil society in which the state and mediating institutions can evolve mutually beneficial relationships.[20]

In spite of these deficiencies, Tocqueville's illumination of the key role of voluntary associations in enriching civic life, promoting social solidarity, and counterbalancing the consolidation of power in the hands of the state is an enduring contribution to contemporary political theory. When seen from the vantage point of Tocqueville's primary concern— the establishment and strengthening of civil liberty—the decline of civic and political engagement described in the preceding pages is much more than a minor irritant embedded in a healthy body politic. The vast array of data which indicate that Americans are harboring greater suspicions about one another and their government and choosing more privatized lifestyles suggest that a historic reversal is under way in Americans' conceptions of themselves, their culture, and their government. The problem is particularly acute because the entire American system of governance is predicated upon the enabling presence of grass-roots organizations of the most diverse nature. The withdrawal from civic and political associations is thus far more than a statistical irritant or one of many troubling trends; it is a corrosion at the heart and foundation of the republic.[21]

Tocqueville is often appropriated by conservative commentators as one of their own because of his criticisms of state centralization, but a more nuanced reading of his major writings suggests that he demonstrates affinities with liberal or radical perspectives. Like the views of Jeffersonian democrats or nineteenth-century agrarian populists, Tocqueville's perspective on the rise of capitalism was a critical one; he viewed the expansion of large modern industries as a substantial threat to the fabric of family, church, and small proprietors which humanized economic relationships and provided the backbone of civil society. For Tocqueville, the owners of large corporations were "an exception, a monstrosity, within the general social condition" because "these rich men have neither corporate spirit nor objects in common, neither common traditions nor hopes." If horizontal ties between capitalists are weak, so are the vertical links between employers and workers in a market economy, for "at any moment interest, which brought them together, can tear them apart." Tocqueville explicitly cautioned against the rise of the "manufacturing aristocracy" of corporate magnates, small as it was in the early 1830s, and warned that "the friends of democracy should ever keep their eyes anxiously fixed in that direction. For if ever again permanent inequality of conditions and aristocracy make their way into the world, it will have been by that door that they entered."[22]

Tocqueville's warning adumbrated the sentiment of many citizens in the late twentieth century that large multinational corporations which dispose of greater revenues than those of many nation-states can be just as overpowering, coercive, and impersonal as agencies of their state or federal government. Liberal and radical interpreters of Tocqueville view the rise of large business enterprises and global capitalism as a threat to the equality of condition which underlies much of our democratic and republican heritage as well as the spirit of civic virtue which promotes community solidarity. They continue to hold fast to Tocqueville's commitment to grass-roots political engagement, in other words, but they differ from marketplace conservatives by contending that the rise of modern capitalism can be just as disrespectful of local autonomy, traditions, and associations as the state ever was.[23]

Discussions of the nature of civil society bear an immediate relevance to our observations regarding the erosion of the social fabric of the United States in recent years. Until recently, social analysts were at a loss to describe the breakdown in families, voluntary associations, and civic activism in terms of a coherent and potent theoretical argument. Conservatives argued that the policies of the federal government subverted civil society by enabling low-income citizens to enjoy a paralyzing dependence on welfare hand-outs; liberals and radicals contended that the vagaries of the economy promoted the social cleavages which have widened in the past twenty years and the breakdown in mediating institutions which accompanied them. Most impartial spectators would agree that there was an element of truth in each point of view.

Analysts broadly agree that the texture of civil society is jeopardized in the United States—but why? That query has recently begun to be answered by a broad range of scholars in the fields of economics, sociology, and political science who use the notion of *social capital* as a key organizing concept. The idea of social capital was first expressed in a fleeting but fecund form by Jane Jacobs, the seminal critic of postwar urban planning, and then by economist Glenn Loury. It was elaborated into a more robust concept by sociologist James Coleman, who used it to identify and describe the economic value which resides in human relationships.[24]

Jacobs, Loury, and Coleman all recognized that there are different kinds of capital. *Physical capital* describes the value of buildings and tactile infrastucture; *financial capital* describes the value of money; *human capital* describes the economic value of an individual's physical and intellectual skills. Social capital differs from all of those forms of capital insofar as it proposes that certain kinds of *social relationships* possess economic value. Those relationships can be formal, as in membership in PTAs, labor unions, congregations, or Boy or Girl Scout troops; they can also be informal, as in the case of neighborhood residents or small business owners who keep a watchful eye on the kids on the block when they play outside after school. Those relationships can involve the most intimate sphere of the family, as in the case of a father who reads to his preschoolers on a daily basis, or they can involve the community at large, as in the example of a mother who becomes president of a neighborhood association. They have a *structural* aspect (as in the case of family organization), a particular *density* (how much time parents spend with the children), are *distributed* in identifiable forms (as in patterns of family interaction), and exhibit specific *outcomes* (children whose parents are highly involved in their educations typically demonstrate higher academic achievement). *Homogeneous* social capital designates ties between individuals of the same background and status, and *heterogeneous* social capital refers to bridges which cross the boundaries of class and ethnicity. In general, theories of social capital suggest that cultural behavior manifested in the realm of civil society is of utmost importance for both the economic organization and civic engagement of a population.

In education, the notion of social capital developed explanatory power in the 1980s through James Coleman's comparative studies of high school graduation rates. Coleman observed that students in Catholic high schools graduated at a higher rate than students in either public schools or private high schools. This was true in spite of the fact that Catholic schools had higher student–teacher ratios, spent less money per pupil than public schools, and offered a narrower range of courses that focused primarily on traditional academic achievement. Coleman sought to explain the Catholic schools' success with reference to the stronger social ties which undergird the Catholic school experience for students. He found that in Catholic schools clergy, parishioners, teachers, and parents all dedicate time to mentor young people in a more intense way than occurs in either public or other kinds of private schools. The Catholic schools' higher investment in relationships with students positively correlated with increased academic achievement and higher graduation rates.

In 1993 Robert Putnam's *Making Democracy Work* further enriched the concept of social capital. Although Putnam's book focused on civic traditions in modern Italy, its use of the concept of social capital to explain the difference between strong democratic institutions in northern

Italy and weak civic traditions in the south propelled what might have been an esoteric academic manuscript to the forefront of social policy discussions in the United States. Putnam argued that broadly accepted norms of social trust shaped powerful civic networks in northern Italy; those networks of civic engagement then served as engines of social capital which disseminated norms of reciprocity and trust throughout the region. In the south, on the other hand, social trust was minimal in a context where clientelism was rampant, governmental institutions were corrupt, and those social networks which did exist were hierarchically rather than horizontally ordered.

Rather than using the idea of social capital primarily as a means to better understand and promote the formation of human capital, as Coleman had done, Putnam sought to use social capital theory to explain the power of strong voluntary associations in civil society in determining effective democratic governance in the state. Putnam theorized that northern Italy was characterized by "virtuous circles" in which citizens displayed "generalized reciprocity" with one another and their institutions, whether public or private. "Generalized reciprocity refers to a continuing relationship of exchange that is at any given time unrequited or imbalanced, but that involves mutual expectations that a benefit granted now should be repaid in the future," Putnam wrote. A wealth of horizontally ordered civic networks, which brought "together agents of equivalent status and power," reinforced "robust norms of reciprocity" which promoted effective governance and strong civic participation.[25]

Southern Italy offered a grim contrast to the north's success, exemplifying the dilemmas of "vicious" rather than "virtuous" civic circles. In the south, social distrust prevented the development of generalized norms of reciprocity; instead, reciprocity was limited to a specific, tit-for-tat exchange of commodities or favors. Vertically ordered civic networks, such as the Mafia and the institutional Catholic Church, predominated over egalitarian horizontal organizations; as a result, social ties between individuals exhibited "asymmetric relations of hierarchy and dependence." "Vicious circles" between individuals and their governmental institutions made opportunistic conduct entirely logical; in an atmosphere of social distrust, why should one confer benefits on another party who could then use them against the donor?[26]

The above presentation of social capital theory is schematic, but it should be substantial enough to convey important ramifications for those concerned about the prospects of American education. Urban schools have long been noted for their hierarchical organization, the structural isolation of teachers, and bureaucratic impenetrability—traits which produce the cynicism and nonreciprocity indicative of vicious circles. Social capital theory suggests that if reformers seek to improve urban schools, they need to cultivate generalized reciprocity and social trust in such a manner that virtuous circles replace vicious ones. In addition—and this is a crucial consequence of the argument—*they must abandon purely internal reforms within the school and emphasize the many potential relationships which can be built (and rebuilt) between a school and its community.* Those relationships must engage parents, whose collaboration has proven to be essential to students' academic success, but they should extend beyond those family members who are immediately concerned with children's learning to reach out to congregations, the business community, and public officials such as the police, school board members, and city councilors. To develop a serious strategy of social capital formation in the educational institutions of our central cities, educators must be bold enough to conceptualize the school as *the center of the community*—as a vital geographical nexus in which friends and neighbors convene to identify, debate, and correct the exasperating proliferation of social problems which have accompanied the economic and social dislocations of the last quarter century.

To date, research on social capital in education has focused on comparisons among institutions (public, Catholic, and independent schools), among ethnic groups (Anglo-Americans and Mexican Americans), and between low and high achievers. The research is heavily quantitative, and although it has done much to illustrate the explanatory power of social capital, it has not articulated a developmental process of change which could promote stronger social ties and improved academic achievement in urban schools and neighborhoods. For those who teach, learn, and study in America's schools, the practical ramifications of social theory and research are matters of urgent concern. The present book is a first attempt to describe and analyze how schools can make a transition from vicious circles of cynicism and disengagement to virtuous circles of trust, solidarity, and reciprocity.[27]

This volume emphasizes the potential of civic action to improve academic achievement in low-income urban neighborhoods, but its arguments concerning social capital bear considerable relevance to the suburban periphery which surrounds our great metropolitan areas as well. Although the decline of social participation and civic ties is evinced in its most acute form in the central cities, the breakdown of the family, the rapid mobility rates of families, and the lack of sustained adult contact with children are problems endemic to all of American society. Lengthening work weeks, women's entrance into the labor force, and the increasingly unreliable presence of fathers in the family have created a gaping "time deficit" for suburban as well as urban youth.[28]

Use of the concept of social capital as a key theoretical construct necessitates several caveats. First, research on social capital is in its infancy, and the current stage of theoretical formulation entails numerous ambiguities which must be clarified if the concept is to develop conceptual rigor. For example, Coleman and Putnam both emphasized the importance of enabling social structures and common norms in the formation of social capital, but they did not specify which kinds of structures and norms are essential, which are contingent, and which are antithetical to social capital formation. Clarifying these ambiguities matters because of the existence of competing interpretations which could lead in radically different directions in terms of social policy.

For instance, consider Coleman's endorsement of Catholic schools as educational sites rich in social capital. In his studies of academic achievement, Coleman concluded that overlapping relationships between the church, the school, and the community were characteristic of Catholic schools and that this milieu fostered a comprehensive sponsoring of young people who grew up culturally embedded in their parishes and their urban neighborhoods. Subsequent research, however, has vitiated Coleman's speculations about the example Catholic schools offer for social capitalization. Tony Bryk, Valerie Lee, and Peter Holland have demonstrated that Catholic high schools recruit youth from broad and geographically diverse urban areas, and that relatively few youth experience the dense and protective social networks which Coleman imagined. Instead, Bryk, Lee, and Holland argue, Catholic school parents are more or less involved in fiduciary relationships with the schools. If one seeks to explain the relevance of Catholic schools for a theory of social capital, one must focus greater attention on the internal school organization and the universality of the norms promulgated by the Catholic Church. The concept of social capital is still preserved, but

Bryk, Lee, and Holland suggest that it is likely to prove more potent theoretically if one uses it to examine the structures and cultures that exist *within* Catholic schools rather than *between* those schools and their communities.[29]

A second example of the need for greater conceptual clarity is the relationship between an individual's human capital and a group's social capital. Coleman tended to treat the two as mutually reinforcing, but social capital and human capital can and do come into conflict with each other. Consider the example of some working-class parents' skepticism toward the value of higher education. Tightly knit families from the most diverse kinds of ethnic backgrounds can prevent human capital formation by emphasizing loyalty to family responsibilities and household economies over individual academic achievement and geographical mobility. Inner-city pupils who are pressured by their parents to drop out of high school or who are discouraged from attending prestigious universities in distant cities can experience strong families as inimical to their future academic success and human capital formation. To take another example, Putnam's observations of "amoral familism" in southern Italy suggest that some kinds of family loyalty impede social capital formation by privileging family ties at the expense of virtually all kinds of broader civic engagement or public accountability.[30]

The ambiguities attenuating Catholic schools' successes and the latent tensions between human capital and social capital development suggest that if one seeks to use social capital theory to improve public education, greater specificity about which norms and structures are essential to community betterment and how they are to be manifested is necessary. This recognition is related to a second caveat: social capital is a relative good, not an absolute one. One might plausibly argue that the South before desegregation had high levels of social capital as represented in strong families and racially circumscribed voluntary associations, but that social capital must be understood against the economic exploitation and political disenfranchisement of African-Americans. Social capital can prove to be a useful construct in reaching other key goals—the formation of human capital in an educated society (as in Coleman), or robust democratic institutions (as in Putnam). In both cases, social capital has an instrumental value which must be gauged in relation to higher norms and principles, such as freedom or justice.

A third warning: if misconstrued, much of the language of social capital theory can be interpreted as indicative of an absence of conflict. Trust, reciprocity, and solidarity suggest harmonious relationships— but the threat or actual expression of conflict can be an invigorating force in building social capital. A mother who demands that a recalci- trant daughter do her homework may experience unpleasant argu- ments with her child, but her persistence and the daughter's subsequent academic success reflect human capital formation for the student and social capital formation in the improved nexus between the student, the parent, and the school. Low-income parents who pressure a school board to terminate an ineffective principal may be angry and confron- tational, but the hiring of a new and dedicated principal can build so- cial trust and reciprocity between the board and the community. To be genuine, trust, reciprocity, and solidarity must be *earned,* not given as charitable gestures. Earning those qualities of social capital will frequently involve conflict; certainly, conflict has played an essential role in moving from vicious to virtuous circles in the case studies re- ported here.[31]

In spite of these caveats, social capital theory appears to offer much to educational theory and practice in the current national context. De- cades of research and policy reforms aimed at purely internal reforms of public schooling have created depressingly minimal results, and new attention is now being focused on the norms that inform civil society, the nature of social networks that can improve the lives of young people, and the development of enhanced communication and collaboration be- tween the school and the home. Teachers and administrators in urban public schools have found themselves swamped with new roles imposed upon them by the unraveling of social fabric in the community. Social capital theory, with its emphasis on the importance of developing norms of reciprocity and robust civic networks, appears to offer one powerful conceptual tool which can help to attack social decapitalization and en- hance the civic capacity of urban schools and neighborhoods.[32]

There are an infinite number of political currents at work in contem- porary discussions on social capital. On the one hand, political conserv- atives are attracted to theories of social capital because of their mistrust of the state as a mechanism for redistribution of wealth. On the other hand, liberals and radicals have anti-etatist traditions of their own and can be attracted to social capital theory insofar as they seek to strengthen community organizations which focus on neighborhood empowerment and issues of social justice.

The Texas Industrial Areas Foundation offers a concrete example of these complex social processes. The Texas IAF is a civic network of political intent which combines conservatives' appreciation of the role of voluntary associations in a free society, liberals' recognition of the contested but nonetheless essential integrity of the political system, and radicals' sense of urgency about and commitment to issues of social justice. The Texas IAF seeks to develop a vision and strategy for civic engagement which is pugnaciously nonsectarian, fiercely pluralistic, and deeply democratic, and which strives to cultivate untapped resources for the reanimation of American culture and politics in the current precarious context.

2

Moving Schools into
the Power Arena

Beginning in 1974 and expanding rapidly over the next two decades, the Industrial Areas Foundation in Texas has forged partnerships with a host of social actors who have been hard hit by economic and cultural pressures on the family. Catalyzed by the Texas IAF, parents, teachers, principals, clergy, parishioners, police officers, bankers, and realtors have come together in collective actions which have enhanced both their own lives and those of city children. Readers eager to get to the heart of the case studies can proceed directly to Chapter 3. For those who care about the historical background, theoretical framework, and forms of social action which the Texas IAF promotes, however, a review of its origins and development provides essential insight into the unusual nature of this school reform effort. Unlike much current school reform, which often defines "effectiveness" in an unreflective and noncontextual manner, the work of the Texas IAF is neither antitheoretical nor ahistorical. On the contrary, the particular historical influences and philosophical underpinnings which guide Texas IAF work provide much of the clout and direction which render the case studies comprehensible.

In this chapter I highlight five facets of the Texas IAF's politics of education. First, although the IAF was founded by Saul Alinsky, one of the United States' most original and provocative political radicals in the twentieth century, Alinsky understood his radicalism in a strikingly complex and multifaceted manner. To understand the work of the Texas IAF, we need to delineate the precise nature of Alinsky's radicalism as well as the transformation of the IAF since his death in 1972. The IAF has retained and jettisoned different parts of Alinsky's legacy to render the contemporary IAF more potent and broad based than it ever was in Alinsky's era.

Second, we need to inquire after the manner in which the Texas IAF first became effective in educational policy matters in Texas. Like many states, Texas was the site of a massive school reform movement in the 1980s, and the IAF was integrally involved in developing Texas House Bill 72, which was passed by the legislature in 1984. The participation of the Texas IAF in House Bill 72 gave the organization a reputation among school administrators and politicians throughout the state and set the stage for later school-based collaborations.

Third, the Texas IAF has developed a systemic approach to organizing low-income parents to engage in improving public schools which should be disaggregated to explain the effectiveness of each of its parts. Its approach begins with house meetings of parents, expands to neighborhood walks, builds up to an assembly which rallies all of the major community stakeholders, and continues through the formation of task forces and action teams which target concrete, winnable goals. Unlike the many presidential commissions, governors' conventions, and business league reports which dominate school reform discussions, the approach of the Texas IAF is focused upon listening to the sentiments of low-income parents in house meetings, parish halls, and public school auditoriums. Parents' grievances are then acted upon with a specific methodology and philosophy of organizing that has been carefully honed through decades of experience.

A fourth component of the Texas IAF which provides essential background to the cases of school reform is the development of an incipient philosophy of education. The modifier "incipient" is appropriate here, for Texas IAF leaders and organizers resist sectarian and programmatic labels. In spite of that proclivity, a number of different theoretical influences have gained ascendency in Texas IAF circles, and those influences manifest themselves in schools which collaborate with the community-based organization.

Finally, a fifth aspect of the Texas IAF which is of crucial importance to its evolution and success is its strong emphasis on expanding the political capacity of citizens. That expansion occurs through a kind of "mini-university" structure of workshops, seminars, and training sessions which convey a critique of contemporary American society, a political philosophy which enables constructive engagement in social change, and tools for analysis and reflection that do not just develop the human capital of individuals but also provide a theoretical framework which weaves together complex issues of personal meaning, social engagement, and political transformation. Leadership training sessions, seminars led by prominent intellectuals, and national gatherings of leaders with a focused civic curriculum create a core culture of engagement, debate, and problem solving. Those kinds of continuing education differ radically from traditional staff development in schools. They provide keys which can explain why Texas IAF leaders and organizers can be particularly focused and effective when entering school settings.

Background in history, theory, and methods of social organization in the Texas IAF is important for understanding the case studies for a number of reasons. A theoretical framework for organizing enables leaders and organizers to make difficult political decisions on a daily basis without falling prey to the vagaries of the moment. Knowledge of history matters because an oral culture exists in the Texas IAF which draws upon forms of social action demonstrated over two decades ago in Texas or even five decades ago in Chicago. Understanding that the Texas IAF approaches urban neighborhoods with specific organizing methods can dispel the mystique of community organizing and convey the tools which organizers use to teach political leadership in even the most disenfranchised of communities. Finally, recognizing that the Texas IAF is approaching school reform with an incipient philosophy of education can correct romanticizations of community organizing which would overemphasize the role of the community in school reform without connecting that to a coherent interpretation and practice of education.

Origins of the Texas IAF

The IAF was founded by Saul Alinsky in 1940 and developed in its first three decades into the most powerful community organizing group in the United States. Under Alinsky's leadership the IAF spearheaded a number of successful initiatives throughout the North in the postwar era and achieved international visibility as one of the most effective grass-roots political organizations in the country during the tumultuous 1960s. Although the vast majority of the work of IAF organizations was accomplished by community activists in inner cities, Saul Alinsky has appropriately received credit for providing an underlying philosophy and method of organizing urban neighborhoods. A brief review of Alinsky's political philosophy and its extension in contemporary Texas is essential if one is to grasp the theoretical and practical coherence behind the Texas IAF's current school reform activities.

Although Saul Alinsky referred to himself as a "radical," his understanding of that sobriquet was unique. He criticized student radicals of the 1960s for attacking the middle class, romanticizing the poor, alienating the white working class, and denigrating patriotism. He insisted that organizers stay within the experience of poor and working-class people and was critical of philanthropists, liberals, and social workers who sought to improve the life situations of the poor without enhancing their political power.

Alinsky made deep and lasting contributions to American politics by modeling an array of new kinds of social action that taught hitherto isolated and disenfranchised citizens how to accumulate and wield political power through strong neighborhood organizations. Particularly through his organizing efforts in Chicago and Rochester, Alinsky guided low-income citizens to develop organizations which could take on multifaceted issues—housing, employment, health care, and schools—and do so in a way which created lasting change. Alinsky taught citizens how to recognize their interests, how to collaborate with one another, how to personalize conflicts, and how to accept compromises. He loved conflict and enjoyed nothing more than a scandal. One of his most famous gambits involved the threat of a mass occupation of all of the toilets at O'Hare airport for a day to force the city to meet the demands of low-income African Americans in the Woodlawn section of Chicago; another involved purchasing a mass of tickets for a performance of the Rochester Symphony Orchestra and literally creating a stink by hosting a massive bean dinner before attendance at a gala event. Both strategies were planned to force city leaders to improve conditions in northern ghettos, and neither strategy was actually ever carried through. For Alinsky, however, the threat or even the rumor of a threat was as good as the real thing, particularly when it got the reaction from the city power holders that he desired.

Alinsky was anything but a dour and programmatic radical. Avoiding the party loyalties and sectarian squabbles that plagued the Left from the 1930s to the 1960s, Alinsky insisted upon a ferociously independent variant of American radicalism that weaved its principles and methods out of a crazy quilt of philosophical and political sources—including everything from the Old Testament to the Declaration of Independence and modern labor union organizing—and which he threw together in two provocative books, *Reveille for Radicals* and *Rules for Radicals*. Alinsky described himself as an "urban populist" and contended that "my philosophy is rooted in an American radical tradition, not in a Marxist tradition." He used ridicule and profanity to attack powerful individuals and corporations, but he also knew how to protect himself and the IAF through collaborations with religious institutions, particularly the Catholic Church. He valued civil society and especially cherished the notion that real politics consisted of *initiating* action and not simply *responding* to candidates, public officials, or issues defined by the media. During the 1960s Alinsky appeared to many student activists as a hero and prophet, but he kept a guarded distance from the countercultural parts of 1960s youth culture and criticized the self-defeating nature of its hostility to middle-class notions of material security, patriotism, and the sanctity of the family.[1]

The IAF never organized in a systematic way in the South in general or Texas in particular in Alinsky's lifetime, but the social movements which swept America in the 1960s did not leave Texas untouched. Ernesto Cortés, Jr., a native of San Antonio, was one individual who was inspired and challenged by many of the civil rights and farm workers' movements of the 1960s, and who was to develop into the central leader of IAF organizing in Texas. Cortés' grandparents were Mexican immigrants; his father managed a drug store and his uncle ran the first Spanish-language radio station in the United States. Cortés graduated from a parochial high school at sixteen and became the first member of his family to go to college. He enrolled at Texas A&M University in the fall of 1959, where he experienced anti-Mexican racism firsthand from his first college roommate and a band instructor who referred to Mexicans as "greasers."

Cortés graduated from Texas A&M when he was nineteen with a double major in English and economics. He then entered graduate studies in economics at the University of Texas, but the confluence of a number of factors, including his father's death, led him to abandon academics and to commit himself to social activism. He organized with the United Farm Workers in the Rio Grande Valley, supported the civil rights movement from a base in an African American church in Beaumont, Texas, and spearheaded the efforts of the Mexican American Unity Council to create minority-owned businesses in San Antonio. Throughout this period he developed his political leadership skills and immersed himself in the literature of social change and theology. While working with the United Farm Workers he met Gilbert Padilla, a former organizer with an IAF organization called the Community Service Organization in Los Angeles; from Padilla he learned of the impressive organizing legacy of IAF organizers Fred Ross and César Chávez in California. While active in Beaumont he studied leading twentieth-century theologians who had grappled with problems of social justice, such as Reinhold Niebuhr, Paul Tillich, Dietrich Bonhoeffer, and Rudolf Bultmann.[2]

Cortés was impatient with the pace of change in Texas. He began preliminary conversations with IAF organizers in Chicago in 1971 and attended a leadership training institute there with about fifteen other community activists from San Antonio in June 1972. After the training session, he spent a further two weeks in Chicago in August, trailing an IAF organizer to learn more about the nature of this kind of political engagement. He then returned to San Antonio briefly before returning north in 1973 to spend a full year organizing with IAF leaders in Milwaukee, Wisconsin, and East Chicago, Indiana. Throughout this period he was observing, experimenting, and planning to acquire the skills he would need to build the first IAF organization in Texas.

Cortés joined the IAF at a crucial turning point in the organization's history. For all of his strengths, Saul Alinsky alienated many potential supporters through his bombastic egocentrism, his pleasure at upsetting even those who were his most loyal allies, and his difficulty with truly listening to those who were trying to learn from him. Ernie Cortés was one of many who was nonplussed by Alinsky in their first encounter in Austin in the early 1960s. "I didn't like him, and he didn't like me," Cortés recalled. "I kept asking him questions he didn't want to get into, such as 'How do you actually *do* this stuff?' He wanted to talk about Lyndon Johnson."[3]

Saul Alinsky died in June 1972, but even before his death, his protégé Ed Chambers had effectively taken over the leadership of the IAF and brought new talent and vision to it. It was Chambers who had actually led the successful IAF organizing drive in Rochester in the 1960s, and it was Chambers' tenacious organizing experience which Alinsky drew upon (and claimed full credit for) when he wrote *Rules for Radicals*. Chambers quickly recognized the organizing talent of Ernie Cortés and brought him into the IAF at a time when the organization was maturing into a healthy culture of self-criticism which frankly recognized its many shortcomings.

Chambers strove to develop a new strategy for the IAF based less on spectacular assaults on the status quo and more on a patient building of power through collaborations based on mutual interests. Chambers recognized that Alinsky had stereotyped views of women, and he created an opening for women to receive training as organizers. Alinsky's political radicalism was rendered more complex by broadening IAF politics to address the needs of middle-class families, congregations, and neighborhoods. Chambers recognized another shortcoming of the IAF when he learned that he had so neglected his own health that he was too weak to make a blood donation. He subsequently repudiated Alinsky's neglect of the economic needs of organizers and worked successfully to provide them with strong middle-class salaries through dues gathered by churches and foundation grants.[4]

The boldest IAF transformation wrought by Chambers was to base the organization in religious institutions. Alinsky had always benefited from powerful patrons in the Catholic Church and he had developed a style of organizing that was immensely respectful of citizens' religious commitments. "To know a people is to know their religions," Alinsky wrote. "If the organizer believes in democracy and is concerned with what Jefferson referred to as 'a decent respect for the opinions of mankind,' there is no reason to oppose or try to break down local traditions." Chambers saw that although Alinsky had identified a powerful social base in religious institutions in low-income communities, the IAF could go much further in expanding its constituency if it would explicitly reclaim the emancipatory currents of the Judeo-Christian heritage. As a result of that new heightened commitment to religious institutions, the IAF recruited hosts of talented new leaders and organizers from clergy, many of whom had decades of experience in inner-city ministries, the civil rights movement, and the United Farm Workers.[5]

Ernie Cortés benefited from the new energy Chambers brought to the IAF and helped to reconceptualize the future of the organization with the IAF leadership. To start the first IAF organization in Texas, Cortés made regular visits to San Antonio from his northern base in 1973 to establish a sponsoring committee of Methodist, Episcopalian, Presbyterian, and Catholic clergy who would raise the funds and develop a contract to start an IAF group. In addition to the support of clergy and their congregations, the sponsoring committee's initiative was endorsed by Archbishop Francis Furey and Auxiliary Bishop Patrick Flores of the San Antonio Catholic Archdiocese. Flores was the son of migrant laborers and the first Mexican American prelate in the United States, and he brought a particularly intense passion to his work on the sponsoring committee. Both Furey and Flores were alarmed about the failure of San Antonio to provide minimal public services to its working-class, Mexican American citizens.[6]

Cortés returned to San Antonio in January 1974 and immediately began conversing with hundreds of civic and neighborhood leaders on the West Side to learn about which public issues troubled them the most. He learned that the residents of the West Side of San Antonio had a long list of changes they had desired for years. Neighborhood residents wanted new sewer systems to prevent flooding, sidewalk installation or repair to help children get to school safely, and bank loans to low-income homeowners victimized by redlining. They wanted respect from city council members and mayors who routinely ignored their neighborhoods when funds were assigned to different urban renewal projects. They knew that a powerful "Good Government League" dominated by Anglo-American politicians and business elites decided most of the key political issues in San Antonio, but they did not know how to challenge the league by establishing broad-based political organizations of their own.[7]

Rather than starting by organizing the entire city, Cortés decided to begin on a parish-by-parish basis. One of his first meetings was with Bishop Flores, who in addition to his work at the chancellory had become the presiding priest at the Church of Immaculate Conception on the West Side. Immaculate Conception had three major problems in the early 1970s. First, the church stood in close proximity to a hide processing plant which emitted terrible odors when the grease from inside the skin was burned; many services were ruined when the stench came wafting through the congregation. Second, a privately owned junkyard across the street from the church hosted large numbers of rats that were a health threat. Third, every time it rained, water would render intersections impassable, flood into neighborhood homes, and damage property.

Ernie Cortés worked with Bishop Flores and his parishioners to attack these three problems. When a letter-writing campaign was fruitless, Cortés organized a visit for the congregation with John Hill, the state's attorney general. Flores and his congregation rented two buses, traveled to Austin, and invited Hill to visit their parish. When Hill came to San Antonio shortly afterward, a strong wind blew the intolerable smell directly in his face. Hill gave the plant owner ten days to acquire and implement air pollution controls; thereafter, the plant would be fined a thousand dollars a day for violating state laws.

The Immaculate Conception parish was elated at the support and thrilled when the plant purchased the air pollution equipment and the community had clean air to breathe for the first time in decades. Galvanized by its success, the parish quickly moved on to take care of the junkyard, which eventually was purchased by the city and turned into a lovely park for the neighborhood. The problem with flooding was a larger issue, however, that could not be solved by the parish alone. Flooding was rampant on the West Side. To deal with community-wide issues, the parish would need to work with others to start a new organization which would force the ruling powers in San Antonio to include them in all of the key issues which confronted their city.

Fortunately for Immaculate Conception, similar civic momentum was under way at numerous other West Side parishes. Sparked by Cortés' leadership, but also committed to the idea that community leaders must learn to fight their own battles, a host of community groups initiated civic reforms on the West Side. Leaders in Holy Family parish fought for and won a footbridge over a drainage canal so that their children could walk in safety to Garza Elementary School. Another church, San Martín de Porres, acquired city funds so that its parishioners could build a walkway over a major thoroughfare to reach a popular day-care center. Other churches acquired traffic lights at dangerous intersections and crossing guards for schools.

The West Side was slowly learning how to challenge San Antonio's public service sector in order to receive its fair share of city revenues. After dozens of victories on neighborhood issues, the first Texas IAF organization, Communities Organized for Public Services (COPS), planned its founding convention for November 24, 1974. Although many issues had been won on the West Side in the months before the convention, one major problem persisted: the terrible flooding which occurred whenever a heavy storm hit the community. Although funds had been pledged by the city as far back as 1945 to rectify the problem, the West Side had languished over the intervening decades. In 1974 the city was hit with unusually severe rains and over 150 West Side residents were compelled to abandon their homes for shelter after one relentless storm in May.[8]

Recognizing the increasing frustration and anger in the community, Archbishop Furey sought to channel it to develop political capacity for COPS. He wrote a letter to all of the priests in the archdiocese, urging them to attend the founding convention: "The COPS approach seems to be the most effective model for citizens to have a voice in their community. The amount of support the church gives means life or death to the organization. Your presence, even for a while, would be a great encouragement for the people."[9]

As a result of the hard work of the sponsoring committee and Ernie Cortés, over two thousand citizens came to the founding convention at Jefferson High School on the West Side. It was attended by representatives from twenty-seven churches; they were husbands and housewives, workers at Kelly Air Force Base and Levi-Strauss, teachers, small business owners, and nurses. Bishop Flores spoke to the audience:

> You are not here today as supplicants with downcast eyes, not as welfare recipients, not as beggars. You are here as equals, as responsible, law-abiding, tax-paying people. You are a people that with your sweat have helped shape this country, this state, and this particular city. You seek no special favors. You seek a just share of your tax monies to have a decent community.[10]

The working-class Mexican American community was galvanized by the creation of COPS, but San Antonio's business and political elite paid no attention to it initially. For decades San Antonio had elite Mexican American leadership, but the *ricos*, as they were called, generally scorned working-class activism and espoused a paternalistic Mexican nationalism. The first Chicano political party, La Raza Unida, had developed substantial political clout in the late 1960s and early 1970s, and had forced Anglo powerholders throughout the Southwest to accommodate Mexican American demands for more inclusive political participation, but La Raza collapsed after 1973, undermined by self-destructive infighting. In spite of important challenges to the city establishment from a wide array of groups such as the League of United Latin American Citizens, the Mexican-American Legal Defense and Education Fund, and the

Mexican-American Student Organization, most of the blue-collar Mexican American constituents who made up COPS' membership still felt shut out of political power in San Antonio. As for the political establishment, its members saw no need to transform a system of governance that had served the affluent, Anglo-American elite.

COPS presented a phenomenon unfamiliar to San Antonio's ruling class. For years disgruntled citizens on the West Side had complained about the lack of infrastructural repairs; COPS was the first organization which took the time to study the city's budget and to come up with a detailed "counter budget" that allocated millions of dollars for drainage improvements, sidewalks, parks, and libraries on the West Side. The Good Government League had outlasted the challenges presented by La Raza Unida. It was less certain, however, of ways to stereotype and dismiss COPS leaders, who emphasized their commitment to Judeo-Christian values rather than their ethnic distinctiveness.[11]

Initially, COPS' counterbudget was ignored by Mayor Charles Becker, city council members, and San Antonio's business leaders, all of whom refused to meet with COPS to discuss its recommendations. Cortés proposed that COPS respond with a "tie-up" action that he had used in Indiana, and COPS leaders assented. In early February 1975, COPS activists filled the lobby at one of San Antonio's major banks, the Frost National Bank, and blocked all business by changing pennies into dollars and dollars into pennies for two straight days. At the same time, over five hundred other activists, all wearing red, white, and blue COPS buttons, filled one of downtown's largest and most elegant department stores, located within a stone's throw of the Alamo. They explored different combinations of make-up at the cosmetics counter, visited dressing rooms to try on expensive clothes, and tested beds in the furniture section—all without purchasing anything. COPS members were careful not to do anything illegal, but they thoroughly disrupted all business operations at these two prominent institutions for two days.

San Antonio was in an uproar about COPS' tie-up actions. Knowing that the Catholic Church supported COPS, conservative business owners visited Bishop Flores to express their indignation. "We were accused of being communists," Flores recalled, "but I said, 'We're not communists, we're Americans! We're Democrats and Republicans who have legitimate grievances.' I asked them whether they had ever been to the West Side to see the real conditions in which people are living, but most of them lived on the North Side and had no idea how poor the public services were in this part of the city."

At the end of the second day, San Antonio's power elite got the point and agreed to meet with COPS leaders. In subsequent meetings with the mayor, city council members, and business leaders, COPS won over $100 million in capital expenditures for the West Side. More than the sheer cash amount, however, the victory showed the city's Mexican American community that it had earned a new level of respect and power for itself in the fractious world of urban politics.

In 1977 COPS turned out more than six thousand citizens at its annual convention, with the theme of "San Antonio COPS Versus Cheap Labor." COPS had consolidated its position as a major political player in San Antonio. Previous IAF efforts had shown that the IAF could gain victories in northern states where unions were strong and neighborhoods had long traditions of working-class activism; COPS marked a turning point by demonstrating that an IAF organization could flourish in a southern state in which organized labor was weak but religious institutions were strong. COPS was not an anomaly in national politics; powerful new IAF groups developed simultaneously in Los Angeles, Baltimore, and New York City. The new IAF strategy of anchoring organizations in religious institutions was working.

In March 1978 the IAF codified its new commitment to partnerships with religious institutions in a succinct paper entitled "Organizing for Family and Congregation." The paper analyzed the changes in American politics and society that threatened to undermine the family and secondary associations. Although the paper retained Alinsky's emphasis on grass-roots political participation, "Organizing for Family and Congregation" shared little with the overall development of American radicalism in the 1970s. Unlike the rising politics of group identity which emphasized race, class, and gender differences, "Organizing for Family and Congregation" sought common ground by defending the sanctity of the family, highlighting the endangered status of American youth, and championing the role of secondary associations in enriching American social and spiritual life. Unlike the proclivity of liberals and radicals to expand the powers of the state to address social problems, the IAF developed a synthetic attack upon "the huge corporations, mass media, and 'benevolent' government" to which "we have given over control of much of our lives." Eschewing the romanticization characteristic of the social movements of the 1960s, the IAF, like Alinsky, decried the "lack of collective leadership, the reliance on charismatic leaders, the lack of a solid dues base, the tendency toward unaccountable action, and the alienation of the moderates and conservatives" which characterized 1960s movements.[12]

The IAF's radicalism, always unique in the American political landscape, continued to develop its independent path and accrued more populist hues. However much secular perspectives may prevail among liberal and radical intellectuals, "Organizing for Family and Congregation" recognized that "in our country one of the largest reservoirs of untapped power is the institution of the parish and congregation" and proclaimed that "the citizens' organization of this type respects and builds on the traditions and patterns of the community." Unlike Marxism's single-minded focus on the conditions of wage laborers, "Organizing for Family and Congregation" was concerned with all sectors of society, ranging from ironworkers in Pittsburgh to housewives in Chicago to Long Island executives burdened with college tuition payments. The IAF retained its traditional profile as a secondary association primarily promoting the interests of poor and working-class citizens, but it tempered its tactics and used them in a more deliberate, focused, and patient fashion to build its new organizations.[13]

In Texas the new strategy paid off. Although many other factors also played a role, COPS sounded the death knell of the Good Government League in San Antonio and compelled the city's business and political elite to accommodate the legitimate demands of low-income citizens. Inspired by the example of COPS, clergy and parishioners in other nearby metropolitan areas soon began forming sponsoring committees. In 1976 a coalition of Protestant and Catholic clergy in Houston wanted to replicate COPS' successes in the sprawling working-class neighborhoods of that city, and by 1978, Cortés and Sister Christine Stephens had brought together a network of thirty-two churches in The Metropolitan Organization (TMO). By 1982 a third IAF organization, Valley Interfaith, was established in the lower Rio Grande Valley, where its organizers and leaders focused on issues of clean water provision and sewage drainage in some of the most impoverished communities in the United States. Further organizing efforts led to the creation of sister IAF organizations in El Paso, Austin, Fort Worth, Dallas, and Beaumont over the next two decades.

The growth of the Texas IAF organizations dovetailed with the decline of older urban regimes that were gradually compelled to share power with minority voters and leaders. For decades, elite social networks of White politicians and business leaders dominated Texas politics through informal, closed-door gatherings. In Houston, the "Suite 8F Crowd" included such magnates as Jesse Jones, Gus Wortham, and Herman and George Brown; Fort Worth had a similar coterie in the "Seventh Street Gang," as did San Antonio in its "Good Government League." In the 1970s and 1980s these older concentrations of power ceded control to more open and pluralistic urban networks in which the economic power of Whites coalesced with more ethnically diverse political leadership.[14]

Because of the intensely local flavor of each Texas IAF organization, idiosyncrasies abound from one metropolitan region to another. Like COPS, Valley Interfaith and the El Paso Interreligious Sponsoring Organization (EPISO) are almost exclusively Catholic and Mexican American in composition, while the organizations in Houston, Austin, Fort Worth, and Dallas encompass Black, White, and Hispanic congregations of the major religious faiths. The organizations in the Rio Grande Valley work in some of the most impoverished counties in the United States, while Texas IAF organizations in suburban Fort Bend County (southwest of Houston), Dallas, and Austin include Episcopalian, Lutheran, and Jewish congregations that are affluent by any measure.

The remarkable heterogeneity of Texas IAF organizations and their evolution from militant Alinsky organizations to more complex and broad-based networks of civic engagement have left many observers perplexed as to their overall nature and trajectory. In part, the Texas IAF organizations appear to both foster and benefit from a deliberate ambiguity that eschews traditional political alignments and endeavors to focus on the pragmatics of bringing diverse constituencies together to address practical and immediate problems of poor and working-class citizens. My own interpretation is that the organizations' structures and intentions are parallel to the "two aspects of the church's life that are both demanding and inseparable: universality and the preference for the poor." The universality of the Texas IAF can be seen in its alliances with affluent suburbanites to protect underground aquifers that provide water to broad metropolitan regions such as San Antonio or Austin; in its advocacy of omnibus education bills that pump vast new revenues into public schools in both privileged and impoverished communities; in its readiness to work with corporate chief executive officers and political leaders to develop comprehensive programs of urban development that enhance all facets of a region's political economy. The "preference for the poor," on the other hand, is manifested in the Texas IAF's advocacy for the provision of water and sewage facilities in unincorporated communities in the Rio Grande Valley, its focus on educational betterment in the lowest-performing schools in working-class neighborhoods, and its creation of job training programs for unskilled workers who need further education to participate in the new global economy. By oscillating between communities that are predominantly low-income and those with greater fiscal and human capital resources, Texas IAF organizations both maintain their traditional ties to disadvantaged Americans and build powerful new relationships with a broader range of community stakeholders.[15]

The economic base of Texas IAF organizations consists of dues paid primarily by religious institutions which pay organizer and staff salaries, rent, and office supplies. Dues are paid on a sliding scale basis, dependent upon the size of a congregation and its revenues. A small Catholic church on the West Side of San Antonio gives five hundred dollars a year to COPS, while a large Lutheran church in Dallas contributes ten thousand dollars each year to its local IAF organization. In between those two extremes may stand some thirty religious institutions whose dues more commonly come to between fifteen hundred and three thousand dollars a year.

Much of the work of starting an IAF organization involves persuading clergy and church councils to raise the funds to support an IAF organizer and staff—a task which can be extremely difficult, given the limited resources and internecine quarrels of many churches in working-class neighborhoods. The example of COPS is instructive here. In spite of Archbishop Furey's letter of endorsement to clergy and the strong popular support in the community, COPS leaders were disappointed to observe that only six pastors attended their founding convention in 1974. The circumstances causing the poor attendance in San Antonio were somewhat unique. Prior to Furey's leadership, his predecessor, Robert Lucey, had combined a bold political commitment to social justice with an authoritarian leadership style which alienated all but his closest friends. After close to thirty years in power, Lucey was expelled from the archbishopric in 1969 in the midst of a clerical rebellion which polarized the Catholic community in San Antonio and revealed latent, long-standing tensions to full public view. It should hardly be surprising that most Catholic clergy would be reluctant to participate in another initiative entailing political engagement after years of subterranean conflict with Lucey.[16]

The process of building a coalition was a slow one, but it began to take hold nonetheless as Cortés and local leaders started winning a host of victories similar to those at Immaculate Conception, Holy Family, and San Martín de Porres. Father Don Hennessey, pastor of Saint James' Church, took on a leadership role in persuading the clergy to join. Hennessey urged his colleagues to recognize that their parishioners "were all flying out to the North Side—the ones who could afford it—and taking a good chunk of our collection with them." Hennessey followed Alinsky's admonition to organize around self-interest rather than high moral principles. "Guys, this is an insurance policy to keep our key leaders here in our parish," he told his fellow clergy. "I'm paying $3,000 a year to the chancery for insurance on these buildings. Fifteen hundred dollars is cheap to keep them from becoming a cemetery." Hennessey's strategy worked: two years after its founding convention COPS had forty member churches.[17]

Once COPS had gained its first successes in San Antonio, the process of building sister IAF organizations in Texas was greatly expedited, in part through the close relationships which exist among the Catholic leadership. Archbishop Patrick Furey, for example, had been raised in the lower Rio Grande Valley, was a priest at Holy Name Catholic Church on Houston's North Side, and bishop of El Paso before moving to San Antonio. Furey had years of collegial relations with parish priests, bishops, and chancellors throughout the state that enabled him to persuade the church's parishioners and leadership in places like Houston and the Rio Grande Valley that IAF organizations would benefit their congregations. Since more than a third of all churchgoers in Texas are Catholic, the endorsement of the Church hierarchy greatly enhanced the expansion of the Texas IAF network. Simply an endorsement from a friendly archbishop was hardly enough to secure the success of an IAF organization, however. The founding of the El Paso Interreligious Sponsoring Organization was marked by tenacious opposition from conservative Catholics, and IAF organizers and leaders had to tolerate everything from slashed tires to death threats from their opponents in the first stages of their organizing effort.[18]

The Catholic Church offered one channel for organizing low- and moderate-income Texans which Ernie Cortés capitalized upon in starting IAF organizations in the Southwest. Another resource, hitherto slighted by the IAF in its northern organizations, was the civic and political power of women. Fred Ross, an organizer for the Community Service Organization in California, had been the first IAF organizer to develop women as organizers in the 1950s, but Ross' efforts had not been duplicated in IAF organizations in other parts of the country. That failure to develop women's potential in IAF groups changed when Cortés began systematically training women as organizers and civic leaders in Texas in the 1970s. Cortés trained nuns such as Christine Stephens, Maribeth Larkin, Consuelo Tovar, and Mignonne Konecny to be IAF organizers, and he worked with housewives throughout urban Texas and the Rio Grande Valley to identify community problems and to develop strategies of attacking and ameliorating them.[19]

Once established, Texas IAF organizations are not entirely dependent upon dues. Texas IAF organizations acquire funding from the Catholic Church's Campaign for Human Development, the Ford Foundation, and the Rockefeller Foundation. The organizations neither solicit nor accept funds from governmental agencies. There are ten lead organizers in the Texas IAF who have the overall responsibility for organizing metropolitan areas such as Dallas, Houston, Austin, El Paso, Fort Worth, and San Antonio; suburban areas such as Fort Bend County, southwest of Houston; and rural areas such as the Rio Grande Valley. The lead organizers generally have over two decades' experience in community or labor union organizing. Seven of the organizations are headed by women and four are led by men; the majority of these leaders are native Texans. Five of the women are nuns. All of them spent years organizing in the Texas IAF before receiving their current assignments. They are well paid; salaries range from $45,000 to $60,000 for lead organizers.

In addition to the lead organizers, Texas IAF organizations usually employ other organizers with less experience who work on issues ranging from education to housing to health. Although no rigid set of guidelines is followed with regard to race or gender, the Texas IAF makes every effort to assure that organizers who work in Mexican American neighborhoods have a command of Spanish and those who are assigned to African American communities are either African American themselves or have extensive backgrounds in working effectively with Black Americans.

The community leaders who work with the Texas IAF organizers are unsalaried and are drawn from religious institutions, neighborhoods, and schools. One of the key tasks of Texas IAF organizers is to identify indigenous community leaders and to develop their political capacities. When Ernie Cortés first began organizing COPS in 1972, he did not seek out political radicals in the community; rather, he asked ministers for the names of leaders who served on parish councils, organized church athletic tournaments, and conducted fund-raising events such as bingo games or cookouts.

Texas IAF organizers never refer to participants in meetings and assemblies as "volunteers"; as part of the organization's emphasis on leadership development, every citizen who participates in Texas IAF actions is referred to as a "leader." Such nomenclature might seem pedantic if one were describing parents who turn out for events intermittently, but it is important if one is to understand what one Texas IAF co-chair, Father John Korscmar, has described as the most distinctive attribute of the Texas IAF—its radical inclusiveness and tenacious commitment to promoting leadership development in low-income communities. "The genius of this thing," Korscmar says, "is that there truly always is room for more people to become leaders." Reflective of that horizontally ordered network, COPS had thirty-eight vice-presidents scattered about San Antonio at one point.[20]

Each Texas IAF organization consists of leaders and organizers who set policy, take action, and hold elected officials accountable. Policies for the organizations are determined largely through a strategy of house meetings in neighborhoods in which local residents come together to speak out on the issues that most concern them. The IAF is founded on the premise that people in a community can solve their own problems, given the requisite training and leadership development. Common phrases in IAF circles are that the IAF is an "organization of organizations" and a "confederation of congregations." Although the number of congregations will vary from city to city, the IAF aspires to be as broad based as possible in its membership. In Austin, for example, the Texas IAF organization's congregational base is one-third Catholic and one-third Baptist; the final third is made up of non-Baptist Protestant and Jewish congregations.

Leadership training is the key part of the work of the Texas IAF. To build the organization, organizers and leaders must identify individuals with latent leadership skills and cultivate them. "At the very beginning," IAF organizer Sister Christine Stephens says, "it's not even that important what the leaders think. What's important is that they have the skills of leaders and are recognized in the community for that." Her point is an essential one which sharply demarcates Alinsky organizing from other kinds of political work. Alinsky recognized that many of the local leaders who make up the daily fabric and vitality of a community may have no visibility outside of that community, and he warned against quick identification of apparent leaders such as business owners or school principals who might work in a community but have no real ties to it beyond their jobs. "Let us look at it this way," Alinsky wrote,

> Joe Dokes, a labor steward, may have a following of thirty or forty people who regard his decisions on labor as final. Ten of them, however, if confronted with a financial problem will look to Robert Rowe, who is in an entirely different field of employment and whom they know through their fraternal society. Ten others may look to John Doe, who is a bartender, for financial advice. Of the twenty last mentioned, thirteen may look to Sidney Smith for political leadership; Sidney is a fireman.
>
> And so the question of determining who is a leader involves a large number of partial leaders or leaders of small groups and particularized aspects of their life. The number of natural leaders therefore is considerable. It is as true in that community as it is in any other segment of the population, including that of the reader. These natural leaders—the "Little Joes"—may, it is clear, occupy the most humble roles in the community. A window trimmer may be the president of the Holy Name Society. Or your "Little Joe" may be a garage mechanic, a bartender, an elevator operator, a bus driver. These are the common people, and among them are to be found the natural leaders of the natural groups which are present among all people.[21]

Aside from the absence of women in leadership positions, Alinsky's description characterizes the kinds of individuals that Texas IAF organizers would first seek to recruit into a community organization. Particularly important is his recognition of the large numbers of partial leaders who exist in any community whose resources can be mobilized to enhance their schools and neighborhoods.

Organizers and leaders establish their own unique dynamics in working with one another. When Ernie Cortés organized COPS in San Antonio, he refused to grant press interviews and made sure that media attention stayed on the indigenous community leaders who were developing their political capacities. "In my mind, if I came forward, it undermined the work they were trying to do—the real work of ordinary people doing extraordinary things," he said. As the Texas IAF has grown and expanded over the past two decades, it has been possible to hire more and more organizers whose first work with local organizations was as community leaders. Those organizers have a special sensitivity to the needs of leaders and ways that they can identify and support new leaders. "The work that organizers do with leaders is part of a very delicate process," COPS organizer Alejandra Rodriguez commented. "We need to agitate leaders without irritating them—because if we irritate them, we've lost them for good." [22]

To stabilize Texas IAF organizations, leaders and organizers develop a rhythm of house meetings, strategic action, and evaluation. Organizers and leaders need to achieve victories that will assure clergy and parishioners that their dues are well spent. Infrastructural repairs—road repairs, better lighting, code compliance—are especially visible facets of urban neighborhoods that affect everyone; Texas IAF organizations have typically addressed these kinds of projects to demonstrate their capacities to promote improvements in working-class communities.

Given this emphasis on issues which are sources of distress to a community and of a concrete, almost tactile nature, the decision of Texas IAF organizations to become involved in issues of school reform represented a departure from tradition. From the beginnings of Alinsky's Back of the Yards Council in the 1930s to the late 1960s, IAF organizers and leaders worked with schools, but most of their work dealt with policy issues relevant to fiscal concerns such as affordable milk or school desegregation. They played no role in rethinking the school's curriculum, methods of instruction, or forms of student assessment.

It was not until the 1960s that one of the most famous of the IAF organizations, The Woodlawn Organization (TWO), tried to improve inner-city schools in Chicago. Distressed by segregated schools, high dropout rates, poor academic achievement, and a proliferation of youth gangs in the neighborhood, TWO worked with the University of Chicago, the local school board, and the federal Department of Education to create the Woodlawn Experimental Schools Project in a vertical team of neighborhood elementary, middle, and high schools. Benefiting from high community support, the experimental schools reduced teacher attrition and showed impressive gains in reading scores at the elementary school level in their first year.[23]

In spite of some successes, however, the experimental schools effort collapsed after only their second year. The project failed for many reasons. First, TWO failed to break through the control of the central office of the Chicago school district over vital decisions concerning teacher evaluation and assignment. That inability in and of itself could have been overcome if TWO had developed a concerted strategy to train teachers and parents in the mutual accountability they would have to have developed with each other if the schools were to be improved, but no such systematic training occurred, and a significant minority of the teaching staff resisted the empowerment of parents. Second, frustrations with the central office over teacher assignments fueled dissent within the Woodlawn community, and schisms developed between community-chosen leaders who directed the overall project and administrators assigned to the schools. TWO's inability to overcome that internal schism opened the door for the district to terminate the project and to reassert its power over the schools in the Woodlawn community.

The IAF learned important lessons from the failure of TWO in school reform. Most urban public schools are embedded in massive bureaucracies which can share or delegate power to community groups but which retain ultimate control over the most important decisions concerning teachers' school assignments and promotions. Even when teachers or administrators are committed to the communities in which they work, their self-interest dictates that they respect the decisions of central office administrators, who can undermine community-based programs by insisting upon the maintenance of city or state rules and regulations that run counter to the spirit of community control.

The IAF learned from its efforts in the Woodlawn Experimental Schools Project that it would need to develop a far more sophisticated approach to school reform than simply massive community involvement. Although TWO consistently turned out high numbers of parents for PTA meetings, school board meetings, and a host of school-based events, those numbers were not sufficient to challenge the power of the central office and organizations such as teacher unions. Because TWO lacked knowledge of the internal culture of the bureaucracy, power in the form of a citywide base of support, and money to provide the flexibility to circumvent rigid district guidelines, the prevailing powers just had to wait until the community-based effort collapsed from fatigue and internal dissent.

In spite of the negative experiences of TWO, the IAF organizations in Texas gradually became involved in school reform in the 1980s. This time, however, a number of different strategies were deployed. Rather than force an experimental project on recalcitrant districts, IAF organizations developed collaborative relationships with power holders such as school superintendents and board members early on in their organizing efforts. Recognizing the power that teachers hold, Texas IAF organizers and leaders conducted lengthy one-on-one discussions with teachers to hear out their grievances and develop relationships of trust and reciprocity. Rather than taking a confrontational approach, Texas IAF leaders emphasized the language of mutual accountability. By developing a more relational approach to schools which accepted the interests and needs of a wide range of community stakeholders, the organization was able to develop legitimacy in the eyes of the many citizens who were alarmed about the low academic achievement of low-income youth.

First Steps in the Politics of Education

None of the Texas IAF's first issues were related to schools, although concern about children's safety walking to school on streets with neither sidewalks nor adequate drainage concerned many parents on the West Side of San Antonio and played a role in advocating those infrastuctural improvements. As COPS grew and became more powerful, however, it took on two educational issues. First, COPS compelled the San Antonio Independent School District to make public its budget—action required by Texas state law but routinely ignored by the district. Second, COPS mobilized effectively to defeat an initiative to commit $1.6 million to a new administrative building in San Antonio at a time when thousands of children in the city were spending their days in dilapidated temporary classrooms.

When COPS compelled the San Antonio Independent School District to make public its budget and defeated the referendum on a new administration building, citizens in the Texas IAF learned that they could play a positive role not only in issues affecting drainage or parks but also in matters concerning public schools and their expenditures. Those victories were of vital importance to low-income, predominantly Mexican American citizens in the early 1980s, because they had been involved in over a decade's worth of fractious litigation attempting to improve the state funding of children in poorer school districts. Especially in San Antonio, Mexican Americans were dissatisfied about the phenomenal resources enjoyed by children in affluent Anglo-American Alamo Heights and the paucity of materials available to Mexican American students on the west, south, and east sides of the city.

In the early 1980s Texas IAF leaders and organizers saw a new opportunity to participate in sweeping changes of the state's educational system. Mark White, a Democrat, was elected governor of Texas in November 1982 with a platform advocating far-reaching improvements in public schools. Seeking to fulfill his campaign promises, White accepted the recommendation of House Speaker Gib Lewis to create a Select Committee on Public Education (SCOPE), and appointed a political novice (at that time) to chair the committee, H. Ross Perot. The purpose of SCOPE was to study the dynamics of public education in Texas, with particular attention to be focused upon teachers' salaries, per-pupil expenditures in poorer districts, and academic achievement. SCOPE was to have no power to implement change on its own; rather, it was asked to propose a detailed list of recommendations to both the Texas House of Representatives and the Senate for approval by the legislators.[24]

Texas IAF leaders and organizers played no role in determining who was appointed to SCOPE, but they are credited by virtually all of the key players on the committee with having had a deep influence on its deliberations. Lieutenant Governor Bill Hobby met with IAF leaders eight times in the summer of 1983 to explain the intricacies of Texas school finances to them, and they met with Perot himself soon after his appointment. Once the leaders and organizers felt familiar enough with the major facets of school reform to teach others, they developed a comprehensive strategy to teach citizens in their home communities about the importance of reform. House meetings, parish meetings, and city-wide conventions were held in San Antonio, El Paso, Houston, and Brownsville to discuss the importance of SCOPE's recommendations.

In November 1983 Perot appeared before a crowd of over two thousand citizens organized by Texas IAF organization Valley Interfaith at the Catholic War Veterans Hall in Weslaco in the Rio Grande Valley. Perot heard a litany of complaints from Valley Interfaith leaders about the failures of the educational system and the inequities of public school funding. Impressed with that grass-roots mobilization, Perot asked Texas IAF leaders and organizers to make a presentation to SCOPE with recommendations on financial issues later that month. Those recommendations were then largely adopted by Texas Comptroller Bob Bullock, who chaired SCOPE's finance subcommittee.[25]

By the summer of 1984, Governor White was pleased with SCOPE's progress and exercised his prerogative to call a special session of the legislature to hammer out legislation enacting comprehensive reform in Texas' public education system. Once the session convened, Texas IAF leaders and organizers capitalized on their months of training and study to hold a series of meetings with their representatives and to advocate reforms that would benefit the poorest school districts, improve the student/teacher ratio, and raise teacher salaries. As a result of their detailed studies of school finances, many of the leaders and organizers demonstrated greater knowledge of the many facets of the issues than their legislators. Texas IAF leaders and organizers were pleased to find that many of their major issues pertaining to higher quality education for children from low-income backgrounds received prominent attention from SCOPE.

The Texas IAF gained more than just its desired recommendations from SCOPE. Through their meetings with legislators, Ernie Cortés and the Texas IAF garnered new respect and visibility among Texas' political leaders. Tom Luce, chief of staff of the select committee, liked the "fact-driven, substantive way" that the Texas IAF organized, and Perot said, "They're the kind of people you need to accomplish things like major changes in the public schools." The harmonious relationship was almost obliterated on June 17, 1984, however, when in a notorious turn of events called "the Father's Day Massacre," the House Public Education Committee gutted every substantive recommendation made by SCOPE that could have enhanced the improvement of public education in Texas.[26]

The House Public Education Committee could not have foreseen the consequences of its actions. On June 18 thousands of Texas IAF leaders gathered in a rally outside of the capital to demand a resuscitation of the reform effort. The rally had been planned in advance to support SCOPE's recommendations, but the sabotage of its agenda turned a supportive rally into a massive public protest against the Father's Day Massacre. A grateful governor and lieutenant governor, both of whom had campaigned on the issue of school reform, went before the crowd to express their commitment to continue the fight, and those legislators who had destroyed the proposals were confronted by hosts of angry Texas IAF leaders who demanded that they support the reform agenda.

According to Tom Luce, the rally and the tenacious advocacy of the Texas IAF saved the reform legislation. Besieged by Texas IAF leaders, legislators promised to give SCOPE's recommendations a second look, and many of the recommendations were restored and approved by the House and the Senate. The final legislation increased per-pupil funding, improved the student/teacher ratio, and raised teacher salaries. Perhaps the most important result of the legislation, which increased school funding by $2.8 billion, was to raise students' academic achievement by enhancing the student/teacher ratio. This achievement, documented by Ronald Ferguson of the Kennedy School of Government at Harvard University, would have been impossible without the key intervention of the Texas IAF in the reform debate at the impasse created by the Father's Day Massacre.[27]

The Texas IAF's advocacy in Austin showed low-income citizens that they could have an impact on public education that would improve the quality of their children's educations. Having experienced victory with House Bill 72, Texas IAF leaders and organizers have intensified their work on issues of public education by challenging low-income parents to break out of their disengagement from their children's schooling, to identify common areas of concern, and to work in a tenacious and focused manner on leveraging change from school boards, city council members, mayors, the state commissioner of education, and the governor. In the process, the Texas IAF has itself matured from the role of outsider mobilizing for change to insider negotiating with school districts, business leaders, and foundations to hammer out realistic, winnable strategies for improving education.

Developing Methods for Organizing Urban Schools and Neighborhoods

Texas IAF organizations have chosen to improve certain kinds of schools and developed a clear strategy to increase parental involvement in them. Texas IAF leaders and organizers target schools which are deeply troubled but which have a fighting chance of turning themselves around. "Deeply troubled" here refers to a litany of problems associated with America's urban youth, including high rates of unemployment and low-paying jobs, low test scores, high rates of academic failure and drop-out, the presence of youth gangs, lack of personal safety, and a high number of single-parent households—all in a state with the highest adult illiteracy rate in the nation. To refer to troubled schools in the Texas context is to refer to schools in neighborhoods in which many parents have had little formal education, have had negative experiences with schools themselves, and see schools as opposed to the culture of the home and the community.

The neighborhoods in which the schools are situated display a range of different demographic and economic characteristics which influence the kinds of community organizing that occurs in schools. In the major metropolitan areas of San Antonio, Houston, and Dallas, neighborhoods tend to be dominated by one ethnic group, with others occupying housing or tenements on a few blocks scattered throughout the community. In part, however, commonalities in ethnicity can mask cultural differences within groups. Mexican Americans who descend from families who have been in the United States for three or more generations may lack linguistic and other cultural ties with *indocumentados* who are firmly rooted in either a Mexican identity or that of other Central American nations. Where White or Black Americans might see a Latino neighborhood, indigenous residents might see a complex mélange of Chicanos, Mexicans, Salvadorans, and Guatemalans, who are themselves stratified by class and demonstrate heterogeneous attitudes toward institutions such as public schools. Although residential segregation is strong, particularly for African Americans, the surge in the Hispanic population in the past two decades generally has resulted in pockets of Mexican American residents even in the heart of historically Black communities such as east San Antonio, the Fifth Ward in Houston, and Oak Cliff in Dallas. In addition, many predominantly Black communities have maintained a sprinkling of older White residents, generally senior citizens who made a commitment to stay in the community when, in the 1960s and 1970s, Whites vacated the cities en masse and moved to the suburbs.[28]

The class composition of the neighborhoods the Texas IAF organizes is relatively consistent. The majority of the neighborhoods are zones of high poverty (in which over 30 percent of the residents fall below the poverty line) but not extreme poverty (over 40 percent). In Dallas, Houston, and San Antonio, the neighborhoods are made up of a mixture of working-class citizens employed in manufacturing industries and the service sector and persons employed on a transient basis who are living in poverty and dependent upon federal programs such as Aid to Families with Dependent Children. Whether one is in a Mexican American community such as the Near North Side in Houston or a Black neighborhood such as Morningside in Fort Worth, per capita income is low (roughly, between seven thousand and nine thousand dollars) and high numbers of parents have less than a high school education. In these neighborhoods, stable single-family, owner-occupied housing inhabited by families who have lived in the community for decades alternate in crazy-quilt patterns with tenements packed with female-headed households and the families of recent Latino immigrants.[29]

Thus, the neighborhoods organized by the Texas IAF are characterized by a mixture of citizens who have steady albeit low incomes and those who are poor and dependent on varying amounts of public assistance for survival. In designating some citizens as "poor," it is important to recall the dynamic and multidimensional nature of social class in the United States; although the majority of Americans who become poor climb out of poverty in less than two years, others are dependent on various forms of federal aid for decades. It is also important to notice who is not included as poor in official definitions; currently, a family of four making $16,000 a year is not poor, for example, although many middle-class Americans would be aghast at the prospect of making ends meet with such limited fiscal resources. At any rate, the West Side of San Antonio, the Fifth Ward in Houston, and other Texas IAF strongholds are not like the South Side of Chicago or the South Bronx in the sense of concentrated poverty and social isolation from middle-class customs and mores. Home ownership, steady work, and stable families are within many citizens' reaches, although the continuing fall of wages for unskilled workers makes participation in the mainstream increasingly difficult.[30]

Although most of the neighborhoods in which the IAF organizes schools do not occupy the extreme represented by the Robert Taylor Homes or Cabrini Green in Chicago, some of the schools are populated by children growing up in extreme poverty. Schools in Brownsville, Laredo, Del Rio, and El Paso, for example, are centered in communities in which the rate of childhood poverty is well over 50 percent (reflecting the fact that the poverty rate is higher for children than it is for the general population). The greatest poverty indicators in the United States are along the Texas–Mexico border. In many of the schools in these communities, virtually all of the children are beneficiaries of federal free and reduced-price breakfast and lunch programs. In the *Segundo Barrio* of El Paso, for example, where IAF organizers work in seven schools, virtually all of the community residents live in small, low-cost tenements. Per capita income is under four thousand dollars, making the neighborhood one of the poorest in the United States.[31]

We are dealing, then, with urban neighborhoods, inhabited by predominantly Mexican American and African American populations, with a mixture of persons who have achieved some economic independence and other who rely heavily on various forms of state assistance. It is important to recall that even in neighborhoods characterized by high rates of poverty, the majority of the population will consist of working-class and some middle-class residents. That heterogeneity of class composition is an important consideration for IAF organizers. "We're trying to organize not only the very poor, but also blue-collar and middle-income people," Dallas organizer Christine Stephens explained. "We're not just looking for ethnic and religious diversity, but we're also looking for class diversity." Accordingly, most of the neighborhoods in which the IAF organizes for educational reform are characterized by a broad range of different human personalities, including citizens who own homes, raise families, work hard, and pay taxes. In the analysis that follows, I will refer to these neighborhoods and their residents as "working-class" and "low-income," asking the reader to keep in mind the subtleties and variations of these designations based on the preceding analysis.

In assessing the approach of Texas IAF organizations to schools in urban neighborhoods, it is crucial to appreciate that the organizations are not beginning from scratch. Texas IAF organizations now have over two decades of involvement in Texas politics and have marshaled a great deal of public support through issue-oriented politics. By avoiding divisive ideological positions, and by focusing on visible, concrete improvements—such as providing storm sewers and traffic signs, shutting down crack houses, and securing better police protection—the Texas IAF developed political power years before it began its school-related work. "We have people trained now so they feel comfortable going into City Hall and talking to the officials," COPS leader Father Rosendo Urrabazo said in 1990, "But they don't feel comfortable going into the schools. What we did in City Hall, we have to do now in the schools." The hard-won political legitimacy of the Texas IAF, forged in two decades of struggle, has facilitated the Texas IAF's entrance into schools and given it multiple entry points to influence educational policy.[32]

The cases which follow illustrate that the Texas IAF has begun its work in schools in myriad ways: through recommendations by a school's corporate partners, by listening to a parent from a congregation in which the Texas IAF is anchored, and by choosing a middle school with the lowest test scores in a city and targeting it for reform in consultation with a superintendent and a school board. At the same time that there is diversity regarding points of entry, however, there is a clear and consistent logic to all of the Texas IAF school collaborations.

Texas IAF leaders and organizers strive to keep their fingers on the pulse of the communities they seek to organize. Access to that pulse is gained by constant involvement in member congregations. Every Sunday Texas IAF organizers and leaders attend services at member churches, meet with lay leaders, solicit opinions about issues confronting the community, and seek to identify those individuals with leadership potential who can help to articulate the needs of their community. When educational issues are brought forth, the Texas IAF must gauge the depth of community sentiment and explore whether some vital criteria are met by the school which could make it suitable for focused attention. Factors which can influence the selection of a school include dedicated faculty, a supportive school board, corporate partnerships, and latent parental support which can be made manifest through effective organizing.

Once a school is identified as a focus for community organizing, Texas IAF leaders and organizers plan one-on-one meetings in the homes of those parents who are most active in their churches or in the targeted schools. "One-on-one" is literally accurate: one community organizer or leader meets with one parent and spends time searching out the parent's sentiments and grievances about concrete issues which should be addressed in his or her neighborhood and schools. These preliminary meetings provide parents with opportunities to express their feelings about their children's school, the lack of safety in the neighborhood, or their frustration at not being able to offer greater educational support for their children. Texas IAF leaders and organizers do not interpret heavily at this early stage; instead, they place their emphasis on building strong interpersonal and political relationships with the parents.

As soon as a relationship of trust and open communication has been established, leaders and organizers move to the next phase of community organizing: house meetings. House meetings are tremendously important. They are the first forums in which neighbors begin to identify common problems and think of ways in which they could become involved in solving them. House meetings enable organizers to identify natural leaders in a given community and to begin parent training in such issues as preparing an agenda; opening, leading, and concluding a meeting punctually; and evaluation.[33]

Texas IAF leaders and organizers can either convene house meetings in rapid succession or can take several months to identify the most pressing concerns of citizens. In the familiar setting of their homes and neighborhoods, citizens rarely need much encouragement to express themselves about the issues they find most distressing. For one parent, it may be the lack of sidewalks; her children have to walk in the street when they go to school. For another, it may be the prostitutes and drug dealers who ply their trades in a park across the street from the school. For another, it may be the gangs who threaten students on their way to and from school. Each parent views the issues that he or she identifies as an immediate threat to their community that cries out for rectification. Given the numerous problems which confront inner-city residents —such as fear of retaliation from gangs or drug dealers, or lack of knowledge about how to persuade elected officials to perform as public servants—the problems may have plagued the community for years.

House meetings have many important facets. One of the most important of those involves a shift from a culture of civic withdrawal and self-blaming to a culture of conversation and the "public processing of pain." "I've been amazed at how open people can be in our house meetings," Juanita Zamarripa, an IAF leader in San Antonio, commented. "Somehow everyone gets included and we feel just like a family." Teacher Norma Vinton agreed: "A lot of things come out which I know I would never hear outside of a house meeting." She added, "Some people can be so reserved in public, but in those house meetings they blossom and we talk about everything."

How do house meetings enable citizens to drop their reservations about one another? Part of the answer lies with the Socratic method used by organizers, in which the intent is not for the organizer to provide solutions but to agitate citizens so that they themselves think critically about their legitimate grievances and their latent powers as citizens. "If we have a fixed idea in our heads of what our agenda is," Ernie Cortés said, "then there's no point to doing house meetings." At the same time that organizers and leaders engage in dialogue with neighborhood residents, however, they do not patronize them. Part of the house meeting may involve some hard and frank challenges, as occurs when organizers and leaders inform citizens that the voting turnout is so weak in their area that politicians have no motivation to provide them with services. "To a certain point, we have to mug them with reality," Cortés said. "We have to take some very ugly realities and confront parents with them and shove them up against what the future could be like for their kids. People have to get angry that they're getting clobbered."

As an illustration of the catalyzing role of house meetings, consider the situation of Cristian Escobedo in the *Segundo Barrio* of El Paso, one of the poorest neighborhoods in the United States. Cristian was a healthy boy until he turned five years old, at which point he suffered a brain tumor which left him permanently blind in one eye and a slow learner. Cristian's elementary school worked closely with a Texas IAF organization to promote community engagement, and he received the support he needed at that level of his education. Once he hit middle school, however, he was psychologically abused by several of his teachers, who accused him of being lazy and stupid.

Cristian's mother, Lili, was one of a number of mothers in the *Segundo Barrio* who had become regular participants in the house meeting structure created by the Texas IAF. When Cristian began having problems at the middle school, she decided to share her anxieties about her son's experiences with other parents. "As soon as I brought up my problem, all of the other parents said, 'Me, too!'" she recalled. "We had all had bad experiences with the middle school."

"I've always been afraid of public speaking and I've never done it," Lili Escobedo confessed. "But leaders at the house meetings told me that if I really cared about my child I was going to have to speak up for him because nobody else was going to do it. At first it took all of my courage to speak to a teacher or a principal, and I needed lots of support." Escobedo and other parents carefully prepared their comments and grievances with a Texas IAF organizer and then complained to the school board and the superintendent in private and in public meetings. As a result of their activism, the El Paso Independent School District conducted an internal investigation which showed that over one-third of the middle school students failed every year and that over half of them were suspended. As a result of the parents' protests, the superintendent decided to take radical measures to rebuild the middle school. The principal was removed, all of the faculty in the school were required to reapply for their positions, and the parents, including Lili Escobedo, played a key role in selecting a new principal.

Not every parent and not every house meeting results in transformations as radical as those initiated by Lili Escobedo. In most instances, house meetings mark the beginning of a culture of conversations and mutual clarification between a school and its community which lead to greater trust and gradual, evolutionary change. Escobedo recognizes that she never could have emerged into her new public identity as a community leader without support from her friends, neighbors, and the educational organizers of the Texas IAF. "But now it's come to the point where nobody has to push me," she observed. When she feels her children need her advocacy, she proudly affirmed, "I do it on my own." The house meetings in the *Segundo Barrio* served as the community fulcrum in which she and her neighbors expressed their frustrations with their children's school, their neighborhood, and their public officials—and then found political solutions.

The anger and anxiety of Lili Escobedo's friends and neighbors with situations such as those that existed in the middle school are hardly restricted to El Paso or confined to the schools. Drive-by shootings, easy access to guns, unresponsive city officials, abandoned homes used by crack dealers—these are all traumatizing aspects of everyday life for the residents of America's central cities. Concern with these issues has come up repeatedly at Texas IAF house meetings in East San Antonio, South Dallas, South Fort Worth, and the Third and Fifth Wards in Houston. Good house meetings enable parents to get past their isolation from their neighbors and self-blaming in order to develop solidarity with other parents who face the same challenges.

By creating an unusual kind of public space—small and neighborly but with a commitment to change—the house meeting enables citizens to share their concerns and to see their problems less as a reflection of their own personal fallibility and more as an expression of economic and political forces. The intimacy of meeting in a neighbor's home is one step toward building new relationships of reciprocity and trust in working-class neighborhoods. Parents who are welfare mothers or work for the minimum wage in the service sector rarely feel confident enough to express their sentiments in large public meetings, but they do feel secure enough to voice their observations and grievances in a neighbor's home. "You can learn a lot more at a house meeting with ten people than in a church meeting with a hundred people," COPS president Pat Ozuna observed.[34]

After sponsoring debate, enabling vulnerability, and then carefully listening to parents, Texas IAF leaders and organizers work together to advance concrete strategies for remedying problems. The strategies which emerge must have a dual nature: they must both attack the issue and resolve it to the community's satisfaction at the same time as the community develops the leadership to go on to other issues once its immediate objective has been reached. Any action which only attends to the first facet while neglecting the second is incomplete and unsuccessful from the vantage point of building long-term, community-based leadership.

It is common at this point in the organizing process for IAF organizers to begin a deliberately didactic phase of their work in communities. In schools, religious institutions, and homes, IAF organizers lead training sessions about a number of key issues that low-income citizens need to understand if they are to develop into powerful advocates for their children and their communities. For example, citizens who are in danger of losing their employment at manufacturing jobs and accepting low-wage service sector jobs without benefits are helpless if they do not understand the globalization of the economy and their need to acquire the education which will enable them to become skilled laborers or professionals. Parents who have always been taught to be deferential to politicians such as school board members and city council members need to learn that public officials should also be public servants, and that parents have rights as citizens and taxpayers to hold elected officials accountable for their conduct. "We rub the parents' noses in some ugly realities—about globalization, wages, and their kids' prospects," Cortés said. Yet the house meeting doesn't stop with compelling citizens to confront realities they would rather evade. The next step is for organizers to teach citizens an empowering politics which emphasizes the importance of mediating institutions, the distinction between unilateral and relational kinds of power, and the centrality of social capital formation for any serious strategy of school and neighborhood improvement.

After conducting training sessions, Texas IAF leaders and organizers often plan a public demonstration of support for the targeted school by visiting with parents and students in their homes. Such visits have many names, such as a "Walk for Success," a "Neighborhood Walk," or a *"Caminata del Vecindario para Exito."* In organizing such events, Texas IAF leaders and the school identify and recruit all of the church and civic leaders at their disposal. Generally, the core leaders are parents and teachers, but they can also include clergy, the school's alumni, sympathetic college students, and students themselves in the case of secondary schools. The Texas IAF leaders and organizers then train teachers, students, alumni, and members of Texas IAF churches in appropriate ways to make home visits, emphasizing role playing to simulate the kinds of transactions that occur when volunteers arrive at students' homes. Texas IAF organizers, teachers, and parents write letters and send them to students' homes prior to the Walk, informing parents of the impending visit. Clergy stress the importance of the Walk from their pulpits at church and emphasize it in their church bulletins. Texas IAF leaders divide up the school zone into blocks and give visitation assignments to the participants.

When the day comes for a Walk for Success, a tremendous amount of enthusiasm can often be felt in the school and community. Students, parents, and teachers wear school colors, carry exhortatory signs conveying a spirit of unity, and may be preceded by police on motorcycles with brightly colored flags waving from their handlebars. After a walk around the periphery of the school, leaders move into the neighborhood and split off onto different blocks, knocking on students' doors to visit their parents. In smaller schools, the goal is usually to visit the home of every student; in larger schools, leaders and organizers may choose a more limited target population, such as the homes of all freshmen from a given school. Usually the participants visit homes in pairs; one volunteer leads the interview and the other takes notes. In Mexican American communities, Texas IAF organizers assure that at least one person in each pair speaks Spanish. When high schools are involved, one of the walkers usually is a student.

Home visits are a cornerstone of Texas IAF organizing for school improvement. The sight of a well-organized and neatly dressed group of parents and teachers moving through a community besieged by gangs and abandoned lots to solicit ideas on school improvement and to inform parents and students about programs that can benefit the community has uplifted the spirits of many low-income parents and students, who are unaccustomed to civic activism in their neighborhoods. Many parents have used the home visits on the Walk for Success to ask questions of the walkers that they have wanted to address previously but never did, fearing that the question would reveal their lack of familiarity with basic knowledge about schools. Some parents, for example, have not known how to read report cards or have not known what a college or university is until Walk for Success participants have explained it to them. Others, particularly immigrants from Central America, may never have had the benefits of one day's formal education in their own childhoods and lack the most fundamental knowledge about the workings of schools in the United States. (Most recent adult Mexican immigrants received less than six years of public education in Mexico.) In other cases, parents might have grievances about one particular teacher or feature of their children's school, but have hesitated to make inquiries or to speak out, worrying that the teachers in question might unfairly punish their children as a consequence. In the security of their homes, they are more vocal, particularly when walkers use surveys about the school and community to gather information about problem areas from the parents' perspectives. Walk for Success participants write down parents' grievances and Walk coordinators arrange for follow-through discussions with educators and civic officials. Through the solicitation of comments from parents, the home visits are a key step in changing the culture of the school from one of institutional rigidity and defensiveness to one of engagement and dialogue.[35]

After the Walk for Success, Texas IAF organizers and key leaders evaluate their effectiveness. Generally, participants in the Walk are pleased with the manner in which parents welcomed them into their homes and discussed their issues with them. Not all parents are happy to receive the walkers, suspecting an ulterior motive or unwanted intrusions into their home life. In those cases organizers and leaders gain new perspective on students' home backgrounds and identify areas for further conversations and clarification. Most of the problems which arise do not come from parental resistance but from mechanical matters such as establishing students' correct home addresses. Follow-through meetings and actions are planned around those issues which have emerged as parents' most salient concerns during the home visits.

As soon as the Walk is over, leaders and organizers begin mobilizing for their first large public action in the form of a parents' assembly at the school. The assembly is a high-stakes proposition in the organizing effort and is usually held two weeks after the Walk. It is advertised through church bulletins, school mailings, posters, and radio announcements. Texas IAF leaders and organizers receive commitments in advance from important school board members, city council members, and other elected officials to participate in the assembly.

In planning the assembly, Texas IAF leaders and organizers carefully work together to design questions and to prepare public speeches that will enable the community to view its school in a new light. While leaders are being prepared, Texas IAF organizers place visits to elected officials to inform them of the exact questions that will be posed to them at the assembly. Those questions will vary from one assembly to another; they usually involve a specific program or budgetary allocation that the community believes will enhance its quality of life. Those programs or allocations should be concrete and visible enough that the community senses that it is establishing a new momentum on behalf of its children. In addition to their pledges of support, elected officials are often asked if they will commit themselves to meet with representatives of the school on a regular monthly basis to ensure that all of the parties who are involved in improving the school are accomplishing the work to which they have committed themselves. These "accountability sessions" are an important mechanism for low-income parents to make certain that their elected officials follow through on their public declarations.

The assembly which follows a Walk for Success has many purposes. One major goal is to recast the community's perspective of itself. "Our large public actions are not just gatherings or forums," Cortés says. "They are public dramas. They not only inform but transform. They get people to see themselves in a different way." To reach that goal of a new self-understanding, leaders and organizers construct a detailed script or program for the assembly in advance. Role playing is an important part of the preparation, as parents and teachers practice reading their state-

d questions in ways that will be powerful in a public setting.
perly planned and executed, the parents' assembly will project
ge of the community before the parents, which will emphasize
th of local leadership and the community's aggressive public
advocacy on behalf of its children.

A second important goal is to advance an agenda. Parents and teachers need to feel that their presence at the assembly is productive and that they are truly engaged in improving the education of their children. They therefore need to see public officials reacting in a committed and respectful way to the community's petitions. Parents and teachers need to experience their efficacy as public actors in a public affirmation of the legitimacy of their grievances and the effectiveness of their advocacy.

From the community's point of view, its parents, teachers, and church leaders are the individuals who introduce the assembly, who ask targeted questions of public officials, and who conclude the proceedings. Assemblies are staged to produce a cathartic effect as parents, teachers, and elected officials commit themselves to concrete actions which will improve educational opportunities in the school and its community. For many leaders, the assemblies have provided the first forum in which they have exercised their constitutional rights to redress their grievances or to advance community-generated solutions to local problems. Texas IAF organizers never appear on stage or address the public during assemblies.

Immediately after the assembly, Texas IAF organizers meet with their leaders to evaluate their work. Two questions are always posed. First, organizers ask whether the assembly accomplished its goals. Did elected officials commit to budgetary expenditures that will create health clinics, after-school programs, or whatever else has been on the agenda for the school and the community? Second, organizers ask leaders to begin thinking about next steps to be taken. Those can take myriad forms, such as scheduling follow-up meetings with elected officials, planning training sessions to inform parents about policies that affect their children, or forming task forces to advance their agenda.

On the day after the assembly, many low-income citizens are viewed differently by their friends and neighbors. They have changed from Mr. Garcia, who reads gas meters, or Mrs. Jones, the housewife, into local public leaders who received a promise from the superintendent to fund a new parents' center for the school or who persuaded the mayor to provide a new after-school program for the neighborhood's children. When ordinary citizens see their work recognized in the ten o'clock news or the Sunday morning headlines—rather than the usual emphasis on crimes in their neighborhoods—the community begins to see itself in a different way. The fatalism which exists in many low-income neighborhoods is confronted with the possibility that things can be different; indeed, things can be better.

Public officials tend to see the assemblies differently. Office holders who are opposed to the concept of a strong public sector generally avoid accountability sessions, whereas those whose principles are closely aligned with the Texas IAF relish the high visibility and the opportunity to garner public support. Public officials of a moderate political stance generally work with the Texas IAF to develop an open-ended questioning strategy in which they commit to a further relationship of the organization and its agenda without specifying exact financial commitments. In the 1970s, the first accountability sessions in San Antonio were sometimes confrontational and embarrassing for officials, who complained of public humiliation at the hands of overzealous IAF leaders. Over the past two decades, IAF organizers and leaders have ceased using accountability sessions to expose political leaders with policies antithetical to their own, and have tended to use them more as forums for consolidating incipient relationships in public assemblies rather than private meeting rooms. Rather than serve as forums for demanding accountability about past actions, the accountability sessions have evolved in such a way that they enhance mutual commitment and support about upcoming neighborhood and educational issues.

Large public assemblies are key venues in which communities can begin the process of assertive self-governance and the nurturance of a proactive civic culture. After such "actions," as they are called in IAF nomenclature, it is imperative that the organizing process continue to build on the momentum in the community. Without sustained effort, large assemblies result in a fleeting epiphany which creates a sense of pride but causes no lasting changes. There is a natural ebb and flow of planning, action, and evaluation in all organizing, but organizers and leaders must pay detailed attention to the rhythm of these processes to sustain a sense of hope and possibilities in the community. Successful organizing involves a perpetual spiral of one-on-one's, house meetings, and large assemblies which in turn spark further one-on-one's, house meetings, and assemblies.

An Emergent Philosophy of Education

The Texas IAF's commitment to a relational approach to power and community organizing means that its politics of education are multi-faceted and contingent upon the most salient issues which confront any particular neighborhood and school at a specific point in time. Given the local and situational approach to school improvement characterizing Texas IAF collaboratives, a dogmatic approach to school reform—one entailing an externally created and imposed checklist of prioritized goals, for example—would be wholly inappropriate. Texas IAF leaders and organizers bristle at the notion that substantial school reform consists of new programs, and are much more intrigued and motivated by the enhancement of political capacity that can change school cultures and of which programs are but one subsidiary part. "We think our primary task is developing leadership," Cortés said, "not just resolving some problem, not just doing good." Yet it would be disingenuous to suggest that Texas IAF organizations are not interested in specific kinds of programs and that they intervene in schools in an unreflective manner which supports community sentiment without critique or nuance. In June 1990 over 150 Texas IAF leaders and organizers convened in San Antonio and composed an essay on education called "The Texas IAF Vision for Public Schools: Communities of Learners." That document, as well as other selected writings of IAF leaders and organizers, articulates why and how the Texas IAF seeks to change the culture of schools.[36]

"The Texas IAF Vision for Public Schools" commences with an affirmation of the Texas IAF organizations' political achievements and their grounding in the dual traditions which frame American society: "They have defended the biblical tradition that a society will be judged by its compassion for the weak and solidarity with the poor. They have defended the republican tradition that extreme inequality threatens community." By extending norms of compassion, solidarity, and democracy to schools, the essay states, "The Texas IAF network shares with the early democrats of our nation a commitment to democratic education and pluralism." No historical myopia is at play: "Public schools first excluded Blacks, Hispanics and Native Americans entirely, then segregated them into inferior institutions." Nonetheless, "the tradition of the democratic 'common school' remains essential to our conception of public schools to this day."

After providing a historical and axiological groundwork for community organizing, "The Texas IAF Vision for Public Schools" addresses the "alarming future" that confronts American youth. The academic achievement of the young is mediocre in an increasingly competitive and materialistic world. The social lives of young people are undermined by weak families, widespread violence among juveniles, and the prevalence of substance abuse. The schools of the young typically prepare them "to be punctual, docile, and adept at routine tasks" while transformations in the global economy demand workers who are restlessly inquisitive, intellectually independent, and socially proactive.

The social crisis of American education, according to the Texas IAF vision paper, requires a threefold change in the culture of public schools. First, schools must abandon the model of the "mass-production assembly line" approach to education which has dominated urban public schools for most of the twentieth century: "In our vision, the model of a school shifts from efficiency to effectiveness: from that of students as passive learners to that of a community whose members are committed to learning the skills of problem solving, teaching themselves and others, and collaboration." Second, schools must free themselves from the top-down directives of the 1980s which mandated a pernicious uniformity in instruction, curriculum, and assessment in public schools. Instead, "Schools should have the authority to design and implement their own program of instruction, including planning curriculum, determining the use of time and space, and choosing instructional materials and classroom management techniques." Third, schools must cease to ignore the crisis confronting American families and design innovative strategies which make the school a resource for families and a cultural center of the community.

The Texas IAF's vision paper proposes a triple revolution for public schools. First, it calls for a transformation of the kind of learning that transpires in schools from an emphasis upon memorization and standardization to critical thinking, collaboration, and alternative forms of assessment. Second, the paper promotes a development of school organization away from centralization and bureaucracy and toward decentralization and democracy. Third, it advocates a transformation of community relations from marginalization and exclusion to participation and empowerment.

The Texas IAF's threefold strategy for change was not designed in a vacuum. Generations of critics of American public education in the twentieth century have attacked the anti-intellectual propensities of urban "factory schools" that emphasize obedience over autonomy, memorization over creativity, and uniform over personalized instruction. Although the democratic localist spirit of public schools has been undermined by the rise of powerful state departments of education, teachers and parents have challenged that hegemony and sought to revitalize community control. In spite of numerous attacks, however, urban school districts have proven to be extraordinarily successful at deflecting criticism and perpetuating centralized control and bureaucratic power.[37]

The originality of the Texas IAF contribution does not stem from its critique of the factory school or its proposals regarding instruction, curriculum, and assessment. Virtually every major school reformer in the country now advocates similar proposals in the same areas as the Texas IAF. Schools collaborate with the Texas IAF experiment with portfolio assessment, interdisciplinary curriculum development, and child-centered pedagogies in a manner entirely congruent with a host of grass-roots reforms which have enlivened and improved American education in the last decade. The unique feature of the Texas IAF approach, which gives its collaboratives a different feel and nuance, lies in its unusually bold interpretation of what it means to engage a community in school improvement.

Texas IAF organizing for community engagement in schools differs from the prevalent paradigms in three ways. First and most importantly, the dominant paradigms of community engagement are *accommodationist.* They assume an uncritical stance of parents toward the dominant culture in the school. In an accurate and concise summary of the literature on parental involvement in schools, Joyce Epstein has identified the five major forms of partnerships that exist between schools and parents. One emphasizes the "positive home conditions" parents can provide to support their children's learning; a second stresses the importance of school communication with parents about children's academic progress; a third seeks to use parents as volunteers in school activities; a fourth teaches parents how to monitor and assist their own children at home; and a fifth stresses parental involvement in "decision making, governance, and advocacy." Although the fifth form shares affinities with Texas IAF organizations' work with parental engagement, its foreshortened notion of political participation, its separation of community issues from school issues, and its lack of grounding in community bases such as religious institutions limits its conceptual utility as a model to describe Texas IAF educational collaborations.[38]

The overall trajectory of parental engagement in Texas IAF collaborations is *radically different* from the prevailing paradigms of parental involvement. Most paradigms are restricted to roles that parents can play in supporting their children's learning: parents learn how to support the school's curriculum or how to sponsor a bake sale for new curtains or computers. Parental involvement in these supportive roles is one part of the Texas IAF collaboration, but it is inextricably interwoven with a larger agenda promoting the cultivation of political leadership in low-income communities. Political leadership, as understood in Texas IAF organizations, consists of a number of factors, including the ability to identify social problems, skill in translating vague grievances into concrete political issues, and talent in coalition building, implementation of change, and evaluation. The deeply political nature of Texas IAF school collaboratives warrants a terminological distinction between *accommodationist* forms of parental *involvement* and *transformational* forms of parental *engagement*. Parental *involvement*—as practiced in most schools and reflected in the research literature—avoids issues of power and assigns parents a passive role in the maintenance of school culture. Parental *engagement* designates parents as citizens in the fullest sense—change agents who can transform urban schools and neighborhoods.[39]

To teach low-income parents how to become active as citizens in issues involving education involves an immense paradigm shift for parents, teachers, and administrators. Research indicates that a substantial minority of low-income parents believe that they can do little to enhance their children's success in schools. Although working-class parents indicate a strong desire to help their children, they often do not know how they can best accomplish that. Contextual factors, such as employers who are unwilling to adapt working hours to accommodate parents' desires to support their children's education, appear to play a large role in keeping parents out of schools. Once students enter middle schools and then go on to high schools, the greater complexity of the curriculum and sheer number of teachers that parents must interact with impede strong relationships between parents and the schools.[40]

However much the public may want and demand systemic changes in its schools, much of the impetus for change regularly becomes defused and routinized in the form of prepackaged programs which are added to the school's curriculum without transforming its underlying culture and organization. The Texas IAF has a critique of education and society that systematically avoids such accommodationist efforts. According to Pearl Caesar, a Texas IAF organizer in the Rio Grande Valley, "We move schools into the power arena rather than just creating programs. In fact, our real work isn't about creating programs. It's about educating parents, teachers, and principals to deal with the political realities of the city in terms of power." Once parents, teachers, and principals understand certain elementary political realities, organizers contend, they can truly begin to become active and effective in advancing the interests of young people in their schools and neighborhoods. Organizers and leaders can then make the transition from encouraging parental *involvement* to initiating and sustaining parental *engagement* with the school and community.

A second distinctive aspect of the Texas IAF's work in schools concerns its institutional base in neighborhood churches. Perhaps because a vocal minority of Americans has challenged the principle of the separation of church and state, many Americans have come to hold that religious institutions should play no role in improving public education. The Texas IAF, on the other hand, holds that religious institutions— which are our country's strongest voluntary associations—represent an untapped social resource which can mentor young people and complement the work of parents and teachers while respecting the independence of the public schools. By enhancing collaboration between religious institutions, families, and schools, the Texas IAF hopes to rebuild the fabric of our communities.

A third important facet of the philosophy of education advanced by the Texas IAF organizations concerns the explicit intention of their leadership to generate social capital. "Our broad-based organizations are trying to build, expand, and agitate the social capital that is embedded in the networks of human relationships," Ernie Cortés has written. "Social capital is not a familiar term in the current debate, but it is as crucial to the resolution of crises and the alleviation of poverty as the other kinds of capital we already understand." Cortés has made explicit reference to Coleman's work on education and social capital and sought to draw out its implications for Texas IAF organizers and leaders in countless leadership training sessions.[41]

Texas IAF organizations self-consciously promote social capitalization through a richly variegated grass-roots strategy. House meetings build social capital between hitherto isolated neighbors as housewives and blue-collar workers begin to understand that issues they have conceived as personal problems are social and systemic in nature. Walks for Success develop social capital between a school's teachers, students, parents, and neighbors as the community begins a process of dialogue and evaluation about the quality of education in the community. Parents' assemblies and the groundwork which leads up to them build social capital between public officials and community members who successfully attack the community's most pressing problems. The Texas IAF also builds social capital within institutions, such as schools and churches, by helping those who are engaged with them to develop more creative ways of sustaining dialogue, transmitting information, implementing social change, and evaluating their results.

The Texas IAF's approach to school reform represents a unique philosophy and practice of education among the multiple contemporary efforts to improve American urban schools. It is an approach which first and foremost engages the community to cultivate local political leadership to enhance education. With the development of local leadership and an informed and active constituency, Texas IAF leaders and organizers advocate the transformation of factory schools into communities of learners in which students, parents, teachers, administrators, clergy, and congregations engage one another in continual conversation about the educational issues facing their community.

Although Joyce Epstein did not have a category for this form of school reform work in her discussion of the relationships between schools and the communities, she did recognize that a nascent kind of relationship was emerging at the time of her article. She noted that community-based organizations were finding new ways to promote parental engagement, and commented that

this type of involvement was not part of the research that helped identify the five major types of involvement in school and family partnerships. The addition of community to the model as a third overlapping sphere of influence opens a complex and relatively unexplored research agenda. New research is needed to determine whether this is a separate type of involvement and, if so, how it differs from the others.

The premise of this book is that the Texas IAF actualizes a distinct new kind of parental engagement, which encompasses and goes beyond other types of involvement by recovering and enlivening the concept of citizenship which has so agitated and enriched the western political tradition. The Texas IAF's work with parental engagement transcends accommodationist approaches to school and community relations by bringing the community into the heart of the school and using the school as a base for the political revitalization of the community.[42]

Expanding Political Capacity

Thus far we have reviewed many facets of the Texas IAF: its history and development, its first efforts in the politics of education, its method of neighborhood organizing, and its incipient philosophy of education. Each of those components of the Texas IAF provides essential keys to its internal dynamics and external efficacy. Left out of the descriptions thus far is the issue of the education and development of individuals *within* the Texas IAF. If one holds that genuine social change involves not simply acting upon others, but also cultivating one's own talents and rendering one's own reflections more complex, then matters of self-education attain the utmost of importance. Unlike many school reform efforts which shy away from abstraction in the interests of nominally "effective" strategies which can raise test scores, the Texas IAF demands high levels of abstract analysis and challenging reflection. That commitment can be seen on many levels, not the least of which are the bookshelves exploding with literature on politics, economics, history, and theology in the main office of the Texas IAF in Austin. Those books are important, for they convey that the Texas IAF has nothing in common with anti-intellectual variants of populism which advocate self-determination without attending to self-education. The Texas IAF has developed a triple strategy for expanding the political capacity of its leaders and organizers.

The first facet of that strategy consists of weekend leadership retreats. Those leadership retreats typically occur in churches or seminaries around the state. They are noteworthy insofar as they do not simply focus on politics in an immediate, ahistorical sense, but rather reach deep into the roots of the Judeo-Christian tradition to challenge organizers and leaders to confront the meaning of their cultural heritage and to use it as a springboard for political action. Emphasizing the theological and political dimension of weekend training sessions is important because so much school reform avoids the most challenging and profound issues of human identity. That very superficiality undermines the most compelling facets of the educational enterprise, which should be centered on the fulfillment of human potential in its broadest and deepest sense. By holding training sessions in religious institutions, and by reconnecting leaders and organizers to half-forgotten foundations of their religious and cultural heritage, the Texas IAF could hardly take a more apposite stance.

In January 1995 I attended a training session Ernie Cortés led for the Triangle Interfaith Project, a new IAF organization which encompasses three depressed industrial cities on the Gulf Coast which border on Louisiana. TIP leaders met at Calder Baptist Church in Beaumont on a Friday evening and began by receiving reports from clergy, teachers, blue-collar workers, and homemakers who are active in improving schools, expanding job opportunities, and upgrading health care in Beaumont, Port Arthur, and Orange. Alton Gallantin, an unemployed Black worker who formerly enjoyed a high-paying manufacturing job, described the thorny path his life has taken since he lost that job several years ago. He struggled to find work all over East Texas and was particularly active in attempting to acquire a job in one of the region's few expanding sectors—state penitentiaries. Manufacturing jobs have been cut all along the Gulf Coast, and the petrochemical unions which once organized workers from Houston to New Orleans have been decimated. In the new economic context, Gallantin battled to support his family in low-paying service sector jobs which provide no benefits and have no future. His lack of education, which was no impediment when he entered the work force twenty years ago, made him unqualified for those jobs in the 1990s which could bring him back into the middle class. He knew many friends and former colleagues who shared his plight, and he spoke movingly of the creeping sense of despair which spread throughout his community. Meanwhile, rumor had it that one of the largest remaining employers in the area recently brought in one hundred low-wage workers from Trinidad who were so vulnerable legally that they would never dream of organizing for higher wages, better schools, or health care.

After Gallantin's presentation, Ernie Cortés took the podium and began his part of the training. Cortés is a stout man of medium build with salt-and-pepper hair and animated dark eyes. A tie which is askew, an uneven shave, and a messy coif gave the impression of someone preoccupied with concerns other than his appearance. Once he began speaking, however, any evidence of personal disorganization fell away. Alternating humor with analysis, Cortés moved rapidly across the podium, stepping into the audience at regular intervals to punctuate his presentations with in-your-face challenges such as "Do you agree?" or "Do you think that's right?"

This evening Cortés began by emphasizing the necessity of finding leaders in East Texas who are angry about their economic plight and lost opportunities for their children. "The kind of anger we want people to have is rooted in loss and grief," he said, distinguishing between anger which is hot and impulsive and that which is cold, calculating, and relational. "If people aren't angry that their kids are getting clobbered, they're not worth much," he said. "And all of you should be angry about Jefferson County. But you also have to know that if you stand up for your dignity and self-respect, some people are going to be offended by that.

"But I'm not talking about just any kind of anger or anger that is impulsive and reactive," Cortés continued, warming to his subject, "but the kind of anger that someone like Moses had." Cortés launched into an exegesis, working the air with his hands as if he could physically connect the plight of Alton Gallantin to the example of the biblical patriarch. "The book of Numbers describes Moses as the meekest man who walks the face of the earth. Now I never understood that. How could Moses be the meekest man who walks the earth and still stand up to the pharoah and lead the Hebrews out of Egypt? Do you think Moses was meek? Of course not! We think of him as a big guy, a hefty guy. Well, I looked it up and found out that 'meekness' comes from a Greek word that means a middle way between two extremes, hatred and apathy. It's the difference between hatred and violence and destruction and no feeling at all. It's defined by some scholars of the scripture as an ability to get angry in an appropriate manner. It implies discipline, control, and accountability. And that's what we need, a kind of anger which is calculating and deliberate and controlled. But like Moses, we need a lot more than just anger. We need calculated action."

Cortés' voice, up until now quiet, almost restrained, suddenly came alive. In the style of an old-time preacher leading a revival, the measured tone of his opening comments provided a backdrop for a deliverance that now delved deeper into the meaning of the Exodus and escalated into booming oratory: "Do you remember how Moses kills an Egyptian and gets the Hebrews out of Egypt? And do you remember how the Hebrews began murmuring against him? And how Moses then says to Yahweh, 'Why have you treated me so badly? Was it I who made a promise to these people to lead them out of Egypt? Where am I going to get meat for all of these people? If this is the way that you want it, why don't you kill me right now and get it over with!'

"Now Yahweh knows he's got to move fast, so he says to Moses, *'Moses, you're a jerk!'*" Cortés mimicked an angry snarl which brought forth peals of laughter from the audience. "'I explained to you before and your father-in-law explained it to you,' Yahweh said. 'Get seventy of your best leaders, people that you've tested out in action, people that you trust, and take the burden that's been put on you and put it on them. And then I'll make sure that they get enough meat for not just one day or two days or ten days but for a whole month, until that meat is coming out of their nostrils!'" After a dramatic pause, Cortés joked, "Yahweh went a little bit far there."

Cortés continued, "So Moses does what he's supposed to do. He gets his key leaders and he agitates them and he pulls them together in small group meetings and he calls them to workshops just like this. And he says, 'You want after-school programs? You want housing? You want jobs? Guess what? I ain't gonna give you none of them! Now, I'll teach you how to do those things. I'll train you, I'll guide you, and I'll mentor you, but I ain't gonna build one house for you. Look on over there, and you'll find some quail. Get yourselves together and get some foraging parties together. You don't know how to do it? I'll show you how to do it—*but I ain't gonna do it for you!*"

Cortés then moved his exegesis from the Hebrews' quest for the promised land to Triangle Interfaith's search for a better quality of life in East Texas. "The point here is that we've got to learn how to act and how to act in collaboration," he said. "We've got to get past the dominant ideology that says that we're clients and consumers and that politics is about electronic plebiscites and that we're all fundamentally disconnected from one another. We've got to develop a civic culture of conversations and house meetings and public actions and negotiations and reciprocity. Developing a civic culture is especially hard for us to do now when so many of us have signed away our birthright. And to understand what that means, we turn to the book of Genesis and look at the story of Jacob and Esau."

Cortés' reading of the story of the exodus offered a lesson on the importance of developing horizontal civic networks—organizations in which all of the responsibility is not piled upon the would-be Moses of a movement for change, but is distributed equitably among citizens. Jacob and Esau offered a different perspective, one which is concerned not so much with the development of shared leadership in community as with one's responsibility to one's self and one's destiny. Yet rather than phrase that message in lofty language, Cortés communicated it in the parlance of street life. "Now, we know that Jacob and Esau are twins, and that Esau was the first born," Cortés said. "And Esau was a big, hairy guy. He was a 'fifties' kind of guy." Cortés imitated the male stereotype of another generation, deepening his voice and waving his arms at his side like a halfback lumbering about the stage.

His voice softened as he continued, "Now, Jacob was his mother's favorite. He was crafty and cunning. He was a 'nineties' kind of guy. He tended to stay inside his parents' tent. Today we'd say that he knew his way around the kitchen. He was a sensitive, new age guy." The audience laughed at the easily recognizable contrast. "One day when Jacob was making a stew, Esau came back from the country famished. He had been unsuccessful in his hunt. He said to Jacob, 'Let me have some of that stew.' Jacob said to Esau, 'Before I give you this wonderful stew, first give me your birthright, your rights as the first born.'

"'Esau answered, 'I'm hungry, I'm starving, I'm famished! What good is this birthright?' Jacob said, 'Swear to me! Give me your oath.' So Esau swore to him and sold his birthright to Jacob. So Jacob gave him bread and stew. And the Bible then says that from this day forward, Esau despised his birthright.

"Now what has this got to do with us?" Cortés asked, moving into the audience. "I'm going to argue that we have a birthright, too, and our birthright is part of our identity and our legacy. A fellow by the name of Sheldon Wolin wrote an essay on this story, and he argues that our birthright is part of our identity as citizens. He says it's an ambiguous legacy. The legacy has in it the founding of the country, but it also has the destruction of the Native Americans. Our legacy has in it slavery, the Mexican War, the mistreatment of freedmen after the Civil War, and vicious wars against working people.[43]

"But our legacy also has in it the Bill of Rights, the Mayflower Compact, the Constitution, and the Emancipation Proclamation. So it's an ambiguous legacy. As citizens, we've inherited this legacy. It's our responsibility and it's also our burden. Esau sees his birthright as a burden. He doesn't accept it. His world is a world of himself, by himself and for himself. He is disconnected.

"The point I'm raising is that if we are going to be citizens we're going to have to go against a culture which teaches us that our legacy is obsolete. Our culture teaches us that we're customers, clients, and taxpayers. What's the difference? Customers and clients and even voters just react. They give us Texaco or Exxon and Bill Clinton or George Bush. But being a citizen means that we initiate, collaborate, and take responsibility. We don't just have rights, but rights and responsibilities. We take risks by initiating action. We don't just passively respond to stimuli and alternatives. We design possibilities, we imagine, we have a constructive critique, we have the gumption to explore different possibilities. We don't just choose between different kinds of schools, but we design the kinds of schools that we want.

"Citizens understand choices and communication and opinion polls, but they also understand that we have to go beyond those. We have to have a culture of conversations. In a culture of conversations I have to understand how you think and how you feel. I have to understand how I'm coming across to you so that I can get inside your situation. I can't just recruit you. I have to listen to you.

"We don't recruit at house meetings and you know why. You'd get people together, and tell them you want to recruit them to your agenda, and they'd agree with you, and then after you left they'd say 'to hell with you!' It doesn't work! We want to listen to what people have to say. We want to develop relationships with people. We want to make offers to people and extend propositions that challenge them to think and act on their interests. We want to develop a culture of conversations, which are based not on exchanging opinions we already have but on sharing ideas and being willing to reassess our preconceived notions.

"Now I can't patronize you. If you say something that I disagree with, I have to interrupt you. I won't just let you talk to be nice to you. In a culture of conversations we ask questions. We're blunt and we're direct, but at the same time we also allow the other person to come back at us. There has to be calculated vulnerability, and we have to be willing to make concessions. And finally, we have to begin a conversation with a disposition for collaborative action."

Cortés' presentation hit home with this audience of clergy, workers, and teachers in Beaumont. Moses, Jacob, and Esau were a cast of characters with whom the audience was familiar and from whom they were willing to learn. At one point, Cortés asserted that "we don't have conversations with each other anymore, in the sense of mutual vulnerability, reflection about what we really want and need from one another as friends and neighbors." He asked why, and one clergyman answered, "We seem to keep ourselves so busy running from one thing to the next that we forget about the most important things." Many participants murmured their agreement.

During a late morning coffee break, I was reminded of how stark our disconnectedness from one another can be. I fell into conversation with an African American teacher. We discussed the regional economic situation, the Triangle Interfaith Project, and his work at a local middle school. He said he was learning a lot from the training session and then paused for a moment. "But do you know what the most amazing thing about this morning is?" he asked me. "It's that we're having this meeting in Calder Baptist Church in the first place. I never thought in my life that I'd be in here. Blacks and Whites still don't mix socially much here, and especially not in our churches."

Cortés' exegesis in Beaumont offered a dramatic contrast with the traditional style of IAF leadership development promoted by Saul Alinsky. Although Alinsky's IAF organizations were heavily dependent on religious institutions, Alinsky himself never entered into sustained engagement with biblical texts except to extract a lesson of direct relevance to the interpretation of power. "You take care of the religion," he told one of his strongest supporters among the clergy. "We'll do the organizing." Alinsky's Jewishness was an asset while he was organizing the Back of the Yards Council insofar as he stood outside of the conflicts between rival groups among Catholics and between Catholics and Protestants in Chicago.[44]

Cortés' stance could not be more different. He professes no neutrality, but advocates constant critical engagement with the Judeo-Christian tradition. Cortés was raised as a Catholic, attended parochial school, and has drawn inspiration from the strength of the Catholic Church as a haven for immigrants and as a bulwark of family rights. In his perspective, Catholicism offers an intellectual tradition which contrasts with modern individualism in economics and politics:

> This tradition locates the development of a human being not within himself or herself, nor in others per se, but in relationships with others. Thus *Gaudum et Spes* taught us that "through man's dealings with others, through reciprocal duties, and through fraternal dialogue he develops all his gifts and is able to rise to his destiny." This conception imagines human beings as "persons," not as "individuals." They are mothers, fathers, brothers, daughters, workers, employers, pastors, governors, and so on, not isolated, self-directed singularities.

Cortés' approach to Catholicism is not without critique. He has taken the Catholic Church to task for giving insufficient guidance on the criteria which should guide the development of social relationships and their organizational manifestations. "Catholic social thought, if it is to be useful, must elaborate a theory and a practice of competent social relationships," Cortés wrote. "The church must be emboldened—not discouraged—by the vacuum that exists in social relations."[45]

While Cortés' personal heritage is Catholic, IAF organizations encompass a spectrum of religious faiths. According to Cortés, "In this context the term 'faith' does not mean particular religious beliefs, but rather a more general affirmation that life has meaning." Religious institutions matter because they are social expressions of a faith which must not be privatized: "Congregations are the conveyors of tradition, which connects people and holds them accountable to both their past and their future. They force us to recognize that we are encumbered beings who have a responsibility to deal regularly with the business of transformation, thereby engendering hope."[46]

By grounding political action in the Judeo-Christian tradition, the

Texas IAF appropriates a rich heritage and language of ethics which informs its deliberations and strategies. It is essential to recognize, however, that the norms of solidarity and reciprocity which are advocated by Cortés and other IAF leaders do not exist in isolation from frank recognition of the brutalities which typify much political conduct. "Sometimes it's hard to work with church people," COPS organizer Alejandra Rodriguez said, "because they believe that we're not supposed to be powerful. They think that we're supposed to be humble." Yet the IAF teaches low-income citizens the imperative of acquiring political power. How is the emphasis on power and its concomitant characteristic, self-interest, linked to the Judeo-Christian tradition?

In spite of the pleasure Alinsky derived from shocking others with fairly crude expressions of power, he actually bequeathed the IAF a sophisticated appreciation of the nuances of power. Alinsky noted that the dictionary definition of power consisted of nothing more than "ability, whether physical, mental, or moral, to act," and quoted the *Federal Papers*: "What is a power, but the ability or faculty of doing a thing? What is the ability to do a thing, but the power of employing the *means* necessary to its execution?" Ernie Cortés has extended that appreciation of power. "Power is nothing more than the ability to act in your own behalf," he wrote. "In Spanish we call the word 'poder,' to have capacity, to be able." Gaining power is essential to human fulfillment because power enables human capacity and expands our abilities. Although it is broadly recognized that, in the words of Lord Acton, "power tends to corrupt," it is also true that "powerlessness also corrupts—perhaps more pervasively than power itself," as Cortés has observed. In other words, individuals who have not developed their capacities tend to act irresponsibly, for they have not learned how to hold either others or themselves accountable for their actions.[47]

In training sessions at religious institutions, Cortés commonly has to confront opposition to the notion of consolidating political power; for many religiously minded individuals, power is inherently suspect. Cortés counters such objections by citing Protestant theologian Paul Tillich, who observed that power is *ontological*—"of the nature of being." In a presentation at the Oblate School of Theology at San Antonio in January 1995, Cortés announced,

> *I want power.* There, I said it! But I want power, and we should want power, not for its own sake, but to enable us to act on our

values, to realize our imagination, and to develop our curiosity. We organize around vision, values, and imagination. We imagine what a good school could be, or a good job training strategy, or a different kind of neighborhood. We ask ourselves, "If we had the power to act differently, how would our community look?" And because we want power that lasts, we base ourselves in institutions. That way any one of us can leave a community, but the institutional base will persist.

Unlike Alinsky, Cortés and current IAF leaders differentiate between various kinds of power. Following an essay by Bernard Loomer entitled "Two Conceptions of Power," Cortés distinguished between "unilateral power" and "relational power." "Unilateral power tends to be coercive and domineering," Cortés wrote, juxtaposing it to "relational power." The IAF teaches people to develop the kind of power that is embedded in relationships, involving not only the capacity to act, but the reciprocal capacity to allow oneself to be acted upon. Both kinds of power are commonly mixed with each other, but the IAF prefers to build relational power—the kind of power that is grounded in Judeo-Christian ethics of the covenant and pentecost; that is, social and religious relationships which tie together communities and faith.[48]

The Texas IAF has gathered power in over two decades of organizing, but that power is mediated by a recognition of the encumbered nature of political work. "One of the worst things you can be is overly principled," Ernie Cortés said. "Everybody has got to compromise, adapt, change." Yet at the same time that there is a quiet modesty and a healthy sense of humor about Cortés' undertakings as they relate to his personal achievements, it is also clear that he has the highest expectations, and indeed a touch of hubris regarding the IAF as a mediating institution. If properly conceived and pursued, IAF organizations should reenliven ancient religious and political traditions in the contemporary context. Cortés wrote:

Much as the *ecclesia* existed for Classical Greece as a forum for speech and action and for the early Christians as a space within which they created the first congregations, the IAF organizations offer a public space in which modern human beings experience the open-endedness of relationships and of themselves. Members meet, discuss, argue, convince others, change their minds; they deliberate collective action and act together. These institutions not only allow families to defend themselves, but to discover and to develop their potential. They enable humans to participate in the kinds of politics that come closest in the contemporary world to the essence of the Athenian *polis.*

In this conception, IAF organizations operate as points of fusion for the Judeo-Christian and democratic-republican traditions, once one has stripped away the ideological superstructures which can corrupt faith and mystify democracy.[49]

When IAF organizers and leaders conduct training sessions in churches and temples throughout Texas, they offer a fundamentally different approach to restructuring schools than do most educational reformers. They base themselves in religious institutions and challenge participants to take the values transmitted in the Judeo-Christian tradition seriously. They provide political education for local leaders and emphasize their interpretation that no serious school reform can occur which is disengaged from parents and the community. They bring together the different ethnic groups in the city and urge them to recognize their common interests and to use them as a basis for common political action. IAF leaders and organizers challenge participants to confront the largest issues which face us as human beings and frame those issues of trust, relationships, and power in the most important political and theological terms. They then connect those issues to the details of community organizing, such as developing effective strategies for voter registration, job training, or school improvement.

A second forum where Texas IAF leaders and organizers continue their self-education is in the ten-day national training sessions led by regional directors of the national IAF. Creating the national training sessions was Saul Alinsky's last achievement; he recognized belatedly that IAF organizations needed far more systematic apprenticeship and seasoning than the spasmodic mentoring which he provided his organizers and leaders. Today, between seventy-five and one hundred participants come to national training sessions three times each year from all over the country and a sister IAF organization in England. The training sessions are a major forum for leaders to reflect on their organizing efforts thus far, to develop their ideas about politics and power, and to build relationships with other leaders and their organizations. These training sessions are the educational vehicle through which IAF organizers articulate the philosophy and method of organizing that they have developed in over fifty years of political action.

In March 1995 I attended a national training session in Fort Worth. The participants represented the many regions, ethnicities, and classes of America. Among our participants were an African American pastor from South Central Los Angeles, an Anglo-American housewife from Omaha, a Mexican American sanitation worker from El Paso, an Anglo-American housing developer from Memphis, and a Philippine American priest from the Rio Grande Valley. We began by introducing ourselves to each other and sharing our political biographies, emphasizing the institutions that most shaped us.

Everyone had a different story. For Reverend James McGriff from Los Angeles, the turning point in his political development began when he watched a friend's father die at the hands of a White police officer as a fourteen-year-old in rural Georgia. For Beverly Oliver from Fort Worth, watching her mother struggle as a single parent to raise her and developing her faith in Christ led her to understand social justice as one constitutive part of the gospel. For Arlene Briscoe from Sacramento, her mother's leadership in founding the California chapter of the Association of Community Organizations for Reform Now was a key influence in her life. My own political education began when my father, a career military officer, went on a tour of duty in Vietnam in 1969 and I began questioning the reasons for the war.

Our introductions forged connections that were to grow deeper and richer throughout the training session and beyond. But IAF training sessions do not remain long on a level of sharing personal stories. We had an assignment to read "The Melian Dialogue," a chapter from Thucydides' *History of the Peloponnesian War*, for our evening session. It was unclear to many participants why we were working with this text, which is difficult to follow and has many obscure references to Argives, Phliasians, Corinthians, and other peoples of the Peloponnese. We read the chapter, discussed it informally over dinner, and wondered about its relevance to our work.

Participants acted out the roles of Athenians and Melians when we returned to the evening session. When the role plays were completed, we discussed how we had acted in the simulations and why the text was chosen as a catalyst for reflections about community organizing. Ernie Cortés challenged us to reread the text and to recognize the manner in which the Melians polarized the attempts of the Athenians to create a dialogue based not on high ideals but on mutual interests. The Melians' appeal to high ideals of liberty or death had seemed more heroic than the Athenians' sober consideration of interests, negotiations, and compromises. Cortés emphasized that the Athenians wanted to meet with the Melians as a whole, following the democratic practices of the Athenian assembly—but the Melian elite refused to allow ordinary Melians to have a voice in the life-and-death decisions that confronted them. As a result of the Melians' opposition to compromise, the Athenians decimated them and took control of their island.

Cortés warned participants to avoid the Melians' fate. Community organizers and their constituents, he said, occupy a position analogous to that of the Melians insofar as they both confront a superior power. The Athenians had interests to pursue, but they were willing to negotiate on the basis of shared interests. The Melian leaders, by contrast, would only consider the polarized alternatives of absolute independence or certain death. The Melians' fixation on rhetoric prevented them from seeing opportunities and flexibility in the Athenian stance; as a result, they were annihilated.

Personal introductions focusing on how institutions had shaped participants and discussion of Thucydides' text provided a framework of personal reflection and political analysis that shaped the rest of the national training session. We discussed the difference between private and public relationships and simple but effective ways of understanding others' interests. We analyzed the difference between unilateral kinds of power and other types of reciprocal power that are based on public relationships and shared interests. We visited a delegates' assembly of Dallas Area Interfaith, at that time a relatively new IAF organization, and observed local leaders' attempts to increase electoral participation, guarantee a living wage for low-income people, and increase funding for innovative schools and after-school programs.

Not all of the training was perfect or harmonious. Some participants complained that the workshops were too didactic and did not allow for enough informal exchange of ideas, and others were offended when Cortés, during a critique of the Dallas assembly, commented that a female IAF leader was "pleasant to look at." Some community leaders came to the training from movements and organizations that were not based in religious institutions, and they had trouble with organizers' references to Judeo-Christian principles and traditions. Cortés sparked a debate among participants when he stated that the "civil rights movement was dead long ago and we should have had the decency to bury it." Contestation, refutation, and elaboration provided much of the spice of the training. At each step of the way, the participants challenged themselves and each other to ask hard questions about what was happening in their neighborhoods and cities—and what their community-based organizations were doing to reverse economic and social declines with strong, broad-based organizing efforts.

Finally, a third forum for expanding the capacity of Texas IAF leaders and organizers has been elaborated through a collaboration with the LBJ School of Public Affairs at the University of Texas at Austin. Using funds from the Ford Foundation and the Rockefeller Foundation, Texas IAF leaders and organizers have since 1989 had the opportunity to study materials written by and attend seminars with many of the leading public intellectuals in the United States. Cornel West, Theda Skocpol, Jean Bethke Elshtain, Mary Ann Glendon, Lester Thurow, James Comer, William Damon, Glenn Loury, Michael Sandel, Chester Finn, Ted Sizer, Robert Putnam, Ted Fiske, and Howard Gardner have all participated in seminars with Texas IAF leaders, helping to expand their intellectual horizons and exploring with them the complexity of the problems they seek to address.

The seminars with public intellectuals do not simply serve to educate Texas IAF leaders and organizers. They also serve to teach the public intellectuals about the concerns of the working class in the Southwest and about the IAF's philosophy and method of community organizing. Texas IAF leaders and organizers prefer to think of the seminars as forums for an exchange of different kinds of knowledge and experience than simply as a one-way street in which intellectuals have a monopoly of expertise regarding the civic problems of American democracy.

There are several striking characteristics of the Texas IAF weekend leadership retreats, national training sessions, and seminars with public intellectuals. First, Texas IAF leaders are compelled to deal with the ambiguity and heterogeneity of perspectives concerning public policy issues. The radical nonpartisanship of the Texas IAF is represented by speakers who advocate a diverse array of political philosophies and are willing to engage others from different perspectives. Second, an underlying theme in the seminars and training sessions relates to an attempt to agitate the emancipatory currents of the Judeo-Christian tradition and the American democratic and federalist legacy. The IAF is a conservative organization insofar as it holds fast to seminal works in the western intellectual canon, ranging from Thucydides to de Tocqueville, as sources of inspiration and civic renewal.

A third noteworthy current of the seminars and the training sessions is the example set by Ernie Cortés as the director of the Texas IAF. Although Cortés appears entirely noncharismatic at first glance, he is an enthralling speaker who sets high standards for himself and others. He has an encyclopedic knowledge of modern history and politics and is unusually talented at weaving together factual references and interpretations in a way which stimulates audiences from diverse social and educational backgrounds. In addition to his personal fascination with history, politics, philosophy, and theology, Cortés incessantly urges Texas IAF leaders and organizers to become voracious readers as well. "Whenever Ernie sees me, he always asks me what I'm reading," one organizer in Dallas laughed. "He's always dragging me off to the bookstore with him." Cortés will assign organizers readings and ask them to submit brief written responses about them to him. And, although he can be tolerant of others' shortcomings and has an animated sense of humor, he is brusque and confrontational when the occasion demands it.

A fourth aspect of the IAF workshops and seminars concerns the complex nature of much of the material. Many Texas IAF leaders were high school dropouts who only later completed a General Equivalency Degree, and others can only speak English with great difficulty. Refusing to condescend to those leaders, the Texas IAF challenges them to study materials that can be difficult even for those with advanced degrees. During the seminars and training sessions, every effort is made to engage and assist those leaders with limited formal education or proficiency with English, but no attempt is made to reduce or explain away the intrinsic complexity of the most challenging civic issues facing the nation today. Instead, organizers and often Cortés himself will begin a process of tutoring organizers. Cortés will recommend specific books or articles for IAF organizers to read, will establish a realistic schedule for them to follow, and will ask that the organizers write brief reports to him interpreting the author's point of view and its relevance for organizing. This feature of the Texas IAF civic curriculum compels organizers and leaders to recognize the difficulty and legitimacy of different points of view concerning the political issues they seek to address; it also establishes a climate of respect for sustained intellectual engagement and reflection.

Taken together, weekend leadership training, national training, and seminars provide a complex web of educational activities which makes Texas IAF organizing unusually reflective and theoretically sophisticated. In contrast to many variants of populism, there is nothing anti-intellectual about the Texas IAF. Grass-roots organizing does not mean that low-income citizens cannot be challenged to develop their intellectual horizons as much as anyone who would seek to master a discipline, or that they should not desire to learn from outside specialists from universities or other forums of public life. Texas IAF leadership training institutes and workshops can be especially beneficial for teachers because they differ so radically from traditional forms of teacher education. Most teacher education courses emphasize new methods and programs to improve instruction and avoid the deepest questions and problems which confront the human condition. As a result of the IAF's ambitious efforts to plumb the most complex religious and political dilemmas, a much more profound side of personal engagement is tapped than is common in most professional development programs attended by teachers. In the Texas IAF, serious study and intellectual engagement are not optional forms of recreation, but a constitutive part of each organization's ongoing development.

Questions of Method

The following account of Texas IAF organizations' school collaborations relies on naturalistic descriptions of schools based upon classroom observations and interviews with parents, teachers, students, clergy, organizers, and leaders conducted in schools, churches, homes, restaurants, and community centers. First, I present four case studies of school change as a result of work with Texas IAF organizations. In each case, I have been particularly interested in describing the politics of change, with some attention given to the turning points which transformed the school from engaging in vicious circles of bureaucracy and low achievement to creating virtuous circles of parental engagement, democratic governance, and improved academic achievement. The goal of the case studies is to capture the trajectory of Texas IAF school organizing as well as the variety entailed in changing the culture of schools. Although there are patterns to be detected in each of the schools—including the use of house meetings, Walks for Success, assemblies, coalition building, and so on—each school is unique in regard to its local politics and history, the nature of its coalitions, and the degree of its success.

The second part of the description which ensues is not based on single case studies; rather, it focuses on systemic change both within the city of San Antonio and across the state of Texas. In San Antonio, the political power of COPS and its younger sister organization, the Metro Alliance, have grown to such strength that both organizations have played major roles in promoting and creating affordable college educations, after-school programs for latchkey children, job training programs, and bank loans for aspiring low-income homeowners. The net effect of the organizing of COPS and Metro Alliance has been to develop a host of low-income community leaders and a multilayered social policy which is in the process of revitalizing working-class communities that have been neglected for decades.

A few words are warranted about the criteria that were used to select the schools described below. The first criterion was some degree of sustained contestation, experimentation, and transformation within a school and its community. I was not looking for success as much as for evidence of struggle—a readiness to confront the critical condition of urban public education and a concerted effort to seek out bold new kinds of solutions. As a teacher educator who is both an instructor and a practitioner, I wanted to find examples of schools that were charting a new and different kind of path to school reform based on community organizing so that I could learn about its strengths and weaknesses. To locate schools that were engaged in unusually intense struggles to overcome problems of low academic achievement and student disengagement, I examined diverse data concerning academic achievement, parental engagement, teacher retention, and (in the case of a high school) the percentage of students going on to higher education. None of the schools that have entered into collaborations with the Texas IAF have experienced progress in any arena without a great deal of soul-searching, without confrontations with their own colleagues as well as with external school authorities, and without constant evaluation. And, although many have experienced success in a number of arenas, most have progressed through a spasmodic "two-steps-forward, one-step-backward" pattern that has blended excitement and hope about small victories with consternation over the persistence of the social problems that confront low-income urban neighborhoods and their schools.

A second criterion in selecting schools was institutional diversity. Although most of the schools I describe are elementary schools, I also investigated middle schools and high schools so that I could explore the possible ways in which differences such as the size of schools and their internal organization might either facilitate or impede the process of community organizing for school change and neighborhood improvement. The evidence suggests that although all schools can be successful sites for community organizing, one is best advised to begin with elementary schools and to progress upward, taking special pains to keep the parents engaged during the transition to middle and high schools.

A third criterion for selecting the schools involved geographical diversity. I wanted to determine if IAF community organizing plays itself out differently in different kinds of cities. The narrative begins in an African American neighborhood in Fort Worth and then moves to Mexican American communities in Austin, El Paso, Houston, and San Antonio. Woven into the narrative are accounts of the ways in which different local cultural, economic, and political conditions inform the process of school change.

If considerable variance exists among the schools and communities described below, all of them shared certain commonalities. As measured by census tract data, income in the different neighborhoods is far below that of the national median, whether measured by per capita income, household income, or family income. Between a quarter and a half of all persons living in each of the neighborhoods are poor. All of the communities are predominantly minority, reflecting asymmetries of race and class in the United States, where the median family income for Hispanic students is 60 percent of that of Whites, and Whites' median family income is more than double that of Blacks.[50]

Finally, rather than simply looking at individual schools, I have also sought to describe larger patterns of change. San Antonio possesses Texas' strongest IAF organizations and has in general gone the furthest in its school collaboratives; I have attempted to describe these in a systemic way which recognizes the interdependent nature of many of its school reform initiatives. In addition, I also describe the Texas IAF's collaboration with the Texas Education Agency, the state's department of education, to create a network of "Alliance Schools" throughout the state with special funds and waivers. Since their inception, those Alliance Schools have fought for preventive health clinics for children, free after-school programs, safer streets and neighborhoods, and transformations of instruction, curricula, and assessment in urban schools. Their struggles, their successes, and their travails offer new kinds of data about the challenges confronting mediating institutions which seek to improve urban schools and communities.

The research design underlying the study is informal. I have relied primarily on in-depth interviews of informants who have been engaged in school reform processes, although I also refer to a variety of other sources when appropriate; these include census tract records, newspaper articles, school district research reports, scholarly research, and the scores of schools on the annual Texas Assessment of Academic Skills test. It may be that this account is susceptible to confirmation bias, in which my sympathies with informants impede the development of a more objective perspective; as with any account of this nature, it may be that it serves primarily as a negative example. Nonetheless, the case studies are compelling enough, and the development of the Alliance Schools is provocative enough, to disseminate accounts of the work of the schools at this point—if only to provoke further research and debate. That contribution may be no small one if it serves to advance larger issues of democratization and education which currently should dominate the national political and civic agenda.

II

Developing
Civic Capacity

3

Morningside Middle School

Starting a Path for Change

By the early 1980s, news of the success of COPS in San Antonio had spread throughout Texas, and sponsoring committees had begun IAF organizations in Houston, El Paso, and the Rio Grande Valley. In spite of the spread of IAF organizations, no activity had yet begun in the dynamic "Metroplex" region in North Texas, comprising Dallas and Fort Worth. Yet it wasn't the case that there was no need for community-based organizations in those cities. As the oil bust demolished banks, wiped out jobs, and drove down property values, more and more citizens in North Texas felt that some kind of organized response to their troubles was crucial.

Reverend Nehemiah Davis, the pastor of Mount Pisgah Missionary Baptist Church in Fort Worth, was alarmed at what he saw happening in the region. Rising unemployment and overall economic instability hit his parishioners and the African American community hard. Davis felt a special responsibility, as an established community leader, to shape a creative and effective response to the region's problems. Mount Pisgah was one of the oldest African American churches in North Texas; it was founded in 1878 to accommodate the religious needs of Black workers who streamed to Fort Worth from East Texas and Louisiana to labor in "Cow Town's" booming stockyards and its packing houses. Reverend Davis had ministered to the congregation at Mount Pisgah since 1963. He had built up a congregation of 650 parishioners, had raised funds to provide for an elegant reconstruction of the chapel, and had served a two-year stint in local politics after being elected to the school board in 1978. In spite of his pride in his congregation and his church, however, he felt that some piece was missing from his ministry. When religious colleagues told him that working-class San Antonio had found a way to organize through COPS, Davis agreed to attend a ten-day IAF national training institute in Lake Forest, Illinois, in 1983.[1]

Davis did not expect to find himself so taken by the IAF's work. He liked the diversity of IAF leaders and organizers, he liked their emphasis on accountability, and he appreciated their pragmatic recognition of the importance of interests, negotiations, and compromise in politics. Shortly after returning to Fort Worth, he began a sponsoring committee for a new IAF group to be called the Allied Communities of Tarrant, or ACT, with the hope that the group would engage citizens not just in metropolitan Fort Worth but also in the larger Tarrant County in which it is situated.

Davis had to work hard to get his fellow ministers to commit to raise the money to bring the IAF to Fort Worth. The biggest problem that he faced was that ministers in affluent parts of the county did not feel any special calling to deal with problems such as unemployment, gangs, and drugs in low-income communities. "Some of the ministers, especially the Anglo ministers, had a difficult time recognizing that poor conditions in one part of the city affect everyone in all parts of the city," Davis said. Davis tried to emphasize to his colleagues that even if their parishioners were affluent, problems with an issue such as crime would hurt their quality of life, even if only in the form of increased private security and raised taxes for incarceration. Patiently and slowly he built a broad-based constituency to support ACT.

As ACT was in the process of becoming established, Davis and other religious leaders began to identify winnable issues in the community. ACT first became mobilized when its leaders discovered that utility rates were about to go up. Working with city council and corporate leaders, ACT challenged the new fee structures successfully. ACT then organized a voter registration drive and added over six thousand new names to the electorate. Finally, ACT leaders learned that many residents were angry about their streets, whose massive potholes broke axles and whose poor drainage blocked intersections and caused accidents. ACT leaders conducted research which showed that Fort Worth had a tradition of focusing its street repairs on avenues leading to the freeways used by upper-middle-class citizens to commute to suburbs. Like many American cities, Fort Worth typically reserved federal Community Development Block Grants to repair inner-city streets.

To ensure that Fort Worth's working-class residents would benefit from city revenues, ACT began mobilizing citizens to identify streets that were in disrepair, to turn out for city council meetings, and to advocate the allocation of city revenues to repair the streets of working-class communities. When Fort Worth city council members held public meetings to discuss a proposed bond for street improvement, they were surprised when hundreds of low-income citizens turned out to advocate the expenditure of funds in their neighborhoods. Thanks to the community's advocacy and the ability of ACT to increase political participation, voters passed a bond in 1985 to allocate over $57 million in capital improvement funds to improve the streets of working-class communities.

ACT's work on utility rates, voter registration, and repair of streets won it credibility and respect from the city's power brokers. ACT needed that respect when it learned that Texas Wesleyan College was considering relocating out of South Fort Worth because of the rampant crime in the area. ACT worked with other community leaders to keep the university in the neighborhood. Even when it succeeded with this short-term goal, ACT was left with the larger issue of community development. There were many areas in which ACT could contribute; they spanned from health care and housing to job creation and community policing. From "one-on-one's" and house meetings, ACT leaders learned that the major issue agitating citizens in South Fort Worth concerned the poor performance of the public schools.

Fort Worth newspapers constantly printed test results from the city which showed that the schools in South Fort Worth were failing their students. Academic achievement was weak, dropout rates were high, and there was high attrition among the teaching staff. The community appeared trapped in a vicious circle of low expectations, unaccountable institutions, and poor academic results.

To determine if there was a contribution which ACT could make to improve school performance, and to use that as a lever to improve the neighborhood, ACT began meeting with key community leaders in Fort Worth. These included business leaders in the Chamber of Commerce, Downtown Fort Worth, Inc., and local foundations. ACT leaders then met with officials from a long-range planning committee of the Texas Education Agency to learn about the state's major concerns with school performance and the changing nature of the regional economy. Finally, they met with Superintendent Donald Roberts from the Fort Worth Independent School District to discuss ways in which ACT could play a role in improving public schools in Fort Worth.

As a result of these meetings, ACT learned that all of the major players in education in Fort Worth—the school district, the business community, and the Texas Education Agency—had clear ideas about instruction, curricula, and standards, but that none of them felt informed about truly effective ways to enhance parental participation in schools. In addition, they learned that parents in urban public schools often would become angry when they felt that their children were punished inappropriately and would attack school personnel personally rather than developing joint strategies to enhance cooperation between the school and the home. Sensing that ACT might be able to address these problems effectively, Davis and Texas IAF organizer Sister Mignonne Konecny prepared a document for the school board of the Fort Worth Independent School District proposing that they provide parental training in low-income communities on educational issues.

As part of their preparation, they met with the local chapter of the American Civil Liberties Union to ensure that they would not in any way be violating the separation between church and state. The Fort Worth branch of the ACLU assured them that as long as there was no propagation of religious doctrine in the schools, ACT should feel free to play a positive role in any way that it chose to improve education. To test the business community's commitment to their engagement, ACT requested financial support to cover salaries and expenses for their initiative. Local foundations and businesses agreed to make the requested contributions. ACT then submitted a proposal to the school board which outlined a strategy for engaging the community to enhance educational achievement. The proposal was immediately approved.

The program that ACT advanced had two facets. First, ACT organized churches to increase cooperation between parents, educators, congregations, and clergy. Second, it wanted to identify a particularly troubled urban school for a major intervention, as a kind of pilot case in which it could gauge its success at transforming a school's culture.

In the past, African American churches in Fort Worth had publicly recognized young people for exceptional academic achievement during Sunday morning services. ACT leaders and organizers now worked with nearly twenty neighborhood churches, ranging from large Baptist and Catholic congregations to small Pentecostal sects, to broaden their recognition programs to honor the special strengths of all of the young people in the community. Fort Worth clergy and congregations were receptive and formed education committees in their churches to make certain that the young people received public recognition for their achievements at a special recognition program held every six weeks. To learn more about the development of the children of their congregations, education committees asked the students to bring their report cards to church to identify areas of achievement. That simple act increased students' sense that their community held them accountable for their schoolwork and enhanced communication about the situation of young people among teachers, clergy, and laity.

When the new push toward recognizing educational progress began, clergy emphasized many aspects of learning. If children had a grade of D in a course but had climbed out of failure, they were praised; if children missed ten days in a semester but had previously missed twenty, their rise in attendance was publicly appreciated; if children did not go to church, clergy and educators invited them to attend services at a religious institution of their choice to receive the community's approbation of their achievements. "We basically tried to recognize any child who had improved each six weeks," Reverend C. M. Singleton of the First Missionary Baptist Church recalled. "Sometimes there wasn't much to recognize them for in terms of academic achievement, but we might find something that they had done well in terms of citizenship, or that their school attendance had improved." Many clergy preached sermons emphasizing the importance of caring for the young, while others made a special effort in their services to recognize parents who had visited or assisted in their children's schools, and still others began expanding their mission to visit the children of their congregations in school. At Mount Pisgah, Reverend Davis commended children who read books on their own during the summer and parents who were particularly active in reading to their children.

ACT's community organizing, the involvement of local clergy and relatives, the encouragement of teachers, and the heightened sense of pride among young people came together to create a new awareness of the challenges and resilience of Fort Worth's youth. "What that started to do was change the culture," ACT organizer Perry Perkins said. "We figured out a way, if only for attendance or citizenship, to encourage all kids." Significantly, this first action was grounded in the spiritual bedrock of the African American community—the church. Once the community felt a new unity toward the young within its congregations, "People started saying that 'we ought to be involved in our schools,'"

Perkins said. "They now said, 'it really is the job of the church and the job of the community to be involved in the schools.'"

While ACT was working with its churches to create and monitor the new recognition programs, it simultaneously looked for a school to work with. One school which stood in strong need of assistance was Morningside Middle School in the Morningside neighborhood in South Fort Worth. Morningside was "intensely segregated," with close to 90 percent of the pupils African American and another 7 percent Latino. Of the twenty middle schools in Fort Worth in 1985, Morningside had the lowest test scores on a criterion-referenced test given throughout Texas, the Texas Educational Assessment of Minimum Skills, or TEAMS test. Half of the nine hundred children at Morningside failed the writing component of TEAMS; half of the students failed at least one subject in the regular academic curriculum. Eighty-five percent of the students at Morningside participated in free or reduced-price lunch programs; almost all of those came from families with incomes well below the poverty line. Few of the students came from families with both parents living at home. The majority lived in single-parent, female-headed households in apartments close by the school; many were living with their grandparents or other extended family members.[2]

Morningside Middle School needed help. In 1985 the Fort Worth school board attempted to respond to its situation by appointing a new principal, Odessa Ravin, to the school. Ravin proved to be an excellent choice, but the manner in which the board appointed her was inauspicious—and typical of urban school bureaucracies. Ravin was not informed that she was even a candidate for the position until after the meeting which had approved her transfer from a high school. When children at her church learned that she had been appointed principal of the middle school, they told their parents "We don't want Sister Ravin to go there—she'll be killed!"[3]

In spite of the unilateral nature of her appointment, Ravin was an ideal individual to take over the leadership of Morningside Middle School. She was known as an effective disciplinarian and a talented instructor who had served successfully as the instructional vice principal for three urban high schools. Ravin worked with teachers who desperately needed assistance to teach effectively, and she had a superb reputation among students, faculty, and parents for fairness and commitment. A diminutive woman in her fifties, Ravin was conservative in her sense of personal accountability and liberal in her intellectual independence and readiness to innovate. If there was anyone in the Fort Worth Independent School District who might have had the skills to improve conditions at Morningside Middle School, Odessa Ravin was that person.

Ravin also had an advantage in that she was no stranger to the school or the community. She had first begun teaching social studies and English at the middle school in 1966 but had been sent to a predominantly White school in 1971 to comply with the school district's desegregation plan. Simultaneously, the school's student body was broken up, as White magnet school students came in and Black Morningside students were bused to a White middle school where they were tracked to the lower level. "That's when I saw community pride leave," Ravin recalled. "The community's view was that 'they took our school.'"

In the 1970s, Ravin had watched in dismay as drugs became increasingly visible in Morningside and morale crumbled. By the early 1980s Fort Worth school officials persuaded the federal government that they had complied with segregation mandates, and Morningside Middle School reverted back to being a predominantly Black neighborhood school, albeit with White and Latino students bused in for ethnic balance in the magnet program. Ravin believed that the disruption that the students from the neighborhood experienced in predominantly White Wedgewood Middle School, as well as the rise of gangs and drugs in Morningside, contributed to an atmosphere in the middle school that was entirely unconducive to learning. It didn't help that the students' home lives were often disorganized, with few adult males available to sponsor the development of the young men and many of the children of her pupils from the 1960s relocated to the homes of their grandparents because of their parents' difficulties. "When the neighborhood kids came back here," Ravin said, "they had no pride, and they were destructive." Ravin discovered shortly after her unsought promotion in the summer of 1985 that her predecessor had had his jaw broken when he tried to break up a fight involving high school dropouts who had attacked a Morningside student after a basketball game. The job of principal was going to be tough.

Ravin was not sure of how to approach her new position, but she was certain of one thing: she would not be able to lead Morningside Middle School without rallying every community stakeholder to improve it. Recognizing the strength of religious conviction and church attendance in the African American community, she resolved to ask for help in Morningside's churches. Shortly after receiving word that she would take over the middle school, Ravin went to the Community Baptist Church, on Mississippi Street, a few blocks down from the school. Community Baptist was presided over by Reverend Finnie Jenkins, whom Ravin had known ever since she moved to Fort Worth from rural East Texas in the 1950s. When Reverend Jenkins asked her as a visitor to his congregation to stand and be recognized, Ravin decided to speak out even though she was out of order. With her voice shaking, she said, "My name is Odessa Ravin, and I've just been assigned to be the new principal at Morningside Middle School. And I'll tell you, that school is out of control! I need help!"

Ravin received the respect and solace of Community Baptist's congregation, but she was not yet clear on how she should engage the community in the day-to-day work of the school. She visited numerous other churches throughout the community and she wrote letters to pastors to ask for their participation in the school. Then, as if in confirmation of her worst fears, the main office of Morningside was firebombed the night before school opened in September. The bomb had been thrown into the nurse's office and the entire front office was blackened and reeking of smoke when children arrived for the first day of school the next morning. "I walked in to school in my new blue knit suit, that I had especially bought for the first day of school," she recalled, "and there was just soot and smoke everywhere."

Although Ravin was shaken, she insisted on holding the first day of school. Until the front office was repaired, she set up her office in the library and asked counselors to advise students in the cafeteria. When Ravin held her first parents' meeting a few days after the firebombing, only one parent attended, tracking soot from the main office into the library. "The place was out of control," ACT organizer Perry Perkins said. "People said you couldn't do anything at this school."

Odessa Ravin was not ready to give up. She drew up a discipline plan with her faculty and challenged the most rebellious students to enter into the learning process or to leave. As part of her effort to alert the community to the problems in the school, Ravin continued her outreach to neighborhood churches. She spoke with area clergy, and those whose churches were members of ACT informed Reverend Davis and Mignonne Konecny of her call for help. For most of her first year at

Morningside, however, Ravin was so preoccupied with crisis management that she never got a chance to attend to issues of instruction and
learning. "We had a fight every time classes changed," she recalled. In
the worst weeks of the year, the police were called to school to arrest
violent and disorderly youths on a daily basis.[4]

In 1986 Davis and Konecny began meeting with Ravin. Most of ACT's
member churches in South Fort Worth were in the Morningside Middle
School attendance zone, and ACT clergy and parishioners had informed
its leaders and organizers of Ravin's outreach to the area's churches.
ACT had interviewed many school principals and found that they responded positively to the idea of a collaboration, but Ravin stood out in
terms of her unusual depth of commitment. "Not only did Mrs. Ravin
have a very positive attitude toward parental involvement," Reverend
Davis recalled, "but she had already been out visiting churches in the
community and beating on our doors, *asking* us to get involved. I don't
know anyone else who was such a pathbreaker in this area as she was."

In addition to their commitment to improving education, Ravin and
Davis both had cultural and generational ties. Both were children of the
depression who had grown up in small towns in East Texas. Both came
from independent farming families and left their rural communities to
look for larger opportunities in Fort Worth. Both had pursued more or
less the only careers available to Black men or women who sought a
professional life: that of the ministry or teaching. Although Davis had
never taught in public schools, he had taught and designed curricula for
Sunday schools, youth ministry, and adult Bible study classes at Mount
Pisgah for years. His work as a minister involved teacher education and
counseling, and those human relations skills prepared him well for the
complex challenge that Morningside presented. Davis was impressed
with Ravin's tenacity and risk taking, and Ravin knew that if Davis participated at Morningside, his special status as a prominent Black minister and former school board member would provide her with valuable
political protection. Finally, Sister Konecny was a former Catholic school
teacher who felt comfortable in working with children and parents. As
a result of a many-sided mutual attraction, ACT leaders asked Morningside Middle School to enter into a sustained collaboration with them.

Once ACT conveyed that it was ready to collaborate with Ravin, the
organization worked to involve community stakeholders in its effort.
ACT met with the Fort Worth citywide PTA leaders and business leaders

to inform them of the partnership and to ask for their support. The business leaders and local philanthropies were eager to increase parental involvement in schools and responded generously to ACT's requests. While these meetings were taking place, Superintendent Roberts received a telephone call from a prominent citizen alleging that ACT was a communist group, and the superintendent felt obliged to call Davis and Konecny to his office to inquire about the accuracy of the charge. Once his concerns were allayed, Roberts presented the collaboration to the school board.

After receiving external support from the superintendent, the school board, and Fort Worth business leaders and philanthropists, ACT began its first discussions with Morningside teachers. Odessa Ravin had impressed her faculty through her outreach to churches in the neighborhood, and faculty were enthusiastic when Reverend Davis began working in their school and community on a daily basis. In their first conversations with teachers, ACT leaders learned that teachers had many negative encounters with parents, who seemed only to show up when they were angry at a perceived injustice. Using that frustration as a wedge, Davis and Konecny sought to persuade teachers that parental engagement which took a positive and proactive stance to support teachers and the learning atmosphere at Morningside could produce hitherto untapped resources for the school. "We're not coming in to tell you how to teach," Davis told the teachers, "but to help parents to come to the school with a positive attitude." Davis and Konecny were careful to convey that they in no way saw their roles as entailing additional demands on teachers.

ACT's next step was to organize community leaders to go from door to door visiting the homes of Morningside students and their parents. ACT designed a survey with questions for its leaders to use during the visits to acquire information about parents' sentiments about the school. Leaders asked parents what they liked best about the school, which areas they felt needed improvement, and what kinds of work they would be willing to do to improve the school. When parents were especially lively, interested, and articulate, leaders identified them as potential future leaders for the middle school.

Rather than simply focusing on improving the school, leaders also asked parents about their church affiliation. If parents' churches were not members of ACT, leaders asked if their churches had education committees which supported the recognition program. Many parents in small pentecostal churches began education committees as a result of the visitations. ACT leaders learned that children at Morningside were affiliated with over one hundred churches, and the recognition program spread not just throughout Fort Worth, but also out to other churches in the Metroplex region with members living on the South Side.

Davis and Konecny began working on a daily basis in Morningside Middle School and its neighborhood. Through coordinating leaders and conducting visitations themselves, they made sure that leaders came to the home of every student in the school and established positive contact with the parents. In many cases an ACT leader and a Morningside teacher conducted the interviews together, symbolizing a new collaboration between churches and public schools.

In a slow but cumulative fashion the labor-intensive, face-to-face, relational approach of ACT leaders and Morningside teachers began to change the attitude of many parents toward their children's school. Reverend Davis recalled that "the parents were always very surprised to see us and very receptive." Many parents were young, unmarried, and had not completed high school, and Ravin observed that usually "they were threatened by people they felt had a lot more knowledge than they did." The fact that teachers and clergy were now making the effort to visit parents in their homes and seeking their ideas on things that could be done to improve Morningside gave the parents a different sense of their role in relationship to the school. Key parents, such as Cordelia Barnes and Lyndia Taylor, who would go on to develop public relationships with school or city officials, were discovered during the visitations. Parents changed from the unsolicited recipients of services to "co-laborers," a term Odessa Ravin used to encourage parental engagement.

ACT leaders and teachers visited students' homes throughout 1986. At the same time, Odessa Ravin began internal school discussions with her faculty about the low academic performance of Morningside students. She refused to blame the students for their achievement level and insisted that the faculty take some responsibility for their role in students' low achievement. Many of her faculty were White, and in spite of years of teaching African American children, knew little about Black American life outside of the classroom. Odessa Ravin helped to "train them in our culture" through everything from bus tours in South Fort Worth to presentations by Black clergy to cultural diversity workshops.

As parents began to feel that Morningside genuinely sought their participation, they began visiting their children's classes with increasing regularity. With increased parental visibility, teachers were less secluded in their classrooms and began to feel more accountable for their instruction.

Simultaneously, Ravin maintained her presence in the churches in her school's zone. Many pastors gave her a forum in their churches to talk about the problems at Morningside. Ravin urged the community to acknowledge and address the many problems faced by its young people, including low academic achievement in the classroom and high crime in the neighborhood. One of the churches she visited was the First Missionary Baptist Church, and Reverend C. M. Singleton observed that his congregation was impressed with Ravin's forthright presentation of the problems at her school. "People were incensed about the firebombing, and they wanted to react," he recalled. To Ravin's delight, ACT's visitations and small group meetings, as well as her outreach into churches, began to yield results, as more and more parents began participating in the life of the school.

During the visitations, ACT leaders and organizers urged parents to attend small assemblies to discuss ways that parents could engage with Morningside Middle School. Before the assemblies they called parents to remind them of the meetings. They provided transportation for those parents who did not own cars, and informed parents of follow-up meetings when their work schedules did not permit them to attend upcoming assemblies. Again and again, leaders told parents that the middle school and their children needed their participation if their children were to have a chance to learn the skills they would need to participate fully in our society.

When the evenings for the first small assemblies at the school arrived, between fifty and one hundred parents came to four separate sessions. ACT leaders organized and led the sessions; they also solicited the services of a facilitator from the Fort Worth Independent School District to make sure that the district assumed some ownership of the assemblies. The first assemblies were open-ended. "We started first with sessions where parents could just vent," Perry Perkins said. "Parents could just talk about what it was that was bothering them." Odessa Ravin welcomed the parents to each session, and said, "I want you to feel free to say whatever is on your mind, whether it is good or bad, about me or anything else about the school. I will receive a report on what was said but not on who said it." She then left the room so that parents would feel no inhibitions about expressing themselves freely.

According to Reverend Davis, simply providing parents with a forum to express their grievances was of vital importance. "We told our leaders not to attempt to answer the parents' questions, but to just keep them talking. We wanted them to answer their own questions." As the sessions progressed, parents shifted from a focus on blaming the school to address their own need to become more engaged to help their children to learn more effectively.

The visitations and training sessions gradually changed Morningside from a school with no ties to the community to a fulcrum of parental involvement. Many parents had never understood the actual course of study for their children in the school or how their children were assessed. ACT leaders prepared training sessions to teach the parents about the structure of the school and to advise them about ways they could reinforce activities at home. At this stage, abstract debates about the legitimacy of the curriculum or the problems of Texas' standardized tests were avoided; the focus was on helping parents to understand the given realities of the school and how they could assist their children within that framework.

As the structure and purposes of the school became more and more transparent to parents, their involvement increased. Parents contributed to the school by providing extra attention to children with special needs, reading aloud to small groups in the library, and sharing concerns at staff development workshops. "Just being able to talk to a teacher, when one had never done that before, meant a lot to the parents," Reverend Singleton recalled, "and it meant even more when the teachers made an effort to reach out to talk with them." The visibility of parents in the school helped to improve instruction, for even teachers resistant to change found that they prepared their classes a little bit better when they knew that a parent would be observing them. ACT leaders and organizers and Ravin and her faculty conducted small group meetings so that parents could understand what their children were studying, how they could set up a positive work atmosphere at home, and how to prepare for tests. Teresa Chaney, who had taught at Morningside for nine years, was amazed at the transformation of the middle school. "Parental involvement was almost nonexistent before," she said. "I've seen more parents this year than in all the years I've taught." Whereas only one parent had shown up for the first PTA meeting after Ravin became principal, over nine hundred parents attended an assembly with Odessa Ravin and Fort Worth Superintendent Donald Roberts at the school in August 1987.

As parents became more involved in the life of the school they began to become more vocal about their concerns and needs. During the first visitations in 1986, many parents told ACT leaders that their children were unsupervised in the late afternoon after school had let out and before parents came home from work. As Davis and Konecny expended more and more of their time at the middle school, it was becoming clear that additional support would be needed to continue the transformation of Morningside. At that point Reverend Davis proposed that ACT use funds donated by local philanthropies and business leaders to create an additional paid position, that of a strictly educational organizer who would work exclusively on school issues. ACT leaders approved the proposal, and Morningside resident Mattie Crompton was hired as the first educational organizer. She quickly established an after-school program which was free for all of the middle school children, with sports, arts, and academic tutoring components.

ACT and Morningside Middle School received their first major indication that visitations, training sessions, parental engagement, and the after-school program were reaping results in December 1988. At that time Odessa Ravin, Reverend Davis, and all of the parents and teachers who had been involved in shaping a new school climate learned that the middle school had moved from dead last place in achievement on the TEAMS test among the twenty middle schools in Fort Worth to third place. From 1986 to 1988, the percentage of students passing the written portion of the state's test jumped from 50 to 83 percent; the percentage passing the math section rose from 53 to 86 percent; and the percentage passing the reading, writing, and math sections climbed from 34 to 71 percent. Other internal indicators reflected positive changes. Previously, half of the students had been failing one subject; now only 6 percent were in that category.[5]

In recognition of its transformation, Morningside Middle School received banner headlines in the Fort Worth press. "Better Times Dawn at Morningside," proclaimed the lead article of the *Fort Worth Star-Telegram* on December 3, 1988. The favorable press coverage conveyed the news of the school's improved discipline, enhanced academic achievement, and parental involvement to readers throughout the city. Parents, students, and teachers celebrated the transformation of Morningside Middle School in parties and awards ceremonies in the schools, churches, and homes in the busy weeks before Christmas. "If we have any school headed in the right direction now, that's one of them," Superintendent Roberts told the press. "I don't think I've seen a relationship between students and faculty that's quite like it." [6]

The increase in parental involvement created new opportunities for Morningside Middle School, but also new dangers. Many urban schools have found one formula for success and failed to explore other promising opportunities for school improvement. In the case of Morningside, parents had become more aware of the need to coach their children at home and more assertive about their right to participate in improving their children's classrooms. The school had dramatically increased parental involvement, and the local press and the Texas Education Agency applauded its successes. Gratifying as that recognition was, Odessa Ravin wasn't ready to stop. She knew that many teachers were traditional in their orientations and emphasized memorization and test-taking skills rather than creativity and critical thinking. She knew that her teachers needed staff development opportunities to learn how to design student-centered classrooms with interdisciplinary curricula and alternative, more accurate measures of assessment. She also knew that, just beyond the boundaries of the school, youth gangs were growing more and more powerful, and that drug dealers were selling crack cocaine in low-rent apartments just around the corner.

In other words, while Ravin was pleased with the changed self-image of the middle school and the rise in test scores, she saw those victories more as an indication that the school was moving in the right direction than as a confirmation that it had already fulfilled its potential. A new opportunity to catalyze Morningside's developmental process presented itself when Mattie Crompton resigned from the educational organizer post in 1989. Davis and Ravin wanted to hire someone who would go beyond using the position to run a program for children—someone who would galvanize the community to radicalize its engagement in the school. They found a strong candidate in Leonora Friend, who would play a pivotal role in taking parents out of the school and into the street-level politics of the Morningside neighborhood.

Like Ravin and Davis, Friend had deep roots in Fort Worth's African American community. Her grandmother—who was a teacher—was one of the first Blacks to move to the Morningside neighborhood in 1958, and she woke up the first morning after her arrival to find that a cross had been burned in her front yard during the night. She persevered, however, and worked in the Fort Worth Independent School District for over forty years. Leonora Friend grew up in a middle-class home which prized education in the Morningside community and attended Morningside Middle School herself in the 1960s.

When Friend first took on the position of educational organizer, she saw that the position had developed in an inappropriate direction in its first trial period. Friend appreciated the contribution of the after-school program, for example, but she also recognized that it violated the IAF's iron rule never to help others when they could help themselves. The IAF heritage does not call upon organizers to run programs for schools or communities, but to challenge citizens to develop their own political resources so that they can develop the programs that they need without reliance on organizers.

Friend began one-on-one meetings and small group discussions with parents to ask them about the after-school program and the issues that they felt were most pressing for their children. She found that parents liked the program but wanted to go beyond reinforcing the school's curriculum at home to deal with issues of code compliance, safety, and political power in the school and the community. Following this imperative, Friend worked with the parents to form action teams to focus on the core issues confronting Morningside Middle School and its neighborhood.

Working with Friend, parents formed one action team to focus on issues of school safety and a second team to improve academic achievement. Parents were concerned with traffic patterns and crime in the neighborhood and wanted to learn about action they could take to create a more wholesome environment for their children. They also wanted to continue to advance the academic achievement of their children by shaping decisions about instruction, curricula, and governance in the school.

Leonora Friend anticipated the formation of the first two action teams. She was pleasantly surprised, however, when Cordelia Barnes, a single mother, proposed creating a third action team that would focus purely on issues of communication. Barnes resided in an apartment complex next to the school filled by over three hundred families dependent on welfare. She was a teenage mother, as her mother had been before her, and she had been poor all of her life. Yet the activity at Morningside had sparked a side of her that she had not known about. "You have a lot of things going on at this school," Barnes said, "but the parents never have the opportunity to talk about how they'll develop. If we had the chance, we could help to communicate to other parents. We could help with communication between parents and teachers. I have to say that I don't know how to talk to teachers who are smarter than I am. That makes me feel low, and then I just don't say anything. If we had a committee to work on this, we could do things better." A "communication action team" was formed and immediately went to work, drawing out parents who felt reluctant and incapable of guiding their children wisely through the middle school years.

One of the first issues that confronted the safety action team concerned a neighborhood issue. In close proximity to the school, a convenience store called "Gents" openly sold alcohol to underaged Morningside students. Under Texas law, no alcohol should be sold within five hundred feet of a public school. Parents such as Cordelia Barnes had observed the problem with the store for years, but did not know about the violation of state law or how to compel its enforcement. With careful guidance from ACT, parents learned how to place concerted pressure on their city council representatives through a barrage of telephone calls and how to circulate petitions among themselves which demanded the enforcement of the law. Parents gathered hundreds of signatures which they presented to the Fort Worth school board at one of its public meetings. As a result of the pressure, Texas Alcoholic Beverage Commission officers shut down the store. It was a victory which brought tremendous exhilaration to the parents.

When the excitement over closing down Gents abated, ACT leaders and organizers asked the parents, "OK, now what did you learn about what was needed at the school, about acting, and about getting other parents involved?" Using the "action" around the convenience store as a teaching tool, ACT leaders and organizers highlighted the sequence of "planning, acting, and evaluating" that the parents had moved through. Perry Perkins emphasized that "the evaluation time is really the most important time because that's the time you learn." As parents throughout South Fort Worth learned of the success of the parents at Morning-side, they also became mobilized, and over the next five years their activism resulted in the closing of over twenty stores selling alcohol to minors in close proximity to schools.

Morningside Middle School's efforts to enhance academic achievement and the quality of life in its neighborhood brought it further recognition in 1990, when it was the recipient of the Texas Governor's Excellence Award. The award carried an honorarium of fifty-three thousand dollars, which Ravin earmarked for staff development in instruction, curricula, and assessment. As a result of its successes, Morningside was one of four schools in Texas in 1990 to win a prestigious Carnegie Initiative Award from the Texas Education Agency and to become a "Carnegie School," which entails additional staff development funds. Ravin now placed all of her emphasis on giving her teachers intellectual resources that would enable them to diversify instruction, plan curricula collaboratively, and develop more precise and accurate forms of assessment. "I have relinquished my power over the schedule and the curriculum," Ravin said, "and all of that work is now happening within the individual teams."

Finally, as part of her own professional development, Odessa Ravin went to the IAF's national training institute in Irving, Texas, in the spring of 1990. At the institute, she was able to refine her skills in organizing the community around its most salient issues. Ravin is explicit about the debt she owes to the Texas IAF. "I could not have done any of this without ACT," she said. "They empowered me, and they taught me how to organize."

In spite of Morningside's achievements and accolades, its struggles were far from over in the early 1990s. Ravin confessed that a key part of her strategy to improve test scores focused on recitation and memorization—skills that are valuable components of cognitive development but that need to be balanced with higher order thinking skills involving creative expression, synthesis, and evaluation to enhance children's many-sided development. In 1990, the Texas Education Agency began using a new test to measure academic achievement which had far higher standards than the old TEAMS instrument, and only 22 percent of Morningside students passed all three sections (reading, writing, and math) of the new test. In spite of faculty training, the struggle has been arduous, and although test scores have gone up each year, by 1995 it was still the case that less than 40 percent of Morningside students passed all three sections of the test, a figure well below the state average. More ominously, youth gangs in the neighborhood have become more and more powerful, and although they have been kept out of the school, they have created a sense of danger and violence in the community.[7]

Odessa Ravin and her faculty responded to the new set of challenges by experimenting with team structures in the school which they hoped would lead students to develop a sense of personal worth and community to foster academic achievement. Teachers began holding advisory periods with students at the start of each day; these combat anonymity by providing explicit time for teachers to mentor students about personal issues and their overall academic development. The governance of the school has been divided into fourteen teams, grouped together by the grade of pupils, the location of teachers, or natural sources of social cohesion such as participation in the school's band. Those teams enable teachers to keep track of individual students better, to align curricula, and to develop joint conversations with parents rather than single parent–teacher conferences. The Carnegie Initiative provides the school with financial support for teachers to have two planning periods a day instead of just one; teachers employ the additional time to confer with parents and to develop new curricula using an interdisciplinary approach. Youth ministers from Mount Olive Baptist Church visit Morningside regularly and assist teachers, tutor students, and confer with parents. Morningside is struggling to develop *network closure*—a term James Coleman used to describe mutual relationships that are strong enough to develop common norms.[8]

The development of Morningside Middle School from 1985 to 1995 is a complex trajectory containing many peaks and valleys. When Odessa Ravin first became principal, the school was in the midst of a crisis, and Ravin worked with ACT and Morningside parents to effect a dramatic rise in test scores within three years. When the Texas Education Agency began requiring higher skill levels from students on its standardized tests, Morningside fared poorly, but it is has worked hard to create a more communal academic environment and is demonstrating signs of continuing progress. Morningside Middle School's experience suggests that community-based organizations can help to catalyze a process of change in urban middle schools, but that they cannot do everything. They need to find principals and teachers who are willing to take risks, who will explore myriad ways to personalize and improve instruction, and who are willing to stay with the hard work of school reform for the many years that it will take to truly improve the situation of youth in working-class communities.

On the basis of ACT's engagement in Morningside's development, the Texas IAF re-evaluated its previous stance toward involvement in the internal culture of public schools. In the past, Texas IAF organizations had only worked on public school issues that were relevant to external issues such as building renovation—issues which did not address the pedagogical atmosphere of the school. The developments at Morning-side suggested to Texas IAF leaders and organizers that they could make an impact at the heart of the school rather than just on the periphery. For Reverend Davis, Morningside's development was well worth the effort. He had committed thousands of hours of work to the creation of ACT, and he had carefully nurtured it through its first years of existence. Although only about ten of his own church's members had students at Morningside Middle School at any given point in time, he had been able to recruit large numbers of them to confront the crisis in the school and community, and together with Odessa Ravin, Morningside teachers, parents, and others from the community, had facilitated a tranformation at the school. The current situation at Morningside is not perfect, but it is a far cry better than the firebombing and fights which traumatized the school in 1985.

One immediate upshot of Morningside's development was that Ernie Cortés systematized Reverend Davis' concept of the educational organizer by approaching the Rockefeller Foundation in 1990 to fund organizers such as Leonora Friend throughout urban Texas. Such organizers would focus on education in the broadest sense—not just on the school, but also on whatever neighborhood issues shape the school's overall development. The Rockefeller Foundation agreed to fund those positions, and IAF leaders and organizers expanded their efforts in other low-income communities in Texas.

4

Jefferson Davis High School

The Struggle for Reform

Jefferson Davis High School is located off busy North Main Street in the midst of Houston's Near North Side. Although the name of the school reflects Houston's troubling continuity with the nomenclature of the Old South, Davis today is more southwestern than southern. Of its seventeen hundred students, approximately 84 percent are Latino, 14 percent are African American, and the remaining 2 percent are Asian American and White. Roughly one quarter of the students are recent immigrants to the United States from Mexico, Guatemala, Honduras, and El Salvador. The school has changed dramatically since its founding in 1925, when the United Confederate Veterans and the Daughters of Confederate Veterans argued before the all-White Houston school board for its current name.[1]

Like many urban schools, Davis experienced "White flight" in the late 1960s and early 1970s as Houston schools became more and more integrated. Throughout the 1970s and 1980s it struggled with the problems of many inner-city and minority schools: a dropout rate of over 50 percent, high staff turnover, and low student and teacher morale. Fights between students culminated with a stabbing in the auditorium in the spring of 1981, and Houstonians began referring to Davis and its environs as "the bloody North." When Myron Greenfield, now the chair of the English Department at Davis, first wanted to teach there in 1977, the administrators at the Houston Independent School District warned him that the school was dangerous and should be avoided. Father Tom Sheehey, the priest at nearby Holy Name, the parish church, counseled parents not to send their children to Davis. As measured by a variety of academic indicators—daily attendance, dropout rates, percentage of graduates going on to college—Davis was rated as the worst performing high school in the city by the Texas Education Agency.

Recognizing the problems at Davis and attempting to help, the Tenneco Corporation, a large Houston-based oil business, took on a leadership role in tutoring and staff development in 1981. Tenneco pumped money into staff retreats, but the ideas generated at the retreats were not implemented by the principal. "We talked a lot, but there was never any follow-through," teacher Suzanne Gager lamented. Community involvement in events at Davis was low, and the school had no academic results to show for its efforts. When Tenneco's chief executive officer, Jim Ketelsen, asked his staff to evaluate what it had accomplished in Davis after seven years of engagement, the results were disheartening. "When I asked the bottom line question, the hard facts showed that we'd made no progress at all," Ketelsen said.[2]

In February 1988, Emily Cole was appointed principal at Jefferson Davis High School. Like Odessa Ravin, Cole was reticent to take on the job of principal, particularly at a high school. For close to a quarter century she had worked in public schools at the elementary school level. Once in her new position, Cole looked for ways to integrate the child-centered philosophy of education that she had previously found successful into the design of the high school. Observing that many freshmen dropped out of Davis because of their poor preparation at the elementary and middle school levels, Cole's first initiative was to design the Bridge Program, a summer program which would help middle school students to prepare for their freshman year at Davis. Disenchanted with Tenneco's previous engagement with the school, Ketelsen responded positively to Cole's request that his corporation pick up the cost for the Bridge Program's funding.

The first session of the Bridge Program in 1988 was a success, and Cole and Ketelsen felt that they had taken an important first step in moving Davis' mission in the right direction by expanding it beyond its traditional nine-month calendar. Yet Cole was troubled that the school's collaboration with the community was so weak. Regardless of how much she publicized meetings, she was never able to get more than twenty parents to attend Davis' PTA meetings. In 1989 Cole mentioned her frustration to Jo Ann Swinney, Tenneco's corporate liaison to Davis, and asked Swinney for suggestions about ways in which she could increase the participation of parents in the school.

One might think it unlikely that a major corporation's community relations officer would recommend an organization founded by the inflammatory Saul Alinsky. Yet just as Marshall Field, the maverick department store owner, had been intrigued by and supportive of Alinsky's work in the late 1930s, so was Tenneco to prove flexible and independent in its assessment of the local Texas IAF organization—The Metropolitan Organization—in the late 1980s. In her work at Tenneco, Swinney had had many occasions to observe the consistently cordial manner in which Jim Ketelsen received TMO leaders and organizers when working-class Houstonians had grievances about raises in utility expenses or other pressing financial concerns. Swinney knew that TMO was a broad-based organization representing more than sixty churches throughout Houston. While she knew that Ketelsen had reservations about TMO's combative nature, she also noted that TMO had established a collaboration with the Houston Independent School District to enhance parental involvement at three troubled middle schools, and that its leaders and organizers were spending increasingly large amounts of time working on conflict resolution at schools troubled by tensions between ethnic groups.

The next time TMO leaders and organizers visited Tenneco to ask for funding to help with their middle school project, Tenneco agreed to make a contribution—contingent upon TMO's readiness to help Davis with parental engagement. Intrigued by ACT's ongoing work at Morningside, and sensing an opportunity to gain a powerful corporate ally which might help to produce similar results in Houston, TMO leaders and organizers agreed to the quid pro quo.

Robert Rivera, TMO's lead organizer in Houston, then met with Emily Cole to determine the seriousness of Cole's interest in community engagement. Cole was reluctant at the outset. She worried that TMO might introduce a radical political agenda into her work that could polarize the school and undermine her legitimacy as a new principal. To teach Cole about the nature of TMO's work and to assuage her fears, Rivera invited Cole to a TMO accountability session with Houston Independent School District Superintendent Joan Raymond and the school board, to be held at Pleasant Hill Baptist Church in Houston's African American Fifth Ward.

When Cole arrived early at Pleasant Hill, she was intrigued by the detailed planning which she saw going into the assembly, as TMO leaders practiced in advance the exact wording of their questions to the school board, with careful coaching from organizers and other leaders. She was also pleased when she was invited to take the platform and to sit between the superintendent and a school board member. "A principal usually doesn't sit next to board members and a superintendent," she said. "The hierarchy of HISD doesn't allow that." The meeting was led with clocklike precision by Maria Emerson, a TMO leader, and in spite of the fact that Superintendent Raymond had to respond to many critical questions from TMO leaders, it was completed in an hour.

Emily Cole was impressed. TMO found a way to get the superintendent to come to the much-maligned Fifth Ward and grilled her with questions which showed a firm grasp of the issues in education facing the community. Cole liked TMO's emphasis on mutual accountability and on compromise as an essential part of politics, and its meticulous sense of timing. Believing that she had found reliable allies, Cole mustered her courage and asked TMO to assume a leadership role in increasing parental engagement at Davis.

TMO leaders and organizers agreed to collaboration and began one-on-one conversations with key parent and community leaders on the Near North Side. Testing the waters to sense whether Davis was really prepared to change its culture, parents began visiting the school to assist in classrooms, and Father Tom Sheehey from Holy Name Church became increasingly visible as he conversed with students in Davis' hallways and cafeteria. Davis began organizing its first Walk for Success in the fall of 1989. Cole sent newsletters home to parents advertising the walk and asked them to be home to receive walkers. Public service announcements filled the airwaves in English and Spanish. TMO organized parents, teachers, and students to go on the walk, and supplemented the Davis community with its leaders, student volunteers from the University of Houston, and Davis alumni. Father Tom Sheehey gave a benediction before the walk began, and walkers visited the the homes of every ninth grader at Davis.

One parishioner from Holy Name who participated in the Walk for Success was Maria Cantu, a leader among the older families on the Near North Side. Cantu had had positive experiences with TMO organizer Robert Rivera, who had helped Holy Name with parish development issues. In his work at Holy Name, Rivera had likewise been impressed with Cantu, and had identified her as a parish leader whose skills should be cultivated on behalf of her community. For Cantu, who possesses only a fleeting knowledge of English, that recognition was an important validation which she initially denied but gradually came to accept.

Maria Cantu is a mother of eight children, and her last three children were attending Davis in the late 1980s. She was particularly worried about her youngest son, Juan, whom she feared she was losing to the street life of the neighborhood. Working in concert with Rivera, Cantu was one of several parents who were invited and carefully prepared to make public statements on behalf of their children in an assembly which was planned to follow the Walk by two weeks. The Near North Side was covered with publicity of the parents' assembly before the event, and Davis' vast auditorium was filled to capacity. Mustering her courage to speak to the hundreds of parents, teachers, and students in the hall, Cantu pledged her constant support to her son to continue his education. At the end of the evening, all of the parents who came to the assembly signed a scroll on which they promised to do all they could to enable their children to gain a high school education. For years afterward that scroll was prominently displayed in Davis' front hallway, providing a constant reminder of the connections between the school and the community.

In the weeks following the parents' assembly, TMO leaders and organizers and the staff at Davis began giving a series of workshops to educate parents about their children's school. Workshop topics included presentations on the school's programs and curricula, effective parenting strategies, and scholarship programs. Some parents felt that their children should work to support their family rather than continue their education to the end of high school or to college; they had an opportunity to express their viewpoints in open-ended discussions and to learn more about the advantages of pursuing higher education. To encourage more reflection on that issue, TMO and Davis faculty invited alumni from Davis who were college students to discuss their experiences and to answer questions from parents. Teachers and counselors became much more active in informing parents about students' poor academic performance and designing mutual strategies to improve study habits. Finally, TMO worked with Davis and other Near North Side schools to promote a conference on health issues, attended by over four hundred parents and students.

The Walk for Success, parents' assembly, and TMO workshops reaped many positive rewards for Davis High School. Parents felt that their concerns were the school's concerns and felt a new solidarity with the teachers at Davis. To celebrate the growing sense of community, Father Tom Sheehey introduced a new graduation ceremony at Holy Name in

June 1990 to recognize the achievements of Davis' students. All of Davis' graduating seniors were invited to attend a special mass in which the valedictorian read passages from scripture and the graduates were honored. The graduation mass has developed into an annual and cherished part of the Near North Side in subsequent years, and parents and students alike look forward to the procession of graduates, dressed in rich purple caps and gowns, participating in church services.

Father Tom found a way to blend Catholic liturgy with the academic achievements of Jefferson Davis graduates, thereby bridging the worlds of school and church while violating no boundaries about church interference in schools. Following that effort to weave together the school and the community, Emily Cole spent the summer and subsequent school year raising funds to revitalize instruction, curriculum design, and assessment at Davis. A grant from the Texas Education Agency in 1991 helped the faculty to study possible ways of restructuring the school to enhance learning, and another grant from the Houston Endowment helped Davis students to attend one month of intensive summer courses to prepare them for college preparatory courses in their high school.

The greatest victory for Davis at this historical juncture was that Jim Ketelsen of the Tenneco Corporation decided to take bold action to escalate his company's commitment to the youth of the Near North Side. "I'd been convinced for some time that inner-city education was the greatest problem our country faced," Ketelsen said. "I felt strongly that if we did not take some strong measures to educate minority, inner-city kids that we would end up creating an underclass that would erode the quality of life for everybody." Impressed with the positive momentum in the Davis community, Ketelsen pledged to raise Tenneco's level of involvement in the high school by creating the Presidential Scholarship Program, which would award one thousand dollars for each year of college education for each Davis senior who maintained a 2.5 grade point average.

The Presidential Scholarship Program greatly helped to change attitudes toward higher education in Davis and the Near North Side. Students, parents, teachers, and Davis alumni worked with TMO to make the Walk for Success an annual event and to promote the scholarships. As word of the funding for college spread throughout the community, students' attitudes toward the feasibility of higher education underwent a sea change. "A lot of our kids have people in their family dependent upon them," observed Donna King, an English teacher. "They might miss school because they have to take their mother to the clinic to translate when their sister is sick, or when there is a problem with the bank. The Tenneco scholarships helped them to see beyond their immediate situation. When I started here in 1982 none of the kids thought about college; now almost all of them do. The kids believe in the future more and are more willing to aspire beyond menial labor at McDonald's."

The Tenneco Presidential Scholarship Program involved more for students than simply cash at the end of high school. To participate in the program, students must attend two summer institutes at the University of Houston after their sophomore and junior years which focus on academic skills and leadership training. Those institutes expose students to life on a college campus and reduce the mystique of higher education for students whose parents may never have completed high school. At the end of the month-long institutes, students are paid $150, a nominal amount which nonetheless helps students to explain to their parents that the institutes may profit them more in the long term than summer jobs.

The Tenneco Presidential Scholarship Program has created new possibilities for higher education for Davis graduates. Yet rather than fall prey to self-congratulation and relax their efforts, Davis faculty began asking hard questions of the school's structure and curriculum in the years immediately following the scholarship bequest. Using self-study funds from the Texas Education Agency, Davis faculty investigated whether their traditional structuring of curriculum into six periods of forty-five minutes each was serving their students well. "We knew that what we were doing wasn't really working, and that we needed a drastic change in the ways we organized our work," mathematics teacher Chris McCuen recalled.

As faculty began exploring different ways of reorganizing school structures, they became increasingly interested in "block scheduling," which expands class time to ninety minutes. "We wanted to narrow down the amount of material that kids had to study at any one point of time," McCuen said. Faculty organized a trip to John Hinckley High School in Aurora, Colorado, and returned with good news: block scheduling, when well conceived and implemented, freed up time for in-depth study of curriculum while enhancing strong interpersonal relationships between students and teachers.

Teachers at Davis knew that if they were serious about implementing block scheduling they would need community support. They held a series of meetings and assemblies to describe block scheduling to the parents. "TMO really helped us turn out the parents," teacher LaVaun French recalled. The parents, who were worried about dropouts and who wanted their children to succeed at Davis, supported the faculty's readiness to change.

In August 1992, Davis began experimenting with block scheduling. In its new form of curriculum organization, the usual bracketing of six or seven high school classes into forty-five-minute classes for an entire year was abolished in favor of four classes of ninety minutes' duration which switch at the semester break in January. Fifteen-minute intersessions were introduced after the first and third periods, and lunch was extended to a full hour, which enabled extracurricular groups to meet in the middle rather than at the end of the day. Science teachers have adequate time to set up laboratories, initiate procedures, correct mistakes, and evaluate experiments with their students. English, foreign language, and science teachers report that the additional time allows them to delve into the material with greater depth, and that they have developed a much greater appreciation of students' needs to review material frequently to keep it fresh and to perceive the relationships between different curricular units. Mathematics teachers are the least enthusiastic; they report difficulties keeping students' attention focused on the curriculum for a full hour and a half. They cannot quarrel with the results, however; only four students were enrolled in precalculus courses at Davis before block scheduling; two years later there were four precalculus classes and one advanced placement calculus class. Students and teachers frequently state that the greatest benefit of block scheduling is that they can get to know one another as individuals better under the new system. "Our classrooms are more like a family now," LaVaun French asserted.

At Davis, the Walks for Success, the Presidential Scholarship Program, and the transition to block scheduling have produced several visible changes in the school. The reduction of passing periods between classes drastically reduced discipline problems; in the first year of block scheduling, discipline referrals dropped from 644 to 238. Before block scheduling, Davis was ranked twenty-fifth in attendance of all high schools in the Houston Independent School District; after block scheduling, it jumped to second. The number of students on the honor roll trebled—from 55 to 186. Enrollment at Davis jumped by three hundred students in the first three years after shifting to block scheduling, as students who previously had opted out of their neighborhood school through magnet programs decided to stay in their community.[3]

The changes in the school are apparent to many students who have found new opportunities in its many programs. José Encinas, for example, characterized himself as a "troublemaker" in middle school, where, he said, "Nothing built my self-esteem." At Davis, on the other hand, he has discovered a sense of direction and a commitment to excellence that he never knew he possessed. "It's so encouraging to have your parents, teachers, and executives from Tenneco all united behind you," he said. "All throughout Davis you're getting support from everyone." Encinas is an enthusiastic advocate of block scheduling and has credited the summer institutes at the University of Houston with teaching him the mental discipline to follow lectures and master complicated curricula. Community liaisons at Davis linked him with an internship at Houston's Museum of Natural Sciences for two summers, and in his senior year at Davis he received a paid staff position at the Cochran Butterfly Collection at the museum, which is the world's largest and most exotic collection of live butterflies. "There's no school out there that supports you as much as Davis," Encinas claimed. "And everything's blossoming for me. But without Davis, I can honestly say that I'd have ended up as a troublemaker in the neighborhood." The son of immigrants from Zaragoza, Mexico, Encinas will be the first member of his family to attend college.

Other students echo Encinas' enthusiasm. "In middle school I had seven classes a day," Rachel Isbell recalled, "and everything was fast and unorganized. We only had five minutes between classes and the teachers always rushed us. Now we don't have to hurry, teachers explain everything to you in detail, and I'm learning much more." Citlally Espinoza observed that teachers now teach only three classes a day and have an hour and a half for planning, and believes the new organization has done much to alter the rhythm of the school and to improve instruction. "The teachers are very thorough and exact in their communication," she said. She believes that her dance and physics classes especially benefited from the additional time available to prepare, instruct, and conclude classes. "But what I like the best is that the teachers work with us one-on-one," she said. "With the extra time they get to know me better. Now they don't see me as just a student in their class but as a person, as an individual."

Students such as Citlally Espinoza view their education at Davis as much broader than the mastering of curriculum. Espinoza has been interviewed by the *Houston Chronicle* about block scheduling and has spoken with many visitors about curriculum and school restructuring. She has participated in the school's Innovations Committee along with other students and teachers and she has visited students' homes as part of Davis' annual Walk for Success. "I found that the parents really like the Walk for Success because their children often forget to tell them about the four-thousand dollar scholarship," she said. "And it's so much fun to tell the parents about everything that's going on. It makes you feel proud of your school."

Jefferson Davis High School is now visited by over fifty schools a year that seek to learn from its innovations. The school has developed an esprit de corps among its student leaders that impresses visitors and gives one a sense of development and pride in the school. "People outside of Davis just see a lot of stereotypes here with guns, gangs, and killing," said one such student, Rachel Isbell, "but it's really not true at all. I have friends in suburban schools who have a lot more problems." Citlally Espinoza agreed: "When I first got to Davis I was so afraid, because I'd heard so much about getting beat up in the bathrooms. But I've been amazed at how much support there is here. It seems like everyone bonds and is close to each other."

In an unusual twist, the momentum that has been developed at Davis has proven irresistible to those TMO organizers who worked hardest to develop social capital in the school. Both Robert Rivera (a Texas IAF organizer for close to two decades) and Louisa Meacham (a former TMO educational organizer) joined the staff at Davis in the fall of 1995. Meacham is an English teacher and Rivera is the manager of a program called "Communities in Schools." He now spends his time mentoring troubled students and devising strategies to keep them from dropping out.

In spite of its many signs of progress, students' disclaimers about Davis' problems, and the recruitment of TMO organizers to full-time school staff, a host of problems persist in the school. Students become pregnant and drop out, gang graffiti has to be cleaned up again and again, and rival gangs such as the Hardy Boys and the Crips get into fights which lead the administration to expel students. "The opportunities are there, but now our problem is in getting the kids to take advantage of them," English teacher Myron Greenfield observed. "I regret the wasted potential of so many of our kids." Davis is still an urban school in a high-poverty community which receives a large number of immigrants with special needs. Although the school has improved in many areas, many indicators show that it still faces a long uphill struggle to meet the pressing needs of its students. The dropout rate at Davis improved moderately from 1986 to 1994, but only 26 percent of Davis students who entered in 1990 graduated four years later. Students' SAT test scores have improved, but only from an average of 695 in 1991 to 717 in 1994 (for the *combined* math and verbal scores). Davis has been unusually successful in graduating on time the students from poor families who enter ninth grade with passing test scores in reading and math, but far too many of its students begin the ninth grade with their academic performance years behind the appropriate level. On the other hand, in regard to the transition from high school to higher education, Davis has experienced unequivocal success; in its first three years the Tenneco scholarship program enabled the percentage of graduating seniors going on to higher education to jump from 20 percent in 1989 to 42 percent in 1992.[4]

In addition to problems with academic achievement within the school, social problems continue to engulf the Near North Side. Emily Cole estimates that roughly one hundred Davis students are in gangs, and many of them spray-painted the front of her school with graffiti when the school opened for a new academic year in August 1994. "Our kids who are in gangs think they're so cool when they do that," one social studies teacher complained. "I try to explain to them that when people see that graffiti they don't think the kids are cool—they think they're idiots. Sometimes it feels like all of the money we need for new programs gets drained off by sandblasting graffiti. I'll tell you, working here is a never-ending struggle."

On occasion, the problems at Davis take a more violent turn. In October 1995, just two days before the annual Walk for Success, a Davis junior was killed in her boyfriend's home when she was caught in the midst of a retaliation for a drug deal that went bad. "Every year we lose one or two kids to something like that killing," teacher Stela Balderas observed. In a recent survey, less than half of Davis' students were able to agree with the statement, "The school is a safe place." One English teacher lamented, "Sometimes when you're trying to teach about subject–verb agreement you feel like an absolute idiot when you know what your kids are up against."

Frustration with the slow pace of academic improvement at Davis is widespread throughout the school and its community. Since research shows that Davis does an unusually fine job of graduating low-income students who enter the school performing at their grade level, the most recent developments at the school have focused on reaching future Davis students before they enter high school. "When we examined our situation, we saw that we can't do all of the change by ourselves," teacher Carmen Villanueva commented. "If we were to be truly successful we needed to pull in the middle school and all of the elementary schools."

Recognizing the need for more fundamental change throughout the neighborhood schools, Davis has worked to bring the eight elementary and middle schools into the school reform process. When in the fall of 1993 Principal Roberto Gonzalez took over Marshall Middle School, which shares its cafeteria with Davis, he was so impressed with Davis' block scheduling that he urged his faculty to adopt it as soon as possible. As a result, Marshall began block scheduling not at the beginning of the next school year, but in January 1994. "I don't believe in waiting for change to happen," Gonzalez said. Block scheduling appears to have helped in many areas, and Gonzalez is especially proud of how the longer periods have made possible more in-depth experimentation in science classes. In other areas, such as math instruction, problems persist, and over 10 percent of the students flunk math each year.

Jim Ketelsen agreed with the teachers' observations. Pleased with the momentum at Davis and eager to continue moving in the right direction, Ketelsen was determined to raise even more funds to support educational reform in the Near North Side. "Education is *the* great national problem," Ketelsen said, "and I wanted to prove that these inner-city minority kids can achieve just as well as anybody else if not better if they were given greater opportunities." Using Tenneco as a base and reaching out to other corporate allies, Ketelsen raised over two million dollars to support staff development programs for all of the schools on the Near North Side in the summer of 1994. Those programs have drawn upon the expertise of ten universities to design and implement innovative programs in hands-on mathematics, collaborative approaches to reading, student self-discipline and self-governance, and continual community engagement in the schools. By the summer of 1995, the teachers in the elementary schools, middle school, and high school had not only experienced over thirty thousand hours of training in new forms of instruction and curriculum development, but they had also been brought into continual contact with one another and recognized the need for sustained interaction and dialogue about their new possibilities of better serving their students. The new educational community—dubbed the "Davis Vertical Team"—developed a powerful spirit of mutual commitment and convened at Davis for staff development days and leadership retreats. The Vertical Team ended the 1995 school year with a parents' assembly at Davis at which students demonstrated their academic achievements in math, writing, and science.

TMO served primarily as a catalyst for change in the Davis community. By increasing community engagement in the school, TMO signaled to Tenneco that broadening the scope of the Presidential Scholarship Program was a worthy investment in a community which was prepared to rally its resources to support its children. The Walk for Success has become an annual event at Davis High School, and as students, teachers, and other community leaders visit the homes of ninth graders throughout the Near North Side, they are greeted by younger children in the community, who shout *"La beca! La beca!"* ("The scholarship!") to their parents as the walkers approach. When walkers visit in students' homes, they show parents lists of all of the beneficiaries of the Tenneco scholarships; many of the parents recognize the names of neighborhood youths who have gone on to to college and are determined that their children will avail themselves of the same opportunities. Thanks to all of the collaborative work that has been accomplished by the Davis Vertical Team, even smaller children in the Near North Side are aware of the opportunities that await them when they become older, attend their neighborhood high school, and aspire to a college education.

In subsequent years, TMO has shifted its efforts away from Davis to other schools in the Near North Side and the city at large. When parents and teachers in the local elementary schools worried that their children were unsupervised after school, for example, TMO took the lead in persuading the Houston City Council to fund six free after-school programs for students in schools, two of which were based in the Near North Side. Health care is another area in which TMO has been active. For years, many of the elementary schools on the Near North Side had a nurse available only one day a week, and working parents, fearful of losing a day's wages, often sent their children to school sick. To respond to this problem, TMO brought together governmental agencies and local philanthropies to implement a pilot program in which a nurse practitioner provides health screenings and immunizations for three elementary schools in the Near North Side. Having achieved that victory, TMO is now working with other elementary schools in predominantly African American neighborhoods to expand school-based health care, and is establishing important liaisons with Houston's massive medical center, the largest complex of hospitals concentrated in one compressed geographical area in the world.

One of TMO's major new initiatives was taken up in response to immigrant parents' wishes to become more fully integrated into the American polity. In August 1994, Javier Parra, a former IAF leader from the Rio Grande Valley, joined TMO to help the many immigrants in Davis' neighborhood to become American citizens. TMO leaders and organizers have designed a unique kind of citizenship training for the immigrants which includes the traditional naturalization curriculum of American history and governance but which also includes concrete training in political leadership skills. Training sessions are held in six schools and two churches, including Holy Name and Saint Patrick's, two parish churches on the North Side. The community's response to the "Padres con Poder" initiative has been strong, and TMO, working with many other grass-roots community organizations, is taking on a new and expanded role in encouraging the over 150,000 Houstonians who can become citizens but have hitherto avoided contact with the Immigration and Naturalization Service to acquire American citizenship.[5]

Despite the many bold and exciting initiatives undertaken at Davis by Emily Cole and her colleagues, the school still faced a disheartening future in 1995. Parental engagement, corporate sponsorship, and block scheduling still had not boosted Davis' test scores on the Texas Assessment of Academic Skills (TAAS) test so that the school could be removed from the Texas Education Agency's list of low-performing schools. In spite of her pride in Davis' many achievements, Emily Cole was exasperated. "I never wanted to teach to the test," she recalled, "but I finally realized that I was going to have to take more time to impress on the teachers and the students that the TAAS was important. I had thought that better results would come in earlier, but it hadn't happened, and I was growing more and more apprehensive."

Cole and her faculty decided to develop a multifaceted strategy to promote academic achievement throughout Davis. First, they took a page from Ted Sizer's Coalition of Essential Schools and created "home groups" of ninety ninth graders who were placed with three core teachers for the full freshman year. Designed to overcome the anonymity experienced by many urban high school students, that initiative has proven to be popular with teachers and students alike. Beginning teachers are especially pleased to enter small, close-knit communities where they can develop teaching and curricular strategies in collaboration with their colleagues.

Second, Cole matched every student in Jefferson Davis with teachers, staff, or community members who would be responsible for monitoring the student's overall academic and social development. This mentoring arrangement was another effort to enhance close personal ties between students and adults and to overcome the institutional nature of a large school like Davis. Third, Cole realized that, while ties with adults were important for students, changing student culture itself was vital for improving academic performance. To this end, she instituted a series of schoolwide meetings throughout the 1995–1996 school year and asked older students to talk to younger students about their experiences with the TAAS. The older students addressed problems that had occurred for some of them when they could not graduate because they had failed the TAAS. They also discussed effective strategies for preparing for the test. "We had kids talking directly to other kids about what happened to them when they were in the twelfth grade, couldn't pass the TAAS, and couldn't graduate," Cole said. "And then we passed out cards and had kids sign up to get assistance on preparing for the test through tutorials and Saturday morning coaching sessions."

Third, Cole encouraged the parents of Jefferson Davis students to come to what was termed a mandatory assembly, which was designed to impress upon the parents the importance of doing well on the TAAS. "That was the moment of truth," one teacher said. "We had to have that community support, and it was so exciting to see that a huge group came. After that, no one could tell me that these parents weren't interested." Emily Cole had had students take a TAAS pretest, and she shared the results with parents at the assembly. Parents were also informed that it was imperative for their sons and daughters to do well on the TAAS if they were to graduate from high school. If students had flunked the TAAS pretest or had done poorly, parents were informed of the exact times and locations of tutoring sessions to prepare their children for the test. "We made some mistakes at the assembly," one teacher said. "It was too crowded, and we didn't do a good job of translating. But the main thing was just that the parents showed up and got some information. We told the parents that if their child had done badly on the pretest, they should take a slip out of the folder we'd given them, sign their student up for a tutoring session, and bring it up to the front of the auditorium. It was almost like an altar call. And one big result was that the turnout at the tutorial sessions was excellent."

Finally, Cole hired the services of a company which helped her faculty to make the connections between skills they taught in classes such as home economics and car repair and preparation for the TAAS test. "Teachers had been teaching critical thinking skills and subjects like geometry in many of our vocational education classes," Cole commented, "but they hadn't done it in such a way that any link was made to the TAAS. But now both the teachers and the kids began to see a connection." Consequently, students and teachers started to learn ways that the skills measured by the TAAS had real-life correlates.

As a result of the surge of experimentation at Davis, Emily Cole's hopes were finally fulfilled in April 1996. On the eve of a large Alliance School conference in Houston to be attended by superintendents, parents, and teachers from throughout the Southwest, Cole received word from the Houston Independent School District that test scores at Davis had increased dramatically. Whereas a mere twenty-four percent of Davis tenth graders had passed all three sections of the TAAS test in 1995, in 1996 the number rose to forty-two percent—a gain matched by only one other high school in Houston. "The hugging and the spirit when those scores came in was fantastic," Cole said, "and the beautiful thing was that the teachers and the students all felt that they had been a big part of it."

The administrators at Davis were determined to capitalize on the momentum created by the rise in test scores by using it to increase student motivation. Recognizing the importance of peer influences among teenagers, an assistant principal, Oscar Garza, organized large assemblies in the school's auditorium in which every student who had passed even one section of the TAAS was publicly recognized with an award or medallion. Garza worked with his colleagues to make sure that all freshmen in the school attended these assemblies to witness the achievements of the older students and to have impressed upon them that academic success at Davis *was* possible. "The freshmen saw this as an opportunity to succeed and be recognized," Stela Balderas commented. "And what was especially amazing for us was that some kids who had passed all three sections but hadn't made the highest marks started asking Mrs. Cole if they could take the test over again so they could score in the higher ranks. And that was something that had *never* happened before."

Emily Cole refused to attribute the gains at Davis to any single program. "No one strategy made the difference," she commented, "but the collaboration worked." For the students who had done well on the TAAS, however, their sense of ownership of the results was absolute. "One big change that I noticed," observed Louisa Meacham, "was that the class of 1998 had gotten pretty cocky, but in a good way. They'll say, 'We rule! We're the smartest class that has ever come through Davis!' They have an interesting and positive confidence about themselves that we haven't seen here before." While it is still too early to determine whether the test scores will continue to rise, a preliminary reading suggests that Davis has created a blend of approaches which improve academic achievement and that the long, hard work of almost a decade of community organizing and school reform is finally paying off.

The examples of Morningside Middle School and Jefferson Davis High School both suggest that change can be facilitated in urban secondary schools through novel strategies of social capitalization in which Texas IAF organizations play a major role. In neither of the cases did ACT or TMO develop a sectarian agenda, in which the IAF organization infiltrated a school and changed its identity; rather, the politics of each school developed over a period of time, and parents, teachers, administrators, clergy, and philanthropists each collaborated with the IAF at key junctures of the organizing process. It was not always easy for the IAF organizations to sustain their momentum; once Morningside became a Carnegie School and Davis became the recipient of the Tenneco presidential scholarships, both of those more high-profile initiatives tended to receive pride of place in the internal identities and external community relations of the schools. Yet without the community-based initiatives that first sparked parents' interests and brought them into Morningside and Davis, it is difficult to conceive why Carnegie and Tenneco would have chosen to make their substantial investments in either school.

In spite of their bold reform efforts and the promising nature of many new initiatives, Morningside and Davis have both experienced abundant setbacks over the years. Morningside's test scores faltered once the Texas Education Agency implemented the more demanding TAAS test in 1990, and while Davis' most recent results are promising, it is still too early to determine if they reflect a long-term improvement of scores or a blip in an otherwise lackluster performance. Both schools have had to contend with gangs and other social problems that undermine their quest for academic achievement, and while both schools have proven remarkably inventive in their responsiveness to challenges, the obstacles to their continued success are formidable. Yet each school has clearly found new ways to engage communities in academic improvement and has demonstrated progress in advancing beyond the low points experienced in the early 1980s.

Morningside and Davis suggest that community organizing as an approach to school reform can catalyze a wide range of reforms at the middle and high school level. It may be, however, that community-organizing strategies play out differently at the institutional level of the elementary school where the age of children and the smaller size of the schools create very different educational atmospheres. To investigate this hypothesis, we now shift our attention and explore two case studies of community organizing for school reform in El Paso and Austin.

5

Ysleta Elementary School

*From Parental Engagement
to a New School*

The El Paso Interreligious Service Organization (EPISO) was perhaps the most difficult of all Texas IAF organizations to establish. Owners of vast agricultural enterprises surrounding El Paso were determined to prevent the organization of their Mexican American work force and saw the arrival of IAF organizers as a direct threat to their control of migrant laborers. The city's major newspaper, *The El Paso Times*, ran a banner headline entitled "Religious Leaders Hire Troublemakers to Better City" on July 5, 1981, with a picture of EPISO organizer Robert Rivera on the front page; at a restaurant that morning an angry customer warned Rivera that he had twenty-four hours to get out of town alive. *The Wanderer*, America's oldest national Catholic weekly newspaper, published a brochure attacking EPISO and rented billboards on interstate highways reading "Cristo Sí, EPISO No!" Death threats against EPISO leaders and organizers escalated, vandals smashed car windshields and slashed tires during EPISO gatherings, and Rivera hired a security guard to attend meetings.[1]

EPISO might have collapsed in the early stages of its organizing effort without outside assistance. The manner in which it received support is instructive as to the benefits of developing public relationships with politicians and a network of civic associations throughout a geographical region. The key political figure in this regard was Lieutenant Governor Bill Hobby, a moderate Democrat from Houston, who was facing reelection in the fall of 1982 after a decade's service in office. Conservative on most matters, Hobby had a reputation for fair-mindedness and a number of overlapping political interests with the Texas IAF. Appalled by the heartbreaking poverty of the Rio Grande Valley, Hobby had worked successfully with Valley Interfaith, the local IAF organization, to supply water and clean up raw sewage which ran through the dirt roads of shanty towns called *colonias*. Hobby had been impressed with the spirit and organizing capabilities of Valley Interfaith and believed that another IAF organization in the El Paso area could help to secure water and adequate sewer drainage for residents of Socorro, an impoverished settlement dotted with *colonias* southeast of El Paso.

In addition to his desire to cultivate grass-roots allies who would improve conditions in the *colonias*, Hobby wanted to participate in Texas IAF assemblies in Fort Worth and Houston to enhance his chances in the fall elections. Texas IAF leaders in both cities agreed to include Hobby in assemblies, but did so on the condition that he also attend an EPISO assembly in El Paso. As soon as Hobby agreed to those terms, the animus against EPISO began dissipating in El Paso. "When it was announced Bill Hobby would be here, we received a flood of phone calls from politicians who wanted to be on the same stage with him," Robert Rivera recalled. "It was very gratifying." [2]

Hobby not only appeared in a large public rally and endorsed the goals and methods of the Texas IAF, but he also persuaded local politicians that working with Texas IAF organizations could expand their public support. As a result of his support of Mexican Americans on a number of key issues, of which EPISO's struggle was just one facet, Hobby harvested close to 90 percent of the Mexican American vote in the 1982 election. Subsequently, EPISO was able to begin organizing in some of the most impoverished communities in the United States, advocating against a rise in utility rates, against the deportation of illegal aliens, and for improvements in the *colonias*. [3]

EPISO organizers saw that their sister Texas IAF organizations were becoming active in schools and chose Ysleta Elementary in south El Paso as one of their first educational partners. Ysleta Elementary is made up almost exclusively of Hispanic students, and the majority of them are first-generation immigrants. Over 90 percent of the students in the schools are on free or reduced-price lunch programs. As recently as 1993, test scores of Ysleta students were so low that less than 20 percent of its students passed all three sections of the state's standardized test, earning it a "clearly unacceptable" designation by the Texas Education Agency. Its parents work in factories or as farm workers, tending huge agricultural enterprises outside of El Paso which grow onions, chili peppers, and cotton. Because of the nature of farm work, Ysleta has a highly transitional population. [4]

In spite of its problems with low academic achievement, Ysleta Elementary was an easy school for EPISO to support. Its principal, Dolores de Avila, was a life-long resident of El Paso who first began teaching at Ysleta in 1969. De Avila first became active in EPISO in 1982 when it began pressuring the city of El Paso to improve drainage in front of her church, Santa Lucia, which flooded every time it rained. "It was a turbulent time," she recalled, "but I had to be involved. The church and my family had always been important to me, and EPISO's ideals and my ideals were identical." De Avila subsequently supported EPISO's bond election work, its housing initiatives, and its commitment to supplying sanitary water to residents in the *colonias.*

De Avila quickly saw that the IAF philosophy of citizenship organization could enhance her skill as an educator in building bridges to low-income communities in El Paso. Like Odessa Ravin, de Avila attended one of the IAF's ten-day training sessions—but she did so in 1983, years before Ysleta Elementary School had an official link with EPISO. De Avila was one of the hundreds of citizens who traveled by bus to Austin the day after the "Father's Day Massacre" gutted House Bill 72, and she was exhilarated by the presence of citizens from Brownsville, San Antonio, and Houston who held their elected officials accountable and revived the jeopardized legislation. Those experiences taught her that the IAF could offer much to her school, her church, and her community.

De Avila became the principal of Ysleta Elementary School in 1989, after a stint in the central office of the El Paso Independent School District. In 1992 she was approached by EPISO organizers to discuss the possibility of a partnership in improving the school's relationship with the community. De Avila was immediately enthusiastic, but recognized that she would have to call upon her powers of persuasion to unite her faculty behind a collaborative undertaking with the community-based organization. To facilitate matters she circulated the Texas IAF vision paper, which teachers studied, discussed, and affirmed as a positive direction for their school. Teachers had little reason to be skeptical of de Avila; they had seen how hard she worked with teachers and parents during the 1991–1992 year to apply for Chapter I status for the entire school—an effort which added a quarter of a million dollars and many new staff positions to Ysleta Elementary's resources.[5]

The major issue confronting EPISO organizers after they entered into a relationship with Ysleta Elementary in the spring of 1992 concerned traffic safety. Although Ysleta is adjacent to a bustling business area at the intersection of Alameda Avenue and Zaragosa Street, city officials had never provided the school with traffic safety lights and crosswalks—measures that were automatic for other schools in the district. Dolores de Avila had placed phone calls to the appropriate officials for years to improve the traffic situation, but to no avail. Lupe Meils, an Ysleta mother, had written to J. J. Armes, her city council representative for the Lower Valley in El Paso, asking for assistance. She received a written response in March 1992 saying that the situation would be rectified, but nothing happened.

Through home visits in the fall of 1992, EPISO organizer Sister Maribeth Larkin heard that the traffic safety issue was the major concern of the community. When a girl attending a nearby parochial school, Mount Carmel, was hit by a truck on Zaragosa Street, Ysleta parents became angry at the lack of response by the city and district. Norma Silva, Ysleta's parent coordinator, then called parents to circulate a petition demanding that the city and school district take immediate action to rectify the hazardous traffic situation. For the parents, the fact that the school was reaching out to them for the first time to organize concerted action to help with the traffic issue was a breakthrough. "Norma's receptiveness made me feel that it was OK to keep working on this," Meils said. "And I was discouraged because I wasn't getting any response from the city."

Meils and other parents gathered over four hundred signatures on their petition. To capitalize on the momentum, EPISO convened an assembly in the gymnasium at Ysleta in November 1992; over two hundred parents attended to meet with city council representative J. J. Armes, Ysleta Independent School District Superintendent Anthony Trujillo, area school board representative Fred Sanchez, Assistant School Superintendent for Building Jim Barnett, and other individuals representing the Traffic and Safety Department of the El Paso Police Department and the Texas State Highway Department. To prepare for the assembly, EPISO worked carefully with parents to help them formulate questions they wished to address to their civic leaders and to practice asking them with clarity and force.

When the evening arrived, the parents conveyed a newly found unity that impressed the councillor and superintendent. J. J. Armes still sought to pacify the parents, however, assuring them that if they would only direct their complaints through the proper channels, their concerns would be addressed. Anticipating that Armes would attempt to deflect parental concerns in this way, Lupe Meils had prepared a copy of Armes' March letter promising action, which she displayed on an overhead transparency. "You could just feel the tension," Larkin recalled, "because Armes was nailed and all of those bureaucrats were nailed." Armes, deeply embarrassed, promised that he really would respond this time.

At the end of the meeting, the parents asked their public officials to join them in monthly accountability sessions to monitor the progress the city would be making in implementing improvements. Parents then formed a traffic committee and began a door-to-door campaign to gather petitions to demand improvements.

One vital element of this organizing effort was the community's insistence on accountability sessions; this was of key importance because of the fragmented manner in which civic power is distributed in American cities. Busy Alameda Avenue was maintained by the Texas Department of Highways, and some aspects of traffic safety were the responsibility of the school district, while others fell within the city's purview. When Ysleta parents met with traffic safety officers from one office, those officers typically tried to pass the buck to other public officials. "Most bureaucrats obfuscate the rules," Larkin observed, "so that regular people can't hold them accountable." EPISO organizers educated the traffic committee on how to conduct research on the traffic issue so that all of the key public officials would have to accept their responsibility to create a safer community.

The traffic safety problem was more than just a bureaucratic one. Area homeowners welcomed the prospect of creating one-way streets on side streets, but business owners felt that rerouting traffic would make it more difficult for them to attract customers and would damage their sales. All of the diverse neighborhood constituencies and local and state political officials had to be tackled separately to hammer out acceptable solutions.

The strategy of holding monthly accountability sessions paid impressive dividends. Usually, no improvements were made in the first three weeks after each meeting. Whenever the deadline drew near for an accountability session, however, Ysleta parents discovered that a construction crew would arrive at Ysleta to install lights and signs or to paint crosswalks that would enhance the safety of the children. Public officials would then come to the accountability sessions, take credit for the progress that was being made, and do nothing until a week before the next accountability session. At that point they once again made sure that they would have some concrete results to present at the upcoming meeting.

As a result of EPISO's organizing, by the time Ysleta Elementary opened for a new school year in August 1993, the traffic patterns around the school had been totally transformed. For the first time, there were school crossing zones and a new traffic light on one of the busiest corners. A two-way street, Schutz Street, was converted into a one-way street to cut down on traffic congestion. The school district rerouted school bus entries so that the children disembarked directly on the school campus rather than into the street. "We totally changed the external traffic situation for that campus, and consequently things are a lot safer for the children," Larkin said. "But the most important thing is that there is a whole new level of ownership that the parents feel."

As part of the process of working on external safety, the internal dynamics of Ysleta changed. There had always been a room for parents in the school, but it was a remote room on the third floor of the old building. "Parents never felt connected to the rest of the school," parent education coordinator Norma Silva recalled. Dolores de Avila had visited Hollibrook Elementary School in Spring Branch, Texas, in the spring of 1992, and had been impressed with the centrality of its parents' center in the building. De Avila decided to replicate Hollibrook's example and moved Ysleta's parents' center right next to the main office at the front entrance of the school in September 1992. De Avila acquired a grant from a local foundation to supply the center with a comfortable couch, tables, and chairs for adult classes, and a rich array of materials promoting literacy, numeracy, and academic development.[6]

Even with the parents' center relocated to the front of the school, some parents were hesitant to become involved. "It took about six weeks before parents started really saying, 'This is our room,'" Silva recalls. "The parents were not always comfortable with other parents. There used to be a lady who would monopolize the room, so I needed to educate her about how to build relationships and trust with others. We have to remember that the parental involvement component is developmental."

To respond to parents' concerns about their children's safety, de Avila worked with the police department to designate a special office in the building for police who are trained in community-based policing. Officer George Salas recalled that when he first learned that he was going to be assigned to a school that worked with EPISO, "The hairs on my back stood up. But since then I've learned that they're really involved in helping people who cannot yet speak up for themselves. I've developed a lot of respect for what they're doing and my work with the school has become the most fulfilling part of my life as an officer. I'm the chair of the school's Campus Educational Improvement Council and I really feel that we're providing so much for our kids and our parents." Officer Salas has taken Dolores de Avila on patrol with him, which taught de Avila new respect for the skills and commitment that officers must sustain as they face dangerous situations on a daily basis. He is a constant presence in the school and community who helps parents with income tax forms, public service referrals, and advice about their children.

In October 1993, Superintendent Trujillo visited Ysleta parents to discuss strategies for enhancing the future of the school. In dialogue with the parents, Trujillo extended them the opportunity to relocate to an entirely new school that he would build in a residential neighborhood far removed from the thoroughfares which run by Ysleta en route to Mexico. Ysleta parent leaders designed a survey to solicit parent opinions, parents held fourteen house meetings to discuss the pros and cons of a move, and they took field trips to the proposed location of the new school and schools recently constructed by the district.

In late February, two-thirds of Ysleta parents voted to relocate to a new building scheduled to be completed in 1996. Trujillo encouraged the community to draw up a wish list of all of the features they would like to see in the new school. The parents have responded by expanding and renaming their traffic committee the "Parent Action Committee." They have designed and circulated surveys to solicit parent opinions and have had several meetings with the superintendent to keep him informed of their wishes.

As a result of their deliberations with the parents from Ysleta Elementary School, Trujillo and Assistant Superintendent for Building Jim Barnett increased their commitment to the community in the summer of 1994. Trujillo and Barnett understood that Ysleta Elementary parents sought immediate action to improve the education of their children and that it would take several years to build a new school. As a result, Trujillo and Barnett decided to remodel Ysleta Elementary—not just with their own plan, but with constant consultation and joint planning with the Parent Action Committee. Subsequently, the parents' center has expanded into a second room to contain its growing resources on adult education. In addition, a wellness center providing health screenings has been integrated into the school. The district not only renovated much of the internal structure of Ysleta Elementary, but also planted fresh grass in the rear of the building and over a dozen palm trees at the school's front entrance.

The district now is planning to convert Ysleta Elementary into a pre-kindergarten center and adult education program for the community, while the elementary school children will be moved to the new site. The features of the new school are being designed by the Parent Action Committee, which is eager to retain and expand the parents' center and community police facilities of the old building. The Parent Action Committee is also exploring innovative aspects of middle-class schools from their area that they would like their own children to enjoy, such as a museum wing.

As part of its research into the possibilities which could be cultivated in the new school, Ysleta's parents developed a survey of children's health in the school in the fall of 1993. Fifty-nine percent of Ysleta's parents said that there were times when their children did not receive medical attention because they could not pay for it. Thirty-seven percent of the parents said that their children do not receive dental care. Eighty-nine percent said that they wanted health services expanded in the school, and 69 percent said that they were willing to participate in efforts to improve health services. As a result of the parents' survey and their ongoing research on the new school, parents are developing powerful arguments to persuade the district to build a high-quality wellness center for the children at the new school location.

The series of external changes in the school—relating to traffic safety, community policing, renovation, and the new building—have also had pedagogical analogues within the classroom. Ysleta teachers have introduced two multi-aged dual language classrooms for children who are from five to eight years old, and have found that students and parents have responded well to the many different kinds of interaction that are opened up by this arrangement. Almost all of the teachers at the school now organize student work in portfolios, and many of them ask parents to comment in detail on the portfolios every six weeks to keep them fully abreast of their children's development. Some teachers, such as Rosa Marquez, have designed innovative projects such as the "Parents as Authors" initiative, in which parents are asked to compile biographies of their children. By enabling parents to write in both Spanish and English, Marquez found a way to build strong community relationships in the classroom. Parents came to her class and read the biographies aloud in a forum which was tremendously popular for both the students and their parents. Teachers such as Marquez have also designed Parent Response Forms in both Spanish and English, which ask parents to review the portfolio with the child, to identify which of the children's papers they like the most, and to ask any questions they may have about the portfolio. Many teachers have developed their pedagogy and curricula in similar fashions such that the children's immediate and extended family members participate in classroom activities on a regular basis.

As parents have become more informed about their children's academic progress, they have wanted to know more about the school's curriculum, which has produced greater awareness among teachers of the need to align their curricula with one another to ensure that children receive a balanced and comprehensive education. As part of that effort, Ysleta has abandoned the orthodox practice of placing all classes of the same grade level in adjoining parts of the building. In its stead, Ysleta has developed vertical teams of teachers from kindergarten through fifth grade who plan together and teach in a common area. Each vertical team consists of six or seven teachers who are matched with roughly 130 children.

The intent of the teams is to build social capital within the schools in three ways. First, teachers are able to develop personal relationships with children over six years, so they can make certain that children's cognitive development is facilitated in an orderly and sequential developmental fashion. Second, according to Dolores de Avila, "By creating a vertical team that works together with the same kids for six years, we're creating a family inside the school. Our students are used to taking care of each other; older siblings are used to taking care of younger ones as an important part of their culture. So if we can find ways to create that same relationship inside the school, we are reinforcing something good. We're saying that we want strong relationships between older and younger students, and that they should take care of each other." Third, it should be easier for parents who meet all of the vertical team's teachers when their children enter kindergarten to work more effectively with those teachers as their children progress through the different grade levels.

Two of the vertical teams focus on thematic instruction in math and science and two of them use multi-aged grouping of children to take advantage of peer instruction and the strong family networks which characterize the Ysleta community. The vertical team arrangement has challenged the teachers, and particularly those at the lower grades, who have wondered how they can teach units on more complex topics, such as culture, that teachers in the upper grades want to include. As teachers have become more accustomed to the team framework and their colleagues, however, they report that this new organization has helped them to have a much more comprehensive overview of the work that is going on in the school. By working collaboratively on curricula across grades, each teacher has a better grasp of the developmental sequencing of curriculum and finds it easier to hold her or his colleagues accountable by making sure that each child enters his or her class performing at the appropriate grade level.

Recent rises in academic achievement have validated the internal and external changes at Ysleta Elementary School. In 1993, only 27 percent of Ysleta's fourth-grade students passed the reading portion of the state's criterion-referenced test; in 1994, 61 percent passed the same portion. Students' writing scores jumped from 49 to 70 percent, and their math scores leaped from 21 percent to 51 percent. When the results were made available in the summer of 1994, Texas Governor Ann Richards visited the school to congratulate the parents. She saw a school where community police officers referred adults to social service agencies, where a parents' center bursting with materials conducted adult education classes in English as a Second Language, and where a wellness center administered health screenings. She saw a school which for years had never been able to rally the clout to gain minimal traffic safety provisions and which now had not only an impressive safety zone but also a renovated and beautifully landscaped building. She saw empirical evidence of children's improved learning, reflected in test scores, and she saw a school which had evolved into the center of its community. "This program is one of the greatest things that has happened to public schools," Richards exulted.[7]

Although support by powerful public figures might seem to crown Ysleta's dramatic transformations over the past half decade, it is important to note that none of its changes have come without a struggle. Although the teachers were initially supportive of their school's partnership with EPISO, once the parents actually became active in the school, a cluster of teachers responded with suspicion and hostility. Dolores de Avila fears that good teachers may avoid applying to teach at her school because she has developed a reputation of maintaining unswervingly high standards for her staff. She is concerned that her own constant engagement with the community makes it hard for her to provide the support for the staff that they need as they undergo the self-questioning and doubt that school reform necessarily entails.

Broader political changes have also challenged the momentum of reform in Ysleta Elementary. Ann Richards was defeated in her gubernatorial campaign in November 1994, and the passage of Proposition 187 in California at the same time created a wave of anxiety among Hispanics throughout the Southwest. Hundreds of thousands of immigrants who had lived in the United States for years now decided to become American citizens in order to secure their children's access to public schooling and other public services. To accommodate their needs, Ysleta Elementary School began conducting naturalization classes for the community.

Only forty parents enrolled in the first naturalization classes, which were offered in February 1995; over 220 enrolled in the second set of classes, offered in April. Parent educator Myrna Castrejón, who taught the classes, was puzzled at the booming enrollment. When she asked her students why they had come, she learned that "the word on the street is that in this school people care about what happens in the community, and that people here will help the community to get whatever assistance they need." She believed that the fact that Ysleta parents and teachers have conducted voter registration drives wearing the school's T-shirts may have helped with the response. Still, she was startled when she learned that some of the students came from as far away as Reynosa, New Mexico, a trip of well over two hours' duration. When she told the students that they could take the classes in their own community, she learned something about the power of Ysleta's reputation: "They told me that they knew that they would be treated with respect here," she recalled. "And if you know something about the value that is placed upon respect in the Latino community, you recognize that this is no small thing. Evidently, our school has had more far-reaching implications for this area than we had ever imagined."

In subsequent years, the successes at Ysleta have led to an expansion of the schools working with EPISO in the Ysleta Independent School District. By the summer of 1996, six additional elementary schools and the local middle school were all developing new collaboratives with the community-based organization. Although a residue of caution remains from EPISO's controversial founding in El Paso, the indications of progress at Ysleta Elementary are such that many educators are taking a new look at community outreach, and are finding that EPISO offers a valuable model for galvanizing community support.

The path of change at Ysleta offers an interesting contrast to those of Morningside and Davis. Ysleta began with relatively straightforward safety issues of broad concern to all sectors of the school community and used those as a fulcrum for galvanizing parental engagement. Once the community had experienced victory with the safety issues, Dolores de Avila and her staff quickly moved to transfer the momentum acquired through parental engagement on safety to take on a series of pedagogical and curricular reforms that are improving academic achievement slowly but steadily. Unlike the dramatic breakthrough at Morningside, which was followed by a more problematic period entailing a gradual recovery, and unlike the contested progress at Davis, Ysleta offers a counterexample of relatively steady academic improvement. It would appear that organizing on the elementary school level might be more conducive to the kind of community-based school reform supported by Texas IAF organizations. To further explore this hypothesis, another case study, this time from Austin, can provide additional data to compare and contrast the myriad facets of community organizing for school reform.

6

Zavala Elementary School

Learning the Tools of Democracy

Most Americans who have ever visited Austin, Texas, have not lost much time falling in love with it. Unlike uncompromising automotive cities such as Houston or Los Angeles, Austin has splendid pedestrian zones. On Guadalupe Street near the campus of the University of Texas, street musicians, craft vendors, and local artists entertain passersby and ply their wares at all hours of the day; the recently renovated state capitol is gracefully situated upon a gentle promontory and is brilliantly illuminated every night; downtown's Sixth Street is an exciting mélange of country western honky-tonks, jazz bistros, and elegant French, Tex-Mex, and Cajun restaurants. Just outside of Austin to the west, the mundane flatness of East Texas disappears and is replaced by spectacular precipices which surround Lake Travis with enticing resorts and hilltop restaurants. In a state well known for its procapitalist spirit, exemplified in the no-zoning laws of Houston, Dallas' progrowth "Citizen's Council," and statewide anti-union laws, Austin is a liberal island which has placed a strong emphasis on quality-of-life issues such as historical preservation and environmental protection.

For all of its liberal spirit, however, Austin is no stranger to the economic inequalities which characterize American cities. Sixth Street, the state capitol, and the University of Texas are all on the west side of Interstate 35, the dividing line which separates Austin's haves from the have-nots. If one drives east on First Street, which has recently been renamed César Chávez Street, one arrives in the heart of the East Austin barrio. That name change can possess a special meaning for a visitor en route to Zavala Elementary School, for César Chávez was trained by the Community Service Organization, an IAF organization, in 1952 and remained close to it until his death in 1993.[1]

Zavala Elementary School enrolls 440 neighborhood students; 95 percent of them are served by free or reduced-price lunch programs. The majority of its students live in two public housing projects adjacent to the school in which the average family income is under $5,200 per year. One-third of Zavala's students are in bilingual education classes, and 64 percent of all students are taught in eighteen portable classrooms outside of the main building. For many years, Zavala never promoted students into honor programs in middle or high schools and never sent students to one of the jewels of the Austin Independent School District, the Secondary Science Academy. The school was always at the bottom of district rankings in academic achievement, and it was routine for between one-half and one-third of Zavala's teachers to transfer to another school at the end of the year. Participation of under a dozen parents at PTA meetings was common.

In December 1990, Alejandro Mindiz Melton was appointed principal of Zavala. Melton had taught and served as assistant principal at Zavala since 1985 and had quietly sought different ways to serve the children and the community effectively. Although he loyally supported the previous principal, inwardly he grew dissatisfied. "Really, we were just a holding institution for children all that time, not an educational institution," he said. "We kept the children here for a number of years and then we discharged them."

Melton wanted to become the principal of Zavala Elementary School and won the appointment through the support of a small handful of parents who did play a role in the school. Once he assumed the leadership of the school, Melton began exploring different ways to change its culture to promote higher levels of academic achievement. He learned that a community-based organization called "Austin Interfaith" had collaborated with two local elementary schools in previous years and had successfully written school bond issues that had been passed by the Austin Independent School District in 1989. He was favorably disposed when he first learned that Austin Interfaith might be interested in working with him to improve Zavala.

Melton was not initially aware that Father John Korcsmar, Oralia Garza de Cortés, and Joe Higgs from Austin Interfaith were intensely dissatisfied with their first school collaborations. Unlike the positive experiences of other Texas IAF organizations with public schools, Austin Interfaith's first cooperative ventures with the two elementary schools had been stymied. Korcsmar, Cortés, and Higgs all had years of experience working in Austin's low-income communities and they were aware of the positive school initiatives the IAF had begun in Fort Worth, Houston, and El Paso. When they began their own initiatives, however, they found that their collaborating principals had a restricted interpretation of the role that Austin Interfaith should play in their schools. They liked it when Austin Interfaith rallied parents to attend a PTA meeting or took on limited projects such as collating paperwork for teachers or improving playground equipment, but they balked when parents began discussing ways in which the culture of the schools could become more democratic and participatory for the community.

Ethnic tensions appear to have created part of the problem in the elementary schools. One of the schools, Blackshear Elementary, was experiencing a rapid transition from a predominantly Black to a majority Hispanic population—a relatively common phenomenon in Texas' urban schools in the 1980s and 1990s. The school's principal and staff were not certain how they should respond to the new ethnic composition of the school. An older Black principal in the school was reluctant to create a large opening for the Hispanic parents; when she retired, a new principal, who was also African American, was also reticent to promote community engagement. Each principal wanted Austin Interfaith's organizers to reinforce the school's traditional culture—not to challenge it. Neither principal was willing to work with the community-based organization to confront the schools' problems with low academic achievement and the need for sustained reflection and reorganization. After years of one-on-one's, house meetings, and parents' assemblies, Austin Interfaith leaders and organizers felt that their work had been used by the administrations of both schools to reinforce a bankrupt status quo. When they evaluated their past work and their future prospects, Austin Interfaith organizers and leaders decided that their likelihood of creating deeper cultural change in the schools was small. Exasperated by the recognition that their hard work was not likely to create enduring results, Austin Interfaith opted to terminate its relationships with the schools.

After those frustrating experiences, Father John Korcsmar of Nuestra Señora de Dolores Church was not in a charitable frame of mind when he went to his first meeting with Alejandro Melton:

> When I went to Zavala I was a real stick-in-the-mud. In my
> mind, the only purpose of the meeting was to back Al up against

a wall and to ask him if he was *really* committed to collaborating with us to do things differently. We'd been in other schools where the principals wanted help and wanted parents in the school. But when they did get parents in the school they'd lecture them and tell them what they were doing wrong. And that's no way to get parents to participate!

Melton wasn't bothered by Father John's demand for accountability. On the contrary, he was pleased to discover leaders and organizers who were interested in radical change in the school's culture. "I think it's good when you're challenged," he said of Austin Interfaith's first conversation with him. "It means that people are taking you seriously." Melton was glad to learn that Austin Interfaith wasn't trying to impose a prepackaged program on his school, and was delighted when he discovered that Austin Interfaith was an IAF organization. He had read *Rules for Radicals* as a student at Santa Monica College in California in the 1970s, was impressed by Saul Alinsky's accomplishments, and felt confident that an Alinsky organization would not promote tepid reforms which bandaged over rather than confronted Zavala's critical issues.

For its part, Austin Interfaith was satisfied with Melton's earnestness. "From the beginning Al said, 'This school is in trouble,'" organizer Joe Higgs recalled. "There was no 'rah-rah.'" Father Korcsmar liked Melton's attitude: "It didn't faze him to be challenged," he observed. In addition, Higgs was pleased with Melton's readiness to embrace the values of his school's Mexican American and Catholic community. "I could tell he was different," Higgs remembered, "since he was a Sephardic Jew who had images of our Lady of Guadalupe up in his office." [2]

Austin Interfaith was soon to witness something of the readiness of Melton to tackle Zavala's problems. Zavala had scored poorly on the state's criterion-referenced test in 1991 in spite of the fact that most Zavala students were on the principal's honor roll and were earning A's and B's. Instead of denying the discrepancy between the teachers' high evaluations of their students and the state's low assessment of their skills, Melton took the initiative to invite a disgruntled father, Albert Soto, to read out the test results and to speak out about the problem at a PTA meeting in December 1991. "I thought that was necessary," Melton stated, "to raise the critical concern of everyone about student achievement. We had had a crisis in terms of achievement for years, but we had refused to acknowledge it."

Albert Soto used the invitation to the PTA meeting to demand greater accountability from the teachers for the education of their pupils. Soto accused the teachers of deceiving the parents about how weak their students' academic achievement really was and how low the school's test scores were. He observed that some Spanish-speaking parents did not even have enough information to know which grade level their children were at. Many parents were sympathetic with Soto. "My child was in the third grade," Lourdes Zamarron recalls, "but no one had told me that he was working on a first-grade level. We hadn't been made aware of things like that."

Most teachers were shocked by the aggressive tone of Soto and other angry parents. "He opened a wound," bilingual teacher Claudia Santamaria recalled. "I had been one of the teachers giving A's and B's because I was a beginning teacher and I didn't want my kids to stand out for low performance. We teachers just sat there shaking." Others felt that Soto himself was partially to blame for the situation he decried. "I had had his child in the first grade," Samantha Bednarski remembered, "and I had never seen that man during the whole year." Santamaria said, "He *assumed* that we knew what the kids' tests scores were, but in the old days we didn't know. That wasn't part of how we did things." In spite of her misgivings, Bednarski acknowledged that "he really did what needed to be done, and jolted us out of our complacency." "There were hard feelings after that meeting," Melton recalled, "but I felt that could provide the opportunity for us to have a cathartic experience around student achievement. It could reenergize us to change the school, but to change the school you have to feel a *need* to do that."

Melton had invited Austin Interfaith leaders to attend that pivotal PTA meeting, and Oralia Garza de Cortés offered teachers and parents Austin Interfaith's services in improving parental engagement at Zavala. Austin Interfaith promised to help the teachers to respond to Soto's accusations not with defensiveness, but with action. In the days following the meeting, organizer Kathleen Davis began asking teachers about local parents who could develop into leaders. She paid home visits to have one-on-one conversations with parents and asked them to become more engaged in the school.

One parent Davis discovered was Toña Vasquez, a mother whose three oldest children had all passed through Zavala and whose youngest daughter, Dorothy, was a first grader. Vasquez was an important neighborhood figure. Her extended family had two additional homes on the same block right across the street from the school, she had long championed her children's right to a high-quality education, and she had tutored other parents' children on lunch breaks. Her husband had attended Zavala as a child and had planted a tree which still stands in front of the school.

Toña Vasquez had much in common with other East Side parents. She knew what it was like to come from a tough background: her mother had dropped out of school in the fourth grade to work as a migrant laborer; her mother and father had divorced when she was six years old; her mother had had a nervous breakdown when she was a sophomore and Toña spent the last two years of high school in a foster home. She knew what it was like to have a son who was disengaged from his education and to do everything in her power to keep him in school. She was unusual in the neighborhood inasmuch as she had completed high school, had a strong and happy marriage, and was a tireless advocate of her children's right to receive a top-notch education.

Toña Vasquez had wanted to assist Zavala Elementary School years before Kathleen Davis ever arrived on her doorstep. "Before Mr. Melton came to Zavala I had gone to the previous principal and asked him what parents could do for the school, and he just smiled and told me everything was fine," she recalled. "And I didn't know any better, so I just believed him." Vasquez agreed to work with Davis and Austin Interfaith leaders and began encouraging Zavala teachers to make home visits to ask parents for suggestions about ways in which the school could improve.

The home visits represented a dramatic transformation in Zavala's culture. Vasquez recalled,

> The home visits created a different view of the teacher in the eyes of the parents. Parents thought, 'Look at this: she's actually coming to my house, instead of my having to come to the school all of the time.' And the teachers also were really surprised at how friendly the parents were. But best of all, the kids were just ecstatic, because the teachers were in their neighborhood, and it was something totally new.

When Claudia Santamaria made home visits, she asked one parent why she did not participate in the school's PTA meetings. The woman, who was a single mother with two preschoolers, explained that she could not afford the child care to come to the meetings. Santamaria asked the mother if she could come if the school provided child care, and when the mother agreed, Santamaria did the necessary follow-through so that the many single mothers with young children could participate in PTA meetings.

Alejandro Melton also began visiting homes—not to address discipline problems, as he had done in the past, but to ask parents for their impressions of things that could be done to improve the school. "I discovered that parents had some real ideas about what this school could be," Melton recalled. "I learned that they knew what good teaching was and what bad teaching was, and I learned that they had definite aspirations for their children's careers. And I learned that the parents were so pleased that I visited with them, because their experiences told them that school is a place where you're not treated well and where you fail. They needed to know that a principal could treat them differently."

Following the home visits, Austin Interfaith escalated its presence on the East Side by sponsoring a school board accountability session at Cristo Rey, the local parish church, in January 1992. The organizers hoped that if they held the session at a church just two blocks away from Zavala, neighborhood residents would come out in force. Yet in spite of the proximity of the church to the school, only about five parents from Zavala Elementary attended the assembly, which drew over five hundred people from throughout Austin.

Undaunted, Austin Interfaith continued its house meetings and individual meetings with parents and teachers throughout the spring of 1992. In April Zavala held its first Walk for Success, followed by another series of home visits to Zavala parents to solicit their participation in shaping a new culture in the school. On May 25, Zavala held its first Rally for Success, which was attended by Mayor Bruce Todd and prominent public officials from the Texas Education Agency, the Austin School Board, and the Austin Police Department. At that meeting, Toña Vasquez passed over the boundary from *parental involvement*—a term that aptly characterizes her past advocacy for her children—to *parental engagement*: she began to advocate for changes in the political culture which surrounded the school. Working with organizer Kathleen Davis, Vasquez prepared a carefully worded statement asking public officials to commit to improving conditions at Zavala. "I was a nervous wreck before I went up there," she recalled, "but I pulled it off." She made a succinct presentation and the public officials committed to help. "That hooked me," she said. "It was a turning point. I had spoken up for my own kids before, but now I felt like I was making a difference for everyone. And my neighbors made me feel wonderful because they kept on telling me how brave I was."

Toña Vasquez was developing new leadership skills which would expand her identity beyond that of a mother concerned about her child to a community leader who would wrest concessions from public officials. She was far ahead of her neighborhood at that point, however. In spite of the overtures Austin Interfaith made to the parents in the Walk for Success, many parents were still hesitant to become engaged in Zavala after six months of constant organizing in the neighborhood. Even though over three hundred people attended the rally, only forty of them were parents from Zavala Elementary. The vast majority were Austin Interfaith leaders. "So many parents said that 'other parents won't help, this isn't going to work, and I've tried it before,'" Joe Higgs recalled. "The parents had given up on themselves." In spite of the discouraging participation in the rally, Austin Interfaith continued to organize in the neighborhood.

Why were the parents reluctant to collaborate with Zavala Elementary School? Many parents felt overwhelmed with problems. Academic achievement was one issue, but they were also troubled by flagrant drug dealing in two public housing projects next to the school. The parents wanted the drug dealing to stop, but they were afraid to become too vocal because of the possibility of retribution. There was a third issue that came up in meeting after meeting with parents, however, and that concerned their children's health. On that issue the parents appeared to be ready to act, and with good reason.

During the 1991 school year, only one nurse attended to the 440 children at Zavala on a quarter time basis. She was not empowered to help children with pressing medical needs such as immunizations. Most Zavala parents received very low wages and no health-care benefits, so the only time their children received medical care was for emergencies. Roughly one-third of the students had not received vaccinations against such dangerous and preventable diseases as measles, mumps, and tuberculosis. In spite of the fact that Texas state law requires that all children be immunized against these contagious diseases before attending school, the law is almost completely ignored, with the result that Texas is ranked forty-ninth of all fifty states in immunizing preschoolers.

The issue of health care for children became particularly acute in the summer of 1992, when parents learned that the East Austin clinic run by the Travis Country Health Department was scheduled to be closed for repairs due to a faulty duct system. Since that clinic served over 2,000 neighborhood residents each month and was the vehicle for allocating food coupons for a Women, Infant, and Children (WIC) nutritional program run by the Texas Department of Health, the county's plan to relocate the clinic in northeast Austin on a temporary basis foreshadowed a terrible setback to many low-income mothers without private transportation. Working closely with Austin Interfaith and Melton, parents began advocating for the creation of a clinic in the school that would provide comprehensive, preventive health care for children.

Fighting for a clinic in an inner-city school is a formidable task for low-income parents, the majority of whom speak Spanish at home and are not accustomed to challenging the status quo. Nonetheless, with sufficient support from Melton and Austin Interfaith, Zavala parents created a proposal for a clinic with an immunization program in their children's school. Toña Vasquez became part of the early organizing process. She attended countless meetings with city health officials, individual school board members, the Austin Independent School District superintendent, and Mayor Bruce Todd.

By August 1992, Zavala parents had persuaded the city council to fund a preventive health clinic in their school, with salaries allocated for a full-time nurse and social worker and a part-time medical records clerk. When the next large assembly was held at Zavala in October, over two hundred parents and teachers attended, along with fifty Austin Interfaith leaders. In a newfound show of power, the parents at that meeting were effective in securing a commitment from the Texas Department of Health to provide preventive children's health services and WIC at Zavala while providing transportation for more severe, primarily adult services (related to the treatment of diseases such as tuberculosis and AIDS) at other area clinics.

The major opposition to the parents then came from an unexpected quarter: the school board. The board's resistance to the clinic at Zavala had two sources. First, school board members objected to the city council's decision to fund a clinic in a public school without prior consent from the board. The issue was not a trivial one, since in the event of an injury in the clinic, the Austin Independent School District would have to assume liability. Second, the Austin district at that time had a task force on sex education in which Lidia Perez, a former school board member, had a great deal of influence. Perez persuaded conservative members of the task force that opening a clinic in a school might prepare the way for condoms and abortion counseling to be provided in schools at a later date. At a November school board meeting, Perez organized ten speakers who opposed the clinic on grounds that it would open the way for distributing information and materials relevant to birth control to students. Perez found supporters to pack the meeting who wore buttons with slogans such as "Save Our Children," and "Say No to Condoms." Zavala teachers, students, and parents, who wore their aqua blue Zavala Mustang T-shirts in a sign of solidarity with each other, were completely taken aback by the amount of opposition to the clinic. Most of them had never been to a school board meeting before and could not understand why people whose lives would not be affected by a clinic in their school expressed such intense opposition to it.

In spite of the fact that the Austin Independent School District would not be asked to contribute any financial resources to the clinic, and in spite of the fact that at issue was a clinic in an elementary school in which reproductive services were almost entirely irrelevant, a major battle between the parents and Christian fundamentalists took place. Debates were sponsored on local television channels, radio talk shows gave the story prominence, and the newspapers kept a close watch on developments. The school board members felt themselves uncomfortably caught in the middle, hoping to appease Zavala parents but worried about adverse publicity by the clinic's opponents.[3]

Zavala teachers, such as Claudia Santamaria, were discouraged by the fundamentalists' attacks: "I thought we were in over our heads," she recalled. Lourdes Zamarron, a Zavala mother, agreed: "I didn't think we were going to get the clinic when all of the opposition began. After all, we're on the East Side, and we're not used to getting anything."

The waging of the conflict at this phase is instructive with regard to the manner in which community-based organizations can mediate school politics advanced by different political interests. A variety of constituencies were now involved in adjudicating the school clinic issue. First, the mayor and city council had approved funding the clinic, not anticipating any opposition from the school board. Austin's mayor, a strong supporter of Planned Parenthood for many years, was particularly adamant that no restrictions be placed on the provision of reproductive services in schools. Second, the school board—which had not been consulted when the city council approved the clinic—felt intimidated by a vocal minority opposed to reproductive services in the schools. Third, Zavala parents—many of whose children lacked proper immunizations—felt themselves pulled into a larger polemical struggle irrelevant to their fundamental concern for vaccinations and quality health care for their children.

On December 7, 1992, the Austin School Board met again to discuss the health clinic at Zavala. For the meeting, Austin Interfaith organized clergy to testify regarding the importance of the clinic for the children who attended Zavala. When priests and nuns from Cristo Rey, Zavala's parish church, came dressed in traditional vestments and habits and took the microphone to emphasize the importance of health services for children, the fundamentalist opposition dissipated. Yet one complication remained. In its last written formulation of the health services proposal, the Travis County Health Department mentioned the possibility of staffing the clinic not just with a nurse but with a doctor. "When the board discovered this, total chaos broke out," Father John Korcsmar recalls. "They just didn't know what to do."

After several moments of tense exchanges among her colleagues, school board vice-president Kathy Rider stepped down from the podium, confessed the confusion of the board, and asked Zavala parents to decide whether they wanted a doctor. The parents then caucused in the front of the auditorium, determined that they had never asked for a doctor, and asked only that their original request for a school-based clinic be granted. The school board then voted unanimously to approve the opening of the clinic, without the addition of the doctor.

It was an emotional moment. "I was crying, and many other people were crying too," Toña Vasquez recalled. "We couldn't believe it." Immunizations, health screenings, and referrals were given at Zavala the very next day, and the morale of the students and teachers at Zavala soared. "The teachers now saw the parents in a new light," Joe Higgs said. "They hadn't realized that the parents were so capable." The sight of Zavala's low-income parents resolving an impasse between the city council, the county health department, and the school board demonstrated in the most palpable way to the community the new respect and power the parents had earned. For their part, parents' perspectives of the teachers had changed. Zavala teachers had come to school board meetings until late at night, met with officials from myriad city departments, and stood side by side with the parents as they fought to improve their children's health. For the first time, Higgs recalled, "parents began to see that the teachers really cared about the kids."

Zavala Elementary had broken through the vicious circle of civic disengagement to create a virtuous circle of solidarity and mutual accountability. "It was a turning point for this community," Alejandro Melton said, "because this was the first time that they had organized around an issue which they had identified, faced opposition, persisted, and won. They had learned the basic tools of democracy and petitioned their government for a redress of their grievances. They petitioned vigorously, eloquently, and continuously, and secured the services that they wanted."

Galvanized by their victory, the parents and teachers of Zavala Elementary were now ready to focus their attention on a second issue that had been discussed in many home visits with parents and at the acrimonious PTA meeting in December 1991: academic achievement. Austin Interfaith leaders and organizers held workshops for parents and teachers to address the test scores on the Texas Assessment of Academic Skills test. In the next year, scores at Zavala rose dramatically. For third and fourth graders, scores climbed from 23 percent to 43 percent in reading, from 40 percent to 92 percent in writing, and from 17 percent to 50 percent in math. As for teacher retention, Zavala closed the gap from a 50-percent turnover rate in 1991 to 0 percent in 1993.

Academic scores and teacher retention rates are crucial indicators of school improvement, but there are deeper indices of cultural changes at Zavala. First, the teachers and parents at the school know that all of the children are now fully immunized. The disheartening situation from the spring of 1992, in which a majority of Zavala children's basic health needs had not been attended to, has been radically transformed. In 1993 Zavala won the Award for Excellence in Texas School Health from the Texas Health Foundation and the Texas Department of Health for its new clinic; in 1994 it won a second award for a dental health program that it installed in the clinic with assistance from a religious charity called the Manos de Cristo.

Second, one of the simplest and most profound changes in the school has ensued from the recognition that every effort must be made by the school to communicate with parents in the only language which many of them speak—Spanish. Before 1992, all of the letters home to parents were written only in English, and PTA meetings were held in English with no translation available. "You could always hear the parents whispering, '*¿Qué dice él? ¿Qué está pasando?*'" Claudia Santamaria recalled, "and some teachers thought the parents were just being rude, but the truth was that they couldn't understand what was being said and were just trying to help each other. But now my parents all come to our meetings, and are proud to speak Spanish."

By the end of 1992, Zavala's monolingualism had been superseded, with all report cards and letters home composed in both Spanish and English and regular two-way translations provided at all public meetings. As a result, the community has responded with hitherto unheard-of events, as when two mothers who speak only Spanish invited all of the Zavala faculty to their homes for an end-of-the-year party in June 1993. "These things never happened here before," Melton said. "It is going to cost those parents a lot of money to feed the fifty people on our staff. It's a real sacrifice on their part to do this." Yet the parents are willing to make the sacrifice because of the commitment that the teachers have shown to their children. Reflecting the new appreciation of Spanish, a group of African American parents have requested the creation of Spanish language classes for adults so that they can improve communication with Spanish-speaking parents.

A third dramatic change in the culture concerns Zavala students' perceptions of themselves. Santamaria explained,

> You have to understand that usually whenever you heard anything about East Austin in the news before, it's always been about crime, drugs, and low test scores. And when our fifth graders would go to visit Murchison, our partner school in northwest Austin, they would chatter their heads off in the bus going there, but were completely silent on the way back. They realized that those other kids have everything—cars, computers, even polo, and that they had nothing. It's not fair to match the richest of the rich with the poorest of the poor. It really shot our kids down. And now, *finally*, we have something. *Finally*, our students, and especially our older ones, see that we're in the news for positive things. We have our students read every article about us in the paper, and they talk about seeing Mr. Melton on television. They

see that visitors come to the school and take notes. We *never* used to have visitors; we've had more visitors to the school this year than ever before. All of this has lifted the spirits of the parents, too.

Additional changes in the school culture have come about through the creation of a vibrant tutoring program which brought more than one hundred regular community volunteers to the school in its first year to help children to improve their reading comprehension.

Changes in academic achievement, student health, parental engagement, language usage, a tutoring program, and school spirit are major indicators of a sea change in Zavala's culture. These changes have also had a direct impact upon how teachers instruct and how students learn. According to Melton, the victory regarding the acquisition of the clinic empowered Zavala's parents to take a fresh look at the educational standing of their children and the range of services available to them in the public schools:

> After their success, the parents felt emboldened to make other demands on us and on their city for their community. Their level of expectation increased. Now they started asking, "Why aren't our children in honors programs in secondary schools? What are you doing to prepare our kids for college preparatory courses? Why can't our kids participate in the same after-school programs that they have at other schools?" They started focusing on solutions to community problems instead of just acquiescing to the status quo.

Parental interest led the teachers to reexamine their instructional styles and curricula, and to develop new attitudes and techniques to teach their students better. "We've gotten away from the stereotypical idea of minority children which led many of us to water down the curriculum," Samantha Bednarski says, "and we're using materials from the city's gifted and talented schools to teach our kids literacy skills." Following the example of the Walks for Success, the school's librarian has organized "Reading Rallies," in which Zavala's children parade through the neighborhood with signs they have written promoting literacy. Melton believes that providing better instruction in reading and writing to his students will ensure that his students achieve greater successes in middle school. In addition to the emphasis on literacy, Zavala teachers are using discretionary funds to transform their curricula to focus on interdisciplinary topics which will emphasize conceptual development rather than memorization.

A further change in the culture of Zavala Elementary has had to do with the creation of new programs. In their assessment of their children's educations, Zavala parents learned that in the past decade only one of their graduates had attended a prestigious magnet school in Austin called Kealing Junior High School, which prepares students for the Lyndon Baines Johnson Secondary Science Academy. Their lack of representation at Kealing concerned Zavala parents, particularly because Kealing is located only eight blocks away from their children's school. In addition, parents such as Toña Vasquez began to question the routine manner in which the Mexican American children were always tracked to the lowest level at Murchison Middle School while the Anglo children were tracked to the honors program. Vasquez made sure that her own daughter, Cynthia, was tracked to the honors program and encouraged Cynthia to participate in extracurricular activities such as the swim team and the band to make new friends. In spite of her best efforts, however, Cynthia found that her new classmates had a hard time understanding or appreciating her background. When they learned that she lived in East Austin, for example, they assumed that she must be frightened to live there and asked her why she didn't move out. Cynthia began feeling that she would never fit in with her classmates in the honors progam and began deliberately flunking her classes so that she could join her friends from the East Side in the lower level courses.

Confronted with stories like these, Zavala parents and teachers sought a way not only for the children of the most vigilant parents to enjoy academically challenging programs, but also for a critical mass of students to be able to participate each year who would support each other and pave a new relationship between Zavala and Austin's secondary schools. Through a fortuitous turn of events, Alejandro Melton learned that the National Science Foundation was supporting a research program at the University of Texas which needed an outreach component. Melton began negotiating with Pamela Cooke, the liaison from the university, to begin a new program for a class of sixth graders called "Zavala Young Scientists." The National Science Foundation could not cover all of the expenses of the program, however, and Zavala parents and teachers had to wrest a commitment from the school board to spend an additional twenty thousand dollars a year on the program. The school board was constrained by financial limitations, but by February 1993, the Zavala community had learned how to do effective advocacy. Toña Vasquez and many other parents organized meetings with the school board and the superintendent, and in spite of their reluctance, secured funding. "We forced it on the superintendent, who clearly didn't want it," Joe Higgs said.

Liberal critics of tracking may wonder at the choice of Zavala parents to create a kind of gifted and talented program for their young people; in point of fact, the Austin superintendent and school board raised objections based on their opposition to tracking. So that the program is not misunderstood, it is crucial to understand the context informing the parents' support for Zavala Young Scientists. To demonstrate that Austin complies with federal school desegregation mandates, most middle school children from the Zavala neighborhood are bused to a middle school in the northwest of Austin populated by affluent Anglo children. There they are almost always tracked to the lower levels. Zavala parents understood that if their children were ever going to have a crack at success in the upper levels, they needed some differentiation at the end of their elementary school experience. Significantly, there was no opposition from the parents: "I was so impressed," Austin Interfaith leader Oralia Garza de Cortés recalled, "with how clearly the parents understood the need to address the larger public good in their community. It didn't matter so much to them that their own children could attend Zavala Young Scientists as it did that some children from their community would have opportunities they had never had before."

As a result of the new program, eighteen Zavala students now receive superb instruction in the sciences each year from teacher Todd McDowell, a passionate advocate of hands-on learning who cares far more about stimulating children's curiosities and critical thinking skills than the memorization of terms, which characterizes so many contemporary science classes. McDowell has set up a visually rich classroom filled with microscopes, computers, fish tanks, maps, and encyclopedias; he likes to get the kids out in the hallways trying out projects, such as measuring wind resistance on toy cars they've designed to stimulate their interest in mass and velocity.

In the spring of 1995, McDowell sponsored a competition among his students. The students were to design small wooden bridges; the goal was to design the bridge that would carry the most weight. The students had to think about why walls are usually built on bridges and effective means of distributing weight. Once their projects were completed, they took a field trip to the University of Texas where scientists applied pressure to the different bridges and identified the strongest one. Understanding that learning is developmental, McDowell then had the students redesign the bridges so that they could implement the principles that they had learned after their first ventures. On a rainy April day, his class was a beehive of activity as students transferred their plans on paper into three-dimensional bridges, busily cutting and pasting wood together as incipient civil engineers. The work is intrinsically rewarding, but beyond its immediate pleasures lie larger opportunities. Zavala's young scientists participate in summer programs at the University of Texas, and every Zavala student who attends the LBJ Secondary Science Academy and graduates is promised a full scholarship to the university, thanks to the support of the National Science Foundation.

Programs such as Zavala Young Scientists have given the children at Zavala a new sense that the best educational resources our society has to offer are within their reach if they can demonstrate the right amount of motivation and self-discipline to acquire them. For those students who are not yet in the program, however, certain immediate needs have required attention. As a result of their many conversations in house meetings, Zavala parents and teachers identified a key weakness in the education of their children in 1993. Most Zavala children had working parents and went home to unsupervised residences until their parents arrived shortly before dinner. Although many Zavala parents disliked that hazardous situation, their lack of resources compelled them to cope as best they could.

Concern about both the safety of Zavala's children and the new focus on academic achievement led Zavala parents and teachers to seek out new strategies for capitalizing on children's hitherto unsupervised time in the late afternoons on school days. Working closely with Austin Interfaith, Zavala parents and teachers learned that the issue of after-school care was salient throughout Austin's low-income neighborhoods. Teachers found that many of their students did not want to go home to empty houses in the afternoon, and parents were frustrated that they had to work rather than attend to their children. Working with Austin

Interfaith, Zavala parents and teachers began meeting with city council members to identify funds which could support free after-school programs in four city elementary schools. As a result of tenacious organizing and constant political pressure, the city council agreed to draw funds from its Parks and Recreation Department budget to support the four new programs commencing in October 1993.

The after-school program has relieved parents of their anxieties about their children's safety in the late afternoon; in addition, it is giving the children new opportunities to enjoy academic enrichment activities. "We didn't want the baby-sitting that we saw in most extended care programs," Toña Vasquez recalled. "We wanted something that was interesting to the kids and would really extend their learning." Parents and teachers asked the children what classes they would like to take and then created classes in cooking, sewing, computer literacy, magic, and the martial arts. As a result of this process, many children who were marginally attached to the school previously have formed new ties to it through special relationships with instructors in the after-school program. Parents and Austin Interfaith leaders teach some of the afternoon classes, and teachers are strong supporters of the program, believing that it accelerates students' intellectual development in their regular morning and afternoon classes.

The result of so many successes on so many fronts has been an utter transformation of the culture of Zavala Elementary as well as its relationship with the community. Melton said, "It used to be that we saw ourselves *apart from* the community rather than as an integral part *in* the community." The boundaries between school and community have become so porous that they have almost dissolved. Zavala parents are now deeply involved in advocacy work with Austin Interfaith and have broadened their perspectives to reach beyond the immediate needs of their own children. In 1994, parents worked with Austin Interfaith to argue successfuly for the creation of twenty new free after-school programs at schools in low-income neighborhoods throughout Austin, sixteen health clinics at other schools, and five hundred summer jobs for adolescents, all to be created in fiscal year 1995. "It really worked," Toña Vasquez said, "because the mayor's big theme is 'opportunities for youth.' When we approached him with these proposals and had our individual meetings with each city council member, the mayor couldn't really say 'no.' And it was another big breakthrough." Austin Interfaith is moving beyond its previous focus on the city's funds to ensure that Travis County, of which Austin is a part, makes a generous contribution to the creation of new programs.

In spite of its many successes, Zavala Elementary continues to face challenges. Sixty-four percent of its students receive instruction in eighteen portable classrooms. "It breaks my heart to see the little ones going through the rain to the portables," lamented Alice Hernandez, president of the PTA. In the spring of 1995, Zavala learned that it would lose eighty thousand dollars of additional funding that it had acquired when it was a low-performing school. The school's shared decision-making team went through a wrenching process of deliberation before finally deciding which teachers to cut; one of them was a popular physical education teacher who had worked at the school for years. Zavala teachers and parents wanted to continue to emphasize academic achievement, and the classroom teachers were ready to try to teach physical education on their own. The change was difficult for all of the parties concerned in the deliberative process. "Money makes a big difference, in spite of what some people say," Melton commented. "Right now we don't have money, and it's really hurting us."

As a result of Zavala's many reforms and its students' improved achievement, Alejandro Melton has won nationwide visibility, which he hopes to use to make further improvements in his school. Melton appeared on the nationally syndicated television program *Good Morning, America* in April 1993 as an exemplary principal; he also received the prestigious American Hero in Education award from the Reader's Digest Foundation. Yet Melton is different from many of the educational figures who attract national media attention, such as Jaime Escalante or Joe Clark. "This work isn't about charisma," he said. "It's about people learning to work together who understand that the school can be a vehicle for political organizing and social change. School doesn't have to be a place where children just learn to read and write."[4]

Claudia Santamaria, the bilingual education teacher, feels that she has changed profoundly as a result of her work at Zavala:

> When I used to go to parties and people asked me how I liked teaching, I'd always tell them that I hated the politics of it. But now I love politics! Who would have ever thought that I would be asking the mayor of Austin to commit thousands of dollars to

our after-school program—and that he would do it? But don't get me wrong—this process has not been easy. We teachers did a lot of soul-searching and a lot of crying. Sometimes I'd just break down in my classroom and say to myself, "God, are we ever going to get anywhere?" But I guess this makes it all the better now that we've come so far in such a short period of time.

In the future, Santamaria plans to attend an IAF national training session to further cultivate her growing political skills.

Perhaps no one has changed more as a result of Zavala's development than Toña Vasquez. She has testified before the House and Senate Committees on Education of the Texas legislature and brought her daughters, Cynthia and Dorothy, with her on each occasion. She has written articles that have appeared in the local press, has addressed hundreds of Texas IAF leaders at annual Alliance School assemblies, and has appeared on television numerous times. For her friends and neighbors she is a champion of their community who has worked with many others to create new kinds of hope for the children of East Austin. To expand her skills and continue to improve the community, Vasquez began working as a VISTA volunteer in two other East Austin elementary schools in the spring of 1995. She attended a week of training in preparation for her work, but stated, "It was completely unnecessary. I had already learned all of that and more in my work with Austin Interfaith." In her case, her growth into citizenship operated as a kind of job training which now enables her to mentor other parents in East Austin to improve their schools and neighborhoods.

7

San Antonio

Building Networks of Reform
throughout the City

S an Antonio is unlike any city in either Texas or the nation in that its IAF organizations are so powerful that they are consulted by the mayor and city council on virtually every major piece of legislation which can impact the city. The oldest Texas IAF organization, Communities Organized for Public Services (COPS), has over two decades of successful experience in urban politics and has achieved a national reputation as the country's best example of effective community organizing. Thanks to its efforts, over seven hundred million dollars of federal, state, and local funds have been invested in public goods projects in working-class neighborhoods in San Antonio that traditionally had been used to enhance San Antonio's downtown. In particular, COPS has effectively steered funds for improvements in drainage, flood control, lighting, and street improvement toward working-class neighborhoods. COPS' younger sister organization, the Metro Alliance, was not founded until 1989; because it was not as multifaceted in its initial outreach, the Metro Alliance has been able to focus more intensively on educational issues than has COPS. Each organization draws on large congregational bases, with twenty-eight churches in COPS and thirty-seven in the Metro Alliance. The Catholic archbishop for the archdiocese of San Antonio, Patrick Flores, has been a tenacious defender of the work of the IAF for over two decades and is one of the six members on its national board of trustees.[1]

San Antonio is a city in which community-based organizations have not simply taken first steps to reform one or two urban schools; rather, they have transformed the lives of hundreds of citizens by radically enhancing their political capacity. The majority of leaders in COPS and Metro Alliance are working-class Mexican American women who vividly recall from their own childhoods the indignities of another era, in which they and their siblings received corporal punishment at school for speaking Spanish or attended segregated schools. It is therefore a dramatic testimony to those women's resilience that one generation later, they have made tremendous strides in recovering the dignity of their cultures and their communities. These women provide the community base which has introduced systemic community-based change into the public schools that vastly exceeds any of the transformations in other cities in Texas.[2]

Annette Ytuarte, for example, is a COPS leader who was identified as a special education student when she moved from a predominantly Mexican American inner-city school to a predominantly Anglo suburban neighborhood in her own childhood. She now feels that her involvement in COPS is one way that she can make sure that her own children do not suffer the same stigma. "I never imagined myself meeting with the mayor. I never imagined myself in the position that I'm in now, as a leader in the community," she says. "But one thing I do know is that I had a lot of anger in me. I wasn't less intelligent than those other kids, but I didn't have the same opportunities they had." After her marriage, Ytuarte moved back to the same inner-city neighborhood that she had grown up in and sent her children to the same schools. "But this time it was going to be different," she said. "Things had not changed, but I was determined to do something, and I also knew that I couldn't do it alone. I also knew that a lot of people felt the same anger that I did. That is when I came into COPS."

Terri Morado, now co-chair of the Committee on Education for COPS, experienced similar injustices in her childhood. In 1972, during her senior year at Memorial High School in San Antonio, Morado was accepted to Yale University. Her Anglo guidance counselor, however, advised her against attending, since he was sure that she would fail. Morado went to Yale anyway, and returned to San Antonio to work in her home community after graduation. In the summer of 1994 it was her role to ask the comptroller of the state of Texas at the twentieth anniversary COPS convention if he would make every effort to expand the number of urban schools working with the Texas IAF. He responded in the affirmative.

Virginia Ramirez, another COPS co-chair, also has been transformed through her work with the Texas IAF. Ramirez was a high school dropout who initially was intimidated in dealing with public officials but became emboldened through the leadership training she acquired in her work with COPS. When she was forty-four she returned to school to earn her general equivalency degree; she then continued on to college. Today, she is a respected civic leader in San Antonio, and has had a series of meetings with the mayor, the school superintendent, and corporate leaders to articulate COPS' issues. "We live in our neighborhoods, so we know exactly what is going on and what we need," she affirmed. "This is not something we have to learn from somebody else. And we're making sure that the system is changed." [3]

Those parents who are active in San Antonio schools which collaborate with COPS and Metro Alliance now have the opportunity to make sure that their own children receive better educations and become politically involved. Children go on Walks for Success with their parents, learn about their parents' meetings with public officials, and watch their parents ask their mayors, school superintendents, and other public officials to make commitments to improving public services in their communities. Because many low-income students have never before had the experience of watching their parents, and particularly their mothers, being taken seriously by public officials in mainstream institutions, the transformation of their parents in becoming public figures has had a dramatic impact. "Over the years it has been very important to me to see the role model of strong Hispanic women in COPS," Terri Morado said. "It's not something that you see anywhere else." Parents have derived a special satisfaction from watching their children learn political skills when they testify before the city council about the conditions of their neighborhoods. "They're learning politics at a very early age," Annette Ytuarte affirmed.

Carried by the organizing efforts of women like Ytuarte, Morado, and Ramirez, COPS and Metro Alliance have created a culture of civic engagement in urban schools and neighborhoods in San Antonio that is reshaping the experience of growing up in working-class communities. COPS and Metro Alliance have opened up new avenues to higher education, increased neighborhood safety, created over one hundred after-school programs, persuaded banks to provide low-interest mortgage loans to low-income citizens, and created an ambitious job training program known as QUEST. Each of their programs has emerged out of the identification of a direct need in working-class communities, and each program endeavors to address the major dilemmas of low-income urban Americans—from quality employment to reduced crime to home ownership to parental engagement with the school.

Access to College

In 1985, Reverend David Semrad of the United Methodist Campus Ministries in San Antonio began a Bible studies class by asking a student at San Antonio College to read aloud a section of scripture. To his dismay, the student was not literate enough to read the passage, although he had graduated from one of San Antonio's high schools. "It really was very painful," Semrad recalled, "and the students began to talk about classmates of theirs who had not known how to read in the ninth grade. By the time most of my students were graduating from high school, half of their former classmates had dropped out. The students had a lot of sadness in them, and our conversation really touched some chords in me." For Reverend Semrad, the experience compelled him to think about what he could do to improve the quality of education in San Antonio so that "all of us can share in God's bounty."

Semrad was not alone in his desire to act. In the late 1980s, many San Antonians from all walks of life—the business community, clergy, parents, and the students themselves—were observing that much needed to be done to improve the quality of education in the city. COPS and Metro Alliance were particularly concerned about the high dropout rates in low-income neighborhoods in San Antonio. They conducted research into ways to help students to graduate from high school, and found that an IAF sister organization, Baltimoreans United in Leadership and Development (BUILD), had forged an intriguing coalition with their corporate sector, the mayor, and sixteen institutions of higher learning in Maryland. Similar to Jefferson Davis' Tenneco scholarships, BUILD's "Commonwealth Agreement" required students to have excellent attendance and a strong grade point average to become eligible for scholarships at area colleges. If students in the Commonwealth program chose not to go to college, BUILD had received commitments from corporate leaders that the students' high standing in their classes would guarantee them a job in the private sector. Texas IAF leaders and organizers were especially interested in the extensive community participation of Baltimoreans in the Commonwealth Agreement, which not only enhanced job placement and increased access to higher education, but also trained thousands of parents in effective ways that they could improve their children's academic achievement.[4]

COPS and Metro Alliance then approached Henry Cisneros, the mayor of San Antonio at that time, about creating a similar program for their city. Cisneros subsequently flew to Baltimore to investigate BUILD's work. He returned persuaded that a replication of Baltimore's initiative could work in San Antonio, and began a series of meetings with the Texas IAF organizations and San Antonio's Chamber of Commerce to raise funds for "Education Partnerships." That coalition targeted the eight high schools in San Antonio with the highest rate of student drop-outs. Students in those schools were informed that if they maintained a 95-percent attendance rate and a B average, they would either gain a job with a sponsoring corporation or one thousand dollars a year of paid college education at any San Antonio college for four years.

One result of the Education Partnership has been an improvement in the graduation rate at those eight high schools from 81 percent in 1988 to 94 percent in 1996. In 1988, only 19 percent of students in those schools qualified for Education Partnership awards; by 1996 that figure had leaped to over 60 percent. As a result of the Education Partnership, over thirty-two hundred students have gone on to college. In 1994, COPS and Metro Alliance succeeded in expanding the program to two other high schools, and San Antonio's corporate sector is trying to raise the money to fund additional schools. For Betty Williams, principal of Sam Houston High School, the Education Partnership has been an un-mitigated blessing. "It's given our kids a whole new sense of possibili-ties," she says. "They see their older brothers and sisters going on and graduating from college. Many of them who never would have thought it was possible for themselves are beginning to see it as within their reach for the first time."

Increasing Neighborhood Safety

Smith Elementary School is located on the East Side of San Antonio. It is 73 percent Hispanic and 27 percent African American, with 98 per-cent of the students receiving free or reduced-price lunches. Although its elegant red brick facade and pillared portico suggest an architect's understanding of ordered harmony, Smith was confronted with terrible community problems in the early 1990s. Substance abuse, vacant homes and lots, litter, and a large transient population all played a role in creating a high-crime area. "My students would come to me telling me that someone in their family had been shot, or that the family felt that they had to leave the neighborhood because they had been threatened with violence," teacher Celinda Garza recalled. "They were often so traumatized by what was going on in the community that there was no way that they could learn anything in my class." To improve the situation, Principal Sharon Eiter asked Metro Alliance to begin a series of house meetings and school gatherings in the fall of 1991 to determine what issues most concerned parents.

Metro Alliance leader Marcia Welch and organizer Julia Lerma played key roles in coordinating and leading the numerous meetings that autumn. Many themes were discussed by the parents, but two emerged as the most salient. First, many parents had to work until five o'clock in the evening. They worried about their children's safety walking home through the neighborhood, and they worried about the children's safety at home without adult supervision. "Our community has lots of very young children and lots of elderly people," parent Louie Brown observed, "and we were sick and tired of all of the vacant buildings occupied by people we didn't know who used them for dealing drugs. We knew we needed to do something." In addition to safety concerns, many parents had received little formal education and were frustrated with their inability to help their children with their schoolwork. Perhaps it would be possible to create some kind of an after-school program that would give children a safe place to be until their parents came home, and would also provide them with classes that would strengthen their academic skills.

The theme of after-school classes was an important one for Smith parents and one that would play a dramatic role in recasting San Antonio's educational system. Yet far more urgent for the parents was the issue of safety. Assisted by Metro Alliance, parents and teachers learned how to identify vacant buildings and lots in the neighborhood that violated San Antonio's code compliance laws. Parents and teachers formed teams to survey the neighborhood for dark areas that needed additional street lighting. They then met with Police Chief William Gibson to discuss their desire for added protection. "We were thrilled to find that the police were so willing to work with us," Celinda Garza recalled. "People from the Smith neighborhood had never come to them as an organized group before, and we feel going as a group made a big difference."

Teachers and parents then planned and held a large rally at Holy Redeemer Catholic Church, a predominantly African American church on the East Side, on January 12, 1992. The sense of anticipation and excitement at the meeting was palpable—yet so was the sense of anxiety. Eight days before the assembly an elderly parishioner from Holy Redeemer had been killed while waiting for a bus; she was caught in the crossfire between rival gangs in the neighborhood. A few days later a sixteen-year-old, Samuel Cunningham, was shot twice in the head by a gang and left to die on an expressway. Drug dealers angry about the possibility of losing territory had threatened parents and parishioners with reprisals if they attended the meeting.

In spite of the threats, Garza recalled, "the church was packed. All of the people who had been so afraid before came to the meeting." Over four hundred parents, teachers, principals, pastors, and lay leaders attended and watched as Smith parents, Holy Redeemer parishioners, Metro Alliance leaders, and neighborhood residents bombarded the mayor, police chief, and other public officials with their grievances and challenges to improve the neighborhood. "Education is a great concern, but first we must deal with the fear that fills our neighborhoods," Reverend Arthur Hollis of the Revelation Bible Study Group said. "Children cannot study mathematics when madness and mayhem menace their neighborhoods." East Side resident Mary Johnson testified that her son was shot three times by gangs in the previous year. "Crime is on our minds," Reverend Semrad concurred. "We can't think about education until this is resolved." Would the police increase their visibility in the neighborhood, not just through reaction to crises, but also through proactive community policing? Would code compliance officers work with the parents to enforce existing codes? Would the mayor work with parents to explore the feasibility of creating an after-school program? Would the city improve lighting in the neighborhood?

Following the format of Texas IAF actions, all of the public officials who attended the meeting promised to play a role in rejuvenating the neighborhood. "I promise to work to identify additional funds for youth-oriented programs," Mayor Nelson Wolff said. "This is a priority." Police Chief William Gibson promised to help the community by adding more officers to the neighborhood; the director of Parks and Recreation agreed to work with Metro Alliance to give young people programs which would keep them away from gangs, and City Councillor Frank Pierce promised to help the community to improve housing. The neighborhood audience was thrilled with both its newfound sense of unity and the public officials' readiness to work with them. "We were so excited," Metro Alliance leader Marcia Welch said. "It was the first time that anything like this had happened, and it was a powerful evening for the whole community."

In the months following the Holy Redeemer assembly, the city rallied its forces to accommodate the community's requests. "The city really followed through," Smith principal Sharon Eiter said. "They added police, and they added new lighting. Code compliance made a big difference. But best of all, it changed the relationship between the school and the parents. We saw how much strong support was in the community, and the parents looked at us differently because they saw that we really were interested in them. They saw that we cared about their lives and their safety."[5]

In April 1992, Smith Elementary School held a press conference, in Eiter's words, "to let the public know that the city had followed through on its commitments." Honoring the accountability of public officials who had fulfilled their promises, Metro Alliance made every effort to assure that their public officials understood that they were appreciative allies. "We were trying to show that if you do get organized, the city will listen," Eiter said, "and the public needed to know that." Louie Brown said, "We're proud of what we've achieved, and we see a better city evolving."

Creating After-School Programs

Encouraged by their close cooperation with the city, Smith parents next turned to the issue of after-school programs. As with almost all working-class Americans, quality child care and education for their children in the late afternoons is a matter of utmost concern. Nearly half of American youth under eighteen are now growing up in single-parent homes in which the parent, almost invariably the mother, works full time. Only 7 percent of students today come from homes with two parents in the home and in which only one is a wage-earner and the other is a homemaker. In spite of dramatic changes in students' domestic lives, public schools have been slow to adjust their schedules to their pupils' needs. Schools with strong after-school programs are much more the exception than the rule; often, urban schools charge a tuition for after-school activities.[6]

Seventy percent of students in communities served by Metro Alliance and COPS in San Antonio are either from homes where both parents work or are raised by just one parent. Many parents have been alarmed by the rise of gangs and juvenile violence in their neighborhoods, and especially by their inability to provide adequate supervision for young-sters between the time school lets out and the time parents arrive home from work. The parents' concerns are legitimate: nationally, the peak time during which juvenile violence occurs is between 3:00 P.M. and 6:00 P.M. In addition, because many working-class parents received little formal education and feel handicapped in terms of their academic abilities, they expressed a strong desire to have high-quality academic instruction as one part of after-school programs for their children.[7]

To serve their clientele and the larger public interest, Metro Alliance and COPS had already organized to urge the city to fund three middle schools with after-school programs in 1991. When objections were raised about the expense of the programs, COPS and the Metro Alliance organized teachers, principals, and parents to conduct research to iden-tify revenues for the programs. The research team found that the city's Department of Parks and Recreation had suffered over five million dol-lars in budget cuts in the last two years.[8]

COPS and the Metro Alliance leaders and organizers then pressured the city to restore one million dollars to the department's budget, and integrated that request into a budget plan they had been developing over years for neighborhood development in San Antonio. The plan focused on improving housing, expanding jobs, and enforcing code compliance. To complicate matters, San Antonio has an unusually fragmented pub-lic school system; the metropolitan area is divided into eighteen separate independent school districts. COPS and Metro Alliance activists thus needed to meet with many different sets of school administrators.[9]

Galvanized by the mobilization of the Smith community, a new coa-lition of leaders developed within COPS and Metro Alliance who were determined to use their organizations to improve public education in San Antonio. COPS leader Maria Diaz attended "meetings upon meet-ings" with city council representatives and with her fellow leaders urged the council to set a top priority on the creation of after-school programs. "Of course, the first response was 'No, there is no money,'" she stated. Yet because Mayor Nelson Wolff had set a high priority on youth in his electoral campaign—and because Metro Alliance had made sure that he received favorable publicity after cleaning up the Smith neighborhood—Wolff agreed to open up the city's budget to work with COPS and Metro Alliance leaders to find the funds to support an expansion of after-school programs. As San Antonio began to come back from the recession in the early 1990s, funds were restored to the Department of Parks and Recreation; these funds were then targeted for the new After-School Challenge Program.

As a result of constant grass-roots advocacy, Mayor Wolff and the San Antonio city council agreed to fund a plan proposed by COPS and the Metro Alliance for twenty free after-school programs in the 1992–1993 school year. The city allocated fourteen thousand dollars to hire a staff of two after-school coordinators for each school site out of its Parks and Recreation budget. Those positions were matched by a third position paid for by the school district, which also provided games and equipment for the programs. Each school worked with COPS and Metro Alliance to recruit parents to provide additional staffing for the programs, which varied on the basis of participation from school to school.

In the first year of its funding, between one-quarter to one-third of all children in each school in San Antonio with an after-school program took advantage of the new program. Children were tutored in material that they had studied during the regular school day and participated in a host of offerings involving the arts, athletics, and the sciences. There was such vocal public support for the programs in their first year that Metro Alliance and COPS convened another large assembly of over five hundred activists in February 1993. Recognizing the widespread popularity of the after-school program, Mayor Wolff and the city council created programs in an additional forty schools for the following year. When the school year opened in August 1993, sixty schools sponsored free after-school programs for the children of San Antonio for a total cost of $1.3 million.

COPS and Metro Alliance leaders made certain that parents played a major role in shaping the after-school programs in their children's schools. Parents and community leaders not only helped to recruit staff, select curricula, and monitor the programs, but they are also highly visible on a day-to-day basis as they offer courses, provide refreshments, and serve as teacher's aides. Some after-school programs emphasize academics; others allow children to play in a variety of organized games; and most are a blend of tutorials and recreation. In all of them, the community plays an integral role in directing the program.

In addition to providing a safe environment for the children, the after-school program began to change students' attitudes toward school and academic achievement. "Students who previously hadn't done their homework began turning it in every day," according to Julia Lerma, educational organizer for the Metro Alliance. "As a result, their grades were improving, and so was their self-esteem." Laura Villanueva, a fifth-grade teacher at Woodrow Wilson Elementary, credited the after-school program with greater student and community ownership of the school: "Instead of the school being a place where students came for eight hours a day and then left, now it is *their* place, now it is *their* home."

Not only do the children benefit from the after-school program, but their parents are also enthusiastic supporters. Those who have to work until the evening are relieved to know that their children not only are safe at school, but are also learning. As Villanueva testified: "Time after time parents would come up to us and were so grateful that their children were *finally* getting the help that they needed to be in a safe environment and socially interact with other children. They didn't have to worry so much about their kids being at home by themselves."

Yet it would be a mistake to construe the after-school program just as a child-care program. As COPS leader Maria Diaz stated, "Our concern was that the after-school program shouldn't feel like a day-care center. We really wanted it to get the community more involved in the schools. And it *has* led to more parental involvement, and a new kind of development in the schools." Parents who teach in the after-school program testify that they have a much greater awareness of the children, teachers, and challenges in the school, and are in a better position to contribute to their children's educational development. Because the parents battled for the program in a combined effort with teachers and administrators, they feel a sense of ownership of it and are determined to develop it to its full potential.

The combined efforts of COPS and the Metro Alliance have revolutionized the process of growing up in San Antonio. In 1994–1995, the number of schools with after-school programs rose to close to one hundred, although a major failure by the San Antonio school board to match the city's $2 million contribution with $170,000 meant that the program did not reach the over 130 schools that COPS and Metro Alliance had hoped to support. In spite of that blunder by the board, teachers such as Laura Villanueva are inspired by the after-school program and the civic energy which infuses it. "I've always prided myself on my work as a teacher," she said. "But now I see how much change we've really created, and how much potential we really have. It's not just small changes for a small number of children. We've effected change for all of San Antonio."

A Chain of Change in Urban Schools

Change has not just happened at the macro level in San Antonio. To understand what some of the larger organizing efforts of COPS and Metro Alliance have wrought, examples of cultural change in individual schools are instructive. One of the schools which has gone the farthest in transforming its culture is Herff Elementary School, a preschool through second-grade school with over four hundred students located in the Alamodome neighborhood of east San Antonio. Although the school is a charming turn-of-the-century edifice with its original wood floors and slate blackboards remarkably intact, its neighborhood has been afflicted with problems in recent years. During the day, traffic raced back and forth in the front of the school and jeopardized the safety of children. After dark there was almost no lighting and two gangs, the LA Kings and Puro Ocho, terrified residents with drive-by shootings. One evening shots were fired through the windows on the front of the school. Substance abuse was rampant, and teachers found themselves cleaning up syringes and broken wine and beer bottles on the school grounds each morning. Gangs, drug dealers, and drug addicts occupied abandoned buildings on side streets adjacent to the school. Less than half of the parents at Herff had completed high school, more than half of its students had limited English proficiency, and virtually all of the pupils were on free or reduced-price lunches. Parental involvement and ties to the community were close to nonexistent.

Herff Elementary School began its transformation in 1989, when Pamela Ahart Walls became principal. Whereas her predecessor had responded with resignation to the problems in the community and attempted to cover up its many problems, Walls went on the offensive. One of her first acts was to call upon the Metro Alliance for assistance. Metro Alliance helped Walls and her faculty and parents to make house visits, to hold Walks for Success, and to challenge parents to improve their school and community. Walls also engaged the media to cover the problems at Herff and to create a momentum which would demand change. She told a reporter from the *San Antonio Express-News* about the problems at her school:

> Herff is a school where we must check the grounds daily for drug paraphernalia; where parents are afraid for their children, so they don't leave until the bell rings and they are safely escorted indoors; where a gang threatened in the past to snatch a four-year-old and use her for satanic sacrifice; where the principal must keep Mace on her key ring for protection; where domestic violence has left blood in this very cafeteria; where children have witnessed so many negative role models that I've removed three knives from my young students in the past two days.[10]

To confront the problems, Walls and her faculty worked with Metro Alliance to convene a large parents' assembly which over five hundred parents attended in November 1992. As with Smith's assembly, public officials promised to act on parents' requests, and to act quickly. Only one week after the assembly, Herff parents won on one of the key issues they had long sought to address, which was the transformation of traffic patterns in the immediate vicinity of the school.

A second issue that was brought before the parents' assembly concerned the community's relationship with the police. As Officer Bobbie Adams bluntly put it, "Before that assembly, everyone hated me." It was Adams' role to move into the community to arrest fathers who beat spouses and to take uncles and brothers to the police station for questioning when they were suspects in crimes. The police felt that many parents raised their children to be suspicious of and hostile to law enforcement officers.

Two parents, Rosemary Davila and Maria Rivera, led the effort to introduce community policing into their Alamodome neighborhood. They worked with Pamela Walls to recruit two officers to befriend the children at Herff. Although the police were hesitant at first, they have grown into their roles as mentors for the children and now find their frequent visits to Herff and their friendships with the children one of their favorite aspects of their work. Officer Bobbie Adams, a tall African American previously feared by the children, now visits Herff twice a week. He has developed a host of young admirers who rush up to hug him when he arrives at the school, and he enjoys collaborating with the teachers when they are developing curricula. When teachers at Herff were working on an interdisciplinary unit on transportation, for example, Adams provided for a helicopter to land near the school so that the children could explore it up close; he also arranged for fire engines to come to the school for the children. For a unit on careers, he organized a field trip to the police academy for the children. He has escorted the children on foot in field trips to the nearby public library and has visited children's homes on Herff's Walks for Success. As a result of these numerous new connections between Adams and the community, the children and their parents see the police in a new light, and Adams feels a new emotional stake in the well-being of the neighborhood.

A third issue addressed by the November assembly concerned code compliance, housing, and neighborhood development in the community surrounding Herff. In the six months following the assembly, more than sixteen vacant houses near Herff were demolished and long-abandoned vehicles were removed from vacant lots. Teachers such as Anita Cortez and administrators such as Anita O'Neal, who have worked on the Code Compliance Committee, have developed a detailed knowledge of their pupils' community and the problems experienced by children in their neighborhood.

In their most sweeping and systemic effort, parents and teachers from Herff played a key role in designing a comprehensive proposal with Metro Alliance to protect their neighborhood from commercial developers. The Alamodome sports facility, directly on the other side of a nearby interstate highway, could easily have spawned a limitless profusion of mini-malls and gas stations to serve consumers from the suburbs. "This area was already downgraded before the dome got here," Metro Alliance leader Claude Black observed. "Ninety percent of the business owners did not live in the community and therefore had no real ties with the people who live here." Metro Alliance worked closely with San Antonio's city council to protect the residential character of the Herff neighborhood.

San Antonio's powerful business elite resisted the notion that a small working-class community could circumscribe commercial growth in the proximity of the Alamodome. In February 1993, the Alamodome East Property Owners Association sued San Antonio while the city was developing the Alamodome Neighborhood Plan in cooperation with Metro

Alliance. Without any community opposition, the property owners would have profited, but the precarious fabric of the community would have suffered further and perhaps irreversible decline. Metro Alliance continued to plan with the city for residential zoning, the property owners lost their lawsuit, and in December 1993 the city council put the motion for residential zoning to a vote. With city hall packed with 150 Metro Alliance leaders, the city council voted unanimously to pass the resolution. "We saved the neighborhood!" Pamela Walls affirmed. Parents who were thinking of moving out of the neighborhood, such as Rosemary Davila, have now decided to stay to contribute to the new vitality.[11]

Change in Herff's neighborhood has also stimulated change within its classrooms. Pamela Walls has used discretionary funds to acquire consultants who can teach Herff teachers how to plan, instruct, and evaluate interdisciplinary units, and the result has been "richer, longer, in-depth study" of units from multifaceted angles which enable children with different learning styles to participate easily in the curriculum. Reflecting the dynamic interaction between the school and community issues, Herff teachers have planned a wide range of interdisciplinary curricular units on housing and shelter with their students. "We're integrating the curriculum and the community," Julia Lerma commented, "and that's another way to get parents involved."

Education at Herff has changed not only for the children and their teachers, but also for parents. Walls and her teachers created adult education classes in English as a second language and basic education, as well as a program for parents to earn general equivalency degrees. A portion of Herff's library has been turned into a parents' center, and to give parents full insight into the ongoing development of the schools, Walls invites parents to attend staff development programs. From her perspective, the presence of parents in staff development workshops "keeps teachers from going too deeply into jargon. It really makes one stop and make sure that everyone understands all of the issues that are being raised." More importantly, however, Walls believes that "it really doesn't matter what we would do with the curriculum if we didn't have the parents involved" because "teachers must address the issue of what parents can do in the home to enhance units of instruction." It is Walls' conviction that simply focusing on what happens in the school, while neglecting the home life of children, might make for interesting workshops but is ineffective if one wants high academic achievement for the children who attend Herff. In Walls' experience, including parents in staff development workshops is particularly important because workshop leaders will often model for the teachers ways in which they can be most effective in communicating with children, and most Herff parents have not had the opportunity to pursue higher education or to reflect upon all of the issues involved in stimulating children's cognitive growth.

For parents such as Maria Rivera, participation in staff development workshops gives her the chance not only to understand current developments in instruction and curriculum, but also to enhance teachers' awareness of their pupils as whole individuals with a home life outside of the school. "There are schools where it would be a really big deal to have parents involved in staff development," Pamela Walls said, "but Herff has evolved in such a way that no one sees it as an issue." Including parents in staff development has removed the mystique of teacher training and expanded the educational mission of the school into the homes of the children.

The result of so much social capitalization has buoyed the community's spirits. "Leaders from the Metro Alliance encouraged me to speak to the mayor about our neighborhood's needs," Maria Rivera said, "and I was terrified at first. But Julia Lerma, the organizer, made me feel very comfortable. We ended up writing my presentation at midnight while lying on my living room floor and eating ice cream! And the presentation went very well." Rivera has attended staff development workshops, organized Walks for Success, attended Metro Alliance sessions on preparing students for state-administered tests, and been an enthusiastic supporter of the school's after-school program. She has traveled to Houston to hear Howard Gardner speak at Texas IAF conventions; she felt that his theory of multiple intelligences validated her own observations of the different learning styles of her children. As a result of all of her work in the school, she has switched churches and her family now attends Saint Michael's Catholic Church, which has housed summer programs for Herff children. As a result of the engagement of parents such as Rivera, Pamela Walls feels confirmed in her conviction that "this school really *is* the center of the community."

As Smith and Herff discovered new ways to connect to their communities through their work with Metro Alliance, even skeptical educators who had been hostile to COPS and Metro Alliance—who saw them as combative, intrusive political organizations—found themselves intrigued by the new school collaboratives. Richard Alvarado, principal of Beacon Hill Elementary School, had grown up in San Antonio and had criticized his own parents for their support of COPS. As a high school and college student, he deplored COPS' disruptive, attention-getting interruption of normal business routines in its first protest actions.

In spite of those early impressions, Alvarado knew that Saint Anne's, a parish church right next to Beacon Hill, was a member of Metro Alliance, and he knew that a positive relationship to the church and its congregation could only help his work as a principal. As a consequence, he agreed to a series of meetings with Metro Alliance leaders and organizers in the early 1990s, in which he learned about programs such as the Education Partnership, the After-School Challenge Grant, and the ongoing work at Smith and Herff. Those conversations piqued his curiosity. "I recognized that I didn't know anything about community organizing and that acquiring those skills was essential if I was going to increase parental involvement at Beacon Hill," he said.

Increasing parental participation was not the only issue that Alvarado faced as principal of Beacon Hill. Close to 100 percent of his students were on free or reduced-price lunches. He has six hundred students in his school, but only one bathroom for boys and one for girls. Twenty of his twenty-nine classrooms are in ten temporary buildings where a playground should be. Alvarado knew that his children did not have the same opportunities that most American children have, and he was eager to do all he could to improve their circumstances.

Alvarado first tried to have meetings for parents at the school to begin building better ties to the community. Those meetings were failures; almost no parents came. Drawing on its familiarity with this problem, Metro Alliance helped Alvarado to reconceptualize his outreach. The new strategy was to set up "block meetings," in which all of the blocks in his school attendance zone held meetings in a parent's home to learn what the parents' major concerns were about their children and the school. Teachers telephoned parents to ask them if they would agree to host meetings. Once they had set up a schedule, Alvarado and a small cluster of teachers and parents moved from home to home soliciting parents' ideas and doing whatever they could to encourage parents to advance their children's education.

For Alvarado, the block meetings were a time of excitement and personal growth. He recalled,

> We arrived with refreshments, and we would meet anywhere—
> on the front lawn if there was nice weather, or in the living room,
> and the parents had it all organized. One mother would look after
> the children while we all talked about ways we could help the
> children. I saw that what we were doing was so badly wanted
> and needed—it was just that the parents didn't want to come to
> the school! And after the meeting I'd get phone calls in my office
> from people saying, "I want the meeting to be held at my home
> the next time!"

After the block meetings, the parents held a number of meetings with the mayor, the chief of police, and the director of Parks and Recreation. They then worked to hold a public assembly at Beacon Hill in October 1992.

Over five hundred parents turned out for that first large assembly at the school, attended by Mayor Nelson Wolff. The parents' attention was clearly focused on the presence of vacant buildings and a bunkhouse occupied by transients in the neighborhood. Parents complained about drug dealers and users who inhabited the buildings, individuals who defecated publicly in front of their children while they walked to and from school, and sidewalks littered with syringes. "The parents and children were frightened, because one of the worst buildings was right on a major pathway on the way to school," Alvarado recalled. Rebecca Schwartz was in the middle of teaching her third-grade class one morning when a homeless man wandered into the class and asked her for money. Other vagrants loitered in the restrooms and frightened children when they needed to use them.

Before their assembly, Alvarado and the parents had tried to get code compliance officers to board up the vacant buildings or at least to pledge to close the buildings quickly. Parents such as Juanita Zamarripa and teachers such as Norma Vinton covered the neighborhood, noting buildings which violated the code, and informed the appropriate officials. Regrettably, the officers refused to make any greater commitment than to attend to the buildings as quickly as circumstances allowed.

As a result of the city's intransigence, Alvarado and the parents decided to go to the public. They invited the media to film their assembly and to tour the buildings with them. They found syringes, pornography, and a host of filthy conditions that should be nowhere in the proximity of elementary school children—and the television stations projected it all in living color on the ten o'clock news. Mayor Nelson Wolff and other public officials promised action. The very next day, code compliance officers boarded up the buildings.[12]

For Alvarado, the rapidity of response of those code compliance officers after the negative media coverage "completely blew the door open" at Beacon Hill. "I think that's when the parents really understood the power of an informed and organized constituency," he said. Seeking to capitalize on that momentum, Alvarado and his staff have strongly promoted political education at Beacon Hill. Alvarado had noted that electoral participation in his school zone was abysmally low—as low as 10 percent in some elections. As a result, Beacon Hill mobilized on a schoolwide basis to educate students about how the political process works, to conduct voting drives in the neighborhood, and to educate parents about the importance of their electoral engagement. Educating the school and the community is a dual mandate at Beacon Hill, and Alvarado hopes that a new level of citizenship awareness, in terms of both rights and responsibilities, is changing a culture of disengagement in the community.

Within the school, Alvarado feels that "the classroom looks totally different." Like Herff, his school has focused on the development of interdisciplinary themes in recent years. Part of the pleasure and motivating power of interdisciplinary approaches to curriculum involves the myriad topics that teams of teachers can select and shape into curriculum units. At Beacon Hill, elections were one such interdisciplinary unit; another one was birds, which a teacher introduced with such gusto that she and her students painted the entire front foyer of the school with bright representations of exotic birds. Other topics such as housing, health, and community are ongoing interdisciplinary themes which are helping to weave together the worlds of the school and its neighborhood.

A third school touched by the chain of change in San Antonio is Flanders Elementary School on the South Side. Cynthia Castillo was a new principal at Flanders in the fall of 1992 who had herself grown up in the neighborhood. "I'm a Southsider at heart," she said, "and while I see that positively, I also know something about the pain that is here. When my grandparents first bought a house in this neighborhood, they couldn't live in it for the first two years because of restricted covenants." Although she brought empathy and commitment to her work, Castillo found herself more than fully challenged by leading Flanders. The school's achievement was designated unacceptable by the Texas Education Agency because a large majority of the children failed to pass all three sections of the state's standardized test. The problems the school faced were not just academic, but social in origin. Ninety-four percent of Flanders' children were on free or reduced-price lunches and 40 percent of the students who were in the school each September had relocated elsewhere by the end of the school year.

COPS leaders and organizers had worked successfully in the South Side for years on issues of drainage, lighting, and traffic safety before beginning a collaboration with Flanders. Their victories had helped to preserve a large number of owner-occupied residences in the neighborhood, largely filled by older, retired blue-collar workers and their families. COPS leaders and organizers approached Castillo about building a partnership in the fall of 1992, and Castillo moved rapidly to take advantage of that opportunity. "I knew that educators have not been trained to know how to work with parents," she said, "and I also knew that if anybody could help us with that, it was going to be COPS." Castillo built social capital by leading neighborhood walks in which teachers, parents, clergy, and COPS leaders visited the homes of every child in Flanders. She held special evening meetings to register parents to vote, to provide them with library cards, and to recruit them to improve the school. "We worked very hard to reshift the focus of the community and to get the parents to feel that this school is a community center," teacher Edward Mendez recalled. "We wanted the parents to feel that Flanders isn't just a building where they send their kids, but that it really is *their* school."

As a result of its new surge of energy, Flanders became one of the first schools to benefit from the After-School Challenge Program. Castillo said that the program has "made all of the difference in the world" by enhancing her students' academic success and providing them with adult supervision in the late afternoon. Instead of going home to empty houses, Flanders students now take classes on dance, karate, cooking, and computing. "Our kids are so much more involved now in the school than they ever were before," teacher Norma Ibarra observed. Parents are involved in establishing the after-school curriculum, teaching courses, and serving as teachers' aides. Castillo credited the after-school program, as well as the work with Flanders parents, with improving Flanders' test scores and raising them to the "acceptable" level in the 1993–1994 school year.[13]

As parents began to become more visible in the school and a new culture of conversations was developing, Flanders' staff and parents learned that they all shared one frustration in common. The Harlandale Independent School District had converted to a year-round schedule in 1992, but district officials had failed to recognize that none of their eighteen elementary schools was equipped with a gymnasium. When teachers tried to do physical education with the students on rainy days, they ended up using hallways and the cafeteria. Not only were the hallways and cafeteria unsafe for the children, but the building also took a beating from all of the activity. Teachers and parents were especially troubled when the children played outside during the scorching summer months. Several children fainted during physical education classes in June and July in the first year of year-round schooling, when average daily temperatures were often over one hundred degrees.

Flanders parents and teachers visited other schools in surrounding districts and found that virtually all of them were equipped with gymnasiums. Through conversations they developed the idea that they wanted more than a gymnasium; they wanted a building spacious enough that it could be a genuine community center which could host large assemblies and performances. When they raised their proposal for such a multipurpose center to school board members, however, their representatives noted that the latest school bond referendum had been voted down for fiscal reasons in 1992 by the district's voters. The path to a multipurpose center looked difficult, if not impossible. Yet just as other schools in San Antonio have learned, political organizing offers an entirely new vista of possibilities for urban schools and communities.

COPS organizer Joe Rubio conducted much of the detailed work with the Flanders community around the service center issue. Working with parents in 1993, he discovered that the Harlandale district was planning on building a three-million-dollar maintenance building—at the same time that it claimed that the less than two hundred thousand dollars it would cost to build the service center was unaffordable. Given COPS' clout on the South Side, it didn't take much pressure to persuade the district that the maintenance building was a bad idea—but the district still claimed that the funds for the service center were unavailable.

From 1993 to 1995, the Harlandale Independent School District experienced three different superintendents, with the same interim superintendent filling in twice between the appointments. Throughout that time period, Flanders teachers and parents conducted constant advocacy for their school with the school board and the different superintendents. At times the advocacy was grueling work. Parents and teachers would develop a promising relationship with a superintendent only to learn that he would soon be leaving for a better position elsewhere. Some school board members got tired of hearing grievances about the same issue and refused to meet with Flanders parents; others visited the school and told the community that they should use the hallways or the cafeteria for games and exercises. "Some of our board members really upset me," parent Janie Benavides recalled. "I saw that before elections they would come to our meetings and say whatever we wanted, but after the election they can be very disrespectful with you. My daughter, Lee Anne, had been in one of the classes in which a girl had fainted. I wasn't going to let the issue drop." Marta Avalos, with a second-grade daughter in Flanders, was another parent who tenaciously pursued school board members to keep the multipurpose service center idea alive.

Flanders parents and teachers decided that if they were to have a prayer of success in gaining their multipurpose center, they would have to mobilize not just their own resources but those of the whole community. Joe Rubio led an intense series of training sessions with parents and teachers on the essence of IAF community organizing, including strategies for meeting with public officials, the importance of developing political power, the distinction between public and private lives, and the utility of self-interest as an organizing tactic. He also taught parents and teachers how to conduct research actions—those strategies with which low-income citizens develop the political sophistication to solicit budgets from public officials and to work with them on reallocating revenues.

One of the key developments that emerged from the training sessions was the decision to organize even those neighborhood residents and business owners that did not have children in Flanders Elementary School. "We decided that we would have to go beyond parental involvement to reach the whole community," teacher Edward Mendez recalled.

Rather than simply visiting the homes of Flanders students in the neighborhood, Flanders parents and teachers began making house visits to every neighborhood resident and business to raise community support for the multipurpose center. "At first, a lot of people told us that they didn't have kids at Flanders anymore or that they didn't have children, so that they didn't really care what happened to the school," Mendez said. "But then I told them that 'the way the school goes is the same way that your property value goes. If this school goes down the tubes, what's going to happen to your property values? If a young family with kids was interested in buying your house, do you think they'd still want it when they found out the school was terrible?' And then they gave me a second look and said that they'd never thought about it that way before."

Flanders announced its first schoolwide parents' assembly in June 1994, and parents and teachers made an all-out effort to mobilize the community. Parents and teachers who had been working with COPS on increasing community engagement put hundreds of hours of detailed work into the assembly. They canvassed the neighborhood, made telephone calls, and sent flyers home with the children. "We worked without a break on preparing that assembly," teacher Barbara Jones recalled, "including weekends."

The work was exhausting but exhilarating. For the first time, the politicial capacity of many parents and teachers blossomed. "I used to be the kind of person who wouldn't talk to anybody, and I always just said 'yes' to the teachers," parent Marta Avalos recalled. "I couldn't stand up in front of a lot of people. Even though it still makes me nervous, COPS taught me how to do that." Avalos and other parents prepared presentations, rehearsed them with a parent task force, revised them on the basis of its members' recommendations, and made public presentations at the assembly. Teachers also credit the community organizing with catalyzing their growth as public actors. "Before we began all of our outreach into the neighborhood, we didn't really know how to build relationships with the community," teacher Esther Tomez recalled. "But by doing all of our neighborhood walks we did learn that there really is a right way to go about it if you want to get results. I've gained a lot from this, and I know that other teachers have, too."

As a result of the parents' and teachers' hard work, over five hundred parents—in a school with 520 students—came to the assembly. Harlandale superintendent Pablo Perez attended the assembly, and so did Sonia Hernandez, a former COPS chair who had been appointed the director of education policy under Governor Ann Richards. "We had 100 percent participation from the parents of the kids in my class," Ibarra recalled, "and it was the same way with most of the classes." The assembly was a turning point for the neighborhood and the school, which had never experienced such unified resolve to improve the education of their children.

After the assembly, Flanders parents and teachers continued organizing the community and advocating for the provision of a multipurpose center for their school throughout the summer. At the opening assembly in the fall, over seven hundred parents attended; many took advantage of voter registration tables in the front lobby. Parents and teachers were excited when a new superintendent came to their district from Dallas in January 1995, and they hoped his background as a Hispanic would help them to gain a sympathetic ear. Regretfully, he quickly fell into line with the long history of district intransigence. He told the parents and teachers that they simply needed to order different kinds of lunchroom tables that folded up more easily; then the cafeteria would make a fine gym. "I continued meeting roadblocks with the board," Benavides stated. "They told me that they had nothing more to say to us."

By the spring of 1995, Flanders parents and teachers had nothing to show for their two years of tenacious organizing around the multipurpose center issue. Joe Rubio thought it important to check with the parents and teachers to see if they still wanted to keep advocating for the center; over seventy parents and teachers attended a meeting and asserted that they wanted to keep holding out. In April 1995 they held a research action with the district's chief financial officer to examine the district's resources and allocations to identify possible points of leverage. Demonstrating true concern for the parents and their children, the official worked with them until eleven o'clock one Wednesday night to help them to understand the nuances of the budget and areas of fungibility.

The turning point came in May 1995, when, with no prior warning, Flanders parents and teachers learned that the issue of their multipurpose service center would be voted on at a school board meeting that very day. Quickly rallying whoever was available, the Flanders community brought forty parents and teachers to the meeting, all decked out in bright blue "Flanders Falcons" T-shirts. One teacher and two parents spoke in favor of the service center. The Flanders parents and teachers were then exhilarated to watch as the school board voted unanimously to approve the center. "It was unbelievably amazing!" teacher Edward Mendez said. "We never expected that in a million years, and at first we couldn't figure it out."

What had happened to change the school board's position on the multipurpose service center? Many factors played a role, but the most important related to a school board election. Two of the most intractable opponents of the multipurpose service center had almost been defeated in spring elections and were forced to engage in run-off campaigns in June. They needed to demonstrate that they were committed to serving the community, and the multipurpose service center was one opportunity to do so. The community issue was especially salient for those board members because Flanders had demonstrated that it could turn out parents in large numbers for its assemblies and because of the ongoing community organizing in the neighborhood. Given the traditionally low voter turnout for school board elections, Flanders could provide the difference between victory and loss in the election, and the board members knew it.

Other factors also played important parts in explaining Flanders' victory. The financial officer for the school district was a member of a COPS parish, and he made special efforts to explain to Flanders parents the status of the district's finances so that they could do more than just petition the board for a multipurpose center; they could also suggest ways of finding the resources to fund it. The administrator—who had twice served as an interim superintendent—had observed the commitment of Flanders teachers and parents to their children's education and was genuinely moved by their fortitude and their idealism. Flanders' principal, Cynthia Castillo, proved unusually talented and committed at uniting the school and the community on behalf of their children.

Flanders' victory at the school board meeting was greater than simply serving its own children. Before taking the vote, school board members expressed recognition of the need for year-round schools to have athletic facilities and community centers available for children so that the hot summer months do not jeopardize their health. Parents from two other elementary schools which worked with COPS then played a leadership role in keeping the issue alive, and within a year the school board had agreed to fund gymnasiums for all of the elementary schools in the district. As for Flanders parents and teachers, however, they did not see their work as completed. In the week following the school board's vote, they convened with architects to look at different ways of designing the center and to choose the best part of the school yard to expand the building. Flanders parents and teachers want to make sure that they will be an integral part of all planning for the building so that it can serve not just as a gym or a set of classrooms but also as a fully realized community center.

Stabilizing the Neighborhood to Improve the School

The San Antonio Education Partnership, the after-school programs, and a chain of changes in schools as geographically dispersed as Smith, Herff, Beacon Hill, and Flanders have each helped to shape a new educational environment for youth in San Antonio. Each transformation has attacked a gap in the education of American youth and broadened the scope of education for working-class students. Yet COPS and Metro Alliance have not restricted their work to these domains. Although they might initially seem remote to education, two of their most important areas of activity—neighborhood preservation and job training—have had direct ramifications for the education of urban students.

The quality of neighborhood life is of tremendous importance to young children. If children are forced to walk in the street on rainy days due to the lack of sidewalks and are thereby exposed to traffic in a hazardous way, the anxiety aroused by the lack of safe pathways to school affects their ability to learn once school commences. If low-income parents feel that a poverty-stricken neighborhood is unsafe and frequently change residences in search of slightly better conditions for their children, their children's learning is interrupted. Research indicates that children from low-income households who experience repeated transitions in and out of school typically experience low self-concept, frequent absences, and low academic achievement. To prevent this situation, Texas IAF organizations have played a role in stabilizing and improving neighborhoods threatened by the decline of the country's manufacturing base and the rise of undesirable forms of commercial development which threaten the quality of community life.[14]

COPS has a long history of battling for infrastructural improvements in working-class neighborhoods in San Antonio. Until COPS became a force in San Antonio, the vast majority of city, state, and federal funds available for urban renewal were targeted by the city's elite for projects which would enhance commercial development and the tourist industry in downtown San Antonio. COPS' greatest and most uncompromised victory in the policy arena has been to capture Community Development Block Grants allocated by the federal government to preserve and expand public services on the Mexican American West Side. It thus came as no surprise when commercial interests began advocating the use of public funds to build a domed athletic stadium in southeast San Antonio that COPS would urge voters to defeat a referendum on the issue. COPS argued that the city had greater priorities in education, housing, and employment than a domed stadium, and that the majority of the jobs generated by the stadium would be low waged and without benefits to San Antonio's working class.

The battle for the "Alamodome," as the stadium was to be called, raged throughout 1988, with each side drawing on a host of economic and political considerations in marshaling their arguments. When election day came, however, COPS' opposition to the building of the stadium failed. Popular Mayor Henry Cisneros had promoted the project, and Mexican American voters who identified with his leadership turned out to support the stadium with a greater percentage than Anglos. Overall, voters believed that the economic and recreational opportunities that it would provide outweighed its disadvantages.[15]

COPS and Metro Alliance had warned that construction of the stadium posed a threat to low-income neighborhoods adjoining the stadium on its eastern flank. On the one hand, those neighborhoods had major problems of their own, such as homeless families, substance abuse, and gang control of key blocks and buildings. On the other hand, unrestricted development of mini-malls, gas stations, and fast-food chains to serve the Alamodome's clientele would only further corrode the fragile social capital which existed in the neighborhood.

COPS and Metro Alliance leaders created a proposal for integrated housing and commercial development in the Alamodome neighborhood that would protect and enhance it rather than demolish it. Marcia Welch, a retired African American teacher on the East Side and parishioner at Holy Redeemer, played a major role in spearheading this effort. "It was funny that I didn't see it as a teacher, but as soon as I retired I was shocked at how far the deterioration of the community had gone,"

Welch recalled. "It was only then that I really recognized for the first time that our children were finishing school with no marketable skills. It was only then that I saw that our areas were being gutted of people who had any kind of leadership ability or vision for the future." Welch was a prominent leader in the Metro Alliance, and she took notice when she began receiving phone calls from principals on the East Side, such as Pamela Walls at Herff Elementary, asking her organization to help parents to do something about housing to prevent the further deterioration of the community.

The more that Marcia Welch examined the Alamodome situation, the more she became aware of citizens' concerns throughout San Antonio for safe and affordable housing. As a result of that public sentiment, COPS and Metro Alliance leaders and organizers decided to develop a citywide strategy to work with banks, realtors, and public officials to enhance home ownership for low-income neighborhoods that traditionally had been "redlined" and prevented from receiving mortgages. Marcia Welch coordinated hundreds of meetings between community leaders, business leaders, principals, teachers, parents, and public officials. As a result of that concentrated effort, in the summer of 1994 leading banks in San Antonio committed ninety-five million dollars in funds to help low-income parents to either make the transition to home ownership or to take out low-interest loans to improve their homes.

Parents and teachers throughout San Antonio have been thrilled by the new opportunities entailed in the banks' promise to invest in working-class neighborhoods. Herff Elementary School was the first school to sponsor housing fairs to help its low-income parents to become homeowners. Parents submitted over 250 applications either to become homeowners or to improve their current homes, and the majority of them were at least partially approved by the banks. "A lot of the success of our housing fairs is due to how we've set them up," Marcia Welch stated. "We've made it easier for our parents because they already have a personal relationship with teachers and the principal in the school, whereas they might not know anyone at the bank." For parents who speak limited English, the housing fairs have presented a new opportunity for teachers or neighbors to support them in a familiar environment by translating.

Edna Rodriguez at Herff was one of the first parents to acquire the loan she needed to become a homeowner. "The bankers have been great," she said. "They didn't just come to our housing fair, but they've been coming in every week for one-on-ones with the parents. It's creating a whole new vision for our community." Parent Rosemarie Davila observed, "We had over 150 children move out of Herff's zone in the last year, and by creating affordable housing, we see a new opportunity for parents to put down roots in our community and to give it more stability. And our next step will be to make sure that those parents get involved in the school."[16]

Smith Elementary and Beacon Hill Elementary both had housing fairs of their own in rapid succession after Herff and had equally impressive results. "We had over three hundred applicants for mortgages and other forms of housing assistance even before our fair," Smith parent Louie Brown observed. "And now our low-income parents finally have a chance to get a decent place to live." Unlike the other elementary schools, teachers and parents at P. F. Stewart Elementary School on the East Side were able to combine issues of code compliance with new opportunities for home ownership from the very beginning of their organizing effort. In this undertaking, they have found ready allies in realtors. Real estate agents have joined with the parents and teachers to make sure that the city enforces its code compliance laws, and they have also participated in the school's first Walk for Success. Stewart's principal, Linda Holloman, carefully documented the change process in the neighborhood with before-and-after photographs which she has shared with parents, teachers, and students at school assemblies. With greater stability and commitment to urban neighborhoods such as those surrounding Herff and Stewart, the staggering mobility rates of city schools should be reduced, and homeowners will have greater interest in ensuring that the public schools are of a high quality—if for no other reason than to enhance their property values.

Another program that has strengthened families and neighborhoods in San Antonio that has been sponsored by COPS and Metro Alliance is Project QUEST. QUEST stands for "Quality Employment Through Skills Training." COPS leaders first began thinking about the need for effective job training programs in their city when the city's Economic Development Foundation began advertising San Antonio in the 1970s as a good place to do business because of its plentiful cheap labor. COPS wanted a different future for San Antonio, one that would create and market a trained and highly qualified work force. Yet because of its more astute awareness of the nuances of marketing urban economic development, and damaging publicity about COPS' agenda, the Economic Development Foundation basically outmaneuvered the IAF organization.[17]

The real precipitating incident which sparked the creation of Project QUEST was not in the area of advertisement, however, but the decision by Levi Strauss to close a cut-and-sew factory on San Antonio's South Side in 1990. The Levi's plant terminated over one thousand workers, mostly Mexican American women, and relocated to Costa Rica, where it paid its workers six dollars a day. As a result, the American workers lost high-paying manufacturing jobs with health insurance. The marketplace, following long-term trends in the United States economy, was only offering low-paying jobs in the service sector, without benefits. Working-class women such as Mary Moreno, who had worked at Levi's for twelve years, found themselves looking for work for almost a year before finally accepting a job which paid far less; single mothers, such as Oralia Gonzalez, with only a grade school education and limited English, were threatened with losing their mortgages and their homes as they struggled to make ends meet in the new economy. To make matters worse, layoffs occurred among several other major employers at roughly the same time, including San Antonio Shoe, Kelly Air Force Base, and the Roeglein meat packing plant.[18]

Social science research suggests that one of the major factors, if not the major factor, determining the destabilization of the family, the rise of juvenile delinquency, and a host of other social ills has to do with high rates of unemployment in concentrated areas of the central cities. "The problem of joblessness should be a top-priority item in any public policy discussion focusing on enhancing the status of families," William Julius Wilson wrote in his widely acclaimed *The Truly Disadvantaged.* Wilson's recommendations have been disputed by policymakers, but clergy at the street level in San Antonio saw the direct ramifications of the unemployment he described in their communities. According to Father Will Wauters of Santa Fe Episcopal, a Metro Alliance church on the South Side,

> You could see the changes that unemployment brought to our families: an increase in alcoholism and domestic violence among the parents, an increase in gang activity among the youth. The main reason that I decided that I had to do something is because kids from the local high school were constantly getting into gang

fights in my church's parking lot. It really hurt that at the same time that the jobs were lost the city was cutting back on its funding for youth programs. People felt a huge cloud over their heads. Their hopes for the future were gone.[19]

It wasn't the case that the displaced workers happily consigned themselves to the dole. Seven hundred of them sought opportunities through Job Training Partnership Act programs, but after ten months, only fourteen of them had found new employment through that avenue. Over a thousand former Levi's workers were still unemployed.[20]

COPS and Metro Alliance leaders were themselves hit by the crisis. To respond, they began holding hundreds of training sessions in churches, schools, and homes throughout the city to educate citizens on the transformations of the global economy that were having a direct impact on their jobs and economic prospects. As the training sessions got under way and thousands of conversations began coalescing into sharply identifiable problems concerning education, job training, and employment, COPS and Metro Alliance leaders and organizers decided to collaborate with the city's business elite and public officials, as well as with state representatives and the governor's office, to express their grievances and to develop joint strategies. As a result of those meetings, community leaders identified high-paying jobs requiring training that the private sector had trouble filling in occupations ranging from legal research to health care. "San Antonio *was* producing jobs," Father Will said, "but the jobs required higher skills, and most of them were on the more affluent North Side." COPS and Metro Alliance then deliberated on what steps could be taken to provide high-quality training that would enable San Antonians to have flexible skills rather than just to be trained to, and held captive by, one specific job.

As a result of their work, COPS and Metro Alliance launched Project QUEST in 1992. The project mixed a variety of funding revenues and drew most heavily upon a discretionary budget controlled by Governor Ann Richards. It contained a series of steps bridging the skills of applicants, training (usually at the community college level), and employment. To give the program a chance of success, COPS and Metro Alliance agreed to restrict the applicant pool to individuals who had either a high school diploma or a general equivalency degree. The targeted jobs needed to pay a minimum of eight dollars per hour and had to include health-care benefits. Private sector employers agreed to provide jobs to 650 applicants who would complete training through Project QUEST.

The application process was controlled by COPS and Metro Alliance, whose leaders devoted thousands of hours on weekends and evenings to interviewing applicants and explaining QUEST to them. In its first year, over two thousand people applied to the program. COPS and Metro Alliance leaders chose twelve hundred of them as most appropriate for QUEST. At the end of its second year, 85 percent of those twelve hundred had stayed in the program and 90 percent of those had begun job placements. By March 1996, a total of 396 QUEST participants had found and been placed in jobs in which the average salary paid was $7.83 an hour. Roughly fifty others had graduated and not found work, and thirty-six others graduated but elected to continue pursuing their education, with many striving for a bachelor's degree.[21]

Project QUEST is still too young to determine its overall efficacy as a job development strategy in San Antonio or other American cities. Given the historic weakness of apprenticeships in the United States compared to Germanic Europe and Japan, however, QUEST represents an exciting innovation which combines the American tradition of grass-roots civic participation with human capital development for a global economy increasingly dependent upon skilled labor. For Texas IAF organizations and their efforts in schools, the development of QUEST is an essential component of an overall approach to urban improvement, for even the best public schools will be undermined if the youth who attend them believe that no economic opportunities await them at the end of their studies.[22]

Project QUEST, community policing, after-school programs, interdisciplinary curriculum development, accessible college educations, and low-income housing are all part of an integrated, systemic strategy by COPS and Metro Alliance for school improvement and neighborhood development in San Antonio. The result of all of these efforts is the creation of virtuous civic circles among schools, neighborhoods, and congregations in which San Antonians visit one another, learn from each other's experiments, and encourage each other to continue reinventing their methods of educating and engaging the community. "We still have plenty of drugs, alcoholism, and gang violence in our communities," Father Will said. "But little by little, people are seeing that they can play a role in rebuilding the community. They see that our community organizations are having an impact, and that's why we get such high turnout when we meet at a school like Flanders. As for the kids, what they see is that their school, their parents, and their church all care about the same things: a good education, good jobs, and good housing. For those of us who are pastors, our self-interest is met, too, because a stable community means a stable congregation."

8

Texas

*Alliance Schools throughout
the State*

When the Allied Communities of Tarrant (ACT) experienced success at Morningside Middle School in 1988 with the dramatic jump in test scores, the Texas IAF received its first indication that community engagement could promote academic achievement. That success compelled Texas IAF organizers to reflect on their accomplishments and to see if they could be developed in a more deliberate fashion. "We were trying to figure out how to replicate Morningside," Ernie Cortés recalled, "but at the same time we didn't want to get bogged down in school-by-school work without having an overall strategy."

The search for a more reflective and rigorous approach led Cortés and his colleagues through a series of developments. One important step was the articulation of their paper, "The Texas IAF Vision for Public Schools: Communities of Learners." That paper served several purposes. First, it helped with self-clarification for Texas IAF leaders and organizers, who recognized the need not just for relentless action but also for democratic principles to anchor and catalyze their work. Second, it was written in a way both to reassure urban school superintendents and to intrigue powerful philanthropists, such as those at the Rockefeller Foundation, who subsequently provided funding for Texas IAF educational organizers. Third, it provided a manifesto for parents, principals, teachers, and students to study and to debate as they thought about reshaping their schools and communities.

In the late 1980s, the Texas IAF began a number of meetings with Texas Commissioner of Schools William Kirby. Cortés hoped that he could formalize a partnership with the Texas Education Agency (TEA) which would both release funds to schools in partnership with the Texas IAF and enhance the process of innovation in each school by giving it an official blessing from the TEA. In spite of a positive tone to the discussions, Commissioner Kirby did not make any commitments to the Texas IAF.

In November 1990, Ann Richards was elected governor of Texas. A former public school teacher herself, Richards was eager to improve Texas' schools. She quickly appointed former COPS chair Sonia Hernandez as the Director of Education Policy in her office, terminated Kirby's appointment, and approved the appointment of a new commissioner, Skip Meno, from New York.

According to Meno, his previous experience as a commissioner had alerted him to two major problems besetting urban schools. The first problem was "the stranglehold that urban school bureaucracies can place on school reform," and the second was "the tremendous void in inner-city schools concerning parental and community involvement." When he first came to Texas, he immediately began working to build coalitions with individuals and groups who could help him to deal with both issues. As part of that effort, he met with Texas IAF leaders and organizers in the fall of 1991. While he was curious about their work, he was also cautious. To allay his concerns, he made inquiries to assure that the foundation support behind the Texas IAF from donors such as the Rockefeller Foundation was genuine. He learned that Texas IAF politics were not partisan, but were driven by issues determined by the community's immediate needs. He came to understand that while churches provided the institutional base for the Texas IAF, they did not prescribe a religious agenda for schools. Next, he attended three Texas IAF public actions. The first assembly was held at Saint Mary Magdalen in San Antonio, the second was at Cristo Rey in Austin, and the third was at Holy Redeemer, again in San Antonio. At each assembly, Meno was impressed with the large community attendance, spirited participation, and quality of the local leadership.

As a result of the assemblies, Meno agreed to meet with Ernie Cortés and other Texas IAF leaders and organizers in February. Cortés then asked Meno to commit the TEA to develop a collaboration with nine schools with which the Texas IAF had cultivated special relationships. The TEA had established a precedent for coalitions with eighty "Partnership Schools" that dispensed funds for staff development and waivers to selected urban schools, but funds for the Partnership Schools had already been allocated. In addition, they were controlled by regional service centers throughout the state that were notorious bulwarks of the educational status quo. Meno abstained from making any commitments at the February meeting, but agreed to meet with Texas IAF leaders and organizers again to hammer out a solution.

In the following months, representatives from the TEA and the Texas IAF held a series of meetings to explore the possibility of a collaboration. One of Meno's concerns was the pioneering nature of the venture. "I wasn't aware of anything else like it on a statewide level, and I had talked to my fellow commissioners about it," he said. "While individual communities have done things like this, it's never before happened on a statewide level." The lack of precedent did not discourage Meno from moving ahead with the coalition with the Texas IAF. "You have to take risks in this business, or things will never get better," he said.

As a result of that enterprising attitude, Meno consolidated a relationship with the Texas IAF. On June 6, 1992, the TEA and the Texas IAF designated twenty-one schools in low-income neighborhoods as "Alliance Schools." Meno allocated $350,000 on a one-year, pilot basis from TEA funds for staff development to support the creation of a new network of schools in low-income areas that were willing to innovate and engage parents to enhance students' academic achievement. Schools accepted into that network would receive special waivers from the TEA to overcome impediments to innovation and could apply for up to ten thousand dollars in TEA funding for their campus. In exchange for TEA support, Texans would benefit by receiving the assistance of Texas IAF organizers in increasing parental and community participation in low-income neighborhood schools. "The Texas IAF had shown us that they had developed a methodology that worked to get inner-city parents involved in their kids' educations," Meno said, "and that is something we hadn't been able to do." Meno also hoped that the Texas IAF would teach low-income parents the citizenship skills needed to wrest their "fair share" of funding that was sometimes misappropriated by urban school bureaucracies.

The first twenty-one Alliance Schools sought to develop social capital through the one-on-one's, house meetings, Walks for Success, and parents' assemblies, which are the hallmarks of IAF educational organizing. As one might expect, many of the schools were in the poorest communities in Texas, ranging from urban African American neighborhoods in metropolitan areas like Dallas and Houston to Chicano communities in border cities such as El Paso, Laredo, Del Rio, and Brownsville. Each community was grappling with the traditional indicators of academic failure: high rates of low-achieving students, low test scores, and dropouts.

To bolster the morale of the new Alliance Schools, the TEA held a special "Capacity Enhancement Institute" on education in the summer of 1992. TEA educators and Texas IAF leaders and organizers presented workshops to principals and teachers which discussed the philosophies and strategies that could enhance the internal development and external community organizing work of the Alliance Schools. Yet more than transmitting the information in the presentations, the purpose of the enhancement institute was to bring the Alliance School educators to recognize common problems, to brainstorm possible solutions, and to raise expectations about the potential for academic excellence in each Alliance School and community.

The Alliance School initiative was a milestone in the Texas IAF's work in schools. School change can be easily blocked on many levels when it is undertaken in isolation from broader movements and coalitions which support reform. The individual parent, teacher, or even principal who attempts to bring about change faces a battery of bureaucratic restraints concerning innocuous issues, such as the selection of new tables for a school's cafeteria, and the vital educational matters which relate to instruction, curricula, and assessment. With the formalization of the relationship between the Texas IAF and the TEA, Texas IAF schools had new credibility in their districts. They had funds and they had waivers which would help them to cut through bureaucratic guidelines that strangle flexible and child-centered responses to young people's manifold needs. With these resources, the Texas IAF took a major step forward in its effort to create a civic community of parents and teachers at schools throughout the state which could share ideas, develop common strategies, fight for change, and evaluate successes and failures with one another. As a result of the Alliance School project, the many bureaucratic impediments which obstruct successful school reform could begin to be swept aside, and funds could facilitate the process of change.

While the Alliance School initiative represented a potentially great victory for the Texas IAF, it also entailed sizable risk. Until the Alliance Schools were launched, IAF organizations had focused their efforts on individual schools in working-class neighborhoods that rarely received much attention. If an effort resulted in failure, as occurred with the two elementary schools that Austin Interfaith worked in before turning to Zavala, the withdrawal of the organization was little noted. By developing a network of schools in low-income neighborhoods throughout the state, however, the Texas IAF took on a much higher level of risk.

Consider the vast array of challenges entailed in a project such as the Alliance Schools. The schools chosen were concentrated overwhelmingly in low-income communities in which many parents had little formal education and a significant number were functionally illiterate. Research on Texas schools shows that few highly qualified teachers choose to teach in low-income communities; the vast majority opt to work in higher paying and more affluent suburban communities. In many of the Mexican American communities, English is the children's second language; those in the Rio Grande Valley experience unusually high rates of student mobility due to the large number of families employed as migrant laborers. Even if the Texas IAF were able to work with the schools to raise their test scores out of the rock-bottom, low-performing status attributed to most of them by the TEA, their academic achievement was still likely to lag far behind the achievement levels in the state's most academically successful schools.[1]

In addition to the internal problems confronting each Alliance School community, the Texas IAF also had to attend to the complex political realities of different metropolitan areas. In a culturally diverse city like Houston, The Metropolitan Organization (TMO) could start off in a school like Jefferson Davis with an enterprising principal like Emily Cole, but for reasons of ethnic balance would need to identify schools in African American neighborhoods which might be working on their own agendas within the school and consider parental engagement to be important but not a real priority. Some of the early Alliance School principals were eager to take advantage of the TEA's money and waivers but either misunderstood the concept of parental engagement for school reform or never intended to cultivate it in the first place. Texas IAF organizations had to be patient and diplomatic in working with those principals, but they also had to establish frameworks of mutual accountability and terminate relationships with some of the first schools when it was clear that community engagement would remain more of a slogan than a reality in the relevant school and neighborhood settings.

In other schools, principals' understanding of the ideas behind the Alliance Schools appeared to be partial—sufficient to participate in the program to learn more and to raise funds, but insufficient to grasp just how radically Texas IAF organizers and leaders sought to make schools true community centers.

For Ernie Cortés, the Alliance School initiative had many complex facets, but none of them should dilute the focus on reflection and initiative at the heart of the enterprise. "Frankly, the main thing that we're after with this work is to encourage the different constituents—teachers, parents, principals—to experiment, to try new things," he said. "The new stuff that people might try out doesn't have to be perfect and probably won't be. But at least we'll be recognizing the gravity of the problem and understanding that it's not going to get better if we keep on doing what we've always been doing."

Of course, the readiness to experiment and the reality of urban school politics are such that numerous impediments often stand in the way of reform. Consider the following example. When Emily Cole tried to implement block scheduling at Davis High School, she quickly ran into bureaucratic barriers about contact hours with business partners in her school's vocational education program. Traditionally, vocational education students had a set number of weekly contact hours with employers whom they worked with from August to June of each academic year. With block scheduling, students would double their number of off-campus contact hours in one semester but not take any hours the next semester. The total number of contact hours was exactly the same from the vantage point of the whole academic year. Regrettably, that flexibility did not show up well on forms required by the TEA and the Houston Independent School District, which asked for weekly reports. In October 1992—just two months after block scheduling began—district officials notified Cole that her vocational education program was in jeopardy of losing its funding unless she returned to a traditional ten-month schedule.

Ordinarily, principals at this point enter into the educational equivalent of trench warfare. Principals can follow district mandates; they can attempt to massage the system, usually with the help of a friendly colleague at the central office; they can give up and return to the old system. Such trench warfare makes up a good deal of the daily work load of innovative educators throughout the United States. In this case, however, Cole referred the problem to TMO lead organizer Robert Rivera. Rivera called James Johnson, who oversaw the Alliance Schools project at the TEA, and two days later an official from the TEA visited Houston and clarified the matter with administrators in the Houston Independent School District. Block scheduling was preserved, the new structure for the vocational education program was approved, and the staff at Davis could focus on serving their students rather than battling the district bureaucracy.

The Davis example illuminates just how essential it is that urban schools have organized political allies that can provide innovative principals and teachers with protection from middle-level bureaucrats who attempt to stifle the process of change. Without TMO's intervention, Cole and her faculty could have lost not only their vocational education program but all of their block scheduling. Creative urban educators who attempt to engender change and growth in their schools without establishing strong links with community-based organizations may be courageous, but the evidence from the Alliance Schools suggests that they may also be somewhat foolhardy. Innovators need protection, and they need it from allies with organized political power.

There are many other examples of the ways in which the Alliance Schools' partnership with the Texas IAF has cut through bureaucratic obstacles and promoted a better educational climate for children. In January 1994, an assistant principal from an Alliance School in Fort Worth wanted to attend a lecture by Howard Gardner organized by the Texas IAF in Houston. Her central office superviser told her she could not attend the conference. ACT organizer Perry Perkins then called Superintendent Donald Roberts. The assistant principal was freed to attend the conference; using the knowledge which she acquired, she has coached her teachers to implement more differentiated instructional strategies for their pupils. Likewise, Jefferson Davis and Marshall Middle School were besieged by the graffiti of the North Side Central Posse, the area's largest gang, in the fall of 1994. The principals of both schools could not get the graffiti cleaned up through the regular administrative channels, but when Robert Rivera of TMO brought the matter to the attention of Houston superintendent Rodney Paige, the graffiti was gone in two days. Since that time, the district has maintained a punctual record in responding to problems with gang vandalism at Davis.

There were problems with the Alliance Schools, particularly in their first year. At that time they were funded through regional service centers of the TEA, which exemplified the worst features of the state's educational bureaucracy and demonstrated little commitment to helping a new, innovative program to succeed. By the spring of 1993 it was clear that in spite of Meno's support, the commissioner did not feel that he could move the bureaucracy to support the program or draw on his teacher education budget permanently to fund the Alliance Schools. Only one year into the project, the Texas IAF was going to have to find other ways to keep it afloat financially.

Texas IAF leaders and organizers decided to turn their political skills to advocacy on their own behalf in the Texas legislature. They asked State Senator Gonzalo Barrientos of Travis County to write an amendment to other education legislation to provide funding for the Alliance Schools, which he did, but the amendment was voted down by the Senate Education Committee. Alliance School leaders then wrote their own amendment to legislation under discussion in the House Education Committee. The house committee was chaired by Representative Libby Linebarger, whom the Texas IAF had supported in her efforts to redistribute school financing more equitably. Linebarger was able to guide the amendment through the house committee and the house, and it subsequently was approved by the senate. As a result, Alliance Schools were allocated two million dollars in state revenues for the next two years. Alliance Schools could now apply for up to fifteen thousand dollars per year, and the number of schools doubled and trebled in the second and third years, respectively. At the same time, the Alliance Schools were able to break their dependence on the regional service centers and were funded directly through the TEA.

Although the sums allocated to the Alliance Schools by the TEA are paltry given the magnitude of their problems, principals nonetheless credit them with promoting major changes within their schools. Odessa Ravin, Pamela Walls, and Richard Alvarado used their funds to train their faculty in the development of interdisciplinary curricula. Houston area Alliance Schools credit Rice University's Center for Education programs in mathematics and writing with deepening their faculty's content-area knowledge and expanding their repertoire of teaching methods, and the Rice University Summer School for Middle School and High School Students extended scholarships to thirty Alliance School students in the summer of 1994. Zavala's partnership with the

LBJ Science and Technology Center at the University of Texas has infused hitherto nonexistent vitality into its science education curriculum. Since research demonstrates a correlation between the extent of teachers' higher education and students' academic achievement, the investment in teachers' continued education is an essential contribution to an improved learning environment.[2]

Alliance Schools have generated social capital as they have mediated new relationships between parents, teachers, and clergy which focus increased adult attention on children. While the forging of new relationships within a community is an important step, the Alliance Schools have also developed social capital between schools as they chart their different paths to reform. Alliance School seminars have been a major fulcrum for sharing ideas and borrowing successful concepts among schools. The Texas IAF has aggressively recruited top-notch school reformers to educate its leaders and organizers. Cognitive psychologist Howard Gardner, school reformer Ted Sizer, and child psychologist James Comer have all shared their philosophies of education and policy recommendations in forums organized by the Texas IAF. The structure of those conferences is designed in such a manner that representatives from each Alliance School can question presenters on the basis of their immediate needs—a structure which enables a dynamic cross-fertilization of experiences and innovations among parents, teachers, and principals. By bringing in advocates of school change who have a larger agenda than the creation of smoothly operating "factory schools," the Texas IAF agitates its partners to pursue cultural change in schools rather than reinforcing the status quo.

Not all Alliance School conferences feature academic luminaries flown in from the nation's leading universities. Smaller conferences, organized just for Alliance School principals or education organizers and accompanied by readings about school organization, political power, and curriculum development, promote a broadening of participants' horizons concerning current developments in school reform and neighborhood revitalization. Principal Melvin Traylor of Franklin D. Roosevelt High School in an African American neighborhood in Dallas first learned about Jefferson Davis' experiments with block scheduling at an Alliance School conference organized by the Texas IAF. Roosevelt had been designated a low-performing school by the Texas Education Agency, and Traylor was eager to find a way to improve academic achievement. In February 1993 Traylor sent a team of Roosevelt students, faculty, parents, and counselors to Houston to learn more about block scheduling. When that team returned convinced that longer class periods would help Roosevelt, Traylor organized a series of assemblies for students, teachers, and parents to educate the community about the advantages and disadvantages of block scheduling. The Roosevelt community strongly backed the change to block scheduling. Traylor used his Alliance Schools waivers and funds to prepare his faculty for the transition to block scheduling in August 1993.

Roosevelt's transition to block scheduling was a turbulent one. The administrators at the Dallas Independent School District had a difficult time understanding the new scheduling arrangement, and many students and teachers began their fall semester confused about their course assignments. To make matters even worse, a student was shot and killed in the school by another student in the first weeks of school.

Traylor and the school's teachers, students, and parents struggled to regain their equilibrium. Leonora Friend, the educational organizer who had played a key role in organizing Morningside Middle School, transferred from ACT to Dallas Area Interfaith, which was still in the sponsoring committee phase of organization. Friend worked with everyone in the school, including teachers, custodians, parents, and students, to examine new ways of forging leadership and breaking through the structures which impeded students' success.

Eventually, the benefits of Dallas Area Interfaith's organizing and block scheduling kicked in. Attendance rose and Roosevelt received accolades from the school district and Commissioner Meno. Two years after the change to block scheduling, academic achievement climbed from a mere 13 percent of students passing all three sections of the state's standardized test to over 30 percent passing, lifting the school out of the state's low-performing list. In addition, Roosevelt began making important cultural changes in its organization, seeking to become more responsive to Hispanic students who had recently moved into the neighborhood by offering English as a Second Language classes and hiring Hispanic staff. None of the changes were easy, but they were all expedited by the fact that a network of Alliance Schools had laid the groundwork for Roosevelt to build upon successes, specifically those at Morningside and Davis.

Other Alliance Schools have also borrowed successful concepts from one another, drawing upon the dialogues furthered through participation in the Alliance Schools network. Marshall Middle School in Houston, a feeder pattern middle school for Davis High School, changed to block scheduling in January 1994, thereby creating a bridge between the middle and high school levels. Aoy, Roosevelt, and Alamo Elementary Schools in El Paso learned from the power of parental engagement exhibited at Ysleta and created parents' centers in the school on the Ysleta model. Virtually every elementary school in San Antonio has been in dialogue with others about the optimal manner to develop after-school programs, and many have taken their cues from the first twenty schools with programs, such as Herff Elementary. Following the example of COPS and Metro Alliance, Austin Interfaith persuaded Austin's city council to provide over twenty after-school programs in the city, which are now in more than one-third of Austin's elementary schools at a cost of over five hundred thousand dollars per year. Houston also has six free after-school programs based upon the San Antonio model. Dallas Area Interfaith has developed a job training program based on Project QUEST in San Antonio.

While Alliance Schools have borrowed concepts from one another, their greatest potential resides in the independence shown by each institution in evaluating one's own school, learning from others, and developing new programs to meet the needs of its own community. In the *Segundo Barrio* of El Paso, one of the country's poorest neighborhoods, Robert Hemphill, the principal of Alamo Elementary School, was impressed with the growing community engagement he saw at Ysleta Elementary in the early 1990s. Hemphill and his faculty worked with EPISO to begin house meetings with parents and quickly learned that many parents were upset with the school's suspension policy. Parents saw the policy as too strict, arbitrary, and destructive of their children's learning. Research indicated that the parents were right: the El Paso Independent School District had the highest suspension and expulsion rates of any of the more than one thousand school districts in the state. Determined to improve the situation, Hemphill and Alamo teachers worked with the parents to develop a new approach to discipline in which parents play a key role in counseling students. As a result of that policy, Alamo has eliminated suspensions and expulsions, and students have a supportive community network made up of their parents and neighbors which makes sure that they contribute to a positive learning environment in their school.

Alamo internalized the deepest lesson of this learning experience, which was not that it should borrow strategies from Ysleta Elementary but that it should open up its own lines of communication with Alamo parents and respond to parents' deepest concerns. In dialogue with the parents, Robert Hemphill and Alamo teachers learned that the parents felt that house meetings were so important that they should become a regular part of Alamo's culture rather than occasional catalysts for change. As a result, Hemphill and Alamo teachers began meeting with parents at their homes two or three times a week throughout the entire 1994–1995 school year. One of the first issues they brought up concerned academic achievement.

The parents of children at Alamo Elementary School knew that for many years, through some slow, opaque, and seemingly inexorable process, their children always ended up tracked to the lowest level when they arrived in middle school and high school. The parents refused to believe that that tracking was a reflection of students' natural abilities rather than the culture of their schools, but they were reticent to pin responsibility on their children's teachers and principal. Working with EPISO organizers and leaders, Alamo parents decided to address the problem of academic standards by looking neither to the "Essential Elements" mandated by the TEA nor to the curriculum experts of the El Paso Independent School District. They decided that they wanted to play a major role in setting the curriculum standards for the school themselves. In a series of house meetings, parents discussed what they wanted their children to know at the end of each grade level. Robert Hemphill, Alamo teachers and staff, and EPISO leaders and organizers attended the meetings. The parents spoke in Spanish with one another about their desires for their children to learn to read, write, and understand the world about them. Hemphill and the teachers dedicated themselves to listening and construed their role as participating in the conversations but not leading them. The parents would need time and a supportive environment to develop their leadership and to establish those curricular goals which most deeply emanated from their own thoughts and experiences.

What kinds of curricular themes did the parents identify? Parents wanted their children to be literate and skilled in arithmetic, science, and social studies. As the conversations evolved, there was an almost perfect overlapping between the parents' curriculum and that which traditionally was taught at Alamo. Yet simply to focus on the content of

the curriculum is to miss the point. There is a world of difference between following a curriculum established by the TEA and a curriculum
established by parents and teachers working together. The first curriculum carries no relationship to the community, whereas the second has
emerged from conversations and relationships; the first is delegated,
whereas the second is a creative act, based in democratic localist educational traditions, which firmly and explicitly articulates the community's aspirations for its children.

At Alamo Elementary School, the curriculum taught in the school is
in the process of becoming fully transparent to the community. As
parents learn what is taught at each grade level, their ability to engage children around curricular issues at home expands. Teachers feel
freer—not more constrained—because they can engage the parents to
help them to shape lesson plans and to support the curriculum at home.
The opposition between school culture and neighborhood culture that
exists in many neighborhoods has diminished, and has been replaced by
a constant exchange of ideas and proposals about ways to improve
education.

There are many schools all over Texas which are not formally part of
the Alliance Schools but have been stimulated by the process of change
they see taking place in schools with increased parental engagement.
Yet just as the process of change was truly becoming synergistic, many
parents and teachers feared that their victories were all for naught when
a Republican majority swept control of the Texas legislature in November 1994. George W. Bush, the son of the former president, was elected
governor, and after he took office in January 1995, Bush quickly terminated Skip Meno's position as commissioner of the TEA. Supporters of
the Alliance Schools anticipated that they were in for a major political
battle and expected that the schools would be vulnerable to funding cuts
promised by the Republicans as part of a pledge for fiscal responsibility.

The Texas IAF was determined to fight to protect, and, if possible, to
expand the Alliance Schools. "We will fight all of the efforts to balance the
budget on the backs of our low-income children," Oralia Garza de Cortés
of Austin Interfaith pledged. Leaders such as Toña Vasquez, Father John
Korscmar, Richard Alvarado, and Emily Cole testified before the Senate
Education Committee. To their surprise and delight, they won the support of Republican Senator Bill Ratliff, the powerful and frugal committee chair. Ratliff and his colleagues liked the Alliance Schools' emphasis

on increased parental engagement, collaborative approaches to neighborhood revitalization, and improved academic achievement. They also liked the wording of the proposed legislation written by Texas IAF organizers, which did not refer specifically to the Texas IAF or Alliance Schools, but simply to a pool of money which could be approved for any "community-based organizations" that applied for them. Ratliff and his colleagues appeared to be ready to raise the revenues allocated for this purpose to ten million dollars for the 1995–1997 school years.

Before the final vote was called, however, Ratliff and his colleagues heard strong attacks against allocating ten million dollars to the fund. The opposition came neither from fiscal conservatives nor from liberals concerned about the separation of church and state; rather, the superintendents of the largest school districts in the state opposed the rise in funding. The superintendents objected because conservatives on the Appropriations Committee had determined that money for schools in collaboration with community-based organizations would be withdrawn from schools' compensatory education funds, which the large districts traditionally have controlled. In spite of the fact that Texas allocates close to one billion dollars a year to compensatory education, and in spite of the fact that virtually all of the Alliance Schools are in high-poverty areas, the superintendents wanted to keep discretionary control of that funding in their own hands.

Instead of ten million dollars, the Texas legislature allocated five million dollars to the fund available to community organizations over a two-year period—less than they had asked for, but still an increase of more than 100 percent over previous funding. Neither Republicans nor Democrats waged any kind of ideological attack on the Alliance Schools or the Texas IAF. Individual schools were able to apply for grants of up to fifty thousand dollars in 1996 and 1997, and the number of Alliance Schools is anticipated to treble to over two hundred schools.

Although the open-ended wording probably helped to raise the five million dollars, it naturally raised problems for the Texas IAF. For although "community-based organizations" has a nice ring to it, it is so vague that virtually any entity could proclaim itself to be a community-based organization. By the end of 1995, the TEA had even received applications for school programs which listed large corporations such as General Dynamics as "community-based organizations"! In spite of such idiosyncratic definitions, TEA officials estimate that over two-thirds of the applications received and approved by January 1996 concerned the Alliance Schools.

In August 1996, test score results for Texas' schools were published by the Texas Education Agency (see Table 1). If one investigates the percentage of students who passed all three sections (reading, writing, and math) of the Texas Assessment of Academic Skills test, one finds a number of trends in the twenty-two schools which have been with the Alliance Schools network from 1993 to 1996 and which have had their students take the TAAS (some elementary schools, like Herff, teach only grades K–2, and the TAAS begins with third grade).

Table 1

Percentages of Students Passing All Three Sections of the Texas Assessment of Academic Standards for Selected Alliance Schools, 1993–1996

	1993	1994	1995	1996
I. Fourth Graders				
Austin				
Becker	33	54	40	81
Zavala	26	32	63	53
Brownsville				
Canales	23	39	48	53
Dallas				
Harlee	0	17	18	48
Knight	32	58	61	49
El Paso				
Alamo	18	26	26	46
Ysleta	18	43	43	38
Fort Worth				
Briscoe	9	24	28	19
Carroll Peak	25	15	32	17
Morningside	45	54	63	63
San Antonio				
Beacon Hill	21	31	28	46
Flanders	14	28	29	29
Neal	16	33	20	41
Smith	21	16	26	37
Texas State Average	46	54	64	66
Disadvantaged Students	31	40	49	54
Alliance School Average	21.5	33.6	37.5	44.3

Before the data are considered, some contextual information is important. First, the TAAS test was first implemented in 1990, but Texas Commissioner of Education Skip Meno changed the design of the test, the test-taking pupils, and the time of year the test was to be taken after he took office in 1992. As a result, TAAS scores from 1990 to 1992 and from 1993 to 1996 cannot be compared.

Second, one cannot know to what degree community-based organizations and the Alliance Schools network operate as an independent variable in the data. In the case of Morningside Middle School and Jefferson Davis High School, for example, it may be the case that the Car-

Table 1

(Continued)

II. Eighth Graders	1993	1994	1995	1996
Fort Bend				
Missouri City	29	28	28	32
Fort Worth				
Elder	32	41	33	34
Morningside	29	28	33	34
Houston				
Hogg	24	29	17	31
Pharr-San Juan-Alamo				
Alamo	29	35	31	50
Texas State Average	45	49	50	58
Disadvantaged Students	25	31	31	41
Alliance School Average	28.6	32.2	28.4	36.2
III. Tenth Graders				
Dallas				
Roosevelt	17	14	29	63
Houston				
Jefferson Davis	28	28	24	42
Jack Yates	22	14	29	63
Texas State Average	51	52	54	60
Disadvantaged Students	31	33	35	42
Alliance School Average	22.3	22	23.3	42.3

negie Schools initiative and the Tenneco Presidential Scholarships account for test score results more than the Alliance School partnerships with ACT and TMO. Self-selection processes might also play a role in influencing test score results, such as when bright students elect to attend an improving neighborhood school rather than commute across town to a magnet school with high academic standards. One might also expect that test scores would rise as teachers and administrators become more deliberate about teaching to the test.

In December 1994, a court order required the Texas Education Agency to make public TAAS tests after they have been administered each year. Many principals throughout the state seized on the tests and used them as a template for restructuring their schools' curricula around test-taking skills. Under these circumstances, it would be astonishing if many schools did not register gains in achievement on the TAAS. Finally, in analyzing the test scores, we are working with small sample sizes. Differences in achievement should be taken as indications rather than as generalizations.

Thus there are many limitations on the test scores. Nonetheless, they do provide one resource for attempting to gauge academic progress. Recognizing the above qualifications, one may explore the TAAS results to ascertain if they provide clues about the development of the Alliance Schools.

A number of intriguing findings are revealed in the test score data. To commence with the fourth graders, one notes that the gains of Alliance Schools are consistent with percentage gains for average Texas fourth graders and average disadvantaged students. From 1993 to 1996, Texas fourth graders' scores rose an average of 20 percent, disadvantaged students' scores rose an average of 23 percent, and the scores of fourth-grade students in Alliance Schools rose an average of 23 percent as well. (Disadvantaged students are defined as those who are eligible for free or reduced-price meals.) The Alliance Schools' results are far below those of Texas students in general and close to ten points below those of disadvantaged fourth-grade students; there is still plenty of room for progress. As an aggregate, however, the schools are moving in the right direction, and with the exceptions of Carroll Peake and Briscoe in Fort Worth, have emerged from the rock-bottom achievement which led them to join the Alliance Schools in the first place.

Eighth-grade scores reveal a more troubled picture. Although the Alliance Schools all show some progress, they have not kept up with rises in test scores for both Texas students in general and disadvantaged students as a cohort. For all Texas eighth graders, scores rose an average of 13 percent from 1993 to 1996, and for disadvantaged students they rose an average of 16 percent. But for the Alliance School eighth graders, the gain was less than 8 percent.

What might account for the different rates of progress between the elementary and middle schools that are in the Alliance School network? Although one cannot know for certain, one can speculate that it is much harder to capitalize on the kind of parental engagement that is the cornerstone of IAF organizing in middle schools. For many parents, the transition from one primary teacher to a cluster of different teachers for their child is confusing, and the child's achievements become more difficult to monitor. Academic subject matter also becomes more complex, which makes it more difficult for parents with little education to provide the kind of guidance and tutoring that is possible for elementary school children. Young adolescents also generally show more reluctance to see their parents in school, as they struggle to develop their independence and strong peer networks. Middle schools can experience dramatic change, as Morningside demonstrated in 1988, but it may be more difficult to sustain that change over years than it would be in an elementary school.

How have the three high schools fared that have been Alliance Schools since 1993? The test scores of Jefferson Davis in Houston and Roosevelt in Dallas were relatively stagnant until 1996. Both schools were stuck on the Texas Education Agency's list of low-performing schools, and in spite of tenacious struggles to increase parental and community engagement, neither seemed to have nourished the kinds of cognitive skills that would reflect well on standardized tests. The breakthrough came in 1996, when each school had the largest gains in their districts at the high school level—a striking achievement for schools that had been seeking to demonstrate academic improvement over many years.

What were the factors that promoted the leap in scores at Davis and Roosevelt? Davis' achievement was already described in chapter four; it was catalyzed by an unusual matrix of community support, innovative curricular and scheduling reforms, and an increasingly academic focus in the school. Roosevelt in many ways followed Davis' lead. Principal Melvin Traylor took his first risk with the Alliance School network when he borrowed the concept of block scheduling from Davis in 1993. Two years later the scores at Roosevelt had more than doubled, but Roosevelt was still on the TEA's list of low-performing schools. Working with Dallas Area Interfaith, Traylor and his colleagues decided that they were ready to take additional risks. Leonora Friend worked around the clock, setting up core teams of parents, teachers, and community leaders to assess the situation at Roosevelt and to devise a school improvement plan with two foci: to increase parental engagement and to get Roosevelt off the list of low-performing schools.

Of the different core teams that Friend organized, the most difficult was the parents' team. The reason was not the parents' attendance; over forty parents regularly came to weekly meetings to address the ongoing challenges of the school. The problem was much more the fragmentation of parents, based on their long-standing interests. Friend had to train the parents to help them to expand their horizons beyond the success of the band, the football team, or other facets of school life to which the parents had traditionally devoted their energies. It became Friend's task to embolden the parents to inquire after their children's academic success and to establish an atmosphere of high expectations and supportive encouragement.

Throughout the 1995–1996 school year, Roosevelt parents and teachers conducted neighborhood walks and held special tutoring sessions for students over lunch, after school, and on Saturdays. Reverend David Henderson of the Greater Mount Pleasant Baptist Church and Brother Cephus Northcutt of the Cedar Crest Church of Christ both used their pulpits on Sunday mornings to urge parents to become engaged in their children's education. "We did what site-based management is supposed to do, but almost never really does," Friend recalled. "We created collective ownership between parents, teachers, and community leaders, and that feeling of working together gave people a new sense of confidence." Dallas Area Interfaith's concerted organizing in the Oak Cliff neighborhood and the energetic recruitment of parents and teachers into the spirit of the Alliance School collaborative appear to have made a major difference in academic achievement in a single year.

Jack Yates, the lone high school in the Alliance School network which has made no progress for four years, has been unable to capitalize on the network for a multitude of reasons. Perhaps the major problem at Yates has been administrative instability; Yates has had three different principals from 1993 to 1996. Each of the principals has been more preoccupied with trying to stabilize his or her authority in the school than with empowering parents to engage in school and community development. TMO organizers indicate that crime has been a greater concern than school improvement among member churches in the Third Ward, and that school reform subsequently has taken a lower priority in terms of neighborhood organizing. The fact that TMO organizer Robert Rivera himself grew up on Houston's Near North Side, and that Davis was especially responsive to the Alliance School concept, also probably played roles in directing TMO's school reform efforts to Davis rather than to Yates. Yates is still a member of the Alliance School network, but the school needs an instructional leader who is ready to take risks to involve the community to the same degree evinced by Davis and Roosevelt.

The test scores from Davis and Roosevelt do indicate that gains in academic progress can be garnered by Alliance Schools that are high schools, but the delayed effect from organizing suggests that the process of school improvement is on the whole more difficult and more in need of multifaceted collaboratives than is the case at the elementary school level. High school students come from a wider, more geographically dispersed catchment area; peer culture often discourages parental engagement; impediments to academic achievement, from pregnancy to gang membership, threaten to subvert a focus on one's studies. The lesson from Davis and Roosevelt would appear to be that change is possible, but that it must be undergirded by patience and tenacity, for it is not likely to come quickly.

If one compares Black and Hispanic achievement in the Alliance Schools, the data show that Hispanics made greater gains than Blacks until the high school level. Ten of the elementary schools are predominantly Hispanic and four are predominantly Black. The Hispanic schools gained a mean of 25.1 points on the TAAS from 1993 to 1996, but the four predominantly Black schools gained only 16.75 points. Although the data are less reliable for secondary schools because of our small sample, the four predominantly Hispanic schools gained 8.25 points and Morningside, the sole predominantly Black middle school, gained only 5 points in the same period. At the high school level, Yates' scores stagnated while Roosevelt's skyrocketed 46 points, with Davis in between with a 14-point gain.

The differences between Black and Hispanic achievement in the Alliance Schools are striking, but appear to have little to do with Alliance

Schools. Hispanics scored higher than Blacks on the reading, writing, and mathematics tests of the TAAS at the fourth- and eighth-grade level each year the test has been given since 1993. In general, Hispanics have also received higher scores at the tenth-grade level, surpassed by Blacks by a slim margin only in writing in 1995 and reading in 1996. Overall, the greater Hispanic gains reflect well-established statewide trends.

Even though the Alliance Schools have made headway in many areas, they have not provided a "magic bullet" solution to the myriad problems of school reform in low-income communities. Some schools, such as Briscoe, Carroll Peak, and Yates, have shown little or no progress on their test scores since joining the network; the middle schools have posted gains, but they have not kept up with the percentage of gains either for all students or for disadvantaged students in Texas; even those schools which have shown improvement may have benefited most from testing artifacts, which we have no controls for. Yet, on the other hand, as the case studies demonstrate, a host of teachers, parents, administrators, and community leaders credit the Alliance School network with revitalizing their schools and neighborhoods, and test scores hardly provide a comprehensive measure for assessing cognitive development or community improvement. Entirely left out of any analysis which relies only on test scores are the wide range of health, safety, housing, and employment issues which the Texas IAF has addressed in and around low-income neighborhoods and which do not directly translate into test score results. Further explorations in community engagement and school improvement will be necessary to capture the potential of low-income youth to succeed academically in the Alliance School network. At this juncture, it is important that we shift our attention to examine in greater detail the many factors that have obstructed and can further impede school improvement in the Alliance Schools.

III
Analysis and Critique

9

Resistance to Change

The process of changing school cultures is developmental and requires a fortuitous interplay of many social forces and talented leaders if it is to be successful. Most urban school cultures are resistant to change, even when there is widespread recognition that children are poorly served under current conditions—partially because fear is more likely to breed defensiveness and rigidity than to foster risk-taking behaviors. It is therefore crucial to reflect upon the various factors that can undermine and prevent the process of cultural change promoted by Texas IAF organizations. Essentially, three factors—social actors, community problems, and the organization of the school—can play important roles in arresting the process of change.

The major social actor who determines whether parental engagement and school change will be successful for an Alliance School is the principal. Consequently, one of the biggest problems for Texas IAF leaders and organizers involves gauging whether principals truly wish to engage parents in the heart of the school, or whether, when the moment of reckoning arrives, principals will delegate tasks to parents which help with lunchroom supervision or shelving library books but which make no use of their knowledge of their children and their community. The grievance that surfaces most frequently for Texas IAF leaders and organizers is that principals state in advance that they want high community engagement in their schools but undermine it when Texas IAF leaders and organizers actually bring the parents to the school. Although some of that resistance is deliberate, much of it appears to be an almost unconscious extension of principals' everyday understandings of how they should exercise their authority and how schools should be run. It takes talented organizing and patience to help urban principals to imagine alternative forms of school organization and to initiate the innovations that might produce the rises in academic achievement they would like to create.

What are some of the ways in which principals can prevent school change? Some principals have scheduled meetings for faculty at times that conflict with meetings the parents have established to further collaboration with the school. Others have expressed interest in parental concerns but have provided no follow-through on grievances expressed by parents on surveys collected during a Walk for Success. Sometimes the principals have not provided the supportive work that can create positive results from a Walk for Success. Robert Rivera stated that one Walk for Success in Houston failed utterly because the school's principal had made no effort to confirm his students' addresses in the community. Because the mobility rate in the community was so high, more than half of the walkers visited homes where the high school's freshmen no longer resided.

School and community change can easily be undercut through seemingly innocuous acts in which principals break the momentum for reform. One principal sent representatives to key decision-making meetings with Texas IAF organizers and public officials, yet would not empower the representatives to make decisions about programs badly needed by their children. As a result, the implementation of the programs was stalled. A principal at an Alliance School in Houston prevented the creation of an academic after-school program in her school, even though the school district and city council assumed all of the costs. She argued that instead of the programs being housed in her large middle school, they should be based in local Black Baptist churches. These churches, however, were not large enough to accommodate the children; nor could they afford the insurance to cover liability in the event of accidents. The IAF organizer who worked with the school felt that the principal simply did not want to stay on her campus into the late afternoon and did not want to take on additional responsibilities, even when an after-school program would have met with overwhelming community support and would have attended to vital needs of the children. By throwing up such barriers to reform, principals thwart the creation of programs that can give urban youth alternatives to the violence which characterizes street life in many urban neighborhoods.

Perhaps the most noteworthy case of a principal creating an obstacle to reform occurred in Austin in the fall of 1994. Austin Interfaith had obtained funding for after-school programs for half of the city's elementary school children, but one principal objected to the mediating role that Austin Interfaith played in the distribution of funds. He went before the Austin School Board, accused the Texas IAF organization of bringing illegitimate political pressure based in religious institutions to the public school arena, and argued against the disbursement of money to the after-school program. At that point, far too many parents, teachers, and clergy wanted the after-school program to let this principal stop Austin Interfaith's success, but a city that was less well organized could have lost the program as the result of his opposition.

Why would principals resist parental engagement in their schools? For one thing, untrained parents who bring a host of personal and social problems to the school clearly can destabilize the learning process. One aggressive, vocal parent who demands special favors for his or her child or is an outspoken but uninformed critic of sound educational practices can compel an already overworked teacher or principal to lose sight of the children while attending to the parent's demands. At Morningside, some of the first parents to become involved hit children or verbally abused them when the children were undisciplined. Others took Odessa Ravin's welcoming attitude as a sign of weakness and sought special privileges for themselves. At Ysleta, one parent sought to take over the parents' center and made other parents feel as if they were intruding into her domain. In these circumstances, schools need to provide training for parents to curtail social decapitalization and to teach them appropriate ways to develop their educational role in the school.

Another reason that principals resist parental engagement is because organized parents can threaten their job security. In the spring of 1994, a Mexican American parishioner from Resurrection Catholic Church in Houston's Fifth Ward asked TMO lead organizer Robert Rivera if he would help to get her child transferred out of Wheatley High School. Although Wheatley had graduated some of Houston's strongest African American leaders, such as Barbara Jordan and Mickey Leland, parents at Wheatley kept hearing from their children that the school had terrible problems with disorganization and youth gangs. Upon reviewing the situation with Superintendent Frank Petruzielo of the Houston Independent School District, Rivera was asked to lead a TMO delegation in assessing the school. The parents found an institution in which no textbooks had been issued during the entire year, hallways were unlit in the middle of the day, and over two-thirds of the eighteen hundred students who had entered Wheatley in August of 1993 had either transferred out or dropped out. "It was like a ghost town," Rivera recalled. "If you went in the afternoon you just didn't see any kids at all." Instruction consisted almost entirely of fill-in-the-blank worksheets and was given at an insultingly remedial level. TMO issued ten recommendations for improving low-performing schools such as Wheatley, and as a result of its mobilization of the community, Wheatley's principal was replaced in the summer of 1994. The school is now struggling to return it to its former stature.

Wheatley was an extreme case, but extreme cases are relatively common in urban public schools. A similar incident occurred at Guillen Junior High School in El Paso in the spring of 1995. Just like Wheatley, Guillen had developed into more of a holding institution than a school; roughly one-third of its seventh graders and eighth graders flunked and the school led the district in the number of disciplinary suspensions. In the Guillen case, however, three of the elementary schools which sent children on to Guillen were Alliance Schools. Parents from Aoy, Roosevelt, and Alamo elementary schools had become accustomed to high levels of engagement in their children's education and unusually intensive house meetings in the community. When those Alliance School parents moved from the supportive environment that they had hitherto experienced at the elementary school level to the bureaucratic and punitive atmosphere at Guillen Junior High School, they began sharing their experiences with one another at house meetings and became increasingly angry at the maltreatment of their children. Lili Escobedo, the mother of a special education student, was particularly upset with the abusive behavior that her son Cristian reported to her about teachers at Guillen. Escobedo and other parents informed the school board and Superintendent Stan Paz of their grievances, and the district conducted a study of Guillen which validated their concerns. Paz was deeply shaken by the parents' reports of their children's experiences and the parents were impressed by his sincerity and commitment to change. In the summer of 1995, Paz transferred the principal out of Guillen and told all of the teachers that they would need to reapply for their positions.

Parents from the Alliance Schools in the *Segundo Barrio* played a major role in interviewing applicants for the position of principal at the middle school. After many hours of work, they hired Tonie Kreye, who had grown up in the neighborhood herself and attended all three of its elementary schools, which are now Alliance Schools. Kreye rehired less than a third of all of the teachers for their positions, created advisory periods and block scheduling, designed a new uniform policy which undermines the practice of wearing clothes as an expression of gang loyalty, and began a new tutorial program using high school students from the neighborhood. Alamo Elementary School principal Robert Hemphill couldn't be happier about the transformation. "We used to have students from the middle school coming to our playgrounds and parks in the middle of the day and hanging around because they'd been suspended," he said. "We don't see that anymore."

The Guillen case is illuminating because it illustrates that once parents are mobilized and understand that their children's school *can* be responsive to the community, parents can transfer the advocacy skills that they learned on the elementary school level to a troubled middle school. Guillen demonstrates that a gradual, evolutionary approach to school transformation at the secondary school level can be initiated by helping low-income parents to develop their advocacy skills while their children are at the elementary level. The skills developed can have a ripple effect that spreads upward through a feeder pattern. Another aspect of the Guillen case that is striking is that the parents in the *Segundo Barrio* exercised their advocacy at Guillen without any collaboration from EPISO. The training they had received from EPISO organizers and leaders at the elementary school level enabled them to develop the initiative and the confidence to radically transform a school that was poorly serving their children.

At Wheatley and Guillen, the internal dysfunction of the schools compelled superintendents to take strong action against ineffective principals on behalf of the children who were poorly served by them. Yet it is not always the case that low-income parents target troubled schools and their leaders accurately; principals as committed and talented as Odessa Ravin have experienced challenges from parents. Shortly after Ravin became principal at Morningside, one mother became convinced that Ravin was harboring vast sums of money which were not used to benefit the children. The parent was vocal in her conviction and began breaking down the trust that Ravin had established with the community. Rather than engage in acrimonious debate with the parent, or obfuscate the issue with bureaucratic jargon, Ravin took a calculated risk and offered to share all of the information she had about the school's fiscal situation with the parent. Ravin then invited the parent to attend the annual school board meeting in which Morningside's budget was reviewed. In the PTA meeting following that school board meeting, the parent stood up, publicly apologized for her suspicions about Ravin, and told other parents that they all needed to help the school by raising additional revenues for it. Innovative principals need to understand that low-income parents may respond to their new openness with suspicion, and that the kinds of sustained engagement with parents demonstrated by Ravin can help to consolidate the trust which is an indispensable component of social capital.

Principals can experience difficulties with parents even when the parents are not challenging them directly. Parents in one Alliance School became upset with their superintendent after he waffled back and forth about promising them a new school building. When the parents publicly challenged the superintendent, he decided to take out his frustration on the principal directly after the meeting. "Don't you ever let your parents talk to me like that again!" he told the startled principal. Subsequent discussions helped to depolarize the situation, but for a brief period the principal became the scapegoat of an administrator who was incapable of dealing with a community of newly empowered parents.

It is impossible to overestimate the role of the principal in accelerating or blocking change. At the same time, it is important to recognize that teachers also can resist change in powerful ways. Even under the best of circumstances, teaching is a complex, unpredictable, and deeply emotive experience. The craft of teaching has been described as "the educational equivalent of whitewater rafting"; it is "marked by the absence of concrete models for emulation, unclear lines of influence, multiple and controversial criteria, ambiguity about assessment timing, and instability in the product." Balancing the needs of children with widely disparate learning styles, abilities, and mother tongues; following the shifting guidelines of administrators; and interacting with a wide array of constituents in the form of parents and community members, even the best teachers are fully challenged by the dynamic circumstances of their work. In Philip Jackson's felicitous phrase, teachers are "gladiators of ambiguity," professionals who have to negotiate a dizzying array of issues to enhance their students' personal growth and academic achievement.[1]

Most new teachers take several years to control and regulate the ever-present threat of chaos entailed in working with large numbers of children and adolescents. Once teachers have found those techniques which work best for them, the techniques tend to coalesce into more or less obdurate forms of practice. Urban teachers follow this pattern just as much as suburban teachers or professors in universities. Transforming the nature of teaching by encouraging parental engagement, developing team-teaching strategies and advisory periods, and other forms of social capitalization can provoke resistance from urban teachers who have become comfortable with the received organization of the school, however dysfunctional it may appear to outsiders. Teachers in urban schools need concentrated training to acquire effective ways of dealing with politically empowered parents, clergy who visit their classrooms, and school-specific innovations which can build community and social capital in their workplace.

Virtually all of the principals and parents who have sought to create a new civic culture in their schools and communities have faced some opposition from teachers. Older teachers generally find it harder to change and are more resistant. In one extreme case, a teacher threatened to sue her district when her Alliance School principal suggested that she would be more comfortable teaching in a traditional school with less community engagement; the superintendent responded to the threat by asking the principal if she herself would be willing to transfer to another school. While the principal remained in her position, so did the teacher, and their tense relationship has added another challenge to a community struggling to develop a new relationship of civic engagement in the school. In less polarized examples, teachers have found subtle ways of quietly discouraging parents from visiting in their classrooms or have suggested to younger teachers that engaging the community constitutes more of a distraction to education than an enrichment.

Even though there are problems with rallying teacher engagement with the community, the case studies presented here suggest that the most tenacious opposition to changing the culture of schools does not come from teachers. If principals are willing to model calculated risk taking which promotes parental engagement, the tendency is for teachers to follow, and to find new levels of dedication and enthusiasm for their work. Innovative principals have found ways to help teachers to overcome their fears and to begin a process of reconceptualizing their professions to engage the community. Teacher education workshops which provide teachers with new ways to design curricula and to work on teams can provide part of the answer. Just as house meetings enable parents to overcome their isolation from one another and to identify areas of common concern, so can a team structure facilitate greater teacher trust and collaboration. For this reason, virtually all of the Alliance Schools have begun a process of greater teacher collaboration through new programs which emphasize team teaching or block scheduling.

The most effective means of helping veteran teachers in the Alliance Schools to overcome their resistance to change has come not through abstract discussions in seminars or workshops but through the experience of actually participating in Walks for Success and house meetings. When teachers observe the responsiveness of communities and recognize that house meetings can enhance relationships of trust and reciprocity with parents, they appear more able to appreciate the special needs of an individual family or child and to be more flexible in rethinking the relationship between the school's curriculum and the social realities of the neighborhood. Many Alliance School teachers have stated that a good house meeting, introduced to the teacher as an invitation to get to know the community, goes a lot further than exhortations in workshops for teachers to take the initiative to reach out to the community.

Some teachers have voiced fears that their involvement in community-based organizations could be seen as a threat to their school districts and could result in punitive action which could jeapordize their jobs. On the whole, such fears appear to be overstated, but examples of district reprisals have occurred, especially when an IAF organization has weak roots in the community. Manuela Cadena, now an educational organizer with EPISO, taught elementary school for many years in Fort Hancock in Hudspeth County in West Texas in the 1980s. When she learned that the state was planning on leasing state lands in her community to dump nuclear waste and sludge from New York City, she contacted EPISO and became an outspoken leader against the waste storage program. Cadena was successful in keeping the waste out of her home community, where her parents lived. Shortly after the victory, however, Cadena's position in the school was terminated. Although one cannot be certain, Cadena feels strongly that her activism cost her her job. She subsequently relocated to El Paso, where she now organizes low-income parents in Alliance Schools in the *Segundo Barrio*. Cadena's work inspires parents through her tenacious commitment to protect their community, but her story may also intimidate teachers who are already afraid of reprisals.

It is imperative to recognize that resistance to changing the culture of an Alliance School does not stem just from stubborn principals or teachers but can also come from parents. Their resistance can take many forms, of which four are the most salient. First, many low-income parents are preoccupied with personal and social issues which block their engagement in schools. Some parents feel ashamed of their lack of academic skills, had terrible experiences in schools themselves, and cannot imagine wanting to discuss their child's learning with a teacher or a principal. They are aware of their lack of education and fear that they will be stigmatized or humiliated in the school. Other parents are confident about their own skills but do not believe that it is their responsibility to attend to their child's academic success; they have delegated that task to the school to accomplish on its own. Many Spanish-speaking parents in Texas are frustrated by their lack of English proficiency and do not feel the confidence to challenge inappropriate or ineffective instruction of their children by teachers.

A second form of opposition to greater parental engagement can come from parents who have found ways to develop a close relationship with a principal and seek to use that to secure special individual favors for their children. Such parents can be threatened when community-based organizations bring more parents into the school and ask them to think about the needs of all of the children rather than just their own. This is especially true because part of the process of mobilizing a community in the IAF tradition is to find community leaders who are not happy with public institutions but feel angry and shut out from them. Parents who have enjoyed privileged relationships with principals can feel that their special status in the school is threatened when new parents become involved who are less happy with the ways in which relationships traditionally have been organized.

Third, some parents fear that the academic goals of the school will be displaced as teachers and parents focus increasing amounts of their attention on the needs of adults and the community. Those fears can have a basis in reality. Some Alliance School principals have found that as soon as they established an open-door policy for parents, it became much more difficult for them to maintain their visibility in the important public spaces of their school; they were too preoccupied with conversing with parents one-on-one in their offices. Other principals have become so enthusiastic about their new ties to the community that they have neglected their responsibility to supervise and improve teachers' instruction. At issue here are important questions of balance. Principals need to play many roles, and engaging the community should always be seen as a way of enhancing children's education rather than a preferential option for those who have grown tired of classrooms and corridors. Principals need guidance and support in developing social capital between the school and the community as they go through their own challenging developmental process of growth and change.

A fourth, particularly pernicious form of opposition to increased parental engagement can come from husbands who resent their wives' enhanced leadership and self-confidence. Husbands who insist upon their uncompromised authority in the household have felt threatened by their wives' meetings with public officials, their growing assertiveness at school board meetings, and their coverage by local media as they become community leaders. "Sometimes it feels like just when we get the mothers organized, they're forced to make really painful decisions between choosing their new public selves or their marriages," Elsy Fierro-Suttmiller of EPISO said. One Texas IAF organizer described a mother whose husband resented her growing leadership in spite of the fact that it was benefiting their children. On one occasion, the woman told her husband that she was going grocery shopping; she took care of a few errands quickly and then went to make a key presentation at an accountability session. That mother had the courage to ask important questions of public officials in front of hundreds of people, but all the while she was afraid that the media would take pictures of her, her husband would learn of her participation, and he would subsequently beat her. Real and deep problems exist not only between schools and communities, but also within communities and within families themselves. Until those problems are confronted and eradicated, parental engagement in urban public schools will never be able to reach its full potential.

Although they are not usually considered to be a part of the problem, it is worth noting that most clergy, through their disengagement from schools, perpetuate intolerable conditions. Even within the Alliance Schools, educators have expressed disappointment with the restricted role that many clergy choose to play in the schools. "Where are the priests? Where are the ministers?" one Alliance School principal asked.

"When we have our assemblies, they're not there." The clergy in the Morningside neighborhood of Fort Worth and on the East Side of Austin demonstrated that a concerted effort by religious and lay leaders can help to transform and improve urban public schools. Still, too many clergy are only involved in schools in an episodic, hit-or-miss fashion which does not cultivate the textured relationships between religious institutions and public schools that develop social capital. On the other hand, it is truly impressive that Catholic clergy in San Antonio, which has the highest parochial school enrollment in the nation, have played such a strong role in the Alliance Schools.[2]

Even though Texas IAF leaders and organizers have played essential and generally positive roles in promoting school change, they are of course fallible human beings, who have at times inadvertently undercut the process of changing school cultures. Occasionally, for example, organizers have violated the "iron rule" and maintained control of a program when parents were capable of doing so on their own. At other times, they have dropped into the background prematurely when local leadership has not matured sufficiently to organize parents. They have also overstepped their boundaries and approached principals in a didactic manner which promoted defensiveness rather than experimentation.

The first educational organizer at Morningside Middle School became deeply involved in an after-school program she established, primarily because she loved working with the children. Because she was more focused on serving the children than developing leadership skills in the parents, the program folded when she departed and has not yet been reestablished. One education organizer in the Rio Grande Valley was distraught with the poor quality of instruction in an Alliance School, but because her efforts were seen as infringing upon the principal's academic freedom, he told her she was forbidden to come on his campus. Finally, although the IAF practice of switching lead organizers from one city to another after several years of involvement in a site benefits the long-term vitality of the Texas IAF, it can seem disruptive to principals and teachers who crave stability and who harbor initial skepticism toward outsiders who seek to promote political activism within the neighborhood and the school.

In addition to all of the impediments to change identified above, it is worth noting that students themselves can play a major role in welcoming or discouraging increased community engagement in schools. A number of principals at Alliance Schools which are middle schools have expressed their dismay that many students do not want to see their parents at school during the years of early adolescence. Students at Jefferson Davis High School have been critical of peers who drop out in spite of all of the resources and idealism devoted by the community and staff to the school. "The parents can't be with their kids twenty-four hours a day," senior Gary Ortega observed, "and there's no way that the parents can make a difference unless their kids want them to. Some kids I know expect the community to work for them, but they don't want to work for the community. They expect that once they drop out, the community will try to get them back in school, but once they're back in, they still don't want to work." While more factors may be at play than Ortega recognized, there can be no gainsaying his recognition that student disengagement militates against high levels of community participation in schools.

Principals, teachers, parents, clergy, students, and organizers all play intended and unintended roles in impeding the growth and development of Alliance Schools. Another important factor involves community problems. For example, consider the persistence of high crime rates in the central cities. The continued availability of illegal drugs, the proliferation of delinquent youth gangs, and the easy availability of guns have devastated the social capital of many urban neighborhoods. Morningside Middle School has had a particularly difficult struggle in this area in recent years. Powerful gangs such as the Bloods and the Crips have taken control of portions of the Morningside neighborhood, and many parents are so worried about gang violence that they insist on picking up their children from school even though they live only four blocks away from the campus. Other parents, drawing on their religious convictions, find themselves tutoring up to twenty-five Morningside Middle School students in the afternoons without compensation, both to enhance their academic achievement and to keep them off the streets. ACT has organized information meetings with the Fort Worth Police Department and city council members at the school to inform parents about effective ways of battling gangs' influence, but it has become a tough uphill struggle to reclaim the neighborhood.[3]

For parents who have been involved with Morningside for a long time, it has been a bitter experience to observe that even though they were successful in shutting down one store which sold alcohol to their middle school students, another store with the same proclivities has sprung up in its place. In October 1994, parents were effective in pressuring city officials to close down Glen Garden Apartments, a notorious center for drug dealing in the community, but the drug dealers have simply relocated to other nearby apartments. After they pick up their children from school, some parents of Morningside students find themselves literally running from their cars to their homes due to their fear of gangs. "Morningside is in a much tougher position than it has ever been in before," Perry Perkins observed, "and we've really had to redouble our efforts."[4]

Problems with gangs and drugs are not unique to Morningside. They also afflict Jefferson Davis and Marshall Middle School in Houston, and it is a rare middle or high school in urban Texas that doesn't have to deal with gangs in one manner or another. One survey of the eight largest cities in Texas estimated that roughly thirteen thousand urban youth could be considered members of over seven hundred gangs. Even at the elementary school level, parents, teachers, and children must concern themselves with neighborhood gang activity. Drug dealing has increased in the public housing projects adjacent to Zavala Elementary School, for example, and Zavala parents, fearful of retribution, are trying to gather the courage to press the police to clean up the projects. Toña Vasquez, who is organizing parents in Santa Rita Courts, has been appalled with the climate of distrust and intimidation that exists in the projects. The child of one parent was beaten up by gang members shortly after Vasquez held a house meeting with the parent, presumably as a form of retaliation, and she is struggling to find new ways to reach out to the parents. In a twist on usual IAF organizing methods, she is likely to hold future meetings with parents from the housing projects in the school, since parents feel safer there than they do in their own homes.[5]

The continued popularity of gangs among urban adolescents reflects the alienation which many of them feel from their families, schools, and religious institutions—an alienation resulting in a dissonant state of "multiple marginality" which they seek to escape by creating a a powerful counterschool peer culture. Gangs are a particularly difficult issue to understand, negotiate, and confront because of the wide mixture of activities and attitiudes which can be clustered under the label. Some "gangs" are little more than frightened cliques of students searching for a sense of belonging in a group of peers. Others have developed into truly lethal youth cohorts that terrorize whole neighborhoods. Developing the analytical capacity to discriminate between different kinds of gangs and to create different kinds of youth and neighborhood organizations which can harness and channel the energy of alienated inner-city youth must be key areas for new kinds of policy interventions and experimentation.[6]

Not all of the social problems impeding school change have to do with gangs, drugs, or myriad forms of petty criminality. One of the greatest obstacles to creating momentum for change in schools has to do with the phenomenal rates of mobility in urban schools. It is not unusual for American urban schools to have student mobility rates of over 50 percent in a given year. Although some children from affluent homes with stable families can handle school transitions well, and there is a need for much greater research in this area, available research does suggest that repeated school transference is emotionally traumatic and academically problematic for poor and working-class children. If low-income parents know or even suspect that they will be moving shortly from one neighborhood to another, few or none will choose to become engaged in improving their children's current school and community. Such parents and their children become more or less captive to the circumstances of each school and neighborhood that they move through, usually in search of a slightly better home and more secure, better-paying employment.[7]

Thus, both social actors within schools and social forces in the community can prevent school change and neighborhood development. A third impediment to change can come from the institutional matrices of schools themselves. In general, middle schools and high schools are more resistant to change than elementary schools. Although Morningside and Davis experienced success in bringing parents into the school in the 1980s, the relatively rapid turnover of students in those schools makes it especially difficult to sustain the momentum over time. In elementary schools, teachers and administrators have more time to develop closer personal relationships and the trust which can enhance selective risk taking and innovation.

Why are middle schools and high schools especially hard to change? The organizations of most of the schools themselves block community participation for parents and a sense of belonging for urban youth. In six years of kindergarten through fifth grade, students and parents are likely to interact with six teachers; even when there are auxiliary programs, both children and parents know that the child's teacher is the primary liaison to the school. In six years of middle and high school, parents may have to interact with thirty-six teachers or more (assuming a six-period day in each year). The sheer number of students that high school teachers instruct on a given day—which can reach over 150 students in metropolitan areas such as Houston, San Antonio, and Dallas—make personal relationships with the students and parents extremely difficult if not impossible to establish. When surveyed, a majority of low-income parents agree that one reason for their lack of engagement with their children's secondary school is that "there are too many teachers with whom to talk." Given the structural impediments to strong social ties between teachers and students, it is hardly surprising that students report a major decline in the quality of their participation in the school in middle school and that they fall under the sway of tremendous peer pressure in seeking to develop their new adolescent identities.[8]

Several other factors make middle and high schools harder to change than elementary schools. The higher levels of knowledge which are taught in middle and high schools arouse low-income parents' anxieties about school. On surveys, low-income parents indicate that their lack of mastery of the curriculum is the primary reason why they are less involved in secondary schools. Almost all low-income parents can be trained to coach their children in reading and arithmetic; the same cannot be said for trigonometry or chemistry. In addition, the fact that the children are older and will sometimes express their desires to be independent of their parents can discourage parental engagement. Tragically, the inherent turbulence of adolescence indicates that the young adult years are those in which our youths most need the guidance, mentoring, and supervision of adults—and when it is usually least available to them.[9]

The final factor that can make middle schools and high schools more difficult to change has to do with community expectations of schools. Even when academic achievement is poor in many inner-city secondary schools, students, parents, and teachers can be enthusiastic supporters of athletic programs and musical activities such as the school's band. Many of those programs peripheral to students' cognitive development enjoy widespread community support, garner substantial financial revenues through their activities, and are experienced by the community as more central to the identity of the school than its academic mission. In spite of Texas' legendary emphasis on athletics, this problem is hardly a regional one; when Deborah Meier and her colleagues at Central Park East Secondary School in New York City struggled to create a small and humanistic school with an intellectual focus, they encountered the same problem.[10]

In spite of the problems involved in changing the culture of secondary schools, recent research suggests that students' academic success can be enhanced in impressive ways given the right combination of reforms. A smaller school size and an emphasis on academics, cooperative learning strategies, and parental participation are only a few of the organizational changes and cultural practices that have yielded increased academic achievement in mathematics, history, reading, and science. Although measuring the significance of each of these and many other variables is a research task that is yet to be accomplished, the findings thus far indicate that the struggle for change is well worth the potential benefits for high school students and their communities.[11]

Another structural factor impeding change has to do with the instability of leadership in urban school districts. The current tenure of a superintendent of schools in urban districts is less than two years. The Harlandale Independent School District, which has suffered through five changes of superintendents in less than two years, is an extreme case, but it nonetheless pointedly demonstrates the problems that occur for schools when there is no stable leadership at the district level. Flanders Elementary School parents have spent many hours seeking to build relationships with each new superintendent, only to watch that individual depart after a brief appointment. It is truly impressive that, even though Flanders parents and teachers perceived that instability, they persisted with their quest for a multipurpose service center rather than simply give up.

Instability in urban schools exists not only at their apex, but also at the level of the principalship. Dallas Area Interfaith organizers and leaders put hundreds of hours into organizing one elementary school in Oak Cliff as a new Alliance School. Shortly after TEA funds were assigned to the new school, however, the Dallas Independent School District assigned the school a new principal who felt no particular responsibility for allocating the funds in a collaborative manner which included parents. The Texas IAF organization is working hard to educate the new principal about the possibilities of parental engagement, but if no change in the principal's perspective is forthcoming, the IAF will have to drop the school from the Alliance School network and begin organizing all over again in a more favorable setting.

One potential source of structural resistance to community engagement in schools in many states could come from teachers' unions. In open shop states such as Texas, however, unions' power consists more in their strength as advocacy groups than in their consolidation of power in teachers' labor representatives. Texas IAF leaders and organizers have always made a point of establishing regular meetings with teachers' unions to apprise them of their work, but unions have not played either an especially positive or a negative role in expanding the work of the Alliance Schools. When Robert Rivera and TMO assessed Wheatley High School critically, they had taken important preliminary steps in clearing their procedures with Gayle Fallon, the president of the Houston Federation of Teachers. Wheatley was heavily unionized, but since the principal was the primary recipient of the community's dissatisfaction in that instance, teachers did not object. "Teachers haven't seen us as part of the central administration or in any way as against them," Rivera said, "but that is a concern." TMO had the benefit of strong participation from the Fifth Ward's large and powerful churches, in which many of the school's teachers are members. Community-based organizations which intervene as TMO did in school districts, but without an institutional base in churches and with more militant teacher unions, might have to anticipate more opposition.

In most cases, however, skillful organizing should enable unions to become part of the membership of IAF organizations. In Baltimore, IAF leaders and organizers recruited the major unions representing teachers, principals, and administrators into Baltimoreans United in Leadership Development (BUILD). That collaboration explains in large part the success of Maryland's capital city in piloting the Commonwealth Agreement with schools which provided the prototype for San Antonio's Educational Partnership. Other union participation—such as that of the hospital workers' union—have helped BUILD to develop strong horizontal ties with social service workers.

Bureaucracies crave stability, and urban schools are parts of an immense and powerful bureaucracy. Texas public schools employ over

430,000 teachers, principals, administrators, and staff—one hundred thousand people more than all ten of the largest corporations in Texas combined. The Houston Independent School District employs more people than any other single source of employment in Houston. And, although the rhetoric of change is easy to espouse, the grinding work of school change—reconceptualizing teachers' and parents' roles and responsibilities, learning new ways of engaging the community, developing innovative methods of instruction and assessment, and cultivating a more flexible sense of one's roles and responsibilities—requires a talented and patient mobilization of people and resources. As of this writing, there are over one hundred Alliance Schools in Texas, and many of them are in the process of just beginning to engage their communities. Thus, although we must be aware of the impediments to change, we also must learn from the factors at this early stage of the Alliance School process that appear to promote experimentation and success.[12]

10

The Pursuit of Success

How is it that some urban schools have been able to work effectively with Texas IAF organizations? What are the features of the collaboratives which have produced higher academic achievement, improved personal and social aspects of students' lives, and enhanced neighborhood stability and security? Without implying that the lessons of schools such as Zavala should be applied directly to other settings, what can we learn from a Zavala Elementary School that should inform our approach to school reform in other low-income communities?

To answer these important questions, we need several layers of analysis. First, we must highlight unique features of the IAF theory and practice of politics that fueled school change in settings like Zavala. The rigorous methodology of IAF organizing—from one-on-one's to house meetings to Walks for Success to parents' assemblies—should be disaggregated to illuminate the efficacy and interdependence of each of the component parts. A second layer of analysis concerns the Texas IAF strategy for building social capital. On the one hand, schools could draw upon many civic institutions to develop social capital, such as neighborhood associations, corporations, and nonreligious nonprofit organizations. On the other hand, religious institutions appeal to a unique facet of the human identity and play a specific role in American life. Analyzing the interface between the church and the school, as mediated by the IAF organization, can help us to understand why this model of organizing has helped to change the culture of urban schools in the Texas context, and how it has helped to cultivate social capital between clergy, students, parents, teachers, administrators, and neighbors.

A third layer of analysis focuses on the issue of test scores. The Texas IAF has avoided some of the major contemporary quagmires of school reform, such as arguments about site-based management and literacy strategies based on whole language or phonetics. The reason for that abstinence has less to do with the importance of the issues than their intractability and the difficulty of demonstrating concrete results that will meet the agenda developed in house meetings. Instead, Texas IAF organizations have focused on the interface between parental engagement and academic achievement. That concentration has enabled schools which previously had been trapped in vicious circles to engage in the reflection and experimentation which could enhance the cognitive and social development of low-income youth.

The Internal Dynamics of Texas IAF Culture

IAF organizers are fond of saying that "all organizing is reorganizing" to indicate that all communities are already organized, even if their form of organization is such that they are controlled by forces outside of the neighborhood. It should be clear that for IAF community organizing to succeed, change must occur on a theoretical as well as on a practical and political level. To begin to identify the special kind of social change that is promoted by Texas IAF collaboratives, we must reconceptualize traditional forms of inquiry about education.

Consider the trap involved in the simple question, often asked by principals, teachers, and administrators: how can we increase student attendance and academic achievement? The question is a legitimate one, but it is typically encumbered with a narrow definition of "we" that brackets out vital community resources such as parents, clergy, police, realtors, bankers, philanthropists, and providers of public health services. By excluding those resources, a worthy goal is undermined, leading to frustration, scapegoating, and disengagement.

Texas IAF leaders and organizers ask a different question: *how can we create and develop a political constituency and political leaders to organize the community to improve our schools and community?* This question presupposes a different criterion of success, one that is measured by the formation of an articulate, well-informed, and organized community which engages in powerful and effective public advocacy on behalf of its children. In the case of schools, that advocacy includes the opportunity for all children to receive strong educations—not just the scions of the affluent. In the case of the community, advocacy includes the chance to live in safety with adequate housing and health care. Success in this instance is predicated upon leadership development, political participation, the creation of a constituency, and the strengthening of community-based organizations. That political success can then generate further improvements relevant to academic achievement, immunizations, community policing, after-school programs, job training, and home ownership.

Why does this reframing of the question of success matter? The Texas IAF teaches that the definition of success should be developed through conversations with parents and clergy and not through the programs—however well-intended—of even the most sophisticated experts. When the Texas IAF first began working in schools, its leaders and organizers were most concerned with the quality of instruction and curriculum. Through house meetings, Texas IAF leaders learned that parents had different priorities. Parents were not worried about the advantages of a whole language versus a phonetics-based approach to literacy; they were obsessed with their children's safety in the community. Morningside parents resented a convenience store which sold alcohol to their children; Zavala parents were terrified of the drug dealers in the housing projects; Ysleta parents wanted traffic lights and warning signals to help their children cross busy Zaragosa Street; Smith parents wanted a greater police presence in the neighborhood and community policing in the school. Rather than pursue their initial interest in pedagogy and curriculum, the Texas IAF took the parents' concerns seriously. They then taught parents how they could become political actors who could not just improve safety in their neighborhoods, but also develop the skills to acquire programs which will give their children at least a shot at reaching a decent quality of life in the twenty-first century.

It doesn't take much to observe that *politics* is a dirty word for most Americans today. Yet as long as *all* political activity is vilified, there is no chance of developing an integrated philosophy and strategy of school reform and neighborhood stabilization. Instead, one falls back to the failures of the last two decades, in which the reform of the school is bracketed off from the dynamics and troubles of its surrounding community. One ends up with schools like Ortega Elementary in Austin—a hothouse of reform and innovation surrounded by an eight-foot-high fence topped off with barbed wire to keep out the gangs and drug dealers that bully the law-abiding citizens of the neighborhood. One ends up with an illusion of success rather than the real thing.

By reconceptualizing success along the lines of Texas IAF collaboratives, we recover the original meaning of the word *success* itself. *Success* is a derivative of the Latin *succedere*, meaning "to go from under." By resisting the lure of technical expertise per se as the sine qua non of school reform, Texas IAF organizations literally "go from under" by taking seriously the aspirations low-income citizens have for their children. There is of course a synthesis with sustained and critical analysis in the forms of training and seminars. Nonetheless, house meetings are viewed as the generative point of origin of Texas IAF educational organizing.

We begin, then, by reconceptualizing the definition of success in school reform to posit that the development of a political constituency and political leadership is the first task of serious educational reformers. The next step is to state that the process through which problems are attacked matters. If political leadership and a political constituency are created, but those leaders and those constituents delegate their concerns to political representatives and corporate leaders, one cannot achieve the sense of ownership of the reform process generated among low-income parents in the Alliance Schools.

The first factor explaining the successful school reforms sustained by the Texas IAF is inextricably interwoven with the organizations' approach to civic engagement. One of the most important axioms defining that approach is the "iron rule" to "never do for others what they can do for themselves." The iron rule is indispensable if one is to avoid the famous "free rider" problem in social relations, in which individuals capitalize on the work of others without expending any energy themselves. Community organizers, parents, teachers, principals, and clergy all have to worry about free riders in their schools, families, and congregations. The IAF's insistence on the importance of the iron rule derives from the realization that too many free riders will destroy the community organization by scattering its resources and undermining its accountability. If the community organization is to have a chance to get off the ground, it must strictly separate itself from potential free riders and a culture of entitlement.[1]

That theoretical emphasis and the practice that accompanies it give the Texas IAF credibility with community stakeholders. The IAF must develop an alternative culture of civic action, accountability, and reciprocity if it is to amass power and respect in the volatile and contentious world of urban politics. The constant repetition of the iron rule, which harmonizes well with the dominant Jacksonian political culture in Texas, has been one route to gaining that respect in the urban Southwest.

Once the Texas IAF has helped a school and its community to garner their resources, vocalize grievances, broker reforms, and gain political credibility, it usually is not long until organizers move on to another challenge in the community. This independence, a logical expression of the iron rule, gives Texas IAF organizations a broad base of support in schools in working-class neighborhoods. Educators are reassured that the purpose of the Texas IAF is not to take over a school but to help it through a transition.

The pedagogical analogue to the Texas IAF organizations' movement of engagement and removal is the constructivist principle of "scaffolding" and "fading." Once organizers have helped the community to build a "scaffold" for their own self-mobilization, they will typically "fade" by devoting their attention to other concerns where they are more deeply needed. For some educators, including several at Davis High School in Houston, TMO's withdrawal after the first Walks for Success occurred too rapidly; others, such as principal Emily Cole, recognized that Robert Rivera and his colleagues had determined that the school had become strong enough to sustain and develop its strong community partnerships on its own. TMO did not leave its work on the Near North Side; it refocused it upon health care in elementary schools and citizenship classes for parents. Lupe Meils, a parent leader at Ysleta Elementary in El Paso, grasped the logic of this movement when she said, "We're learning for ourselves that we can organize ourselves. If EPISO was to leave tomorrow, we could take the skills we've learned and go on." Ysleta principal Dolores de Avila agreed, "We've internalized the process." [2]

If the iron rule's emphasis on autonomy and respect is a key aspect of the Texas IAF's success, another important aspect is the emphasis on relational power, a culture of conversations, and connectedness. When Texas IAF leaders and organizers visit homes for one-on-one conversations, house meetings, or as part of the Walk for Success, they do not approach parents with an agenda to sell, although in certain cases they do want parents to know about programs which can benefit their children or themselves. But first and foremost, a successful house meeting is one in which leaders and organizers learn from the community about its most salient issues. When Julia Lerma first began working for Metro Alliance, she spent a full six months just visiting community leaders, local clergy, teachers, and principals before she began formulating an agenda in collaboration with the community leaders. Six months may seem like a long time for this kind of work, but for working-class citizens it indicates something important in terms of follow-through and commitment, which builds a base of trust and solidarity that will be needed for the political struggles that lie ahead.

A third strength of the Texas IAF resides in the kinds of pedagogical interventions leaders and organizers use to help communities identify and circumscribe their grievances to focus on one winnable issue. Organizers are not laissez-faire; they do not promote whatever concepts the community brings forth. A culture of conversations means that the organizers and key leaders listen to the grievances of a community and work with the community to redress those problems. When EPISO first became active at Ysleta Elementary, the parents were bitter about many facets of their school and community. Maribeth Larkin helped the community to choose the most salient problem—traffic and safety—and to keep that in the foreground for an entire year. Austin Interfaith leaders and organizers discovered that the major issue vocalized by parents concerning their East Austin community dealt with the high volume of drug dealing in two public housing projects near Zavala Elementary. The leaders and organizers observed that the community was too afraid of the dealers to confront them, and rather than press the parents to take on an issue that clearly frightened them, worked with them on the more winnable issue of health care and academic achievement for children in the community. Taking on the issue of crime is still an important priority, but one that awaits the development of a more confident public voice for neighborhood residents and their leaders.

One vital part of Texas IAF organizing for community engagement is its emphasis not just on training parents, but also on working with educators to make schools more proactive. In Texas IAF training sessions, teachers are taught not to dismiss parents for their lack of formal education but to capitalize on ways in which parents' life experiences can be infused into the curriculum. Even when parents lack literacy, they can encourage children's imagination by telling them stories; they can find ways to get their children involved in measuring while cooking; they can practice English expressions together if they come from a Spanish-dominant home. By speaking to parents in such a way as to communicate that they are essential partners in the educational enterprise, parents feel valorized, want to spend more time in the school, and are more likely to complete their formal schooling in adult education programs.

Many Texas IAF training sessions are held for parents and educators. They include such diverse topics as changes in the global economy, the key role that education will play in enhancing children's life chances, and the need to move beyond drilling and memorization to develop more multifaceted approaches to teaching, learning, and assessment. Some training sessions are devoted to study and debate, based on materials such as the Texas IAF vision paper or presentations by prominent educators. All of the training sessions work to build a more cohesive sense of community and to teach neighborhood and school leaders the key strategies that they will need to develop if they seek to be effective political actors.

Other types of training help leaders to develop the political savvy to get the results they seek from power holders. COPS organizer Joe Rubio held a training session at Flanders Elementary School in San Antonio in December 1994. In that training session, Rubio and session participants reviewed what had happened over the course of the four changes in school superintendents in the previous year and a half; this turnover had seriously undermined the school's efforts to gain a multipurpose center that would include a gymnasium. During the training, teachers and parents developed a strategy of one-on-one meetings with school board members and the incoming superintendent to ensure that the over four hundred children at Flanders would receive a multipurpose center before the district began to think about allocating its funds to other projects.

Teaching political savvy can involve educating parents about subtle but important political dynamics. "When we were first meeting with the district, Sister Maribeth didn't scold us parents, but she told us not to smile so much," Lupe Meils of Ysleta Elementary recalled. "We were trying to be too friendly." Organizers and leaders can serve to remind parents not to overreach themselves and become confrontational with administrators in ways that damage rather than contribute toward long-term successes. At Ysleta Elementary, when a parent made a strong verbal attack upon Superintendent Trujillo, Maribeth Larkin told the parent, "You need to depolarize," meaning that it was important to talk one-on-one with the superintendent afterward to make sure that he knew that the comments were not intended to be personal attacks. Odessa Ravin has had to work with parents to establish limits and to clarify with them that even though they can play substantial roles in governance, staff development, and curriculum issues at Morningside, they cannot use the school's openness as a platform for attacking the legitimate authority and expertise of the principal and her faculty. Part of community organizing for urban school renewal involves educating parents in the specific ways in which they can build effective relationships that will contribute to the long-term academic success of their children.

One of the most important facets of Texas IAF organizing that promotes its success is the development of an interclass, multiethnic organizing base. On the one hand, there is no question but that ethnic solidarity assisted with the founding and development of COPS, Valley Interfaith, and EPISO at a time when Mexican Americans were thoroughly subordinated to Anglo-American political and economic hegemony. On the other hand, it is virtually impossible to find examples of ways in which exhortations based on racial or ethnic solidarity have played any role at all in Texas IAF education organizing.

It certainly is not the case that awareness of ethnic differences is not salient in community organizing in urban Texas. Many IAF leaders have commented that the first time they have ever been in a specific church or neighborhood populated by groups of a different ethnicity was during a Texas IAF action. When Robert Hemphill, who is African American, first did community outreach in the *Segundo Barrio* of El Paso, he had a difficult time establishing contact with parents who refused to believe that he was the new principal of Alamo Elementary School, and many teachers and leaders have expressed anxiety about their first ventures into low-income communities.

Ethnic differences are not just a matter of identity and perception but also of social organization. To take the example of religious institutions, there is a world of difference between the relationship to the community held by a Black Baptist minister who starts a church from scratch and a Mexican American priest who has the international and hierarchical organizational edifice of the Catholic Church to rely upon. Black clergy typically play a dual role as both religious and political leaders in African American neighborhoods; Mexican American or Anglo clergy almost never personify that linkage in their civic capacities. Differences in family structure, rates of attendance in religious institutions, proficiency in English, labor segmentation, and a host of other issues separate the major ethnic groups which populate urban Texas, and those differences must be recognized as part of any organizing effort.

Because of the real differences which exist among ethnic groups, IAF organizations have sought to transcend ethnic barriers by emphasizing universal themes. Building broad-based organizations with strong Black, Anglo, and Hispanic delegations in large multiethnic urban centers like Dallas, Fort Worth, and Houston is a daunting challenge, and much mutual suspicion and distrust between groups must be overcome to develop organizational strength. Yet for Ernie Cortés, the value of shaping broad-based organizations is obvious if the goal is building political power. "The reality is that the United Farm Workers and the United Auto Workers organized millions more Mexicans than La Raza Unida," Cortés commented. "Everybody knows who the International Ladies' Garment Workers' Union is today; nobody remembers the Jewish Bund. You can get media attention if you confine yourself to your own ethnic group, but you can't get power." Cortés' emphasis on broad-based organizing situates him in a broad and inclusive tradition of Mexican American activists, such as Bert Corona and César Chávez, who expressed disdain for organizing strategies that relied strictly on ethnic identity. For the many citizens who are more concerned with finding common ground with others than with emphasizing their ethnic differences, Texas IAF organizing is a welcome way of experiencing solidarity across class and ethnic lines.[3]

Another reason for the successes of Texas IAF organizations in schools is related to their approach to issues of governance in schools. Texas IAF collaboratives offer an alternative to orthodox models of parental involvement, which assume that the reigning culture of the school is legitimate and that parents only need to learn and apply better parenting skills to improve their children's academic achievement. One of the more famous approaches to parental involvement in recent years was devised by James Comer and applied by his colleagues at Yale University to the public schools of New Haven, Connecticut. Comer implemented a tripartite model of parental engagement to schools in low-income African American communities with dramatic educational results. His model created a school governing structure with parental representation, worked to integrate parents into the life of the school, and created "mental health teams" with parental representation to nourish a humanistic, child-friendly atmosphere in the school. Another important recent innovation in parental involvement was implemented in Chicago, where parents have become empowered decision makers who hire not only the teachers in their neighborhood schools, but also the principal.[4]

Both the Comer model and site-based management with significant power allocated to parents represent significant alterations in the traditional culture of schools and bold efforts to improve community participation in educational settings. When viewed from the vantage point of Texas IAF collaborations, however, they each reveal shortcomings. Neither approach seriously conceptualizes the necessity of *educating* parents to develop political *organizations* which address interrelated issues of housing, jobs, schools, and crime in their communities. According to Father Will Wauters, of Santa Fe Episcopal and the Metro Alliance, "If you're only organized internally in the school with site-based management, you're not able to think strategically about how you can influence the school board or city council. You need a broad-based organization that has a strategy to identify different needs in the school *and* the community to do that."

The most striking contrast between the Comer model and the various site-based decision-making plans and the Texas IAF collaboratives has to do with the different emphases placed upon training and structures of school governance. One of the worst tragedies of the well-intended drive for site-based management can be seen in the goal displacement which occurs when administrators, teachers, and parents battle over issues concerning the distribution of power in a school and fail to attend to the needs of the children in their charge. Although research suggests that parental participation is key in enhancing children's learning, too much emphasis on the ties between parents and a school can obscure the other educational relationships, such as those between teachers and children, which lie at the heart of the learning enterprise in the school.

In spite of the assumptions that one might make about Alinsky organizers and the radical heritage of the IAF, the Texas IAF has been discrete in the battles over site-based management that have characterized American public schools in the 1980s and 1990s. Instead of focusing on *structures* of governance, Texas IAF leaders and organizers have provided *training* to help individuals to maximize their political power in ways that will enhance their long-term goals. In this respect they have recognized an insight articulated by Seymour Sarason, who suggested that "forms of involvement in decision making are in some ultimate, practical sense less important for realization of the spirit of involvement than degree and quality of the mutual trust and respect characterizing that involvement." The Alliance Schools have avoided the goal displacement that occurs when conflicts over governance take precedence over children's gains in safety, health, and academic achievement. Intriguingly, the Alliance Schools appear to mirror Catholic schools in this respect, in which parental involvement has never involved parents dictating to teachers what the curriculum should be or how their children should be assessed. By avoiding those conflicts, Texas IAF organizations have kept their attention fixed on children's academic achievement, issues of neighborhood safety, and the other myriad concerns that have emerged out of house meetings, assemblies, and training sessions.[5]

Another reason why the Texas IAF collaboratives have expanded is related to the financial strategies developed by the organizations. Unlike many of the school restructuring initiatives of the past decade, Texas IAF collaboratives typically have placed few financial demands on school districts. Almost all of the programs sponsored by Texas IAF organizations—such as school health programs, after-school programs, code compliance task forces, community policing, housing for low-income citizens, and the Alliance Schools—draw on financial resources other than the school district. Those financial resources include virtually every sector of society: banks in San Antonio, Tenneco in Houston, the police department in El Paso, and the Texas Education Agency in all of the Alliance Schools. In each case the school district benefits by acquiring additional resources which provide new educational opportunities for its pupils at no additional cost to schools.

By harnessing those new financial resources, IAF organizations have enabled financially strapped districts to enhance education without draining their revenues. In February 1995 I attended a meeting of EPISO leaders with an assistant superintendent of the Ysleta Independent School District who suggested that EPISO repeat its successful support of House Bill 72 in 1984 by organizing busloads of citizens to travel to Austin to advocate increased state funding of education. Given the death threats which EPISO organizers first faced when they arrived in El Paso in the early 1980s, the district's acceptance of their presence, appreciation of their contribution, and encouragement of their mobilization are nothing short of amazing—unless one understands that EPISO is helping the district to accomplish its work more effectively without placing onerous demands on the district's limited funding.

Building Social Capital

Assume that James Coleman's hypothesis was correct, and that one reason for the poor academic performance of American public school students is the declining social capital of their families and communities. In Coleman's account, lack of social capital can be measured by an absence of concentrated and stable adult supervision and tutoring of children at home and a lack of dense social ties between students, parents, teachers, and the community. The net effect of social decapitalization is to undermine the stability and prosocial norms of the family, congregation, school, and workplace.

The Texas IAF has sought to build social capital in urban neighborhoods to promote environments conducive to the stability and success of working-class youth. That strategy has three broad facets. *In the community,* the Texas IAF has led one-on-one house visitations, conducted house and parish meetings, held Walks for Success, and battled for safer streets, code compliance, housing, and job training. *Within schools,* the Texas IAF has sought to bring teachers out of their isolation from one another and encouraged the development of dense social ties through innovative arrangements in which teachers form into teams, develop advisory periods for their students, adopt block scheduling, and create after-school programs. *Between schools and the community,* the Texas IAF has conducted training sessions which promoted dialogue between teachers and parents, helped to bring community policing and housing fairs into the school, and wrought changes in the physical capital of the school by developing parents' centers for adults and health clinics for the children.

We can isolate specific moments in the case studies presented in this book in which schools' cultures changed from vicious circles of civic disengagement to virtuous circles of trust, solidarity, and reciprocity. Once parents and teachers at Zavala had won their health clinic, they saw each other differently. Significantly, they did not see themselves differently because of a more tolerant disposition; they had *earned* each other's respect through their common commitment and struggle to improve the conditions of Zavala's children. Similar processes of *earning* trust and respect occurred when Ysleta parents and teachers collaborated to create school safety zones, when Smith parents and teachers demanded community policing and greater code compliance, and when Alamo parents worked with their children's teachers and principal to revise the school's suspension policy and to help to shape the school's curriculum. In all of these cases, parents were *at the center* of political action and invigorating social capital formation; they were never passive and never allowed themselves to be marginalized. Much of the euphoria described in these case studies can be interpreted as a legitimate psychological release of tension as schools and communities have evolved from cynicism and isolation to cultivate new norms of reciprocity and social trust.

The case studies indicate a wide number of different strategies for building social capital. As one would expect with a community organizing group such as the Texas IAF, the most common strategies for accumulating social capital did not develop within the boundaries of schools, but rather in urban neighborhoods. At Morningside Middle School, social capital was first built between the principal, clergy, and parents; it was then imported into the school, which served as a base for social capital formation in the community by taking action against a store serving alcohol to under-age youths and an apartment complex which was a center of drug dealing and gang activity. At Zavala, parents initially refused to become involved in the school around issues of academic achievement; the transition from a vicious to a virtuous civic circle occurred only by waging conflict against opponents of a school-based clinic. Once that hurdle was crossed and social ties had been strengthened, a host of reforms internal to the school, such as Zavala Young Scientists and the after-school program, enabled the school to concentrate its social capital formation within its campus. Other schools also experienced conflict as an important phase of social capital formation; both Ysleta and Beacon Hill had to embarrass public officials into taking action around traffic safety and code compliance, respectively. Once officials had been shamed into serving their constituents, however, the polarization essentially terminated and virtuous circles of cooperation and public service replaced disengagement and civic neglect.

Social capital formation in the case of the Alliance Schools does not necessarily involve conflict. Jefferson Davis High School and its neighborhood schools in Houston have experienced some opposition from teachers opposed to block scheduling or district officials unsympathetic to the flexibility entailed in school innovation, but the general evolution of Davis and its community have not been marked by the dramatic conflicts experienced by Zavala or Beacon Hill. Part of the smoothness of Davis' evolution may have to do with the collaboration it has enjoyed with the powerful Tenneco Corporation. Financial capital, when properly deployed, can promote social capital formation in schools and communities and human capital formation in individuals. Regrettably, far too many urban schools suffer from inadequate financial capital.

The Texas IAF has not simply accumulated social capital within schools and communities; it has also built social capital by bringing different schools and communities into relationship with one another. Jefferson Davis High School spearheaded the effort to build social capital between its neighborhood schools so that each child can learn at his or her grade level, thus preventing the slippage that undermines the success of urban students. The elementary schools in San Antonio have developed joint strategies for creating after-school programs, community policing, interdisciplinary curricula, and housing subsidies. The health clinic and after-school program that began at Zavala in Austin have spread to other elementary and middle schools throughout the city. As trust and accountability between schools and the community are enhanced, educators feel emboldened to take calculated risks to serve their children more effectively. Block scheduling, interdisciplinary curricula, parents' centers, and multi-aged classrooms are but a few of the internal school changes which have resulted from new social ties between Alliance Schools within a city.

The Texas IAF has also built social capital between schools, governmental agencies, the community, and the private sector. In the Alliance Schools, social capital has been developed by law enforcement officers who do community policing, health-care providers who staff preventive care clinics, bankers and realtors who help working-class citizens to become homeowners, and corporations that donate volunteer time and finances. These groups form a community of citizens dedicated to enhancing the educational opportunities of urban youth. When all of those relationships are brought out of their isolation from one another and mediated through a community-based organization, they strengthen and reinforce one another, changing and enriching each of the constituent parts.

While Texas IAF organizations have played key roles in developing social capital in urban schools, their social base in religious institutions has given them a particularly powerful springboard for school reform and community revitalization. Although there are important differences between the congregations which constitute Texas IAF organizations, IAF leaders and organizers have been able to identify shared concerns in issues of political import to their communities. According to Ernie Cortés, "There's enough common ground among our traditions that we can carve out enough space to create a public square that has moral tradition that isn't sectarian." In the language of social capital theory, Texas IAF organizations promote shared norms grounded in Judeo-Christian traditions of social ethics. Those norms are translated into political practice on issues ranging from public education to quality housing to employment. As evidenced in Cortés' exegeses of passages from the Old Testament in IAF training sessions, the underlying norms which animate those traditions emphasize social justice, reciprocal obligations among individuals, the value of political empowerment and accountability, and the obligation of more affluent citizens to attend to the needs of the poor. Cortés and other Texas IAF leaders elaborate a theological and political critique of opposing norms embedded in the unilateral and unaccountable exercise of power, the privatization of social relationships, and the balkanization of the polity on ethnic and class lines.

The Texas IAF has scrupulously avoided issues of school prayer, creationism, and sex education, which have captured headlines in the media and pitted public school officials against clergy. Instead, Texas IAF organizers have sought to recognize the intrinsic integrity of both the public schools and religious institutions, while using the best in both sectors to upgrade the academic achievement and social conditions of low-income urban youth. Sectarian issues, which could divide low-income African Americans from Latinos, or Protestants from Catholics, must be avoided if the Texas IAF is to maintain its credibility as a broad-based organization with deep roots in low-income communities.

The IAF's social base in religious institutions has led some commentators to view the IAF as more conservative in its current manifestation than in it was under Alinsky's leadership, when liaisons with northern unions lent groups such as the Back of the Yards Council a more militant edge. In point of fact, however, religious institutions in the United States have never been monolithic and have always been animated by radical and liberal parishioners and clergy. Archbishop George Mundelein,

Bishop Bernard Sheil, and countless parish priests were core supporters of Saul Alinsky's first work in the Back of the Yards Council in Chicago in the 1930s and 1940s. That tradition continues today in the form of socially committed clergy such as Archbishop Patrick Flores of San Antonio, who is on the national board of trustees of the IAF and has supported COPS and Metro Alliance in numerous political struggles over the past two decades.[6]

Tapping into the institutional strength of religious institutions in the city for purposes of school change can clearly activate a powerful and commonly overlooked resource for educational reform. Research shows that not only is church attendance strongly correlated to a reduced high school dropout rate, but also that young people whose *neighbors* attend church experience indirect blessings from that contact in terms of increased economic opportunities, law-abiding conduct, and abstinence from drugs. In addition, research also shows that religiosity is a singularly powerful force which can help children adapt in positive ways to stressful life circumstances. For low-income parents, membership in religious institutions not only offers a sacred cosmology and set of robust ethical guidelines, but also enhances the academic achievement of the young and provides them with an orientation which can recognize and take advantage of legitimate economic opportunities. One can question whether Morningside Middle School ever would have turned around had ACT leaders and organizers failed to begin their work with recognition programs that were rooted in African American churches and had Odessa Ravin not demonstrated such tenacious leadership in visiting local churches to recruit support. Likewise, the appearance and testimony of Catholic clergy at a meeting of the Austin School Board represented a turning point securing the health clinic at Zavala Elementary School.[7]

If one seeks to develop policies which are based on the strengths of working-class communities and sees churches as one cornerstone of community resilience, an important policy offshoot would be to organize clergy to develop educational programs in their churches, as occurred in the Morningside neighborhood. Catholic churches, of course, have a strong educational component in their parochial schools, but that does not necessarily help the majority of their youth, who attend public schools. Among urban African American churches, only 44 percent of their clergy allow use of their buildings for nonchurch programs; of those churches, less than 5 percent house school-related or educational groups. Clergy who wish to improve the education of young people in their congregations and neighborhoods could enhance their community leadership by expanding the use of the church as a forum for the academic development of the young.[8]

Educational activism can serve the internal needs of a church for recruitment of new parishioners; many parents joined their current churches as a result of the church's engagement with Alliance Schools in their neighborhood. It is of course imperative that church members respect the division between church and state, but there is no damage done to that boundary if a parent is impressed by a minister during a house meeting and elects to visit his or her church to determine if it offers spiritual solace and community. Reverend Davis in Fort Worth credits his visitations with ACT with enriching his own ministry; after using surveys designed by ACT to elicit parent sentiment about Morningside Middle School, he posed similar questions to his congregation and made house visits to many church members. Close to 90 percent of all Hispanic Catholics in the United States are not active in parish activities; clergy who wish to increase parish participation may discover that school collaborations offer one way to revitalize their congregations. Many parents in Texas IAF organizations testify that their social activism, channeled through their churches and the public schools, has deepened their appreciation of religion.[9]

If churches benefit from their collaboration with the Alliance Schools, the Texas IAF's need to identify community leaders has been excellently served by its institutional base in religious institutions. For those Texas IAF organizations which have been branded as radical in the media, as EPISO was in the 1980s, the church affiliation has also been an essential source of legitimation of the organization's presence in the community. Even when IAF was organizing in low-income neighborhoods among constituencies who have little to lose, many parents and teachers recalled that their initial reaction to Texas IAF organizers was one of fear, driven by the anxiety that Texas IAF organizers might abuse the trust of the community for their own purposes. Those fears have been allayed as parents have observed their neighbors and clergy articulating issues which have long irritated their community—and harvesting results.

If religious institutions can provide a resource for the improvement of public schools, one may well wonder why that resource has been overlooked in so many contemporary discussions of school reform. First and most obviously, there is the longstanding American commitment to a separation between the church and the state, which necessarily limits the role of clergy in public schools. Clergy who would misuse their influence to advance a sectarian agenda in public schools could deeply damage, and indeed destroy, community belief in the impartiality of public schools, and that fear undoubtedly has held back principals and teachers in the past from approaching clergy. Second, clergy often are reticent to expand their mission outside of their church or congregation. Since all Protestant denominations are self-supporting financially, and most Catholic churches rely heavily on donations raised by their parishioners, it lies within the clergy's self-interest to focus their efforts on the congregation which makes their livelihood possible. Third, although religious institutions enjoy high levels of respect from many citizens, their reputations are not entirely positive. "The only thing churches are capable of running are school buses," former Houston mayor Louie Welch told a TMO leader, "and they don't do that very well." [10]

Finally, in spite of the positive examples given in this account, one cannot expect churches to provide a magic elixir that will solve all educational problems. In Wendy Glasgow Winters' study of low-income African American mothers and urban schools, she found no significant difference between the alienation from school experienced by church-going versus unchurched families. When further research is conducted, one may anticipate that the results will require considerable nuance and differentiation to develop the most productive school and church collaborations.[11]

Only those clergy who have a strong foundation of support in the community can afford to expend vast quantities of time in Texas IAF organizations. "In the first five years with ACT I almost abandoned most of my work in the church," Reverend Davis of Fort Worth commented. "And I could only do that because of the strong volunteer staff at Mount Pisgah." Davis' leadership is especially noteworthy because research indicates that a sizable minority of Black Baptists oppose political activism among their clergy. Important issues of personal credibility, power, and independence are also involved in developing effective relationships between schools and churches. Clergy, like anyone else, can be reluctant to expend vast numbers of hours in schools, particularly when they cannot really control the decisions which are made by principals and teachers.[12]

Researchers have not helped to advance the collaboration between religious institutions and schools. There is a vast literature on the interface between the home and the school, but research on the interface between the home, the school, and religious institutions is comparatively sparse. Researchers just as much as practitioners need to challenge themselves to explore new territories which use secondary associations to reweave the fabric of social relationships for urban youth.[13]

One must engage in entirely new sets of challenges, both theoretical and practical, when examining new ways of strengthening relationships between religious institutions, schools, and community. It would be a strange distortion of religious observation to go to church to improve academic achievement. If "faith is the state of being ultimately concerned," as Paul Tillich suggested, then the challenge of religious faith is such that one must plunge deeply within oneself and one's community to discover and develop hitherto uncultivated relationships with a calculated disregard for their extrinsic and material benefits. That which is of "ultimate concern" cannot become an instrument of a more trivial concern without damaging one's personal identity and religious faith. In examining religious questions, many educators and school reformers enter unfamiliar territory. Out of that engagement can emerge social capital, but it would be a tragic extension of our culture's obsession with marketplace values to suggest that our children should be religious so that they will have a greater chance of being successful.[14]

The Texas IAF strategy for building social capital suggests that we reconsider the cultural taboo that implies that discussions about politics and religion are breaches of decorum and inappropriate topics in public schools. It would indeed represent a rupture of trust and civic integrity to use schools as a platform for one-sided, partisan politics or sectarian religious preaching. But schools could gain if they would help parents, students, and teachers to develop a culture of conversations which engage and enliven our religious and political traditions. How those relationships with those traditions could be strengthened lies beyond the scope of this book and should be the topic of invigorating debate. That debate in and of itself might accomplish a great deal in overcoming the trivialization of education and citizenship which afflicts far too many public schools.

It should be clear that the Texas IAF has developed an unusual and potent strategy of social capital formation in urban schools and neighborhoods. An important caveat is necessary at this point, however. It would be a profound misinterpretation of the Texas IAF's work to wager that one could introduce policy reforms to build social capital in schools and low-income neighborhoods without serious parental and community engagement and produce the same results. This point is of the utmost importance because of the unfortunate proclivity of many educators to dash from the diagnosis of problems to program design to implementation. The Texas IAF's emphasis on cultures of conversations, house meetings, parish meetings, and simply vast quantities of time to build personal relationships and social trust is not a populist quirk but a profound understanding that social capital can neither be built nor be effective without deeply engaging a community that will be impacted by policy decisions. To illuminate this essential point, consider three experiences of failed social capital formation in urban schools.

First, in 1993 the city of San Antonio designated two schools as the recipients of after-school programs in school districts in which COPS and the Metro Alliance had no member churches. COPS and the Metro Alliance were fully engaged in their own districts and did not organize the affected communities; nor did the school districts make any efforts to train parents, teachers, administrators, or clergy in the skills and norms needed to organize the programs. The lack of social capital in the communities led to unstable programs which floundered in their conceptualization and implementation and which the districts terminated in less than six months. "One of the reasons that our programs have been successful is because we helped the city to identify communities close to our churches where the parents would understand the programs," Joe Rubio of COPS commented. "In the other communities no one had gone in and done the legwork required to build similar relationships."

A second case of failed reform occurred in Austin. Leaders and organizers in Austin Interfaith worked with principals from two elementary schools in the 1990–1991 school year who claimed to want parental engagement. To their chagrin, they found that the principals insisted on approaching the community in a paternalistic way which reinforced rather than changed the existing school culture. Although Austin Interfaith was able to create some benefits for the schools in terms of programs and improvement of infrastructure, its leaders and organizers felt marginalized by the principals and incapable of developing the relationships of reciprocity and trust which could lead to parental engagement.

As a result, the Texas IAF organization broke off its relationship with both schools at the end of the year.

A third case of failed reform resulting from lack of social capital in schools and communities occurred in Houston. After Jefferson Davis' success with block scheduling, a host of other public high schools all over the city converted to ninety-minute class periods. Yet none of the other high schools preceded the transition to block scheduling with the intensive neighborhood visitations, Walks for Success, and parents' assemblies that created the social capital on the Near North Side which supported innovation and change at Davis. Because most of Houston's principals failed to fully engage their teachers and their community in making that transition, several faced angry criticisms from parents and teachers who felt themselves victimized by unilateral leadership. In addition, many principals have introduced a form of block scheduling in which students maintain six classes but those courses are staggered on a schedule which meets only on Monday, Wednesday, and Friday or on Tuesday and Thursday. As a result, the development of social capital through intense personal relationships is mitigated. "I don't understand why schools have taken up that other kind of block scheduling," Susan Carrizal, a student at Jefferson Davis said. "How can the teachers ever get to know their students that way?" In other words, block scheduling has been disseminated throughout the Houston Independent School District, but most communities feel little ownership of the program and the underlying philosophical commitment to building a sense of community has been compromised.[15]

Texas IAF organizations do not just build social capital in schools and community; they must also attend to their own internal civic culture. The multifaceted relationships between parents, religious institutions, and schools exhibited by the Texas IAF have recently come full circle to transform its internal structure. The executive committee of Metro Alliance in San Antonio voted in the spring of 1994 to include Pamela Walls and Richard Alvarado, the principals of Herff and Beacon Hill Elementary, respectively, on its executive board. The Texas IAF is expanding beyond its reliance on religious institutions to bring public schools into the heart of its decision-making structure. The benefits of the new diversity have already paid off, as one new church has joined Metro Alliance as a result of its parishioners' successful participation in the housing fairs held in the public schools. If the patterns of past years are followed, the San Antonio IAF chapters will lead the way in this important reorganization for other affiliates, thus transforming the internal culture of the Texas IAF, opening new avenues for the recruitment and development of community leaders, and strengthening the organization's ties to urban schools.

Academic Achievement

Although cognitive gains need to be measured on instruments far more complex than the tests used by the state of Texas to gauge children's academic ability, the overall rise in test scores in Alliance Schools does indicate that something is happening to agitate and advance the learning of low-income children. That ability to demonstrate progress in academic achievement has puzzled some observers, who, in spite of the literature linking parental involvement to achievement, have difficulty understanding how the involvement of low-income parents who may themselves be high school dropouts or command limited knowledge of English should increase achievement. A few hypotheses follow about why that linkage is manifest in many of the Texas IAF's school partnerships.

First, one of the major shifts in the cultural change of Alliance Schools involves educating parents about why test scores matter. It is part of the culture of schools in Texas that test scores are not indicated on report cards, and many parents are accustomed to thinking that report cards are the only indicators of academic achievement that matter. Many low-income parents are not aware that poor test scores will be used to track their children to lower tracks of classes once they reach middle school and high school. Those parents who do know something about test scores and tracking may know that colleges and universities do not request TAAS scores as part of the application process. For all of these reasons, many low-income parents have given their children the advice about Texas' tests that Lourdes Zamarron of Zavala Elementary gave her children before the transformation of their school: "I told them not to worry about it, that it really didn't matter," she recalled.

Second, once parents have understood the significance of test scores, Texas IAF organizations have held parent education workshops in which parents learn about how the state's test is designed and how they can help their children to prepare for it. For many parents, those workshops are their first opportunity to learn about standardized tests. Many schools have sponsored evening and weekend events in which parents, teachers, and volunteers coach students to prepare for tests.

Third, as part of the parent education workshops, Texas IAF organizers have worked with teachers to discuss the many ways in which parents can support their children's education. Low-income parents need to learn about the educational strategies employed by academically ambitious middle-class parents—limiting television viewing, establishing routines for doing homework, and talking with their children in ways that encourage their creativity and intellectual curiosity. Texas IAF organizers also give workshops which teach parents about the decline of manufacturing industries, the globalization of the economy, and the need to pay much greater attention to children's education than was necessary in the past.

A fourth reason that test scores have improved in many of the Alliance Schools may have to do with the way Texas IAF leaders and organizers approach the issue of test scores with parents. Although the temptation to denounce test scores as reductionist and inauthentic forms of evaluation is immense, IAF leaders and organizers have generally avoided debates about the reliability or validity of knowledge measured on standardized tests. Instead, they have used the low scores that many of the schools have when they first join the network as a lever for confronting a community with issues of academic achievement and creating a sense of urgency on behalf of school reform. Similarly, IAF leaders and organizers have avoided the many mine fields in contemporary school reform around issues such as multiculturalism, phonetics versus whole language approaches to reading, and outcomes-based versus more traditional forms of assessment. Organizers and leaders may have their own personal preferences on those issues, but they have not chosen to use them as a fulcrum for community organizing. By respecting the autonomy of professional educators on complex pedagogical issues, the Texas IAF has helped to create stability and a focus on academic achievement which constrains the democratic tumult which inevitably accompanies increased community engagement.

The initial response of many low-income parents to the Texas IAF workshops on testing and academic achievement has been anger. "Why didn't anybody ever tell us parents what these test scores mean?" one infuriated Austin parent inquired at a workshop in a new Alliance

School in 1994. Yet IAF organizers and leaders have not let the anger dwell on the issue of test scores. Instead, they have used that anger as a point of departure for reflecting on cultural change within schools, so that the unilateral nature of reports from the school to the community transforms into a richer culture of dialogue between parents, teachers, administrators, and students about instruction, curriculum, and assessment.

Although Texas IAF organizers do explain the significance of the tests to parents, they do not do so in an uncritical way. One of the reasons that Ernie Cortés has invited Howard Gardner, Deborah Meier, and Ted Sizer to speak at Texas IAF assemblies is so that parents and teachers can think more reflectively about the limitations of assessment as it is actually practiced in most public schools. In the short run, low-income parents need to learn about the political realities of standardized testing and the way that it is used to track their children into lower level classes. In the long run, they also need to learn that researchers increasingly view standardized tests as just one partial measure of children's intelligence, and a highly reductionist one at that.

One cannot emphasize enough the contextual nature of Texas IAF school organizing. Consider the example of Zavala Elementary in the spring of 1992, when an angry parent asked the teachers to explain the discrepancy between the high assessments Zavala students received from their teachers and the low results on Texas' state-mandated tests. It was of the utmost importance that *immediately* after that meeting Austin Interfaith organizers and leaders helped Zavala's defensive teachers to reach out to the community to learn more about neighborhood attitudes toward the school, and that Zavala teachers felt that the community was genuinely delighted to welcome them into their homes. It would be a grave misreading of the Zavala case to presume that parents or teachers could agitate the already demoralized staff of an urban school and then leave teachers on their own to find a solution to their dilemma. Such strategies, applied in isolation from the larger dynamic of constructive community building and continual follow-through, would consist of an atomistic and tragic misapplication of the real lessons to be garnered from parental engagement in schools.

11

"A Great Truth
Wants to Be Criticized"

It should be clear that the Texas IAF offers an intriguing new approach to American education at a critical juncture in the history of the public schools, when many commentators advocate a wholesale attack on and privatization of public education. Nonetheless, as the aphorism says, "A great truth wants to be criticized, not idolized." The Texas IAF, like all political organizations, gives evidence of shortcomings which require forthright criticism. For heuristic purposes, the areas of critique can be organized into issues of general political strategy, theoretical issues, and issues specific to school reform.[1]

To begin with issues of general political strategy, I have noted that one of the major transformations wrought by the IAF since Alinsky's death has been to ground local organizations almost exclusively in religious institutions. On the one hand, that strategy has many merits. Religious institutions enable individuals and communities to tap into powerful community networks, liturgical traditions rich in symbolism and meaning, and systems of belief which can provide powerful touchstones of group motivation and solidarity. Religious leaders can also disarm potential opponents of worthy reforms: the presence of nuns testifying on behalf of the health clinic at Zavala effectively undermined the credibility of opponents who feared that the clinic would promote materials advocating particular kinds of birth control.

On the other hand, however, individuals who are nonchurched or practice nonwestern religions are unlikely to experience the same kind of commitment to the brand of community organizing that characterizes the Texas IAF as do those who are in churches which pay dues and welcome the references to the Judeo-Christian tradition which animate Texas IAF conferences and assemblies. While a majority of Americans see themselves as affiliated with religious institutions, a large minority—43 percent—do not. Among ethnic minorities, roughly three-quarters of Hispanic Catholics are not practicing, and 22 percent of Blacks are unchurched. Although teachers, parents, and community members are all encouraged to participate in Texas IAF actions, those who are non-churched may feel like outsiders. This sentiment can occur when seating arrangements at assemblies are established on the basis of church affiliation or when individuals are asked to identify themselves by their congregation at smaller meetings.

Until recently, the Texas IAF had no strategy in terms of its dues-paying structure for organizing agnostics, atheists, nonchurched citizens, or members of other religious faiths such as Islam, Buddhism, or Hinduism. Only the relatively recent incorporation of schools into the organizations has provided an institutional base for recruiting un-churched citizens. On occasion, the overwhelming Christian presence in the Texas IAF can crowd out alternative expressions of faith. At a large Dallas Area Interfaith assembly in March 1996, for example, a clergyman led the assembly of over three thousand delegates in a prayer to Jesus Christ. For Ernie Cortés, such a prayer was entirely unacceptable; in a rare public criticism of an IAF organization, he subsequently stated at an Alliance School conference that "a few weeks ago Dallas Area Interfaith showed us how *not* to do a prayer. There was a prayer that was long and exclusive, in which anybody who was Jewish or Muslim would have felt isolated and excluded. We have to recognize that there are other legitimate traditions, and we've got to be willing to be inter-faith in the way we pray." Although the Texas IAF can expand to include other groups, such as Sikhs and Muslims—as British IAF organizations have done—that inclusion remains a project to be undertaken rather than an achievement already in place.[2]

Further, if religious institutions confer a number of blessings on the Texas IAF, they also bring problems with them. Religious institutions are among the most ethnically and racially segregated of American voluntary associations. And although participation in religious institutions is preponderantly female, women have battled for decades to obtain leadership positions in these institutions and are still blocked from higher positions in the Catholic Church. In the South, thousands of Baptist congregations have a strong evangelical component which challenges the separation of church and state and have sought to dictate school policy in curricular matters such as the treatment of evolution in science textbooks and classes. The movement to establish prayer in schools reflects the difficulty some religious institutions have respecting the separation of church and state that is codified in the First Amendment to the Constitution. Many middle-class and liberal Americans express skepticism about the integration of religious institutions into political life because of traditions of intolerance and authoritarianism that they associate with churches.

In addition to these considerations of nonchurched citizens, women's issues, and issues of church and state, reliance on religious institutions may also entail problems in organizing younger Americans. The traditionalist component of Texas IAF organizing works well with older citizens with families to support who identify themselves with religious institutions. It is not entirely clear, however, how much appeal the religious and political dimension of the Texas IAF carries for younger citizens who are much more immersed in contemporary secular and consumer culture, and whose points of reference may have more to do with MTV and fashion trends than with a grounding in Judeo-Christian traditions. This point is a particularly important one because a growing body of research suggests that parental support for education, though a significant influence on academic achievement, is not as powerful a determinant of students' daily study habits and attitudes toward school as their peer culture. The policy implication appears to be that effective strategies for educational achievement must build interconnected networks of support for schooling between and across families and youth cohorts.[3]

A second area of critique concerns the theoretical orientation of the Texas IAF. Texas IAF organizers and leaders point with pride to the hard-nosed and realistic aspect of IAF strategies. Unlike many organizations concerned with social change, the IAF accepts the idea that self-interest is a core feature of human nature, aims to identify winnable issues rather than ideological coups, distances itself from individuals who aren't willing to fight for themselves, and is willing to engage major power brokers in metropolitan areas rather than stigmatize them on charges of ethical dubiousness. There are advantages to each of these strategies, but there are also costs.

Consider the issue of human self-interest. It is of course essential to recognize that individuals are embedded in concrete political, economic, and social circumstances in which specific transformations can either enhance or damage their quality of life and their prospects. Taking the time to identify individuals' interests can enable organizers and leaders to develop innovative strategies with staying power, for when individuals see that their interests will be advanced, they are more likely to persevere with difficult pursuits. Starting with individuals' interests and expanding them to accommodate the needs of the community makes solid political sense under most any circumstances.

The difficulties commence when the focus on individuals' self-interest becomes exclusive, and organizers and leaders fail to appreciate that many community members become involved in the work of IAF organizations because their work appeals in a fundamental way to their ethical sense of right and wrong. One Alliance School principal stated that "one of the main things that I've learned from this work is that people always act in their self-interest—*always*." This principal, I would argue, has learned an erroneous lesson. For if individuals *always* act in their self-interest, it is difficult to explain not only self-destructive behavior in contemporary cities but also many of the moral and ethical conundrums which have plagued humanity throughout the ages.

A second theoretical issue concerns the IAF's emphasis on pragmatic values and winnable issues. One of the great advantages of organizing around battles that can be won is that it fosters a sense of success which in turn fuels the momentum needed for future victories. Christine Stephens of Dallas Area Interfaith said, "Our people have already experienced failure plenty of times. That's why they're in the shape they're in. They need to experience some victories, not just because that feels good, but primarily because victories enable people to dream. They release the imagination and help us to understand that things could be different."

Stephens' point is well taken, but the realities of politics are such that what is right and what is winnable are often in conflict with each other. Consider the issue of violence in urban neighborhoods and the easy access to firearms that leads inner-city youths to intimidate, wound, and kill each other with frightening regularity. The three cities which sell the highest quantities of guns in the United States are San Antonio, Dallas, and Houston. Surveys indicate that the roughly eighteen million Texans own over sixty million guns; the Texas Rifle Association estimates that there are almost four guns for every adult and child in the state. In 1994 over one hundred thousand Texans were imprisoned, many for offenses involving firearms, and in 1995 the Texas legislature legalized the carrying of concealed firearms. Yet because its leaders have ambivalent feelings about gun control, the Texas IAF is not in a position to take a stance on the issue.[4]

As a political organization, the Texas IAF must avoid issues that would split its constituency if it is to survive as a viable political actor in urban Texas. At the same time that one respects the Texas IAF's need for unity, however, one should not lose sight of the need for individuals to engage in openly partisan politics. Members of COPS can work effectively on the nonpartisan level for the expansion of public services for their children on Monday; on Tuesday they can work as individual citizens for candidates and platforms that will advance their interests and those of their communities. The growing social stratification of American society and the increasing impoverishment of American youth are not happenstance accidents, but the result of deliberate social policy decisions. Citizens need to develop complex political strategies which can have both partisan and nonpartisan, nonelectoral components.

One of the older criticisms of the IAF advanced by political radicals has been that the IAF evades incisive criticisms of capitalism and redirects citizens' grievances away from the causes of economic inequalities to deal with their symptoms. In a review of EPISO's work in El Paso, for example, Sallie Marston and George Towers complained that "EPISO's version of neighborhood politics excludes issues that carry a challenge to the American political and economic system." Mike Miller, himself a veteran community organizer, has lamented the "fundamental discontinuity with the Alinsky past" that is represented by the IAF in its current phase, and he has claimed that the "IAF almost makes a fetish of its commitment to 'moderates.'"[5]

It is certainly true that the Texas IAF, through its trainings, seminars, and assemblies, does not attack capitalism per se. "We recognize the role of the market for the coordination of economic activity," Cortés wrote. "The tools of a market mechanism—money and prices—are effective signals for what is to be produced, how much, and for whom." Yet Cortés has also embraced different strands of Catholic social thought which emphasize the principle of "subsidiarity" and that seek to establish mutually correcting relationships between the state, economy, and civil society. In this interpretation, the market has overextended itself in contemporary America and is in the process of undermining not just civil society but the very social preconditions that undergird capitalism in the first place. Hence, "The market has fundamental limits. It accepts grossly unequal distributions of income and power, which distort the very workings of the market process. The market mechanism seems oblivious to the many examples of market failure that lead to the externalities of pollution, environmental degradation, and social imbalance—what John Kenneth Galbraith pointed out as private splendor in the midst of public squalor." [6]

By dropping an ideological hard line against capitalism and seeking to establish a balance between the market, the state, and civil society, however, the Texas IAF has expanded its political options beyond the inflammatory protest politics of Saul Alinsky. The Texas IAF has never threatened a local city council with an Alinsky-style "shit-in" at the airport or a mass consumption of beans followed by attendance at the symphony, to cite two of the IAF founder's more outrageous gambits. While Ernie Cortés claims "fidelity to the tradition," the Texas IAF generally employs a more nuanced political rhetoric and strategy than that which Alinsky advocated. Commissioner Meno observed, "I don't see the tactics of Saul Alinsky in the Texas IAF, and I don't see protest in any of this."

As an organization, the Texas IAF has developed in such a way that protest is less and less necessary to serve its constituency. Former enemies, such as banker Tom Frost, are now on Project QUEST's board of directors, and the former lieutenant governor, Bill Hobby, has written complimentary articles about Project QUEST on the editorial pages of the *Houston Chronicle*. With the advantage of hindsight, Frost has come to recognize that COPS and other IAF organizations have a positive role to play in Texas politics. "It was too easy here for a long time," he said. "We had cattle, oil, and the military—things that weren't tied to the community. Now we've got to do some things, but we won't be able to go anywhere if we're a divided city." A certain amount of Texas nationalism—a regional force never to be underestimated—appears to have eased Frost's transition to working with Mexican Americans; he quipped to a *Wall Street Journal* reporter that "we can identify much more easily with a Mexican industrial complex like the one in Monterrey than we can with foreign countries like Pennsylvania and New Jersey." [7]

Frost is not alone in his appreciation of the changing dynamics of the Southwest. Other rich and powerful Texans, such as Ross Perot, Tom

Luce, and Bill Hobby, have not only let themselves be persuaded about the legitimacy of the Texas IAF's agendas, but have also become strong supporters of those agendas in the behind-the-scenes work that drives much of state and local politics. By understanding that a willingness to compromise is an indispensable part of all political work, and by appreciating the need for officials to receive public acclaim when they do take risks to deliver public services to low-income citizens, Texas IAF leaders and organizers have won the respect of the state's business and political elite so that protest politics are rarely necessary. Rather than protest political policies, the Texas IAF is much more likely to organize massive voter registration drives to develop the clout of working-class Texans. As part of such an emphasis, over one thousand Texas IAF leaders convened in Austin in December 1995 to develop a coherent strategy for mobilizing low-income citizens who have hitherto failed to use the franchise to advance their communities' interests.

There are dangers in the development of the newer, more relational politics of the Texas IAF, however. The acceptance of capitalism as an economic system can militate against the kinds of incisive critiques which illuminate just how powerfully market principles and the profit motive saturate civil society in the United States. A reluctance to dramatize social injustices through public confrontations can leave one unprepared for attacks from conservative opponents who are unimpressed with the traditionalist facets of the Texas IAF. A number of business and political leaders continue to wage ideological and legislative warfare against the Texas IAF and some of them, such as Tom Pauken, the chair of the Texas Republican Party, insist on defining the Texas IAF as a 1960s-style New Left organization.[8]

That public image can create obstacles to IAF community work. Philanthropist Jim Ketelsen said that even today when he mentions the IAF in a business context, some corporations object, "If you're working with that organization, we don't want to have anything to do with you." Ketelsen said, "There's a residue of feeling out there that this is not an organization that one should be dealing with." EPISO organizers and leaders have experienced similar opposition from principals in El Paso who want to be part of the Alliance Schools but are wary of ties to EPISO. Most political, corporate, and educational leaders, however, are now willing to work with IAF organizations to develop common strategies to improve education, health care, housing, and employment.

Some of the Texas IAF's supporters have expressed disappointment that the organization does not drop its nonpartisan stance during elections. "Ernie always says that 'our candidate is our agenda,'" former Lieutenant Governor Hobby observed. "But you and I know that that isn't the way that politics really works. In this business you need allies, and they [the Texas IAF] ought to support their friends more." To abandon its nonpartisan tradition, however, would be to give up an important facet of the Texas IAF's work, which is its effort to develop into a broad-based organization which includes Republicans as well as Democrats, conservatives as well as liberals. However legitimate Hobby's criticism might be, the Texas IAF could not endorse candidates without undermining one of the strongest foundations of its political power.

There are other limits to the Texas IAF's nonpartisan stance. When Mayor Todd of Austin sought to include sex education and counseling in school health clinics, for example, he was recognizing the hard fact that many Austin youth are both sexually active and ignorant of the consequences of their actions. Austin Interfaith was loyal to the Zavala Elementary School community and restricted the mission of the clinics. An impartial spectator, however, must ask whether the youth in the Austin schools were well served by that decision. The rationale that the community, and in particular the Catholic Church, did not want sex counseling in the schools is inadequate. The community and the church were not willing to address the need of Austin adolescents for forthright counseling and services which could, if properly conveyed, save the lives of youth who could become infected with AIDS or other contagious diseases.

Another point of critique relates to the method of IAF assemblies or actions. On the one hand, it is refreshing to observe public officials appearing in situations in which they respond in a strictly limited time period (often just one minute) to the questions of their constituents rather than upstage their constituents with the power of their office. On the other hand, the brevity of time allowed to public officials precludes public dialogue about their thoughts and relationships with their constituents, and that can strike one as a lost opportunity. "*We* talk, and *they* listen," is the way that one Dallas Area Interfaith leader explained the relationship between the leaders and public officials at an assembly at Munger Avenue Baptist Church in November 1993. Although that message of community empowerment is gratifying for citizens who usually feel excluded from the political process, it does not encourage the culture of conversations and vulnerability that Texas IAF leaders and organizers describe in training sessions and seminars.

The brevity of time available for dialogue can be especially disruptive and damaging in cases in which a public official has not been prepared appropriately for a meeting. Richard Alvarado, principal of Beacon Hill Elementary School, was asked publicly to commit to working with Metro Alliance at an action in San Antonio before he felt that he had had sufficient time to discuss the nature of the collaboration with his staff. The Texas IAF organizer grew angry when Alvarado refused to commit to the collaboration, and Alvarado felt attacked. "I was made to feel like a child in front of my peers and my superintendent," he said. "I was experiencing the negative images I had of COPS when I was younger." It was to take some skillful evaluation and recruitment after the meeting to win Alvarado back to the Texas IAF, but the misunderstanding could have been prevented if he had had more time to elaborate his reservations.

Some critics who are sympathetic to efforts to enliven civil society and reanimate the nation's political life have taken exception to the internal culture of IAF organizations and claimed that the organizations stifle independent thinking. Responding to Peter Skerry's presentation of the IAF in his book *Mexican Americans: The Ambivalent Minority*, Bruce Cain criticized the "highly authoritarian" facets of IAF organizations, in which "individuality and independent thinking are not encouraged." Cain wrote,

> I do not regard Alinsky organizing as good democratic political training for anyone, no matter how backward and uneducated he or she might be. I question whether independent thinking should ever be discouraged, whether the goal of any legitimate community organization should be to harass and humiliate public officials routinely, and whether nonpartisanship is a virtue. To my mind, organizations that teach such things do not appropriately prepare citizens for a democracy.[9]

In my view, Cain's concerns are misplaced, but they are understandable given a superficial knowledge of IAF organizations. Texas IAF assemblies are usually not about the give-and-take of democratic deliberation;

in Cortés' interpretation, they are more "public dramas" than they are forums for reflection and consensus building. The purpose of most of the assemblies is not so much to encourage independent thinking as it is to present to public officials a united front and to mirror back to a community a sense of its own efficacy.

Much of the democratic deliberation that occurs in IAF community organizing *precedes* the assemblies. In training sessions, Ernie Cortés says to organizers and leaders repeatedly that there is no point in holding house meetings if one intends to present a preestablished agenda to citizens; the point, rather, is to develop citizens' capacities to think out potential solutions to their problems themselves. Jean Bethke Elshtain, who has presented her work on political philosophy on three occasions at Texas IAF seminars, found that IAF organizers and leaders showed plenty of feistiness and independence in discussing her texts. "They're not afraid to criticize you, they're not afraid to criticize each other, and they're not afraid to do it hard," she commented. Ernie Cortés models the importance of opening oneself up for critique after the large assemblies he leads, when Texas IAF organizers and leaders evaluate the pros and cons of the efforts he spearheaded. Further, at certain kinds of Texas IAF assemblies—such as a large Alliance School conference in Houston in April 1996—school superintendents from Houston, Brownsville, San Antonio, Austin, and El Paso had extensive opportunities to address large audiences and respond to questions.

Texas IAF organizers and leaders have shown flexibility and the capacity to change their strategies when community stakeholders have indicated opposition and critique of their expectations in organizing neighborhoods. Many organizers have stated that when they first decided to work in schools, they anticipated that they would get involved with issues of teaching and curriculum, but parent leaders redirected them by insisting that they felt greater urgency about neighborhood issues such as crime, housing, and health care. When the parents in the *Segundo Barrio* demanded a change of leadership at Guillen Middle School in El Paso, they did not even bother to check with EPISO, but simply used their training in the house meetings to do the kind of independent advocacy that EPISO organizers always hoped they would develop. It is, in fact, difficult to imagine how IAF organizers could enforce a monolithic sectarian agenda even if they wanted to, for they are ultimately dependent upon their church members for dues and are hardly in a position to impose sanctions on clergy and laity who would insist on preserving particularistic aspects of their own political agendas. Ultimately, IAF organizers have to work with traditional political strategies entailing dialogue, persuasion, compromise, and consensus to maintain the necessary civic solidarity to attain desirable political goals.

Criticisms thus far have concerned the Texas IAF's overall organizing strategy, but one should also focus more specifically on the nature of the organizations' work in schools. One major problem in approaching that work is simply that, by and large, the organizations have not written sufficiently about their school efforts. Aside from its initial 1990 vision paper, the Texas IAF has not produced any sustained analysis of what it is attempting to do in schools, why it is committing so much work to the Alliance Schools, and what it hopes to achieve. As a result, there is a lack of clarity at the heart of the undertaking which makes it difficult to engage in the necessary debates and reformulations that can push school reform efforts to higher levels. This situation contrasts with that of other contemporary school reformers, such as Theodore Sizer, Henry Levin, Deborah Meier, or James Comer, who have set down in print their reflections on their philosophies and experiences, thus opening up the issues for a broad readership.

It is difficult to assess how much the absence of sustained written reflection on the work of the Alliance Schools reflects difficulties about establishing priorities, and how much is derived from other sources, such as time pressures and human resource shortages. On the one hand, it is clear that the Texas IAF seeks to improve academic achievement and prevent high school students from dropping out; on the other hand, the specific components of that struggle sometimes strike one as happenstance, as entirely dependent upon whatever might emerge from the community as a result of house meetings and assemblies. Granted that there is no single path to a better future, hammering out a few key principles, such as Sizer has done for the Coalition of Essential Schools, could give more texture to the Alliance Schools that would make them more readily accessible for potential reformers or those who are already veterans but could learn from the Alliance Schools' development.[10]

In addition to the lack of writing on the Alliance Schools, most Texas IAF leaders and organizers are unfamiliar with the professional world into which teachers are socialized and are unfamiliar with teachers' choices concerning different kinds of instruction, curricula, and assessment. This lack of knowledge can be an advantage; it may make it easier for organizers to share the confusion of parents with some of the unnecessary jargon and mystique of schooling and to demand clarification. Yet, given the vast scope of educational research, lack of knowledge about key findings about issues pertaining to reading or academic achievement in the disciplines can make it difficult to develop an informed strategy that successfully obtains desirable results. Would Morningside Middle School have experimented with advisory periods, or would Ysleta Elementary School have implemented multi-aged classrooms, if parents and educators had been aware of the ambivalent track records of such programs, not just in terms of cognitive development, but also in regard to psychosocial dynamics? [11]

Another potential problem pertains to the manner in which the Texas IAF organizations approach the issue of state test scores. Most educators would agree that memorization and test taking should be part of schoolwork, but most would also agree that schools should strive for a balanced approach which incorporates social skills, artistic creativity, critical analysis, and sustained reflection into the curriculum. Most of the Alliance Schools, just like most public schools in Texas, so heavily emphasize the test-taking skills that are measured on the TAAS that they find it almost impossible to attend to the higher order thinking skills that would require more multidimensional and authentic measures of assessment. As a consequence, many of the citizenship skills that the Texas IAF promotes—such as identifying problems, critical thinking about solutions, small group deliberation, public speaking, and compromise—inevitably are relegated to a low priority in the battle to raise test scores.

In addition to the problems mentioned above, there is a negative side to parental engagement which accompanies every effort to bring parents into schools. All veteran teachers and principals have experienced parents who have sought to advance their children's private interests at the cost of their class or community. Other parents are shrill about high standards in the school but provide no supervision or discipline for their children at home. For principals who already feel beleaguered by their faculty, their students, their district office, and the Texas Education Agency, the prospect of inviting in politically active parents can be intimidating. One principal in an Alliance School in Houston sighed, "It was already hard enough to keep my teachers and the district happy before. Now that we've gone and told the parents we want them in the school, I've got another whole constituency to try to please."

In reviewing the case studies, it is important to recognize that most of the Alliance Schools have had a perverse kind of advantage that many public schools do not share. Because Alliance Schools are concentrated in low-income neighborhoods with relatively homogeneous student populations, they have been able to unify around obvious and pressing community needs. They have largely avoided the divisive politics which can accompany parental engagement when parents come from differing class and ethnic backgrounds. Strategies of parental engagement which are based in more heterogeneous public schools may evince competing and mutually exclusive demands for change that may be more difficult for the community and the school to reconcile, and may result in middle-class or affluent parents exercising their clout to acquire preferential treatment for their own children.[12]

In spite of the infinite number of possible distractions and coalitions for Texas IAF organizations, Texas IAF leaders and organizers have kept their focus on neighborhood schools in low-income urban communities. That commitment has reaped rewards in those communities, but it does indicate that the Alliance School principles and methods of organizing may be of limited value when transferred to other kinds of campuses. The Alliance School strategy of community engagement and political empowerment would be far more difficult to implement (if not impossible) in magnet schools with no strong residential community in the immediate vicinity. The Texas IAF could play a role in developing social capital in such schools, but its forte in neighborhood organizing would require the cultivation of creative new strategies for engaging parents in conversations about their children.

These criticisms of the Texas IAF suggest that the Alliance Schools would do well to develop greater theoretical coherence and more systematic documentation of their work. In addition, they would benefit from cultivating closer relationships with teacher education programs in colleges and universities. Even though almost all teacher education programs in universities encourage community involvement in schools, few actually transmit philosophies and strategies for promoting parental engagement. One survey revealed that only 15 percent of teacher education programs dedicate even part of one course to community involvement and only 4 percent devote an entire course to the subject. Another survey revealed that of the more than eight hundred skills, competencies, and objectives measured in state teacher certification tests, less than 2 percent had anything to do with influences on education outside of the classroom—only one of which concerned parental involvement. Research shows that student teachers recognize the necessity of parental involvement in the process of schooling, but it also suggests that student teachers think of that involvement in terms of what parents can do for the teacher. The concept that teachers might be proactive in cultivating relationships with parents to develop comprehensive strategies for school and neighborhood improvement is not part of student teachers' conceptualization of teaching and is, in general, not a part of teacher education programs. After teachers enter the schools, the lack of dialogue with the community persists; Robert Rivera estimated that a substantial majority of all of the teachers in Houston with whom TMO worked had never visited a student's home before TMO organized a Walk for Success for their school.[13]

One upshot for teacher education programs is that participatory research into the dynamics of urban neighborhoods and communities should become a more pronounced component of teacher preparation. Understanding the social and political geography of urban neighborhoods through visits to homes, churches, recreation centers, youth organizations, and small businesses should become a more visible strand of teacher education. The classroom observations by preservice teachers which are required in most states can be linked by innovative teacher educators with participation in neighborhood and community events beyond the boundaries of the school.

Of all of the Texas IAF organizations, EPISO and TMO have been most energetic in linking Alliance Schools to teacher education programs. EPISO organizer Elsy Fierro-Suttmiller collaborated with Professor Jorge Deskamp at the School of Education at the University of Texas at El Paso in 1994 and the El Paso Alliance Schools to help teacher education students to attend house meetings, develop activities to encourage parental engagement, and study critical theories of education. In 1995 and 1996, I took my own students in the teacher education program at Rice University on Jefferson Davis' Walk for Success. "We felt so defeated when we finished reading Kozol's *Savage Inequalities*," one graduate student said. "But the walk showed us so much hope, and that hope can give you energy." A senior observed, "All of the parents were so excited that we were there, and an especially important thing that I learned was that there wasn't just support by parents for their own kids. Those parents really care about all of the kids in their community."

At the same time that fieldwork should be integrated into teacher preparation, a much greater emphasis on the public and political dimensions of teaching must be infused into preservice studies. Developing the capacity to challenge the received culture, learning to make public presentations, infusing conversational skills into the instructional repertoire of teachers, and other strategies for building social capital should all be facets of any teacher education program which aspires to a robust actualization of civic engagement. Faculty in teacher education programs in Texas should establish links with Alliance Schools so that teacher education students can observe and learn from the development of political leadership in low-income schools and communities.[14]

One challenge for teacher education programs which seek to develop social capital between the school and the community has to do with the penetration of marketplace concepts of choice into the public school arena. On the whole, teacher education programs have followed public schools in accepting the transformation of schools for citizenship into schools for customers, clients, and consumers. Ideology matters, and it is difficult to imagine how the public sector and civic life can ever be reinvigorated if the dominant rhetoric of our society and schools purge the language of citizenship and public life from their discourse. Defining students as consumers, customers, and workers will never provide an adequate foundation for a democratic theory of education which stresses relationships of solidarity, reciprocity, and trust over those of choice, mobility, and exchange value.[15]

One way to assure that Alliance Schools can place pressure upon teacher education programs to change is to emphasize parental engagement in their hiring procedures. Robert Hemphill, the principal of Alamo Elementary School in El Paso, asks all of the applicants for teaching positions in his Alliance School how they feel about parents in the classroom both as learners and as teaching resources. If candidates express reservations about parental engagement, Hemphill knows that that teacher is inappropriate for his school. As teacher education faculty learn that principals select applicants who are committed to parental engagement, their programs should change to accommodate the changing emphases of the schools.

A further point of critique concerns the lack of articulation between the Alliance Schools' work on school and community improvement and curriculum development within the schools. We have seen a few examples of overlap between the school's curriculum and the development of its community in social studies education at Beacon Hill and interdisciplinary units on shelter and the housing initiative at Herff. Far too often, however, the excitement which accompanies a victory in an Alliance School or its neighborhood does not inform or transform the classroom practice that is at the heart of the educational enterprise. Yet it does not take much insight to perceive that many of the skills taught by Texas IAF leaders and organizers—such as identifying an issue, conducting research actions, making public presentations, working on a team, and evaluating policy issues—are intensely pedagogical in nature. Finding ways in which democratic practices in the community and curriculum development in the school can reinforce, invigorate, and transform each other should become yet another part of building social capital and enhancing academic achievement in the Alliance Schools.

Texas' Alliance Schools are only just beginning as a serious school reform effort. The Alliance Schools operate in the context of a huge state educational system. Although the work of the Texas IAF on House Bill 72 and the networks of civic activism created among the Alliance Schools are making an impact, the vast majority of schools in Texas operate beyond the ambit of the Alliance Schools. Of course, the foregoing criticisms of Alliance Schools are offered at an early stage of the undertaking, and many of the comments advanced here will have to be addressed through the continuous evolution and growth of the Alliance School network.

In regard to the criticisms expressed above, several counterpoints should be noted. For one thing, although religious institutions will continue to be privileged as the social base for Texas IAF organizing, the inclusion of schools in the social base of the Metro Alliance in San Antonio signals a new willingness to expand institutional representation into new kinds of social networks. IAF organizations outside of Texas include labor unions and teachers' associations in their dues-paying members, and Texas IAF groups can follow their lead in diversifying their organizational base. Further, although the IAF's emphasis on self-interest may jar with the appeal to conscience that animates much of the Judeo-Christian tradition, it nonetheless fits comfortably with that same tradition's recognition of the darker side of human nature, as well as with the blunt acknowledgment of human shortcomings that undergirds founding national documents of the American political tradition.[16]

There are also several counterpoints to criticisms of the IAF's political strategies. First, even if the structure of some Texas IAF assemblies fore-closes discussion and debate with public officials, it does provide a sense of community efficacy and drama that makes such events provocative and fulfilling. Second, the Texas IAF does not see its role as one of taking a stance on all policy issues, so that although individuals in the organizations may support topics relevant to gun control, the organization cannot afford to endorse divisive issues that would polarize its constituency. Third, although some elected officials may feel that the Texas IAF owes them personal loyalty because of their assistance in supporting the IAF's agenda, a nonpartisan strategy is absolutely indispensable if the IAF is to develop long-term organizational strategies such as the Alliance Schools, which can have a lasting effect on inner-city schools and neighborhoods.

Finally, in regard to the politics of its educational strategies, the Texas IAF does not seek to develop a totalistic philosophy of education which would prescribe the precise route to be taken in improving urban schools. Although certain costs may be attached to its highly process-oriented work in communities—such as the reluctance to articulate a comprehensive agenda for educational reform—the Texas IAF in general prefers to maintain a stance of maximum openness to new kinds of ideas and strategies that can emerge from urban communities. The lack of background in instruction, curriculum, assessment, and educational research which characterizes many leaders and organizers is a limitation which has been identified and which is being addressed through training sessions and conferences.

Thus, the criticisms advanced above can, in general, be countered on several grounds. Further, some of the problems noted are amenable to correcting influences. The social base of the Texas IAF in religious institutions, for example, can be expanded to accommodate Americans who are unchurched and have no interest in participating in religious institutions. In addition, IAF organizers' lack of knowledge about education can be corrected through study, debate, and the experience which comes from hundreds of hours of observation and intervention in schools. In terms of the question of political partisanship, the exclusive emphasis on issue-driven politics within the organization can be balanced through partisan politics by individual members in groups outside of the Texas IAF organization's boundaries. Finally, teacher education programs can be engaged to reflect and accommodate the changes that are occurring in the Alliance Schools, and teachers and Texas IAF leaders can develop conversations and seminars to enhance curriculum development relevant to community change and citizenship skills. Thus, IAF organizations can build on past successes and continue to build stronger alliances throughout cities with new or evolving organizations. All of these changes can be prompted by continued work in Alliance Schools and a continued expansion of the multiethnic, interclass organizing base that is committed to Texas IAF school collaboratives and the generation of a democratic civic culture.

12

Building Laboratories
of Democracy

When Supreme Court Justice Louis D. Brandeis wrote his famous decision which used the phrase "laboratories of democracy" for the first time in 1938, he was referring to the importance of establishing different laws in different states so that the states could learn from others' successes and failures. As used here, a "laboratory of democracy" refers to a site in which citizens come together around common concerns, identify strategies for engaging public servants and the private sector, and negotiate solutions which can enhance the quality of lives in their communities. In this context, "laboratories of democracy" has deep affinities with John Dewey's understanding of democracy. "A democracy is more than a government," Dewey wrote. "It is primarily a mode of associated living, of conjoint, communicative experience." [1]

Where were the "laboratories of democracy" referred to in this account? They were incarnated in the house meetings conducted by Nehemiah Davis and Leonora Friend in the Morningside neighborhood of South Fort Worth, the breakthrough school board meeting attended by Zavala parents in Austin, the Walks for Success in Houston's Near North Side, and the housing fairs at Herff, Beacon Hill, and Stewart elementary schools in San Antonio. They were manifested in Dolores de Avila's visits to Austin to support House Bill 72, Toña Vasquez's testimony before the Texas Senate Education Committee, and the assembly at Holy Name Catholic Church that sparked radical forms of community engagement in schools throughout San Antonio. They occurred whenever the most diverse kinds of citizens who work or live in the central cities found new ways of communicating, negotiating, and holding themselves and others accountable around their community's interests.

When actualized as a center of the community, each Alliance School can become a "laboratory of democracy." Yet one must recall that the Alliance Schools are a young initiative, that the schools are embedded in neighborhoods grappling with a gamut of social problems, and that each school must pass through its own developmental process to evolve from a site of bureaucratic control to a center of civic activism. Created by the Texas Education Agency and the Texas IAF in 1992, many of the Alliance Schools are only now beginning to realize the potential of parental and political engagement to improve their students' academic achievement and their communities. Given their relatively recent appearance on the pedagogical landscape, one must be prudent in the current context in speculating about the larger meaning and import of the Texas IAF school collaboratives. Nonetheless, if the foregoing narrative and analysis have been accurate, and if the Alliance Schools are able to sustain their current momentum, they will raise a number of questions and challenges which can provoke us to think anew about current reform movements in education.

Most educators and school reformers try to keep politics out of discussions about schools—as if that were possible or desirable in a robust democracy. The Alliance Schools take an altogether different stance, and suggest that educators and reformers can better serve urban children and their parents if they frankly recognize the interplay between politics and education in the public schools and consciously endeavor to appeal to constituencies which cross the lines of race, class, and religion. They teach that parents and teachers need political training to become advocates for their children and their communities. Finally, they avoid a narrow sectarianism, and teach that those politics which are practiced by community-based organizations must be nonpartisan and identify salient themes which will appeal to all streams of the political spectrum.

The Alliance Schools offer an intriguing object lesson in their explicit attempt to build social capital. By placing social capital formation at the center of their political organizing, the Alliance Schools not only have contributed to their own development, but also have redirected the trajectory of social capital theory in education. They offer new points of departure not just for parents and public school teachers, in other words, but also for policymakers.

Ironically, much of the thrust for concepts of choice in education in the 1980s came from social capital theorist James Coleman himself, who deplored what he referred to as "the destruction of geographic functional communities" in the United States. For Coleman, the collapse of residential neighborhoods as functional communities was a given which no amount of wishful thinking could undo. High rates of residential mobility, the entrance of women into the waged work force, school busing to achieve racial integration, and the popularity of television were only a few of the major social forces which he identified as having destroyed functional communities in which parents felt and exercised a joint responsibility for the community's children. Coleman saw choice programs as avenues to create what he termed "value communities," in which people with similar orientations from disparate parts of a city could come together to share and sustain common norms.[2]

Coleman's research and recommendations powerfully influenced educational policy debates in the United States in the late 1980s and early 1990s by providing social scientific ammunition for advocates of the privatization of public schooling. "Perhaps the most fundamental policy implication of the social capital concept is that the separation of church and state in the United States has been a disservice to education, especially of disadvantaged children," Myron Lieberman wrote in *Privatization and Educational Choice*. "Such separation has forced our society to avoid utilizing religious institutions to educate our youth. Inasmuch as disadvantaged children are the ones who are most handicapped by the absence of social capital, government inability to provide education through denominational schools has been especially harmful to them." Other policy analysts have shared Lieberman's conviction that social capital theory best supports a privatization of education by enabling citizens to construct "value communities" based on their personal convictions and educational preferences.[3]

The evidence from the Alliance Schools challenges Coleman's dismissal of urban neighborhoods as potential functional communities and Lieberman's suggestion that collaborations between public schools and religious institutions under existing arrangements cannot generate social capital. The Alliance Schools demonstrate that Americans can strengthen already existing functional communities and that they can build bridges between schools and churches without undermining the First Amendment. Contemporary urban communities look different from the middle American town described by Robert and Helen Lynd in *Middletown*, to which Coleman explicitly referred, but that difference may indicate an improvement rather than a deficit. After all, the Lynds were dismayed with the provincialism and self-satisfaction they observed in Middletown. Rather than perpetuate parochialism, the Alliance Schools seek to engage urban schools with larger social forces, and the Texas IAF constantly exposes its organizers and leaders to professionals from a wide range of intellectual backgrounds to overcome the potentially stultifying effect of a strictly local perspective.

It is important to recognize that there is nothing in the Alliance School concept per se that explicitly challenges the issue of choice in public schools as they are now constituted. However, the Alliance Schools *do* challenge the rationale for choice programs in that they strive to develop an educational landscape in which choosing to attend a neighborhood school with a range of beneficial community-based programs can be more appealing than selecting a magnet school in another neighborhood which receives special stipends for its magnet programs from the district. Since so much emphasis has gone into magnet schools and other choice programs in the past two decades, perhaps it is time to emphasize new strategies for making neighborhood schools a genuinely desirable choice, rather than the default option they have too often become.

To develop social capital in urban schools and neighborhoods, the Texas IAF has developed into a broad-based organization which cuts across political allegiances. Conservatives value the Alliance Schools because of their grounding in Judeo-Christian ethics, their appreciation of the role of secondary institutions in American society, and their emphasis on self-reliance, as codified in IAF principles such as the Iron Rule. Liberals who care about the heterogeneity of the American polity and want to use tax dollars wisely to alleviate poverty derive satisfaction from the manner in which Alliance Schools expedite the provision of public services such as health care and education to low-income citizens and their children. Radicals who seek to enhance the political participation and empowerment of low-income citizens see the Alliance Schools as a contribution to a more just society characterized by the control of public institutions by community residents.

While the Alliance Schools have been able to break through political stereotypes about school reform by developing a philosophy and practice of education which cuts across the political spectrum, however, it would be a mistake to suggest that they do not run counter to powerful tendencies and convictions in our society. If cultural conservatives find little to contest in the Alliance Schools, marketplace conservatives will object to the Texas IAF's criticism of unlimited growth, and especially that kind of growth which undermines strong working-class neighborhoods. Advocates of school choice may feel that the Alliance Schools' emphasis on enhancing neighborhood schools rather than promoting choice perpetuates bureaucratic incompetence and abandons a strategy which has shown some success in integrating urban schools. Liberals may feel that the secular nature of public schools is threatened by the Alliance Schools' links to religious institutions; others may feel that the reference to common norms in social capital theory represents a threat to the unorthodox opinions and lifestyles commonly sanctioned by liberal conceptions of individualism and tolerance. Radicals are likely to feel uneasy with the Texas IAF's readiness to collaborate with all kinds of political partners, from corporate CEOs such as Ross Perot and Jim Ketelson to conservative Catholic clergy and fundamentalist Baptists.

The Alliance Schools thus are vulnerable to a wide range of attacks from political opponents. Yet, if many political perspectives do not harmonize easily with the Alliance Schools collaboratives, others do. At the very least, Alliance Schools challenge us to reconsider the configuration of our relationships to schools, religious institutions, and communities; they further seek to reanimate norms embedded in democratic-republican and Judeo-Christian traditions. By infusing those values into a public sphere increasingly dominated by market values, the Alliance Schools strive to provide working-class communities with a language in which they can conceptualize the problems and a form of effective political advocacy with which they can address them.

When one steps back from the ideological issues at hand and turns to the immediate needs of low-income urban communities, of course, the concerns discussed above can seem abstract and unimportant for public school students and their parents. Most communities are far more heterogeneous and pragmatic than one imagines when one characterizes them, in shorthand fashion, as "liberal," "conservative," or "radical." Catholics who are conservative about birth control generally are liberal about government programs to support the poor; African Americans who are liberal about civil rights can be cultural conservatives when it comes to their engagement with religious institutions; White suburbanites who are fiscal conservatives can be liberal about sexual preferences or other lifestyle choices. For those who are dissatisfied with or feel limited by the orthodoxies of the Left and Right, the Alliance Schools are an object lesson in the creativity which can be unleashed when one is willing to engage citizens at the intimate public level of the house meetings, listen to their concerns and their proposals for action, and facilitate political strategies that cut across orthodox political lines.

Just as the Alliance Schools effort confounds our stereotypes of the most common kinds of political alignment in theory, so does it transcend the current orthodoxies of educational policy. In a country with an educational system founded upon the separation of church and state, the Alliance Schools suggest that supportive relationships can be built between public schools and religious institutions which can enhance academic achievement and neighborhood stability. In a time when educational technology is revolutionizing the classroom by creating instant access to resources in Germany and Japan, the Alliance Schools teach us about the value of face-to-face conversations with our immediate neighbors. In a period when Communism has collapsed as a competing political ideology and marketplace values reign uncontested, the Alliance Schools seek to recover and reanimate nonmarket values and lost concepts of citizenship which have enriched the western political tradition. In a period when policymakers by and large condemn neighborhood schools and agree that vouchers and choice are the wave of the future, Alliance Schools teach about building networks of reciprocity between geographically circumscribed neighborhoods and schools to develop social capital.

Alliance Schools as an aggregate are disinterested in both orthodox political alignments and so-called "cutting-edge" educational policies. In practice as in theory, the hybrid ensemble of social forces supporting the Alliance Schools gives this initiative a unique vibrancy. None of the other contemporary movements to reform American education brings together a history of community organizing, a social base in religious institutions, and a commitment to citizenship in such a fecund synthesis. James Comer, Henry Levin, and Ted Sizer all have played major roles in improving American public schools in the past decade, and their school reform efforts have enriched hundreds of American schools, including some Alliance Schools. None of those reformers, however, defines the political empowerment of parents as one of its key criteria of success. Among the major school reform movements, only the Alliance Schools have found a way to engage the community on a political level and to develop it as a catalyst which can improve urban schools.

One must, of course, recognize that there are a wide range of community-based organizations that play one role or another in the nation's schools. As of this writing, the Association of Community Organizations for Reform Now (ACORN) has two partner schools in New York City and is involved in collaborative efforts with schools in Chicago, St. Paul, Boston, and Seattle. ACORN's school reform work shares many similarities with the IAF. ACORN trains low-income parents in political leadership skills to enhance their efficacy as advocates for their children; strives to develop a broad-based civic organization that cuts across class and ethnic lines; and views school reform as integrally connected to larger issues of community development, including home ownership, economic opportunity, and health care.[4]

In spite of the similarities, there are also numerous points of contrast between ACORN and the IAF. ACORN members join as individuals and are not formally linked to religious institutions. Further, ACORN endorses candidates for political office and energetically campaigns on their behalf. Finally, ACORN is much more willing to disrupt public assemblies with protest politics entailing civil disobedience than is the IAF. As ACORN's school reform efforts gain greater momentum, their experiences should offer an intriguing opportunity for comparison and contrast with IAF organizations, and especially with those in Texas, which have gone the furthest in the depth and scope of their educational collaboratives.[5]

The IAF and ACORN are the largest and most successful community-based organizations in the country, but their visibility should not lead one to overlook the wealth of local initiatives which enrich the fabric of community culture in low-income urban neighborhoods. Community-based organizations help with sports, tutoring, and community service programs in working-class neighborhoods throughout the country. They provide linkages between the school and community on the basis of ethnic identification; they serve as bridges to the broader worlds of employment, health, and the arts; and they assist with concrete and pressing needs relating to child care, the education of pregnant teenagers, and the nurturance of young families. All of those efforts are worthy of sustained research and analysis.

In spite of the broad scope of civic engagement in schools, the Alliance Schools occupy a unique position in the contemporary school reform movement. The network of over one hundred schools linked to a state department of education and a host of religious institutions committed to political advocacy represents a novel and potent development in school reform and civic engagement. Their successful development does not mean, however, that they do not need strong allies in other school reform efforts. Alliance Schools have learned much from the Coalition of Essential Schools' attempts to develop student-centered curricula and more authentic forms of assessment than standardized testing. The Comer Schools' recognition of the complexity of each child's individual psychological development and the value of school-based social services adumbrated and contributed to the Alliance Schools' emphasis on the social context of learning and development. Howard Gardner's elaboration of the theory of multiple intelligences at Alliance School conferences has assisted many teachers' pursuit of more sophisticated ways of apprehending, encouraging, and assessing cognition. As of this writing, several Alliance Schools are developing collaborative ties with Bob Moses' innovative work on the Algebra Project. The Alliance Schools should be seen as yet another piece of the complex ensemble of contemporary school reform. They are not and cannot be a totalistic solution to a heterogeneous matrix of educational and civic challenges.[6]

Just as the Alliance Schools add one valuable piece to the mosaic of contemporary school reform, so does the theory of social capital contribute to a dynamic reconceptualization of the relationships between civil society, the state, and the economy. Instead of simply focusing on financial capital—the proclivity of citizens in a capitalist economy—social capital theory enables us to disaggregate the different kinds of capital which can sustain a democratic society. Social capital, paraphrased in IAF work as "relational power," provides a different lens for interpreting kinds of school and political reform, a lens that focuses on human interrelationships and their economic consequences. For too long we have focused simply on the *human* capital of individuals in education rather than the *social* capital which exists between individuals, organizations, and institutions. That theoretical impasse can be overcome as we identify and develop new strategies for creating stronger social ties and trust between the students, teachers, and parents who are engaged with our schools and communities.

The Alliance Schools effort has arisen at a particularly precarious time in American history. It is a time in which it has become acceptable to project hitherto unimaginable public displays of hate on low-income people and their children, not only for radio talk-show hosts but also for leading political figures in the United States Congress. No time in American public life has been so marked by the class supremacy of the rich over the poor since the imposition of Jim Crow rule in the South in the 1890s. Yet in spite of—indeed, because of—the polarized political climate of our country at present, it is imperative that one think and act clearly.

Reflection upon both the serious problems and the significant work accomplished by the Alliance Schools suggests a fourfold political strategy for grappling with this polarized political climate. First, one must defend the simple notion that the public sector *has* to have strong public schools. Although one frequently hears from fiscal conservatives that the United States invests more resources in education than other industrialized nations, the statistics are misleading because of the much larger population in the United States and the inclusion of higher education in the data. When one disaggregates higher education from primary and secondary education and examines education spending as a percentage of the gross domestic product, the United States takes a low rank among industrialized countries. Our higher education system is the best in the world, but our system of public education on the primary and secondary levels consistently is outperformed by other industrialized nations in international comparisons. Further cuts would exacerbate social problems that are already severe and exacerbate the cynicism and disengagement that typify vicious circles. Ideology matters, and commitment to the public sector and public schools in a time when both are under siege is an indispensable point of departure for individuals and groups who care about our common civic culture.[7]

The second strategy is to build strong community-based organizations which can effectively advocate for programs which will benefit poor and working-class children. In 1995, Congress pushed to put many social programs such as free meals for poor children into block grants to the states. Low-income Americans had had bad experiences with this strategy before: in the 1960s, urban school districts and organized middle-class Americans redirected compensatory education funds which had been issued in the form of block grants away from poor children and into programs for the middle class. Strong community-based organizations, however, could play the role of advocates who would make sure that low-income children received the food they needed. COPS and

Metro Alliance control federal block grants to San Antonio for urban renewal, and could do the same with block grants for education.[8]

Of course, it is imperative to ensure that we are systematic in identifying bona fide community organizations. Community organizations may be inconspicuous in appearance, and yet be remarkably powerful in their ability to mobilize people. With the exception of Austin Interfaith, for example, Texas IAF organizations have their offices in blue-collar neighborhoods rarely visited by professional elites. The utmost of caution must be exercised in identifying genuine community organizations, however; simple location in a working-class neighborhood does not mean that the organization possesses any real following in a community. For most of this work, I have used the term "community" to convey a common identity among a group of people in a particular location, but I should emphasize at this point that the unity suggested by the word "community" can mask and distort a wide range of different and even opposing social currents. Urban neighborhoods can be just as divided and competitive in their internal fabric as any other kind of social ensemble. Only an expenditure of considerable amounts of time and identification of popular rather than straw organizations can lead to effective community-based collaborations with schools.

A further complication entailed in identifying community organizations concerns the values and structures of secondary associations, which can have a tremendous positive or negative impact on school reform efforts. A community organization can have a genuine basis of popular support in a neighborhood and espouse racist or misogynistic beliefs, for instance; and although popular support has its merits, it hardly can be posited as a *summum bonum* detached from other legitimate concerns. Alternately, a community organization can espouse democratic values, mobilize communities on behalf of worthy goals, and then fall prey to a factionalism which results in political debacles. The key issue here may have to do with the educability of organizations—whether they are disposed to go through the process of internal learning and external engagement which can produce strong and dynamic civic networks.

Even without a linkage to community organizations, educators can initiate some of the steps utilized by the Texas IAF to identify neighborhood leaders, conduct house meetings, and develop political strategies. The principal and teachers at Lee Elementary School in Houston were so impressed with the momentum they saw generated at Jefferson Davis High School that they decided to implement a parent visitation strategy with no training from TMO and little more than a hearty can-do spirit. The parents received them with enthusiasm and Lee's first Walk for Success generated a tremendous spirit of goodwill. Political education per se was not a part of that Walk for Success, but it did demonstrate the initiative that can be taken with little theoretical superstructure when teachers and administrators are serious about forging strong relationships with the community.

A third strategy of promoting community engagement in schools might be to contact local clergy to begin to develop sponsoring committees to form new IAF organizations or other kinds of community-based organizations. IAF organizations now exist in disparate communities such as Memphis, New York, Chicago, New Orleans, and Los Angeles; there appears to be no reason why they could not exist in the many other communities and cities suffering from high rates of poverty and civic disengagement. One component of this strategy—and one that may perplex traditional educators—is that the community-based organizations must not be too narrowly confined to the schools. If COPS, ACT, EPISO, or TMO focused their efforts exclusively on schools, they would lose much of their clout and their efficacy as agents of social capitalization. It is precisely because they are not captive to the interests of large public bureaucracies and maintain deep roots in local communities that they sustain credibility in working-class neighborhoods. Restricting their efforts to work within schools could render a community-based organization captive to urban school districts and their own, often troubled, internal politics.

Finally, the fourth component of the strategy is theoretical: one must maintain a strict sense of boundaries about what a community-based organization can and cannot do in urban schools and neighborhoods, and develop collaboratives with those organizations and individuals who can supply the many pieces of school reform which are not emphasized by community-based organizations. TMO, the Metro Alliance, and ACT do not pretend to provide expertise to schools in matters of pedagogy, curricula, or assessment—concerns which are at the heart of the educational enterprise. Texas IAF organizations recognize their limitations and seek to educate themselves about leading currents of school reform as articulated by theorists and practitioners such as Deborah Meier,

Howard Gardner, Ted Sizer, and James Comer. Respect for the autonomy of the school and the experience of teachers and administrators is a central precondition for successful collaborations between community-based organizations and urban schools.

Whatever fruits such strategies may produce must remain a matter of speculation for the immediate future. Even with the different setbacks that the Alliance Schools have experienced, one may posit that Texas IAF's work has accrued sufficient momentum and staying power to initiate a reconceptualization of American public education. Instead of pursuing marketplace models of school reform, the Alliance Schools indicate that we need to support neighborhood schools by strengthening their ties to their immediate communities. Instead of focusing on fixing the school in isolation from its environment, the Alliance Schools suggest that one can develop integrated strategies of neighborhood improvement and school revitalization. Instead of asking parents to become involved in strengthening the existing culture of the school, we can challenge parents to become engaged in agitating and transforming the school's culture. Instead of relegating parents and students to the roles of clients, consumers, and recipients of information, we can challenge them to become citizens with the skills and commitment to strengthen our struggling urban schools and neighborhoods. The future is open and there are no guarantees. Nonetheless, the development and popularity of the Alliance Schools in Texas provides a powerful counter-example to the dominant rhetoric of privatization and marketplace models of reform.

The diffusion of the Alliance Schools concept beyond Texas is currently under way. As of this writing, the spread of Alliance Schools has taken its most advanced form in Arizona, where IAF organizations in Tucson and Phoenix have organized twenty Alliance Schools in collaboration with local districts and the state department of education. Unlike the Texas Alliance Schools, however, they have not acquired funds from the commissioner of education or waivers for school development programs. "Our superintendent of schools doesn't have the same power that the commissioner in Texas does," said Frank Pierson of Pima County Interfaith. "And the development of our Alliance Schools will inevitably look different than the Texas network. Still, the central thread which emphasizes a culture of conversations and teaching people about power and their self-interests will be the same." Arizona's Alliance

Schools have already won important victories by gaining funding for after-school programs and youth employment projects; they have also gone further than Texas' Alliance Schools by formalizing relationships with local chapters of the American Federation of Teachers. Arizona will provide an intriguing laboratory for the further dissemination and development of the kind of school improvement and neighborhood organizing promoted by the IAF.

Texas IAF leaders and organizers now have over a decade of intense organizing in education behind them. They have fought for parental engagement, increased school funding, better student–teacher ratios, and a new kind of community-based political power mobilized for public school reform. Although the Alliance Schools are still at an early stage of development, they represent one source for educational and civic renewal that should attract widespread attention in the national quest for prosperous cities with safe, diverse, and thriving schools and neighborhoods.

Notes

Introduction

1. Harold Howe II, *Thinking About Our Kids* (New York: Free Press, 1993), pp. 1–8, 29–54; Edward B. Fiske, *Smart Schools, Smart Kids: Why Do Some Schools Work?* (New York: Simon and Schuster, 1991), pp. 24–25.

2. Jonathan Kozol, *Savage Inequalities: Children in America's Schools* (New York: Crown, 1991), p. 4.

3. On the peculiar alliance between conservatives and radicals in their attacks on public schooling, see Peter S. Hlebowitsh, *Radical Curriculum Theory Reconsidered: A Historical Approach* (New York: Teachers College Press, 1993), pp. 94–116. For a description and analysis of the school restructuring movement of the 1980s, see Thomas Toch, *In the Name of Excellence* (New York: Oxford University Press, 1991). On vouchers and privatization, see John E. Chubb and Terry M. Moe, *Politics, Markets, and America's Schools* (Washington, D.C.: Brookings Institution, 1990); James R. Rinehart and Jackson F. Lee, Jr., *American Education and the Dynamics of Choice* (New York: Praeger, 1991); and Myron Lieberman, *Public Education: An Autopsy* (Cambridge, Mass.: Harvard University Press, 1993).

4. On traditions as arguments, see Alasdair MacIntyre, *After Virtue* (South Bend, Ind.: University of Notre Dame Press, 1981), and David Gross, *The Past in Ruins: Tradition and the Critique of Modernity* (Amherst: University of Massachusetts Press, 1992). On American traditions, see Michael Kammen, *Mystic Chords of Memory: The Transformation of Tradition in American Culture* (New York: Knopf, 1991). The best survey of American educational history remains Lawrence Cremin's three-volume survey: *American Education: The Colonial Experience* (New York: Harper and Row, 1970), *American Education: The National Experience* (New York: Harper and Row, 1980), and *American Education: The Metropolitan Experience* (New York: Harper and Row, 1988). On high school graduation rates, see *The Statistical Abstract of the United States, 1992* (Lanham, Md.: Bernan Press, 1992), p. 137.

5. United States Department of Education, *Digest of Education Statistics* (Washington, D.C.: U.S. Government Printing Office, 1993), p. 95; Jean Johnson

et al., *Assignment Incomplete: The Unfinished Business of Education Reform* (New York: Public Agenda, 1995), p. 13.

6. For cross-national comparisons describing Americans' support of voluntary associations, see James Curtis, "Voluntary Association Joining: A Cross-National Comparative Note," *American Sociological Review*, vol. 36 (1971), pp. 872–880, and Sidney Verba, Norman H. Nie, and Jae-on Kim, *Participation and Political Equality: A Seven Nation Comparison* (New York: Cambridge University Press, 1978).

7. The progress at Herff Elementary is stated in general terms because Herff only educates children on the kindergarten and first- and second-grade levels, and is thus exempt from the standardized tests administered by the Texas Education Agency (Texas' department of education), which commence at the third grade. For this reason one cannot use the state's standardized tests to evaluate Herff's progress in comparison with other schools.

8. There is a vast research literature on the Industrial Areas Foundation. Essential readings include Saul D. Alinsky, *Reveille for Radicals* (Chicago: University of Chicago Press, 1946), and *Rules for Radicals: A Practical Primer for Realistic Radicals* (New York: Vintage, 1971); Marion K. Sanders, *The Professional Radical: Conversations with Saul Alinsky* (New York: Harper and Row, 1970); John Hall Fish, *Black Power/White Control* (Princeton: Princeton University Press, 1973); Robert Bailey, Jr., *Radicals in Urban Politics: The Alinsky Approach* (Chicago: University of Chicago Press, 1974); Ed Chambers, *Organizing for Family and Congregation* (New York: Industrial Areas Foundation, 1978); Joan E. Lancourt, *Confront or Concede: The Alinsky Citizen-Action Organizations* (Lexington, Mass.: Lexington Books, 1979); Carl Tjerandsen, *Education for Citizenship* (Santa Cruz, Calif.: Emil Schwarzhaupt, 1980), pp. 233–330; Robert A. Slayton, *Back of the Yards: The Making of a Local Democracy* (Chicago: University of Chicago Press, 1986); Harry C. Boyte, *Commonwealth: A Return to Citizen Politics* (New York: Free Press, 1989); the Industrial Areas Foundation, *IAF: 50 Years: Organizing for Change* (Franklin Square, N.Y.: n.p., 1990); Sanford D. Horwitt, *Let Them Call Me Rebel: Saul Alinsky—His Life and Legacy* (New York: Vintage, 1992); and Jim Rooney, *Organizing the South Bronx* (Albany: State University of New York Press, 1995). On the Texas IAF, see Mary Beth Rogers, *Cold Anger: A Story of Faith and Power Politics* (Denton: University of North Texas, 1990); the Texas IAF Network, *Vision, Values, Action* (Austin: Texas IAF Network, 1990); William Greider, *Who Will Tell the People: The Betrayal of American Democracy* (New York: Simon and Schuster, 1992), pp. 222–241; Ernesto Cortés, Jr., "Reweaving the Fabric: The Iron Rule and the IAF Strategy for Power and Politics," in Henry G. Cisneros, ed., *Interwoven Destinies: Cities and the Nation* (New York: W. W. Norton, 1993); pp. 294–319, Peter Skerry, *Mexican Americans: The Ambivalent Minority* (New York: Free Press, 1993); and Mark Russell Warren, "Social Capital and Community Empowerment: Religion and Political Organization in the Texas Industrial Areas Foundation" (Ph.D. diss., Harvard University, 1995).

9. See J. Matthews, *Escalante: The Best Teacher in America* (New York: Holt, 1988); LouAnne Johnson, *My Posse Don't Do Homework* (New York: St. Martin's,

1992); and Madeline Cartwright, *For the Children: Lessons from a Visionary Principal* (New York: Doubleday, 1993).

10. Frederick Eby, *The Development of Education in Texas* (New York: Macmillan, 1925), p. 79 and p. 127.

11. Ibid., pp. 157–192; Howard Beeth and Cary D. Wintz, eds., *Black Dixie: Afro-Texan History and Culture in Houston* (College Station: Texas A&M University Press, 1992), p.88.

12. See Herschel T. Manuel, "The Education of Mexican and Spanish-Speaking Children in Texas," and Wilson Little, "Spanish Speaking Children in Texas," both in Carlos E. Cortés, *Education and the Mexican American* (New York: Arno, 1974), and Guadalupe San Miguel, Jr., *"Let All of Them Take Heed": Mexican-Americans and the Campaign for Educational Equality in Texas, 1910–1981* (Austin: University of Texas Press, 1987), which describe the nature and origins of segregated schools for Mexican Americans in Texas. On the influence of right-wing extremists on education in Texas, see Don E. Carleton, *Red Scare!: Right Wing Hysteria, Fifties Fanaticism and Their Legacies in Texas* (Austin: Texas Monthly Press, 1985); for a recent update on the textbook selection process, see J. Dan Marshall, "With a Little Help from Some Friends: Publishers, Protesters, and Texas Textbook Decisions," in Michael W. Apple and Linda K. Christian-Smith, eds., *The Politics of the Textbook* (New York: Routledge, 1991), pp. 56–77.

13. Kozol, *Savage Inequalities*, p. 223; National Center for Education Statistics, *The Nation's Report Card* (Washington, D.C.: United States Department of Education, 1994); Bennett Roth and Cindy Rugeley, "Land of the Illiterate," *Houston Chronicle*, September 9, 1994, p. 1.

14. For two interpretations of the discrepancies between Texas myths and realities, see D. W. Meinig, *Imperial Texas: An Interpretive Essay in Cultural Geography* (Austin: University of Texas Press, 1969), and Walter L. Buenger and Robert A. Calvert, *Texas Through Time: Evolving Interpretations* (College Station: Texas A&M University Press, 1991). On the impact of the Voting Rights Act in Texas, see Robert Brischetto, David R. Richards, Chandler Davidson, and Bernard Grofman, "Texas," in Chandler Davidson and Bernard Grofman, eds., *Quiet Revolution in the South: The Impact of the Voting Rights Act, 1965–1990* (Princeton, N.J.: Princeton University Press, 1994), pp. 233–270. Important works tracing the various manifestations of agrarian and working-class activism in Texas include Lawrence Goodwyn, *Democratic Promise: The Populist Moment in America* (New York: Oxford University Press, 1976); James R. Green, *Grass-Roots Socialism: Radical Movements in the Southwest, 1895–1943* (Baton Rouge: Louisiana University Press, 1978); David Montejano, *Anglos and Mexicans in the Making of Texas, 1836–1986* (Austin: University of Texas Press, 1987); Douglas E. Foley et al., *From Peones to Politicos: Class and Ethnicity in a South Texas Town, 1900–1987* (Austin: University of Texas Press, 1988); Alwyn Barr, "African Americans in Texas: From Stereotypes to Diverse Roles," in Buenger and Calvert, *Texas Through Time*, pp. 50–80; Emilio Zamora, *The World of the Mexican Worker in Texas* (College Station: Texas A&M Press, 1993). On the "primitive years" of Anglo-American supremacy, see George Norris Green, *The Establishment in Texas*

Politics: The Primitive Years, 1938–1957 (Norman: University of Oklahoma Press, 1979); on "the myth of overwhelming conservatism," see Chandler Davidson, *Race and Class in Texas Politics* (Princeton, N.J.: Princeton University Press, 1990).

15. The phrase "laboratories of democracy" is a paraphrase of a dissenting opinion from Supreme Court Justice Louis Brandeis. See Philippa Strum, ed., *Brandeis on Democracy* (Lawrence: University of Kansas Press, 1995), p. 147. I have radicalized Brandeis' phrase—which referred to experiments with policy on the state level—by relocating the core of democracy at the local, grass-roots arena. My research is indebted to and builds upon the extensive scholarship on parental and community involvement in schools. Seminal works in this area include Sara Lawrence Lightfoot, *Worlds Apart: Relationships Between Families and Schools* (New York: Basic, 1978); James Comer, *School Power: Implications of an Intervention Project* (New York: Free Press, 1980); Reginald Clark, *Family Life and School Achievement: Why Poor Black Children Succeed or Fail* (Chicago: University of Chicago Press, 1983); Ron Haskins and Diane Adams, eds., *Parent Education and Public Policy* (Norwood, N.J.: Ablex, 1983); Michael R. Williams, *Neighborhood Organizing for Urban School Reform* (New York: Teachers College, 1989); Annette Lareau, *Home Advantage: Social Class and Parental Intervention in Elementary Education* (Philadelphia: Falmer, 1989); Concha Delgado-Gaitan, *Literacy for Empowerment: The Role of Parents in Children's Education* (Philadelphia: Falmer, 1990); Nancy Feyl Chavkin, ed., *Families and Schools in a Pluralistic Society* (Albany: State University of New York, 1993); Joyce L. Epstein, "School and Family Partnerships," in M. C. Alkin, ed., *Encyclopedia of Educational Research*, 6th ed. (New York: Macmillan, 1992), pp. 1139–1151; Norm Fruchter, Anne Galletta, and J. Lynne White, *New Directions in Parent Involvement* (Washington, D.C.: Academy for Educational Development, Inc., 1992); J. William Rioux and Nancy Berla, *Innovations in Parent and Family Involvement* (Princeton Junction, N.J.: Eye on Education, 1993); Barbara Schneider and James S. Coleman, eds., *Parents, Their Children, and Schools* (Boulder, Colo.: Westview, 1993); Seymour Sarason, *Parental Involvement and the Political Principle: Why the Existing Governance Structure of Schools Should Be Abolished* (San Francisco: Jossey-Bass, 1995).

Chapter 1

1. Howe, *Thinking About Our Kids*, p. 40; Lilian B. Rubin, *Families on the Fault Line* (New York: HarperCollins, 1994), pp. 28–43; Lawrence Mishel and Jared Bernstein, *The State of Working America, 1994–1995* (Westchester, N.Y.: M. E. Sharpe, 1995), pp. 144–147; Joint Center for Housing Studies of Harvard University, "The State of the Nation's Housing: 1994," p. 10.

2. Ray Marshall and Marc Tucker, *Thinking for a Living: Work, Skills, and the Future of the American Economy* (New York: Basic, 1992), p. xvi.

3. Recent analyses of the erosion of the American middle class include Frank Levy, *Dollars and Dreams: The Changing American Income Distribution* (New York: Norton, 1988); Frank Levy and Richard C. Michel, *The Economic*

Future of American Families: Income and Wealth Trends (Washington, D.C.: Urban Institute Press, 1991); Kevin Phillips, *The Politics of Rich and Poor: Wealth and the American Electorate in the Reagan Aftermath* (New York: Harper, 1990), and *Boiling Point: Democrats, Republicans, and the Decline of Middle-Class Prosperity* (New York: Random House, 1993); Barry Bluestone and Irving Bluestone, *Negotiating the Future: A Labor Perspective on American Business* (New York: Basic, 1992); Robert B. Reich, *The Work of Nations* (New York: Vintage, 1992); and Mishel and Bernstein, *Working America*. For the political context, see Theodore R. Marmor, Jerry L. Mashaw, and Philip L. Harvey, *America's Misunderstood Welfare State: Persistent Myths, Enduring Realities* (New York: Basic, 1990). For more optimistic interpretations, see Anandi P. Sahu and Ronald L. Tracy, *The Economic Legacy of the Reagan Years: Euphoria or Chaos?* (New York: Prager, 1991), and Robert L. Bartley, *The Seven Fat Years* (New York: Free Press, 1992). For comparisons of U.S. class stratification with that of other nations, see Keith Bradsher, "Gap in Wealth in U.S. Called Widest in West," *New York Times*, April 17, 1995, p. A1. For comparisons of childhood poverty, see Keith Bradsher, "Low Ranking for Poor American Children: U.S. Youth Among Worst Off in Study of 18 Industrialized Nations," *New York Times*, August 14, 1995, p. A7.

4. Jeffrey M. Berry, Kent E. Portney, and Ken Thomson, *The Rebirth of Urban Democracy* (Washington, D.C.: Brookings Institution, 1993), pp. 1–2; Frances Fox Piven and Richard A. Cloward, *Why Americans Don't Vote* (New York: Pantheon, 1988); Samuel P. Huntington, *The Third Wave: Democratization in the Late Twentieth Century* (Norman: University of Oklahoma Press, 1991); Larry Diamond and Marc F. Plattner, eds., *The Global Resurgence of Democracy* (Baltimore: Johns Hopkins University Press, 1993).

5. David Blankenhorn, *Fatherless America* (New York: Basic, 1995), pp. 1–48; Rubin, *Families on the Fault Line*, p. 70; David A. Hamburg, *Today's Children: Creating a Future for a Generation in Crisis* (New York: Times Books, 1992), p. 33; "Virtually All Adults Want Children, but Many of the Reasons Are Intangible," *The Gallup Poll Monthly* (June 1990), p. 22; William R. Mattox, Jr., "The Parent Trap," *Policy Review* (winter 1991), no. 5, pp. 6–13.

6. Judith Wallerstein and Sandra Blakeslee, *Second Chances: Men, Women, and Children a Decade After Divorce* (New York: Ticknor and Fields, 1989); National Association of Elementary School Principals, Staff Report, "One-Parent Families and Their Children," *Principal*, vol. 60, no. 1 (September 1980), pp. 31–37; Sheila Fitzgerald Krein and Andrea H. Beller, "Educational Attainment of Children from Single-Parent Families: Differences by Exposure, Gender, and Race, *Demography*, vol. 25, no. 2 (May 1988), pp. 221–233; Norma Radin, "The Role of the Father in Cognitive, Academic, and Intellectual Development," in Michael E. Lamb, ed., *The Role of the Father in Child Development* (New York: Wiley, 1981), pp. 410–411; Lyn Carlsmith, "Effect of Early Father Absence on Scholastic Aptitude," *Harvard Educational Review*, vol. 31, no. 1 (1964), pp. 3–21; Jeanne Brooks-Gunn and Frank E. Furstenberg, Jr., "The Children of Adolescent Mothers: Physical, Academic, and Psychological Outcomes," *Developmental Review*, vol. 6, no. 3 (September 1986), pp. 224–251.

7. Sylvia Ann Hewlett, *When the Bough Breaks: The Cost of Neglecting Our Children* (New York: Basic, 1991); Robert Pear, "Lost in the Drive to Survive," *Houston Chronicle*, January 15, 1993, p. 16A; Marshall and Tucker, *Thinking for a Living*, p. 169.

8. For an economic explanation, see William Julius Wilson, *The Truly Disadvantaged: The Inner City, the Underclass, and Public Policy* (Chicago: University of Chicago Press, 1987); for a cultural explanation, see Christopher Jencks, *Rethinking Social Policy: Race, Poverty, and the Underclass* (Cambridge, Mass.: Harvard University Press, 1992), pp. 130–142. Other accounts include Paul E. Zopf, Jr., *American Women in Poverty* (New York: Greenwood, 1989); Harrell R. Rodgers, Jr., *Poor Women, Poor Families: The Economic Plight of America's Female-Headed Households* (London: M. E. Sharpe, 1990); Valerie Polakow, *Lives on the Edge: Single Mothers and Their Children in the Other America* (Chicago: University of Chicago Press, 1993); Robert I. Lerman and Theodora J. Ooms, *Unwed Fathers: Changing Roles and Emerging Policies* (Philadelphia: Temple University Press, 1993).

9. See Charlotte Levin Piuck, "Child-Rearing Patterns of Poverty," *American Journal of Psychotherapy*, vol. 29, no. 4 (October 1975), pp. 485–502, Steven R. Tulkin, "Social Class Differences in Maternal and Infant Behavior," in P. Herbert Leiderman, Steven R. Tulkin, and Anne Rosenfeld, eds., *Culture and Infancy: Variations in the Human Experience* (New York: London, 1977); Ronald C. Kessler and Paul D. Cleary, "Social Class and Psychological Distress," *American Sociological Review*, vol. 45 (June 1980), pp. 463–478; Jacques D. Lempers, Dania Clark-Lempers, and Ronald L. Simon, "Economic Hardship, Parenting, and Distress in Adolescence," *Child Development*, vol. 60 (1989), pp. 25–39; Vonnie C. McLoyd and Constance A. Flanagan, eds., *Economic Stress: Effects on Family Life and Child Development* (San Francisco: Jossey-Bass, 1990); Hamburg, *Today's Children*.

10. Lisbeth B. Schorr, *Within Our Reach: Breaking the Cycle of Disadvantage* (New York: Doubleday, 1989), p. 4; Fox Butterfield, "Grim Forecast Is Offered on Rising Juvenile Crime," *New York Times*, September 8, 1995, p. A6; John Gray, "Does Democracy Have a Future?" *The New York Times Book Review*, January 22, 1995, p. 1; Fox Butterfield, "Survey Finds That Crimes Cost $450 Billion a Year: Report is Called Justification for Spending," *New York Times*, April 22, 1996, p. A8.

11. Robert D. Putnam, "Bowling Alone: America's Declining Social Capital," *Journal of Democracy*, vol. 6, no. 1 (January 1995), pp. 65–78; quotes from pp. 72–73.

12. Joe R. Feagin, *Free Enterprise City: Houston in Political and Economic Perspective* (New Brunswick, N.J.: Rutgers University Press, 1988); Task Force on High School Education of the Texas State Board of Education, *One Student at a Time* (Austin: Texas Education Agency, 1992), p. 12; Bennett Roth and Rad Sallee, "Houston's Much Poorer Now Than It Was in 1980," *Houston Chronicle*, February 10, 1993; Kathy Walt, "30 Percent of Teachers Moonlight," *Houston Chronicle*, April 19, 1996, p. A33; Amy Lowrey, ed., *Building Communities of Learners* (Austin, Tex.: Office of the Governor, 1992), p. 11; United States Gen-

eral Accounting Office, *School Age Demographics: Recent Trends Pose New Educational Challenges* (Washington, D.C.: U.S. General Accounting Office, 1993).

13. Lowrey, *Building Communities of Learners*, p.45; "Seeds of Trouble," *Houston Chronicle*, August 14, 1994 p. 2 and p. 9. Population growth in Texas does not account for the rise in crime; the population grew only 6 percent from 1980 to 1990. On national figures, see Peter Applebome, "Shootings at Schools Prompt New Concerns About Violence, *New York Times*, March 3, 1996.

14. Gary Orfield defines schools with over 90 percent minority youth as intensely segregated. See his *The Growth of Segregation in American Schools: Changing Patterns of Separation and Poverty since 1968* (Alexandria, Va.: National School Boards Association, 1993), p. 5. For a historical analysis of racial segregation and urban education, see Harvey Kantor and Barbara Brenzel, "Urban Education and the 'Truly Disadvantaged': The Historical Roots of the Contemporary Crisis, 1945–1990," in Michael Katz, ed., *The Underclass Debate: Views from History* (Princeton, N.J.: Princeton University Press, 1993), pp. 366–402. For an analysis of Texas' low ranking on the provision of public services, see Davidson, *Race and Class in Texas Politics*, and Char Miller and Heywood T. Sanders, eds., *Urban Texas: Politics and Development* (College Station: Texas A&M University Press, 1990); for Texas' affinity with other southern states on this point, see David R. Goldfield, *Cotton Fields and Skyscrapers: Southern City and Region* (Baltimore: Johns Hopkins University Press, 1982), pp. 139–196.

15. On rising incomes for the affluent, see Rubin, *Families on the Fault Line*, p. 34; on the increase in minority political participation in Texas, see Brischetto et al., "Texas"; on volunteer work, see Berry, Portney, and Thomson, *Urban Democracy*, p. 4; on cross-national comparisons of voluntary associations, see Putnam, "Bowling Alone," p. 74.

16. Alexis de Tocqueville, *Democracy in America* (Garden City, N.Y.: Anchor, 1969), p. 513 and pp. 521–522.

17. Ibid., p. 524.

18. Alexis de Tocqueville, *The Old Régime and the French Revolution* (Garden City, N.Y.: Anchor, 1955), p. 107.

19. These are not just contemporary criticisms of Tocqueville made from the vantage point of the late twentieth century, but were initially offered by John Stuart Mill in a pair of scintillating essays published in 1835 and 1840. See John Stuart Mill, *Essays on Politics and Culture* (Gloucester, Mass.: Peter Smith, 1973), pp. 173–267.

20. Theda Skocpol, *Protecting Soldiers and Mothers: The Political Origins of Social Policy in the United States* (Cambridge, Mass.: Harvard University Press, 1992), and *Social Policy in the United States: Future Possibilities in Historical Perspective* (Princeton, N.J.: Princeton University Press, 1995).

21. Concern with the status of civil society and voluntary associations in the United States has grown in many arenas in recent years. Some of the most important writings include the following: Robert Bellah, *The Broken Covenant: American Civil Religion in Time of Trial* (New York: Seabury, 1975); Peter L. Berger and Richard John Neuhaus, *To Empower People: The Role of Mediating Structures*

in Public Policy (Washington, D.C.: American Enterprise Institute for Public Policy Research, 1977); Michael Novak, ed., *Democracy and Mediating Structures: A Theological Inquiry* (Washington, D.C.: American Enterprise Institute for Public Policy Research, 1980); Benjamin Barber, *Strong Democracy: Participatory Politics for a New Age* (Berkeley: University of California Press, 1984); Robert N. Bellah et al., *Habits of the Heart: Individualism and Commitment in American Life* (Berkeley: University of California Press, 1985); Jean Louise Cohen and Andrew Arato, *Civil Society and Political Theory* (Cambridge, Mass.: MIT University Press, 1992); Putnam, *Making Democracy Work*; Amitai Etzioni, *The Spirit of Community: The Reinvention of American Society* (New York: Simon and Schuster, 1993); Amitai Etzioni, ed., *New Communitarian Thinking: Persons, Virtues, Institutions, and Communities* (Charlottesville: University Press of Virginia, 1995); John A. Hall, ed., *Civil Society: Theory, History, Comparison* (Cambridge, Mass.: Polity, 1995).

22. Tocqueville, *Democracy in America*, pp. 557–558. For an interpretation of Tocqueville which suggests a compatibility between democracy and commercial society, see Stephen Holmes, "Tocqueville and Democracy," in David Copp et al., eds., *The Idea of Democracy* (New York: Cambridge University Press), pp. 23–63.

23. Examples of liberal or radical readings of Tocqueville can be found in Bellah et al., *Habits of the Heart*; Christopher Lasch, *The Revolt of the Elites and the Betrayal of Democracy* (New York: W. W. Norton, 1995); Elshtain, *Democracy on Trial*.

24. On "social capital," see Jane Jacobs, *The Death and Life of Great American Cities* (New York: Vintage, 1961), pp. 137–138; Glenn Loury, "A Dynamic Theory of Racial Income Differences," in P. A. Wallace and A. Le Mund, eds., *Women, Minorities, and Employment Discrimination* (Lexington, Mass.: Lexington Books, 1977), and "Why Should We Care About Group Inequality?" *Social Philosophy and Policy*, vol. 5 (1987), pp. 249–271; James S. Coleman, Thomas Hoffer, and Sally Kilgore, *High School Achievement: Public, Catholic, and Private Schools Compared* (New York: Basic, 1982); James S. Coleman and Thomas Hoffer, *Public and Private High Schools: The Impact of Communities* (New York: Basic Books, 1987); James S. Coleman, "Social Capital in the Formation of Human Capital," *American Journal of Sociology*, vol. 94, supplement (1988), pp. S95–S120; James S. Coleman, *Foundations of Social Theory* (Cambridge, Mass.: Harvard University Press, 1990), pp. 300–321; Anthony S. Bryk, Valerie E. Lee, and Peter B. Holland, *Catholic Schools and the Common Good* (Cambridge, Mass.: Harvard University Press, 1993); Putnam, *Making Democracy Work*; Putnam, "The Prosperous Community: Social Capital and Public Life," *American Prospect*, vol. 13 (1993), pp. 35–42; Putnam, "Bowling Alone"; and Francis Fukuyama, *Trust: The Public Virtues and the Creation of Prosperity* (New York: Free Press, 1995). French sociologist Pierre Bourdieu uses the concept in a different and less rigorous way; see his *Reproduction in Education, Society and Culture* (Beverly Hills, Calif.: Sage, 1977), and many subsequent works.

25. Putnam, *Making Democracy Work*, pp. 172–173.

26. Ibid.

27. For the research on social capital other than that of Coleman, see Angela

Valenzuela and Sanford M. Dornbusch, "Familism and Social Capital in the Academic Achievement of Mexican Origin and Anglo Adolescents," *Social Science Quarterly*, vol. 75, no. 1 (March 1994), pp. 18–36; Ricardo D. Stanton-Salazar and Sanford M. Dornbusch, "Social Capital and the Reproduction of Inequality: Information Networks among Mexican-Origin High School Students," *Sociology of Education*, vol. 68, no. 2 (April 1995), pp. 116–135; and Reginald M. Clark, "Parents as Providers of Linguistic and Social Capital," *Educational Horizons*, vol. 66, no. 2 (winter 1988), pp. 93–95.

28. For descriptions of the problems of middle-class children, see Donna Gaines, *Teenage Wasteland: Suburbia's Dead End Kids* (New York: Pantheon, 1991), and Hewlett, *When the Bough Breaks*, pp. 77–126. Suburban schools have mirrored those of many central-city communities by struggling to accommodate waves of new immigrants. Contrary to popular stereotypes of suburbs as lily-white in racial composition, almost half of the 4.7 million Black, Hispanic, and Asian immigrants who came to the United States between 1975 and 1985 settled in the suburbs. On the ramifications for education in one Houston suburb, see Jan Swellander Rosin, "Suburbia Meets the Third World: The Impact of Immigration on Spring Branch Independent School District, 1970–1990," *The Houston Review*, vol. 15, no. 3 (1993), pp. 131–170.

29. Bryk, Lee, and Holland observed that "The basic argument . . . is predicated on a false premise—that most Catholic high schools are organized around individual parishes. Although most Catholic elementary schools are parochial schools, this is true of less than 20 percent of all Catholic high schools." See *Catholic Schools and the Common Good*, p. 378.

30. Putnam, *Making Democracy Work*, p. 88 and p. 175.

31. On conflict and social capital, see Putnam, *Making Democracy Work*, pp. 117–118.

32. The term "civic capacity" in relationship to urban school reform is the topic of a promising research project directed by Clarence Stone of the University of Maryland and Jeffrey Henig of George Washington University and funded by the National Science Foundation. Stone, Henig, and their colleagues are conducting a comparative analysis of the ability of major political stakeholders in eleven different cities to improve academic achievement in their public schools. The cities are Atlanta, Baltimore, Boston, Denver, Detroit, Houston, Los Angeles, Pittsburgh, Saint Louis, San Francisco, and Washington, D.C.

Chapter 2

1. Alinsky, *Rules for Radicals*, pp. 89–91, 184–196; Sanders and Alinsky, *The Professional Radical*, p. 37. On Alinsky and students in the New Left, see Horwitt, *Let Them Call Me Rebel*, pp. 522–536.

2. On the IAF and the United Farm Workers, see Jacques E. Levy, *César Chávez: Autobiography of La Causa* (New York: W. W. Norton, 1975), pp. 97–150; J. Craig Jenkins, *The Politics of Insurgency: The Farm Worker Movement in the 1960s* (New York: Columbia University Press, 1985), pp. 131–137.

3. Dwight Silverman, "COPS: The Seeds of Power," *San Antonio Light*, November 15, 1983.

4. See Chambers, *Organizing for Family and Congregation*; Mary Beth Rogers, "Gospel Values and Secular Politics," *Texas Observer*, vol. 82, no. 23 (November 22, 1990), pp. 6–8.

5. Alinsky, *Reveille for Radicals*, pp. 77–78.

6. Jan Jarboe, "Building a Movement," *Civil Rights Digest* (spring 1977), pp. 39–46.

7. On the history of the Mexican-American community in San Antonio, see Montejano, *Anglos and Mexicans*; Richard A. Garcia, *Rise of the Mexican American Middle Class: San Antonio, 1929–1941* (College Station: Texas A&M University Press, 1991); and Zamora, *Mexican Worker in Texas*; on the origins and characteristics of the Good Government League, see David R. Johnson, John R. Booth, and Richard J. Harris, *The Politics of San Antonio: Community, Progress, and Power* (Lincoln: University of Nebraska Press, 1983).

8. On COPS, see Joseph D. Sekul, "Communities Organized for Public Service: Citizen Power and Public Policy in San Antonio," in Johnson, Booth, and Harris, *The Politics of San Antonio*, pp. 175–190; Rogers, *Cold Anger*, pp. 105–126; Skerry, *Mexican Americans*; Berry, Portney, and Thomson, *Urban Democracy*; Heywood T. Sanders, "Communities Organized for Public Services and Neighborhood Revitalization in San Antonio," in Robert H. Wilson, ed., *Public Policy and Community: Activism and Governance in Texas* (Austin: University of Texas Press, 1997).

9. Rick Casey, "Church Plays Major Role in Community Groups Forging Progress in San Antonio," *National Catholic Reporter*, March 12, 1976, vol. 12, no. 20, p. 1.

10. Ibid.

11. Richard A. Garcia, *Mexican American Middle Class*, pp. 221–252; Ignacio M. García, *United We Win: The Rise and Fall of La Raza Unida Party* (Tucson: University of Arizona Press, 1989); Foley et al., *From Peones to Politicos*; Carlos Muñoz, Jr., *Youth, Identity, Power: The Chicano Movement* (New York: Verso, 1989), pp. 99–126.

12. Industrial Areas Foundation, "Organizing for Family and Congregation" (Franklin Square, N.Y.: Industrial Areas Foundation, 1978), pp. 3–8.

13. Ibid., pp. 9–18.

14. Feagin, *Free Enterprise City*, pp. 120–127.

15. Gustavo Gutiérrez, *A Theology of Liberation* (Maryknoll, N.Y.: Orbis, 1988), p. xxvi.

16. On Lucey, see Saul E. Bronder, *Social Justice and Church Authority: The Public Life of Archbishop Robert E. Lucey* (Philadelphia: Temple University Press, 1982); for the larger context, see Jay P. Dolan and Gilberto M. Hinojosa, eds., *Mexican Americans and the Catholic Church, 1900–1965* (South Bend, Ind.: University of Notre Dame Press, 1994).

17. Casey, "Church Plays Major Role," p. 1.

18. Joseph Nathan Kane, Janet Podell, and Steven Anzovin, *Facts About the States* (New York: H. W. Wilson, 1993), p. 501; Rogers, *Cold Anger*, pp. 176–177.

19. Since Texas IAF organizations are not gender based, I have chosen not to make gender a key component of the analysis presented here. Given the key role that women's political activism has played in shaping social policy in the United States and other industrialized countries, however, further studies on Texas IAF organizations which focus on the political development of working-class women could add to our understanding of women's political education in the Southwest and the social dynamics of community-based organizations. On the importance of women's engagement in social policy issues, see Linda Gordon, ed., *Women, the State and Welfare* (Madison: University of Wisconsin Press, 1990); Gisela Bock and Pat Thane, eds., *Maternity and Gender Policies: Women and the Rise of the European Welfare States, 1880s–1950s* (London: Routledge, 1991); Skocpol, *Protecting Soldiers and Mothers*, Seth Koven and Sonya Michels, eds., *Mothers of a New World: Maternalist Politics and the Origins of Welfare States* (New York: Routledge, 1993). On Fred Ross and the Community Service Organization, see Mario T. García, *Memories of Chicano History: The Life and Narrative of Bert Corona* (Berkeley: University of California Press, 1994), pp. 163–168.

20. Jarboe, "Building a Movement," pp. 39–46.

21. Alinsky, *Reveille for Radicals*, pp. 73–74.

22. Dwight Silverman, "COPS Founder Cortés 'Incredibly Bright But Not a Snob,'" *San Antonio Light*, November 13, 1983.

23. On the Woodlawn Experimental Schools Project, see Fish, *Black Power/White Control*, pp. 175–234; Arthur M. Brazier, *Black Self-Determination: The Story of The Woodlawn Organization* (Grand Rapids, Mich.: William B. Eerdmans, 1969).

24. The contribution of the Texas IAF to school finance reform is described in Richard Lavine, "School Finance Reform," in Wilson, *Public Policy and Community*. Other accounts of school finance reform include Kozol, *Savage Inequalities*, pp. 206–233; Toch, *In the Name of Excellence*, pp. 72–95; Gregory G. Rocha and Robert H. Webking, *Politics and Public Education: Edgewood v. Kirby and the Reform of Public School Financing in Texas* (Minneapolis and St. Paul: West, 1992).

25. Dwight Silverman, "COPS: The Seeds of Power."

26. Luce is quoted by Levine in "School Finance Reform," p. x; Perot is quoted by Rogers in *Cold Anger*, p. 166.

27. Tom Luce describes the role of the Texas IAF in saving the House Bill 72 legislation in *Now or Never: How We Can Save Our Public Schools* (Dallas: Taylor, 1995), pp. 10–11; on the ramifications of the funding increases, see Ronald F. Ferguson, "Paying for Public Education: New Evidence on How and Why Money Matters," *Harvard Journal of Legislation*, vol. 28, no. 2 (1991), pp. 465–491.

28. On the differentiated Latino population in urban Texas, see Harley L. Browning and Rodolfo O. de la Garza, *Mexican Immigrants and Mexican Americans: An Evolving Relation* (Austin, Tex.: Center for Mexican American Studies, 1986). On different attitudes toward public schools among Chicanos and other Hispanics, see Marcelo M. Suárez-Orozco, "Immigrant Adaptation to Schooling: A Hispanic Case," and Maria E. Matute-Bianchi, "Situational Ethnicity and Patterns of School Performance among Immigrant and Nonimmigrant Mexican-Descent Students," in Margaret A. Gibson and John U. Ogbu, eds., *Minority*

Status and Schooling: A Comparative Study of Immigrant and Involuntary Minorities (New York: Garland, 1991), pp. 37–62 and pp. 205–248, respectively.

29. I follow William Julius Wilson's criteria for distinguishing between high and extreme poverty here; see *The Truly Disadvantaged*, p. 46. Median per capita income in the United States in 1993 was $14,387; see the United States Department of Commerce, *Statistical Abstract of the United States, 1994* (Lanham, Md.: Bernan Press, 1994), p. 474. Data on neighborhoods are taken from the census tracts for Jefferson Davis High School in Houston, Alamo Elementary School in El Paso, Morningside Middle School in Fort Worth, and Roosevelt High School in Dallas. United States Bureau of the Census, *Census of Population and Housing: Summary Type File 3A, 1990* (CD90–3A) (CD-ROM).

30. On the transient nature of poverty, see Mary Jo Bane and David T. Ellwood, "Slipping Into and Out of Poverty: The Dynamics of Spells," *Journal of Human Resources*, vol. 21, no. 1 (winter 1986), pp. 9–13. Part of the difference between poverty in northern and midwestern inner-city neighborhoods and those organized by the Texas IAF has to do with ethnicity. In general, commentators on Latino neighborhoods agree that Latinos are not part of the same kind of "underclass" as that described by William Julius Wilson in *The Truly Disadvantaged*. For example, Jorge Chapa commented that "the distinction I would draw between the Mexican American lower class and the Black underclass is that the underclass is outside of the regular economy and occupational structure. The Mexican American lower class can be characterized as having had a firm grip on the bottom rung of the occupational ladder." See Jorge Chapa, "The Myth of Hispanic Progress: Trends in the Educational and Economic Attainment of Mexican Americans," *Journal of Hispanic Policy*, vol. 4 (1989–1990), pp. 3–18, quote from p. 17. Several other authors who advance this interpretation contributed essays to Joan Moore and Raquel Pinderhughes, eds., *In the Barrios: Latinos and the Underclass Debate* (New York: Russell Sage, 1993).

31. For a description and analysis of the problems confronting the inner-city underclass, see Wilson, *The Truly Disadvantaged*. Although it is often not addressed in discussions concerning low-income neighborhoods, one advantage of southwestern cities entails the much lower population density in metropolitan areas. For the example of Houston in this regard, see Peter Mieszkowski and Barton Smith, "Analyzing Urban Decentralization: The Case of Houston," *Regional Science and Urban Economics*, vol. 21, no. 2 (July 1991), pp. 183–199. Concerning poverty along the border, see Avelardo Valdez, "Persistent Poverty, Crime, and Drugs: U.S.–Mexican Border Region," in Moore and Pinderhughes, *In the Barrios*, pp. 173–194.

32. Father Urrabazo quoted in William Greider, *Who Will Tell the People: The Betrayal of American Democracy* (New York: Simon and Schuster, 1992), p. 231.

33. On the origins and significance of house meetings as an IAF organizing strategy, see Gary Delgado, *Organizing the Movement: The Roots and Growth of ACORN* (Philadelphia: Temple University Press, 1986), p. 40.

34. Ernie Cortés has often used the phrase concerning "the public processing

of pain" to describe the cathartic component of house meetings as individuals move from hiding their grievances to sharing them with one another. The phrase is taken from Walter Brueggemann's *Hope Within History* (Atlanta: John Knox, 1987), p. 16. Pat Ozuna is quoted in Brett Campbell, *Investing in People: The Story of Project QUEST* (San Antonio: n.p., 1994), p. 13.

35. On the educational background of Mexican immigrants, see Frank D. Bean, Jorge Chapa, Ruth R. Berg, and Kathryn A. Sowards, "Educational and Sociodemographic Incorporation among Hispanic Immigrants to the United States," in Barry Edmonston and Jeffrey S. Passel, eds., *Immigration and Ethnicity: The Integration of America's Newest Arrivals* (Washington, D.C.: Urban Institute, 1994), pp. 73–99.

36. Linda Rocawich, "Interview: Ernesto Cortés, Jr.," *Texas Observer*, November 22, 1990, vol. 82, no. 23, p. 11; Texas Interfaith Education Fund, "The Texas IAF Vision for Public Schools: Communities of Learners" (Austin, Tex.: unpub. ms., 1990). On the Texas IAF convention which ratified the vision paper, see Greider, *Who Will Tell the People*, pp. 226–233.

37. On the historical origins of "factory schools," see Raymond E. Callahan, *Education and the Cult of Efficiency* (Chicago: University of Chicago Press, 1962); Samuel Bowles and Herbert Gintis, *Schooling in Capitalist America* (New York: Basic, 1976), pp. 151–179; Arthur G. Powell, Eleanor Farrar, and David K. Cohen, *The Shopping Mall High School* (Boston: Houghton Mifflin, 1985), pp. 233–308; and Michael B. Katz, *Reconstructing American Education* (Cambridge, Mass.: Harvard University Press, 1987). Some of the best recent criticisms include Theodore R. Sizer, *Horace's Compromise: The Dilemma of the American High School* (New York: Houghton Mifflin, 1984); Linda M. McNeil, *Contradictions of Control: School Structure and School Knowledge* (New York: Routledge & Kegan Paul, 1986); Susan Moore Johnson, *Teachers at Work: Achieving Success in Our Schools* (New York: Basic, 1990), pp. 106–147; and Michelle Fine, *Framing Dropouts: Notes on the Politics of an Urban Public High School* (Albany: State University of New York Press, 1991).

38. Epstein, "School and Family Partnerships," pp. 1146–1147.

39. Cortés, "Reweaving the Fabric," p. 298. I am indebted to Elsy Fierro-Suttmiller, a Texas IAF organizer in El Paso, for making the sharp conceptual distinction between parental involvement and parental engagement. A valuable albeit foreshortened analysis of parental engagement may be found in Williams, *Neighborhood Organizing for Urban School Reform*.

40. Nancy Feyl Chavkin and David L. Williams, Jr., "Low-Income Parents' Attitudes toward Parental Involvement in Education," *Journal of Sociology and Social Welfare* (1989), pp. 17–28.

41. Cortés, "Reweaving the Fabric," pp. 305–307.

42. Epstein, "School and Family Partnerships," p. 1147.

43. Sheldon S. Wolin, *The Presence of the Past: Essays on the State and the Constitution* (Baltimore: Johns Hopkins University Press, 1989), pp. 137–150.

44. Rogers, *Cold Anger*, p. 87.

45. Cortés, "Catholic Tradition of Family Rights," p. 160 and p. 157.

46. Cortés, "Reweaving the Fabric," p. 303.

47. Alinsky, *Rules for Radicals*, pp. 49–53; Cortés, "Organizing the Community," p. 38; Cortés, "Reweaving the Fabric," p. 299.

48. Bernard Loomer, "Two Conceptions of Power," *Criterion* (winter 1976), pp. 12–29; Cortés, "Reweaving the Fabric," p. 299.

49. Cortés, "Catholic Tradition of Family Rights," p. 164.

50. Barbara Schneider, "Parents, Their Children, and Schools: An Introduction," in Barbara Schneider and James Coleman, eds., *Parents, Their Children, and Schools* (Boulder, CO: Westview, 1993), pp. 1–12.

Chapter 3

1. Rosa Clay and Mary Brown, "A Brief History of Mount Pisgah Missionary Baptist Church" (Fort Worth, Tex., unpub. ms., n.d.).

2. The poverty line and the requirements for qualifying for free or reduced-price lunches are changed every few years. In 1993, students could get a free meal at school if their family income was at 133 percent of the poverty level or below. They could get a reduced-price meal if their family income was at 185 percent of the poverty level or below. For a family of four, the free-lunch annual income limit was $18,655. For a reduced-price lunch, the income limit was $26,548 for a family of four.

3. Quotes are paraphrased by the memory of the speaker in this and many following passages.

4. Beth Freeking, "Community Answers Call to Save its Schools," *Fort Worth Sunday Star-Ledger*, October 10, 1993.

5. Many convincing studies have been conducted by educators who warn about the reductionist nature of standardized test scores. Regrettably, some of the newer and more promising forms of assessment, which focus on exhibitions, demonstrations, and performances, have not been in place for enough time to measure their efficacy in promoting higher order thinking skills. Two useful critiques of standardized testing and explorations of alternative assessment include Howard Gardner, *The Unschooled Mind: How Children Think and How Schools Should Teach* (New York: Basic, 1991), and Grant P. Wiggins, *Assessing Student Performance: Exploring the Purpose and Limits of Testing* (San Francisco: Jossey-Bass, 1993).

6. Keith Matulich, "Better Times Dawn at Morningside," *Fort Worth Star-Telegram*, December 3, 1988, p. A1.

7. Strictly speaking, one should not compare the results of the Texas Assessment of Academic Skills (TAAS) from 1990 to 1995 because the test was considerably revised and given to different grade levels of students at different times of the year beginning in the 1992–1993 school year. If one separates each cluster of three years appropriately, one does find a pattern of steady improvement. Measuring the students who passed all three sections of the test, the percentage rose from 22% in 1990 to 26% in 1991 to 29% in 1992. With the redesigned TAAS, the scores commenced at 19% passing in 1993 and jumped to 33% in 1994 and

38% in 1995. The issue of test scores in Alliance Schools will be discussed in greater detail in Chapter 8.

8. Coleman and Hoffer, *Public and Private High Schools*, pp. 221–227.

Chapter 4

1. Richard Doina, "The History of Jefferson Davis High School" (University of Houston, unpub. ms., 1993).

2. On the integration of Houston's public schools, see Chandler Davidson, *Biracial Politics: Conflict and Coalition in the Metropolitan South* (Baton Rouge: Louisiana State University Press, 1972), and Robert D. Thomas and Richard W. Murray, *Progrowth Politics: Change and Governance in Houston* (Berkeley: University of California Press, 1991). On the tumultuous climate on the Near North Side in the late 1970s and early 1980s, see Arnoldo De León, *Ethnicity in the Sunbelt: A History of Mexican Americans in Houston* (Houston: University of Houston, 1989), pp. 211–213; on the changing economic context, see Néstor P. Rodríguez, "Economic Restructuring and Latino Growth in Houston," in Moore and Pinderhughes, *In the Barrios*, pp. 101–127.

3. Katie Eckstrom, "A Rationale for Block Scheduling" (Houston, unpub. ms.); Jefferson Davis High School, "Multi-Year School Improvement Plan, Davis High School, 1994–1995" (Houston, unpub. ms.); Susan Besze Wallace, "Building Blocks," *Houston Post*, June 30, 1994, pp. A27–A28.

4. Kwame Opuni, "The Jefferson Davis Educational Collaborative Project: Evaluation Report" (unpub. ms., University of Houston, 1995).

5. On the impediments to naturalization and political enfranchisement in Houston's Hispanic neighborhoods, including an account of TMO's earlier organizing efforts, see Néstor P. Rodríguez et al., "Political Mobilization in Houston's Magnolia," in Rodolfo O. de la Garza, Martha Menchaca, and Louis DeSipio, eds., *Barrio Ballots: Latino Politics in the 1990 Elections* (Boulder, CO: Westview, 1994), pp. 83–114.

Chapter 5

1. On the origins of EPISO, see Rogers, *Cold Anger*, pp. 162–165; see also Molly Fennell and Colleen Heild, "EPISO Meetings Cut Short," *The El Paso Times*, April 22, 1982, p. 1A. *The Wanderer* brochure by Stanley Interrante is entitled *The El Paso Model: A Plan for Revolution through Church Structures and Finance* (St. Paul: Wanderer Press, 1982). Robert Rivera is the same lead organizer who headed the Davis effort with TMO; Texas IAF organizers rotate to different cities on a regular basis to provide them with new opportunities for professional development.

2. Dwight Silverman, "Interfaith Groups Go to Bat for the Poor," *San Antonio Light*, November 14, 1983.

3. See David Crowder, "EPISO Lobbies against Deportation," *The El Paso Times*, April 25, 1982, p. 1D; Robert H. Wilson and Peter Menzies, "The Colonias

Water Bill: Communities Demanding Change," in Wilson, *Public Policy and Community.*

4. For historical information on public education in El Paso, see Mario T. García's *Desert Immigrants: The Mexicans of El Paso, 1880–1920* (New Haven, Conn.: Yale University Press, 1981), pp. 110–126.

5. Chapter I funding has been allocated by the U.S. Department of Education since 1981. From 1965 to 1981 it was known as Title I and was provided under the auspices of the Elementary and Secondary Education Act of 1965.

6. Hollibrook Elementary School is part of Henry Levin's Accelerated Schools program. For descriptions, see Edward Fiske, *Smart Schools, Smart Kids,* pp. 17–20 and pp. 112–113; Pamela Bullard and Barbara Taylor, *Making School Reform Happen* (Boston: Allyn and Bacon, 1993), pp. 31–54; Jane McCarthy and Suzanne Still, "Hollibrook Accelerated Elementary School," in Joseph Murphy and Philip Hallinger, eds., *Restructuring Schooling: Learning from Ongoing Efforts* (Newbury Park, Calif.: Corwin, 1993), pp. 63–83; Wendy S. Hopfenberg, Henry M. Levin et al., *The Accelerated Schools Resource Guide* (San Francisco: Jossey-Bass, 1993), pp. 37–44; and Christine Finnan et al., *Accelerated Schools in Action: Lessons from the Field* (Thousand Oaks, Calif.: Corwin, 1995).

7. Juan A. Lozano, "Richards Praises Ysleta School," *El Paso Herald-Post,* August 20, 1994, p. B1.

Chapter 6

1. On Chávez and the IAF, see Levy, *César Chávez,* pp. 95–148, J. Craig Jenkins, *The Politics of Insurgency: The Farm Worker Movement in the 1960s* (New York: Columbia University Press, 1985), pp. 131–137; Horwitt, *Let Them Call Me Rebel,* pp. 520–522.

2. On the importance of the Virgin of Guadalupe in Mexican American culture, see Alfredo Mirandé, *The Chicano Experience: An Alternative Perspective* (South Bend, Ind.: University of Notre Dame Press, 1985), pp. 122–138.

3. Starita Smith, "Panel Won't Back School Health Plan," *Austin American-Statesman,* November 2, 1992, p. B1; "AISD Trustees Delay Decision on Health Project," *Austin American-Statesman,* November 3, 1994, p. B1.

4. Editors, "Zavala Elementary Earns Recognition for Turnaround," *Austin American-Statesman,* April 10, 1994, p. D2.

Chapter 7

1. On the role of Texas IAF organizations in San Antonio, see Sanders' "Communities Organized for Public Service," Skerry, *Mexican-Americans,* and Johnson, Booth, and Harris, *The Politics of San Antonio.* On the amount of funds raised for inner-city improvements, see Ernie Cortés, "Reflections on the Catholic Tradition of Family Rights," in John Coleman, ed., *One Hundred Years of Catholic Social Thought* (New York: Orbis, 1991), p. 157. COPS is unique among Texas IAF organizations in that it consists wholly of alliances between Catholic churches. Originally, COPS had an ecumenical sponsoring committee, but all of

the Protestant denominations had withdrawn their support by 1978, primarily because COPS was seen by many clergy and parishioners as too militant and confrontational. "Alinsky used to say that the difference between a liberal and radical is that the liberals run for cover as soon as the fight starts," Cortés said. "Those churches that left really defined liberals in that sense." At the same time that Protestant churches did not want to appear as polarizing as COPS, they did want to form community organizations with the IAF. As a result, San Antonians began two other groups in the 1980s called the East Side Alliance and the Metropolitan Congregational Alliance (which was primarily based in the more affluent North Side). Those two groups combined in 1989 to form the Metro Alliance. Although the two groups share the same office and collaborate on virtually every issue, COPS continues to be seen by many San Antonians as the more militant organization.

2. Until 1969 it was illegal to speak Spanish in public schools in Texas except in foreign language classes. No serious efforts were made to integrate Texas schools, which were largely divided into separate schools for Anglos, Blacks, and Mexican Americans until the early 1970s. See Jorge C. Rangel and Carlos M. Alcala, "Project Report: *De Jure* Segregation of Chicanos in Texas Schools," *Harvard Civil Rights/Civil Liberties Law Review*, vol. 7, no. 2 (March 1972), pp. 307–391, and Guadalupe San Miguel, Jr., *"Let All of Them Take Heed": Mexican Americans and the Campaign for Educational Equality in Texas, 1910–1981* (Austin: University of Texas Press, 1987).

3. Ernesto Cortés, "Reweaving the Fabric," p. 307.

4. On BUILD and the Commonwealth Agreement, see Boyte, *Commonwealth*, pp. 101–126; Marion Orr, "Urban Regimes and Human Capital Policies: A Study of Baltimore," *Journal of Urban Affairs*, vol. 14, no. 2 (1992), pp. 173–187, and "Urban Politics and School Reform: The Case of Baltimore," *Urban Affairs Review*, vol. 31, no. 3 (1996), pp. 314–345; and Harold A. McDougall, *Black Baltimore: A New Theory of Community* (Philadelphia: Temple University Press), 126–135.

5. Gilberto Reyes, Jr., "Crime-Fighting Plan Eyed: City Officials, E. Side Leaders Trying to Turn Tide on Gang Violence," *San Antonio Light*, January 13, 1992.

6. Leon Lynn, "Building Parent Involvement," *Brief to Principals*, no. 8 (winter 1994), p. 1.

7. Fox Butterfield, "Grim Forecast Is Offered on Rising Juvenile Crime," *New York Times*, September 8, 1995, p. A6.

8. "Teach Parents to Help Children," *San Antonio Express-News*, September 10, 1993.

9. On COPS' work on housing, see Sanders, "Communities Organized for Public Service."

10. Marty Sabota, "City Officials Promise to Make East Side Area Safe for Children," *San Antonio Express-News*, November 11, 1992.

11. Loydean Thomas, "City Zones Alamodome Area Residential: Neighbors Hail Move as a Way to Give 12-Block Section a New Chance for Life," *San Antonio Express-News*, December 17, 1993.

12. Gilberto Reyes, Jr., "City Pledges Clean-Up Aid," *San Antonio Light,* May 27, 1992.

13. According to the Texas Education Agency in 1993, school scores in which more than 20 percent of the students passed all three sections of the state's TAAS test were acceptable. That guideline is revised on an annual basis as part of an effort to raise standards.

14. Robert D. Felner, J. Primavera, and Ana M. Cauce, "The Impact of School Transitions: A Focus for Preventive Efforts," *American Journal of Community Psychology,* vol. 9 (1981), pp. 449–459; Leonard A. Jason et al., *Helping Transfer Students: Strategies for Educational and Social Readjustment* (San Francisco: Jossey-Bass, 1992).

15. See Nancy Kates, "The Battle of the Alamodome: Henry Cisneros and the San Antonio Stadium" (Cambridge, Mass.: Harvard University, John F. Kennedy School of Government, 1989), and Berry, Portney, and Thomson, *Urban Democracy,* pp. 142–146.

16. Veronica Flores, "Fair Deals Are Found on Housing," *San Antonio Express-News,* October 23, 1994.

17. See David R. Johnson, "San Antonio: The Vicissitudes of Boosterism," in Richard M. Bernard and Bradley R. Rice, eds., *Sunbelt Cities: Politics and Growth Since World War II* (Austin: University of Texas Press, 1983), pp. 235–254, and Campbell, *Investing in People.*

18. Gilberto Cardenas, Jorge Chapa, and Susan Burek, "The Changing Economic Position of Mexican Americans in San Antonio," in Rebecca Morales and Frank Bonilla, eds., *Latinos in a Changing U.S. Economy* (Newbury Park, Calif.: Sage, 1993), pp. 160–183; Bill Hobby, "Easing the Pain: A Job Training Plan that Works," *Houston Chronicle,* March 25, 1996, p. 17A.

19. Wilson, *The Truly Disadvantaged,* p. 105. For a critique of Wilson's correlation between employment and family cohesion, see Christopher Jencks, *Rethinking Social Policy: Race, Poverty, and the Underclass* (Cambridge, Mass.: Harvard University Press, 1992), pp. 133–136.

20. Cardenas, Chapa, and Burek, "Changing Economic Position," p. 182.

21. Hobby, "Easing the Pain."

22. For more information on QUEST, see Paul Osterman and Brenda A. Lautsch, *Project Quest: A Report to the Ford Foundation* (Cambridge, Mass.: MIT Sloan School of Management, 1996).

Chapter 8

1. Ferguson, "Paying for Public Education."

2. *Ibid.*

Chapter 9

1. Stephen D. Brookfield, *The Skillful Teacher: On Technique, Trust, and Responsiveness in the Classroom* (San Francisco: Jossey-Bass, 1990), p. 2; Dan C. Lortie,

Schoolteacher: A Sociological Study (Chicago: University of Chicago Press, 1975), p. 136; Philip Jackson, *Life in Classrooms* (New York: Teachers College Press, 1990), esp. pp. 115–155.

2. Thadeus Herrick, "Catholic Cornerstone: San Antonio Leads Nation in Parochial School Enrollment," *Houston Chronicle*, December 11, 1994, p. 1D.

3. Ruth M. Bond, "Principal Fighting to Protect Students from Gang Influence," *Fort Worth Star-Telegram*, December 19, 1993, p. A1.

4. Ibid.

5. Elizabeth T. Buhmann, *Gangs in Texas Cities: Model Programs Report: No. 1: Parks and Recreation* (Austin, Tex.: Office of the Attorney General, 1991), p. 3.

6. On the "multiple marginality" of urban youth, see James Diego Vigil, "Gangs, Social Control, and Ethnicity: Ways to Redirect," in Shirley Brice Heath and Milbrey W. McLaughlin, eds., *Identity and Inner-City Youth: Beyond Ethnicity and Gender* (New York: Teachers College Press, 1993), pp. 94–119; on youth organizations as strategies for cultivating the strengths of inner-city youths, see Heath and McLaughlin, ibid., entire; on other strategies, see Irving A. Spergel, *The Youth Gang Problem: A Community Approach* (New York: Oxford University Press, 1995), pp. 248–296. On youth gangs in general, see Ruth Horowitz, *Honor and the American Dream: Culture and Identity in a Chicano Community* (New Brunswick, N.J.: Rutgers University Press, 1983); James Diego Vigil, *Barrio Gangs: Street Life and Identity in Southern California* (Austin: University of Texas Press, 1988); Joan W. Moore, *Going Down to the Barrio: Homeboys and Homegirls in Change* (Philadelphia: Temple University Press, 1991); Martín Sánchez Jankowski, *Islands in the Street* (Berkeley: University of California Press, 1991); William B. Sanders, *Gangbangs and Drive-bys: Grounded Culture and Juvenile Gang Violence* (New York: Aldine de Gruyter, 1994); and Spergel, *The Youth Gang Problem*.

7. Colin Lacey and Dudley Blane, "Geographic Mobility and School Attainment—The Confounding Variables," *Educational Research*, vol. 21 (June 1979), pp. 200–206; L. Scott Miller, Mark Fredisdorf, and Daniel C. Humphrey, *Student Mobility and School Reform* (New York: Council for Aid to Education, 1992).

8. Chavkin and Williams, "Low-Income Parents' Attitudes," p. 23; B. J. Hirsch and B. D. Rapkin, "The Transition to Junior High School," *Child Development*, vol. 58 (1987), pp. 1235–1243.

9. Chavkin and Williams, "Low-Income Parents' Attitudes," p. 23.

10. Lawrence Steinberg, *Beyond the Classroom* (New York: Simon and Schuster, 1996). For Deborah Meier's comments on why changing secondary schools is harder than reforming elementary schools, see her book, *The Power of Their Ideas: Lessons for America from a Small School in Harlem* (Boston: Beacon Press, 1995), pp. 30–33.

11. Valerie E. Lee and Julia B. Smith, "Effects of High School Restructuring and Size on Early Gains in Achievement and Engagement," *Sociology of Education*, vol. 68, no. 4 (October 1995), pp. 241–270.

12. Luce, *Now or Never*, p. 8.

Chapter 10

1. Cortés, "Reweaving the Fabric," pp. 300–301.

2. For the original formulation of "scaffolding," see David Wood, Jerome S. Bruner, and Gail Ross, "The Role of Tutoring in Problem Solving," *Journal of Child Psychology and Psychiatry,* vol. 17 (1976), pp. 89–100.

3. On the problems of developing multiracial coalitions, and especially coalitions between Blacks and Hispanics in Texas, see Kenneth J. Meier and Joseph Stewart, Jr., "Cooperation and Conflict in Multiracial School Districts," *The Journal of Politics,* vol. 53, no. 4 (November 1991), pp. 1123–1133, and James Dyer, Arnold Vedlitz, and Stephen Worchel, "Social Distance among Racial and Ethnic Groups," *Social Science Quarterly,* vol. 70 (1989), pp. 607–616. For Corona's perspective on this issue, see Mario T. García, *Memories of Chicano History,* pp. 255–269. On Chávez, see Richard Griswold del Castillo and Richard A. Garcia, *César Chávez: A Triumph of Spirit* (Norman: University of Oklahoma Press, 1995), p. 154. They write, "Chávez himself, in spite of the lens through which Chicano radicals perceived him, said: 'La Raza? Why be racist. Our belief is to help everyone, not just one race. Humanity is our belief.' Steiner wrote that when Chávez made this statement to Chicanos, 'their faces fell' in disbelief."

4. On the Comer model, see Comer, *School Power,* James P. Comer et al., eds., *Rallying the Whole Village: The Comer Process for Reforming Education* (New York: Teachers College Press, 1996). On shared decision making and site-based management, see Fiske, *Smart Schools, Smart Kids,* pp. 29–61; G. Alfred Hess, Jr., "Restructuring the Chicago Public Schools," in Chester E. Finn, Jr., and Theodor Rebarber, eds., *Education Reform in the '90s* (New York: Macmillan, 1992); William T. Pink and Kathryn M. Borman, "Community Involvement and Staff Development in School Improvement," in Kathryn M. Borman and Nancy P. Greenman, eds., *Changing American Education: Recapturing the Past or Inventing the Future?* (Albany: State University of New York Press, 1994), pp. 195–220; Maribeth Vander Weele, *Reclaiming Our Schools: The Struggle for Chicago School Reform* (Chicago: Loyola University Press, 1994); and Michael Katz, *Improving Poor People: The Welfare State, the "Underclass," and Urban Schools as History* (Princeton, N.J.: Princeton University Press, 1995), pp. 99–143.

5. Sarason, *Parental Involvement and the Political Principle,* p. 75. On parents and Catholic schools, see Bryk, Lee, and Holland, *Catholic Schools and the Common Good,* pp. 306–308.

6. On Alinsky and the churches, see Horwitt, *Let Them Call Me Rebel,* pp. 67–76, and Slayton, *Back of the Yards,* pp. 196–229.

7. On the relationship between church attendance and high school graduation, see James S. Coleman, "Social Capital in the Creation of Human Capital," in Christopher Winship and Sherwin Rosen, eds., *Organizations and Institutions: Sociological and Economic Approaches to the Analysis of Social Structure* (Chicago: University of Chicago Press, 1988), pp. 95–120; on the impact of neighbors' churchgoing, see Anne C. Case and Lawrence F. Katz, "The Company You Keep: The Effects of Family and Neighborhood on Disadvantaged Youths"

(NBER Working Paper No. 3705, Cambridge, Mass.: National Bureau of Economic Research, 1991); on the benefits of religiosity for children, see Norman Garmezy, "Stressors of Childhood," in Norman Garmezy and Michael Rutter, eds, *Stress, Coping, and Development in Children* (New York: McGraw-Hill, 1983), pp. 43–84, and William Damon, *Greater Expectations: Overcoming the Culture of Indulgence in America's Homes and Schools* (New York: Free Press, 1995), pp. 81–93.

8. C. Eric Lincoln and Lawrence H. Mamiya, *The Black Church in the African American Experience* (Durham, N.C.: Duke University Press, 199), p. 153.

9. Roberto O. González and Michael J. LaVelle, *The Hispanic Catholic in the United States: A Sociocultural and Religious Profile* (New York: Enquire Press, 1985), pp. 126–131.

10. Dwight Silverman, "Group Tackles Big Problems in Big City," *San Antonio Light*, November 15, 1983.

11. Wendy Glasgow Winters, *African American Mothers and Urban Schools: The Power of Participation* (New York: Lexington, 1993), pp. 96–97.

12. Lincoln and Mamiya, *Black Church*, p. 229.

13. Researchers have recognized that the religious climate in the home can be a tremendous motivator for children but generally have not followed through on their observations in any systemic way. As an example, consider Reginald Clark's statement that "in low-income families a key factor in the educational success of a child may be a strong parental religious-spiritual orientation" in his important *Family Life and School Achievement: Why Poor Black Children Succeed or Fail*. In spite of that claim, the Black church received no attention in his study. Clark, *Family Life*, p. 62.

14. Paul Tillich, *Dynamics of Faith* (New York: Harper Torchbooks, 1958), p. 1.

15. Melanie Markley, "Changing Class," *Houston Chronicle*, February 26, 1995, p. 29A.

Chapter 11

1. Friedrich Nietzsche's aphorism is quoted by Martin Jay, *The Dialectical Imagination: A History of the Frankfurt School and the Institute of Social Research, 1923–1950* (Boston: Little, Brown, 1973), p. 50.

2. Barry A. Kosmin and Seymour P. Lachman, *One Nation Under God: Religion in Contemporary American Society* (New York: Harmony, 1993), p. 9 and pp. 138–139; Lincoln and Mamiya, *Black Church*, p. 160. Increasing the inclusiveness of IAF organizations by expanding them to other faiths can lead to some falloff in membership; see Barry Knight, *Community Organizing in Britain: The First Two Years of the Citizen Organising Foundation* (Bristol: Centre for Research and Innovation in Social Policy and Practice, 1991), p. 23. On the British organizations in general, see Paul Henderson and Harry Salmon, *Community Organising: The UK Context* (London: Community Development Foundation, 1995).

3. Steinberg, *Beyond the Classroom*, pp. 138–162.

4. Ross E. Milloy, "Paths of Texas Gun Bills Follow Myths Not Polls," *New York Times*, April 1, 1993, p. A8.

5. Commentators who criticize the IAF for its lack of a bolder, more systemic and radical political program include William H. Friedland, *Revolutionary Theory* (Totowa, N.J.: Allanheld, Osmun, 1982); Mike Miller, "Saul Alinsky and the Democratic Spirit," *Christianity and Crisis*, vol. 52, no. 8 (May 25, 1992), pp. 180–183; Sallie A. Marston and George Towers, "Private Spaces and the Politics of Places: Spatioeconomic Restructuring and Community Organizing in Tucson and El Paso," in Robert Fisher and Joseph Kling, eds., *Mobilizing the Community: Local Politics in the Era of the Global City* (Newbury Park, Calif.: Sage, 1993), pp. 75–102; and Robert Fisher, *Let the People Decide: Neighborhood Organizing in America* (New York: Twayne, 1994), and "Neighborhood Organizing: The Importance of Historical Context," in Dennis Keating, Norman Krumholz, and Phil Star, eds., *Revitalizing Urban Neighborhoods* (Lawrence: University of Kansas Press, 1997). For a defense of the IAF in terms of efficacy, see Rodolfo Acuña, *Occupied America: A History of Chicanos* (New York: Harper and Row, 1988), pp. 432–436.

6. Cortés, "Catholic Tradition of Family Rights," p. 168.

7. Hobby, "Easing the Pain," p. 17A; John Huey, "Uprising in Texas: Control of San Antonio Is Slowly Being Won by Mexican-Americans," *Wall Street Journal*, July 13, 1977, p. 1.

8. Thomas W. Pauken, *The Thirty Years War: The Politics of the Sixties Generation* (Ottawa, Ill.: Jameson, 1995), pp. 173–192.

9. Bruce E. Cain, "Ambiguous Advice to an 'Ambivalent Minority': Skerry's Critique of Mexican Americans," in Tomás Rivera Center, ed., *Mexican Americans: Are They an Ambivalent Minority?* (Claremont, Calif.: Tomás Rivera Center, 1994), pp. 16–24.

10. Sizer, *Horace's Compromise*, pp. 225–227.

11. On advisory periods, see Winston J. Hagborg, "High School Student Perceptions and Satisfaction with Group Advisory," *Psychology in the Schools*, vol. 32, no. 1 (January 1995), pp. 46–51; on multi-aged classrooms, see Simon Veenman, "Cognitive and Noncognitive Effects of Multigrade and Multiaged Classes: A Best-Evidence Synthesis," *Review of Educational Research*, vol. 65, no. 4 (winter 1995), pp. 319–382.

12. On the political edge enjoyed by middle-class parents, see Lareau, *Home Advantage*; for an example of the manner in which elite parents can subvert promising reforms for low-income, minority youth, see Amy Stuart Wells and Irene Serna, "The Politics of Culture: Understanding Local Political Resistance to Detracking in Racially Mixed Schools," *Harvard Educational Review*, vol. 66, no. 1 (spring 1996), pp. 93–118.

13. Gordon E. Greenwood and Catherine W. Hickman, "Research and Practice in Parent Involvement: Implications for Teacher Education," *The Elementary School Journal*, vol. 91, no. 3 (1991), pp. 279–288; D. Williams and Nancy Feyl Chavkin, *Teacher/Parent Partnerships: Guidelines and Strategies to Train Elementary School Teachers for Parent Involvement* (Austin, Tex.: Southwest

Educational Development Laboratory, 1987); Janet E. Foster and Rachelle G. Loven, "The Need and Directions for Parent Involvement in the '90s: Undergraduate Perspectives and Expectations," *Action in Teacher Education*, vol. 14, no. 3 (fall 1992), pp. 13–19.

14. For one recent effort to elaborate the interface between teacher education and citizenship education, see Daniel P. Liston and Kenneth M. Zeichner, *Teacher Education and the Social Conditions of Schooling* (New York: Routledge, 1991).

15. See Liston and Zeichner, ibid. The vast literature on critical pedagogy deals with similar matters; see Henry A. Giroux, *Theory and Resistance in Education* (South Hadley, Mass.: Bergin and Garvey, 1983), and *Teachers as Intellectuals: Toward a Critical Pedagogy of Learning* (New York: Bergin and Garvey, 1988).

16. See, for example, the famous Federalist Number Ten, which presents an incisive analysis of the foundations of factionalism in human nature, in Jacob E. Cooke, ed., *The Federalist* (Middletown, Conn.: Wesleyan University Press, 1961), pp. 56–65.

Chapter 12

1. John Dewey, *Democracy and Education* (New York: Free Press, 1966), p. 87.

2. Coleman and Hoffer, *Public and Private High Schools*, pp. 6–27, quote from p. 17.

3. Myron Lieberman, *Privatization and Educational Choice* (New York: St. Martin's, 1989), p. 214.

4. "Concept Paper: ACORN and School Reform" (Washington, D.C., unpub. ms., 1995).

5. Madeleine Adamson, "ACORN: The People United/El Pueblo Unido" (Washington, D.C.: Service Employees International Union, n.d.).

6. On the Algebra Project, see Mike Davis, *Possible Lives: The Promise of Public Education in America* (Boston: Houghton Mifflin, 1995), pp. 306–319.

7. M. Edith Rasell and Lawrence Mishel, "Shortchanging Education: How U.S. Spending on Grades K–12 Lags Behind Other Industrial Nations" (Washington, D.C., Economic Policy Institute Briefing Paper, 1993); David C. Berliner and Bruce J. Biddle, *The Manufactured Crisis: Myths, Fraud, and the Attack on America's Public Schools* (Reading, Mass.: Addison-Wesley, 1995), pp. 66–70.

8. See Allen J. Matusow, *The Unraveling of America: A History of Liberalism in the 1960s* (New York: Harper Torchbooks, 1986), pp. 221–226.

Bibliography

Acuña, Rodolfo. *Occupied America: A History of Chicanos.* New York: Harper and Row, 1988.

Alinsky, Saul D. *Reveille for Radicals.* Chicago: University of Chicago Press, 1946.

————. *Rules for Radicals: A Practical Primer for Realistic Radicals.* New York: Vintage, 1971.

Bean, Frank D., Jorge Chapa, Ruth R. Berg, and Kathryn A. Sowards. "Educational and Sociodemographic Incorporation among Hispanic Immigrants to the United States." In Barry Edmonston and Jeffrey S. Passel, eds., *Immigration and Ethnicity: The Integration of America's Newest Arrivals.* Washington, D.C.: Urban Institute, 1994, pp. 73–99.

Beeth, Howard, and Cary D. Wintz, eds. *Black Dixie: Afro-Texan History and Culture in Houston.* College Station: Texas A&M University Press, 1992.

Bellah, Robert N. *The Broken Covenant: American Civil Religion in Time of Trial.* New York: Seabury, 1975.

Bellah, Robert N., et al. *Habits of the Heart: Individualism and Commitment in American Life.* Berkeley: University of California, 1985.

Bernard, Richard M., and Bradley R. Rice, eds. *Sunbelt Cities: Politics and Growth Since World War II.* Austin: University of Texas Press, 1983.

Berry, Jeffrey M., Kent E. Portney, and Ken Thomson. *The Rebirth of Urban Democracy.* Washington, D.C.: Brookings Institution, 1993.

Bourdieu, Pierre. *Reproduction in Education, Society and Culture.* Beverly Hills, Calif.: Sage, 1977.

Bowles, Samuel, and Herbert Gintis. *Schooling in Capitalist America.* New York: Basic, 1976.

Boyte, Harry C. *Commonwealth: A Return to Citizen Politics.* New York: Free Press, 1989.

Bronder, Saul E. *Social Justice and Church Authority: The Public Life of Archbishop Robert E. Lucey.* Philadelphia: Temple University Press, 1982.

Browning, Harley L., and Rodolfo O. de la Garza, eds. *Mexican Immigrants and Mexican Americans: An Evolving Relation.* Austin: Center for Mexican American Studies, University of Texas, 1986.

Brueggemann, Walter. *Hope within History.* Atlanta: John Knox, 1987.

Bryk, Anthony S., Valerie E. Lee, and Peter B. Holland. *Catholic Schools and the Common Good.* Cambridge, Mass.: Harvard University Press, 1993.

Bullard, Pamela, and Barbara Taylor. *Making School Reform Happen.* Boston: Allyn and Bacon, 1993.

Callahan, Raymond E. *Education and the Cult of Efficiency.* Chicago: University of Chicago Press, 1962.

Chapa, Jorge. "The Myth of Hispanic Progress: Trends in the Educational and Economic Attainment of Mexican Americans." *Journal of Hispanic Policy,* vol. 4 (1989–1990), pp. 3–18.

Chavkin, Nancy Feyl. "Debunking the Myth about Minority Parents." *Educational Horizons* (1989), vol. 66, no. 4, pp. 119–123.

———— ed. *Families and Schools in a Pluralistic Society.* Albany: State University of New York Press, 1993.

Chavkin, Nancy Feyl, and David L. Williams, Jr. "Low-Income Parents' Attitudes toward Parental Involvement in Education," *Journal of Sociology and Social Welfare* (1989), pp. 17–28.

Chubb, John E., and Terry M. Moe. *Politics, Markets, and America's Schools.* Washington, D.C.: Brookings Institution, 1990.

Clark, Reginald. *Family Life and School Achievement: Why Poor Black Children Succeed or Fail.* Chicago: University of Chicago Press, 1983.

Cohen, Jean Louise, and Andrew Arato. *Civil Society and Political Theory.* Cambridge, Mass.: MIT University Press, 1992.

Coleman, James S., and Thomas Hoffer. *Public and Private High Schools: The Impact of Communities.* New York: Basic, 1987.

Coleman, James S., Thomas Hoffer, and Sally Kilgore. *High School Achievement: Public, Catholic, and Private Schools Compared.* New York: Basic, 1982.

Comer, James. *School Power: Implications of an Intervention Project.* New York: Free Press, 1980.

Cookson, Peter W., Jr. *School Choice: The Struggle for the Soul of American Education.* New Haven, Conn.: Yale University Press, 1994.

Cortés, Carlos E. *Education and the Mexican American.* New York: Arno, 1974.

Cortés, Ernesto, Jr. "Reflections on the Catholic Tradition of Family Rights." In John Coleman, ed., *One Hundred Years of Catholic Social Thought.* New York: Orbis, 1991.

————. "Reweaving the Fabric: The Iron Rule and the IAF Strategy for Power and Politics." In Henry G. Cisneros, ed., *Interwoven Destinies: Cities and the Nation.* New York: W. W. Norton, 1993.

Damon, William. *Greater Expectations: Overcoming the Culture of Indulgence in America's Homes and Schools.* New York: Free Press, 1995.

Davidson, Chandler. *Biracial Politics: Conflict and Coalition in the Metropolitan South.* Baton Rouge: Louisiana State University Press, 1972.

————. *Race and Class in Texas Politics.* Princeton, N.J.: Princeton University Press, 1990.

De León, Arnoldo. *Ethnicity in the Sunbelt: A History of Mexican Americans in Houston.* Houston: University of Houston, 1989.

Delgado, Gary. *Organizing the Movement: The Roots and Growth of ACORN.* Philadelphia: Temple University Press, 1986.

Delgado-Gaitan, Concha. *Literacy for Empowerment: The Role of Parents in Children's Education.* Philadelphia: Falmer, 1990.

Dewey, John. *Democracy and Education.* New York: Free Press, 1966.

Dornbusch, Sanford M., and Philip L. Ritter. "Parents of High School Students: A Neglected Resource." *Educational Horizons,* vol. 66, no. 2 (1988), pp. 75–75.

Dornbusch, Sanford M., et al. "The Relation of Parenting Style to Adolescent School Performance." *Child Development,* vol. 58, no. 5 (1987), pp. 1244–1257.

Eby, Frederick. *The Development of Education in Texas.* New York, Macmillan, 1925.

Elshtain, Jean Bethke. *Democracy on Trial.* Basic, 1995.

Feagin, Joe R. *Free Enterprise City: Houston in Political and Economic Perspective.* New Brunswick, N.J.: Rutgers University Press, 1988.

Ferguson, Ronald F. "Paying for Public Education: New Evidence on How and Why Money Matters." *Harvard Journal of Legislation,* vol. 28 (1991), pp. 465–491.

Fine, Michelle. *Framing Dropouts: Notes on the Politics of an Urban Public High School.* Albany: State University of New York Press, 1991.

Fish, John Hall. *Black Power/White Control.* Princeton, N.J.: Princeton University Press, 1973.

Fisher, Robert. *Let the People Decide: Neighborhood Organizing in America.* New York: Twayne, 1994.

Fisher, Robert, and Joseph Kling, eds. *Mobilizing the Community: Local Politics in the Era of the Global City.* Newbury Park, Calif.: Sage, 1993.

Fiske, Edward B. *Smart Schools, Smart Kids: Why Do Some Schools Work?* New York: Simon and Schuster, 1991.

Frazier, E. Franklin. *The Negro Church in America.* New York: Schocken Books, 1974.

García, Ignacio M. *United We Win: The Rise and Fall of La Raza Unida Party.* Tucson: University of Arizona, 1989.

García, Mario T. *Memories of Chicano History: The Life and Narrative of Bert Corona.* Berkeley: University of California Press, 1994.

Garcia, Richard A. *Rise of the Mexican American Middle Class: San Antonio, 1929–1941.* College Station: Texas A&M University Press, 1991.

Gardner, Howard. *The Unschooled Mind: How Children Think and How Schools Should Teach.* New York: Basic, 1991.

Gibson, Margaret A., and John U. Ogbu, eds. *Minority Status and Schooling: A Comparative Study of Immigrant and Involuntary Minorities.* New York: Garland, 1991.

González, Roberto O., and Michael J. LaVelle. *The Hispanic Church in the United States: A Sociocultural and Religious Profile.* New York: Enquire Press, 1985.

Green, George Norris. *The Establishment in Texas Politics: The Primitive Years, 1938–1957.* Norman: University of Oklahoma Press, 1979.

Greider, William. *Who Will Tell the People: The Betrayal of American Democracy.* New York: Simon and Schuster, 1992.

Gutiérrez, Gustavo. *A Theology of Liberation.* Maryknoll, N.Y.: Orbis, 1988.

Hall, John A., ed. *Civil Society: Theory, History, Comparison.* Cambridge, Mass.: Polity, 1995.

Hamburg, David A. *Today's Children: Creating a Future for a Generation in Crisis.* New York: Times Books, 1992.

Heath, Shirley Brice, and Milbrey W. McLaughlin, eds. *Identity and Inner-City Youth: Beyond Ethnicity and Gender.* New York: Teachers College Press, 1993.

Henig, Jeffrey R. *Rethinking School Choice: Limits of the Market Metaphor.* Princeton, N.J.: Princeton University Press, 1994.

Hewlett, Sylvia Ann. *When the Bough Breaks: The Cost of Neglecting Our Children.* New York: Basic, 1991.

Hlebowitsh, Peter S. *Radical Curriculum Theory Reconsidered: A Historical Approach.* New York: Teachers College Press, 1993.

Horowitz, Ruth. *Honor and the American Dream: Culture and Identity in a Chicano Community.* New Brunswick, N.J.: Rutgers University Press, 1983.

Horwitt, Sanford D. *Let Them Call Me Rebel: Saul Alinsky—His Life and Legacy.* New York: Vintage, 1992.

Howe, Harold. *Thinking About Our Kids.* New York: Free Press, 1993.

Jankowski, Martín Sánchez. *Islands in the Street: Gangs and American Urban Society.* Berkeley: University of California Press, 1991.

Jencks, Christopher. *Rethinking Social Policy: Race, Poverty, and the Underclass.* Cambridge, Mass.: Harvard University Press, 1992.

Jenkins, J. Craig. *The Politics of Insurgency: The Farm Worker Movement in the 1960s.* New York: Columbia University Press, 1985.

Johnson, David R., John A. Booth, and Richard J. Harris, eds. *The Politics of San Antonio: Community, Progress, and Power.* Lincoln: University of Nebraska Press, 1983.

Katz, Michael. *Reconstructing American Education.* Cambridge, Mass.: Harvard University Press, 1987.

Kosmin, Barry A., and Seymour P. Lachman. *One Nation Under God: Religion in Contemporary American Society.* New York: Harmony, 1993.

Kozol, Jonathan. *Savage Inequalities: Children in America's Schools.* New York: Crown, 1991.

Lamb, Michael E., ed. *The Role of the Father in Child Development.* New York: Wiley, 1981.

Lareau, Annette. *Home Advantage: Social Class and Parental Intervention in Elementary Education.* Philadelphia: Falmer, 1990.

Lasch, Christopher. *The Revolt of the Elites and the Betrayal of Democracy.* New York: W. W. Norton, 1995.

Lee, Valerie E., and Julia B. Smith. "Effects of High School Restructuring and Size on Early Gains in Achievement and Engagement." *Sociology of Education,* vol. 68, no. 4 (October 1985), pp. 241–270.

Levy, Frank. *Dollars and Dreams: The Changing American Income Distribution.* New York: Norton, 1988.

Levy, Jacques. *César Chávez: Autobiography of La Causa.* New York: W. W. Norton, 1975.

Lieberman, Myron. *Privatization and Educational Choice.* New York: St. Martin's, 1989.

———. *Public Education: An Autopsy.* Cambridge, Mass.: Harvard University Press, 1993.

Lincoln, C. Eric. *The Black Church Since Frazier.* New York: Schocken Books, 1974.

Lincoln, C. Eric, and Lawrence H. Mamiya. *The Black Church in the African American Experience.* Durham, N.C.: Duke University Press, 1990.

Liston, Daniel P., and Kenneth M. Zeichner. *Teacher Education and the Social Conditions of Schooling.* New York: Routledge, 1991.

Márquez, Benjamin. *LULAC: The Evolution of a Mexican American Political Organization.* Austin: University of Texas Press, 1993.

Marshall, Ray, and Marc Tucker. *Thinking for a Living: Work, Skills, and the Future of the American Economy.* New York: Basic, 1992.

Matusow, Allen. *The Unraveling of America: A History of Liberalism in the 1960s.* New York: Harper Torchbooks, 1986.

McNeil, Linda. *Contradictions of Control: School Structure and School Knowledge.* New York: Routledge and Kegan Paul, 1986.

Meier, Deborah. *The Power of Their Ideas: Lessons for America from a Small School in Harlem.* Boston: Beacon Press, 1995.

Meinig, D. W. *Imperial Texas: An Interpretive Essay in Cultural Geography.* Austin: University of Texas Press, 1969.

Mirandé, Alfredo. *The Chicano Experience: An Alternative Perspective.* South Bend, Ind.: University of Notre Dame Press, 1985.

Montejano, David. *Anglos and Mexicans in the Making of Texas, 1836–1986.* Austin: University of Texas Press, 1987.

Moore, Joan. *Going Down to the Barrio: Homeboys and Homegirls in Change.* Philadelphia: Temple University Press, 1991.

Moore, Joan, and Raquel Pinderhughes, eds. *In the Barrios: Latinos and the Underclass Debate.* New York: Russell Sage, 1993.

Morales, Rebecca, and Frank Bonilla, eds. *Latinos in a Changing U.S. Economy.* Newbury Park, Calif.: Sage, 1993.

Muñoz, Carlos. *Youth, Identity, Power: The Chicano Movement.* New York: Verso, 1989.

Polakow, Valerie. *Lives on the Edge: Single Mothers and Their Children in the Other America.* Chicago: University of Chicago Press, 1993.

Putnam, Robert D. *Making Democracy Work: Civic Traditions in Modern Italy.* Princeton, N.J.: Princeton University Press, 1993.

———. "Bowling Alone: America's Declining Social Capital." *Journal of Democracy,* vol. 6, no. 1 (January 1995), pp. 65–78.

Reich, Robert B. *The Work of Nations.* New York: Vintage, 1992.

Rogers, Mary Beth. *Cold Anger: A Story of Faith and Power Politics.* Denton: University of North Texas, 1990.

Rubin, Lilian B. *Families on the Fault Line.* New York: HarperCollins, 1994.

San Miguel, Guadalupe. *"Let All of Them Take Heed": Mexican-Americans and the*

Campaign for Educational Equality in Texas, 1910–1981. Austin: University of Texas Press, 1987.

Sanders, Marion K. *The Professional Radical: Conversations with Saul Alinsky.* New York: Harper and Row, 1970.

Sanders, William B. *Gangbangs and Drive-bys: Grounded Culture and Juvenile Gang Violence.* New York: Aldine de Gruyter, 1994.

Sarason, Seymour. *Parental Involvement and the Political Principle: Why the Existing Governance Structure of Schools Should Be Abolished.* San Francisco: Jossey-Bass, 1995.

Schorr, Lisbeth B. *Within Our Reach: Breaking the Cycle of Disadvantage.* New York: Doubleday, 1989.

Sizer, Theodore R. *Horace's Compromise: The Dilemma of the American High School.* New York: Houghton Mifflin, 1984.

Skerry, Peter. *Mexican Americans: The Ambivalent Minority.* New York: Free Press, 1993.

Skocpol, Theda. *Protecting Soldiers and Mothers: The Political Origins of Social Policy in the United States.* Cambridge, Mass.: Harvard University Press, 1992.

———. *Social Policy in the United States: Future Possibilities in Historical Perspective.* Princeton, N.J.: Princeton University Press, 1995.

Slayton, Robert A. *Back of the Yards: The Making of a Local Democracy.* Chicago: University of Chicago Press, 1986.

Spergel, Irving A. *The Youth Gang Problem: A Community Approach.* New York: Oxford University Press, 1995.

Suárez-Orozco, Carola, and Marcelo M. Suárez-Orozco. *Transformations: Immigration, Family Life, and Achievement Motivation among Latino Adolescents.* Stanford, Calif.: Stanford University Press, 1995.

Suárez-Orozco, Marcelo M. *Central American Refugees and U.S. High Schools: A Psychological Study of Motivation and Achievement.* Stanford, Calif.: Stanford University Press, 1989.

Thomas, Robert D., and Richard W. Murray. *Progrowth Politics: Change and Governance in Houston.* Berkeley: University of California Press, 1991.

Tillich, Paul. *Dynamics of Faith.* New York: Harper Torchbooks, 1958.

Tocqueville, Alexis de. *The Old Régime and the French Revolution.* Garden City, N.Y.: Anchor, 1955.

———. *Democracy in America.* Garden City, N.Y.: Doubleday, 1969.

Valencia, Richard R., ed. *Chicano School Failure and Success: Research and Policy Agendas for the 1990s.* Philadelphia: Falmer, 1991.

Washington, Joseph R., Jr. *Black Religion: The Negro and Christianity in the United States.* Boston: Beacon Press, 1964.

Wells, Amy Stuart, and Irene Serna. "The Politics of Culture: Understanding Local Political Resistance to Detracking in Racially Mixed Schools." *Harvard Educational Review,* vol. 66, no. 1 (spring 1996), pp. 93–118.

Williams, Michael R. *Neighborhood Organizing for Urban School Reform.* New York: Teachers College Press, 1989.

Wilson, William Julius. *The Truly Disadvantaged: The Inner City, the Underclass, and Public Policy.* Chicago: University of Chicago Press, 1987.

Winters, Wendy Glasgow. *African American Mothers and Urban Schools: The Power of Participation.* New York: Lexington, 1993.

Wolin, Sheldon S. *The Presence of the Past: Essays on the State and the Constitution.* Baltimore: Johns Hopkins University Press.

Zamora, Emilio. *The World of the Mexican Worker in Texas.* College Station: Texas A&M Press, 1993.

Index